OLD LONDON
Shoreditch to Smithfield

THE
'VILLAGE LONDON'
SERIES
from
THE ALDERMAN PRESS

THE VILLAGE LONDON SERIES

Other titles already published in hard back are:

VILLAGE LONDON Volume I
VILLAGE LONDON Volume II
LONDON RECOLLECTED Volume I
LONDON RECOLLECTED Volume II
LONDON RECOLLECTED Volume III
LONDON RECOLLECTED Volume IV
LONDON RECOLLECTED Volume V

Other titles already published in paperback:

VILLAGE LONDON Pt. 1 West and North
VILLAGE LONDON Pt. 2 North and East
VILLAGE LONDON Pt. 3 South-East
VILLAGE LONDON Pt. 4 South-West

OLD FLEET STREET
CHEAPSIDE AND ST. PAUL'S
THE TOWER AND EAST END
SHOREDITCH to SMITHFIELD
CHARTERHOUSE to HOLBORN
STRAND to SOHO
COVENT GARDEN and the THAMES to WHITEHALL

*The above seven titles are extracts from the
hardback edition of London Recollected.*

OLD LONDON

Shoreditch to Smithfield

by

WALTER THORNBURY

THE ALDERMAN PRESS

British Library Cataloguing in Publication Data.

Thornbury, Walter.
    Old London: Shoreditch to Smithfield.
    1. London (England)_____History
    I. Title II. Thornbury, Walter. Old and
    new London
    942.1   DA677

ISBN 0-946619-28-X

This edition published 1987.

The Alderman Press, 1/7 Church Street,
Edmonton, London, N9 9DR

Printed and bound in Great Britain
by Robert Hartnoll (1985) Ltd., Bodmin.

CONTENTS.

CONTENTS.

CONTENTS.

LIST OF ILLUSTRATIONS.

CHAPTER XXIII.

LEADENHALL STREET AND THE OLD EAST INDIA HOUSE.

"IT does not appear to be ascertained where the East India Company first transacted their business," says an historian of the great Company, "but the tradition of the house is, that it was in the great room of the "Nag's Head Inn," opposite Bishop's-gate Church, where there is now a Quakers' Meeting House. The maps of London constructed soon after the Great Fire place the India House in Leadenhall Street, on a part of its present site. It is probably the house, of which a unique plate is preserved in the British Museum, surmounted by a huge, square-built mariner, and two thick dolphins. In the indenture of conveyance of the dead stock of the Company, dated 22nd July, 1702, we find that Sir William Craven, of Kensington, in the year 1701, leased to the Company his large house in Leadenhall Street, and a tenement in Lime Street, for twenty-one years, at £100 a year. Upon the site of this house what is called the old East India House was built in 1726; and several portions of this old house long remained, although the subsequent front, and great part of the house, were added in 1799, by Mr. Jupp.

The façade of the old building was 200 feet in length, and was of stone. The portico was composed of six large Ionic fluted columns on a raised basement, and it gave an air of much magnificence to the whole, although the closeness of the street made it somewhat gloomy. The pediment was an emblematic sculpture by Bacon, representing the commerce of the East protected by the King of Great Britain, who stood in the centre of a number of figures, holding a shield stretched over them. On the apex of the pediment rose a statue of Britannia. Asia, seated on a dromedary, was at the left corner, and Europe, on horseback, at the right.

"The ground floor," says a writer in "Knight's London," describing the old India House in 1843, "is chiefly occupied by Court and Committee Rooms, and by the Directors' private rooms. The Court of Directors occupy what is usually termed the 'Court Room,' while that in which the Court of Proprietors assemble is called the 'General Court Room.' The Court Room is said to be an exact cube of thirty feet; it is splendidly ornamented by gilding and by large looking-glasses; and the effect of its too great height is much diminished by the position of the windows near the ceiling. Six large pictures hang from the cornice, representing the three Presidencies, the Cape, St. Helena, and Tellicherry. A fine piece of sculpture, in white marble, is fixed over the chimney; Britannia is seated on a globe by the sea-shore, receiving homage from three female figures, intended for Asia, Africa, and India. Asia offers spices with her right hand, and with her left leads a camel; India presents a large box of jewels, which she holds half open; and Africa rests her hand upon the head of a lion. The Thames, as a river-god, stands upon the shore, a labourer appears cording a large bale of merchandise, and ships are sailing in the distance. The whole is supported by two caryatid figures, intended for Brahmins, but really fine old European-looking philosophers.

"The General Court Room, which until the abolition of the trade was the old sale-room, is close to the Court Room. Its east side is occupied by rows of seats which rise from the floor near the middle of the room towards the ceiling, backed by a gallery where the public are admitted. On the floor are the seats for the chairman, secretary, and clerks. Against the west wall, in niches, are six statues of persons who have distinguished themselves in the Company's service; Lord Clive, Warren Hastings, and the Marquis Cornwallis occupy those on the left, and Sir Eyre Coote, General Lawrance, and Sir George Pococke those on the right. It is understood that the statue of the Marquis Wellesley will be placed in the vacant space in the middle. The Finance and Home Committee Room is the best room in the house, with the exception of the Court Rooms, and is decorated with some good pictures. One wall is entirely occupied by a representation of the grant of the Dewannee to the Company in 1765, the foundation of all the British Power in India; portraits of Warren Hastings and of the Marquis Cornwallis stand beside the fireplace; and the remaining walls are occupied by other pictures, among which may be noticed the portrait of Mirza Abul Hassan, the Persian Envoy, who excited a good deal of attention in London in the year 1809. The upper part of the house contains the principal offices and the library and museum. In the former is, perhaps, the most splendid collection of Oriental MSS. in Europe, and, in addition, a copy of almost every printed work relating to Asia."

Our trade with India may date its real commencement from the last day of the sixteenth century, when 215 London merchant adventurers, elated by the capture of a Portuguese ship laden with Indian gold, pearls, spices, silks, and ivory, obtained a charter to trade with Hindostan for fifteen years. King James, with some reluctance (being, no doubt, tampered with by courtiers), renewed the charter, in 1609, "for ever," providing that it might be recalled on three years' notice from the Crown. In

1612, after twelve voyages had been made to the East Indies, the whole capital subscribed, amounting to £429,000, was united, and the management taken out of the hands of the original twenty-four managers. The Company suffered at first from the ordinary rapacity and injustice of the Stuarts. In 1623 (James I.), just as a fleet was starting for India, the Duke of Buckingham, then High Admiral, refused to allow it to sail till the Company had paid up a disputed Admiralty claim of £10,000, and £10,000 claimed by the king. In 1635, Charles I., breaking the charter, allowed a Captain Weddell, for some heavy bribe, to trade to India for five years. In 1640, the same unjust king compelled the Company (on bonds never entirely paid) to sell him their whole stock of Indian pepper in their warehouses, which he instantly re-sold at a lower price, at an eventual loss of £50,000. In 1655 the Republican Government, nobly antagonistic to royal monopolies, from which the people had so long groaned under both the Tudors and the Stuarts, threw the trade to India entirely open, but the Company was reinstated in its power two years afterwards. In 1661, Charles II. (no doubt for a pretty handsome consideration) granted the Company a fresh charter, with the new and great privilege of making peace or war. Now the Company's wings began to grow in earnest. In 1653, Madras was made a presidency; in 1662, Bombay was ceded to England by the Portuguese, who gave it to Charles as part of the dower of poor ill-starred Catherine of Braganza; and in 1692 Calcutta was purchased by the ambitious traders, who now began to feel their power, and the possibilities of their new colony. From 1690 to 1693 there were great disputes as to whether the king or Parliament had the right of granting trade charters; and on William III. granting the Company (rich enough now to excite jealousy) a new charter for twenty-one years, an angry inquiry was instituted by the Tories, who discovered that the Company had distributed £90,000 among the chief officers of state. A prorogation of Parliament dropped the curtain on these shameful disclosures.

In 1698 the old Company was dissolved, and a new Company (which had outbid the old in bribes) was founded, rivalled, in 1700, by the old Company, which had obtained a partial resumption of its powers. In 1708, however, the two Companies, which had only injured each other, were united, and called "The United Company of Merchants of England, trading to the East Indies," a title which it retained till its trading privileges were abolished, in 1834. On the renewal of the charter in 1781 (George III.), the Government made important changes in the charter, and required all despatches to be submitted to them before they were forwarded to India. The Government was already jealous of the imperial power of a Company which had the possibility of conquering 176 millions of people. In 1784 the blow indeed came, with the establishment of the Board of Control, "by which, in everything but patronage and trade," says a well-informed writer on the subject, "the Company's Court of Directors was rendered subordinate to the Government" of the time being. In 1794 private merchants were allowed to export goods in the Company's ships, another big slice out of the cake. By the year 1833 the private trading had begun to exceed, in value of goods, those carried by the Company. In 1833 an Act was passed to enable the Company to retain power until 1854, but abolishing the China monopoly, and all trading. This was cutting off the legs of the Company, and, in fact, preparing it for death. Their warehouses and most of their property were then sold, and the dividend was to be 10½ per cent., chargeable on the revenues of India, and redeemable by Parliament after the year 1874. The amount of dividend guaranteed by the Act was £630,000, being 10½ per cent. on a nominal capital of £6,000,000. The real capital of the Company was estimated, in 1832, at upwards of £21,000,000, including cash, goods, and buildings, and £1,294,768 as the estimated value of the East India House and the Company's warehouses, the prime cost of the latter having been £1,100,000. The Company was henceforth to be entitled the East India Company, and its accounts were to be annually laid before Parliament. The old privileges of the Company were now limited.

The General Court of Proprietors was formerly composed of the owners of India stock. After 1693 no one who had less than £1,000 stock could vote. Later still, the qualification was lowered to £500, and the greatest holders had no more. By the last law (that of 1773) the possession of £1,000 only gave one vote; £3,000, two; £6,000, three; and £10,000 the greatest number allowed—namely, four. The Court of Proprietors elected the Court of Directors, framed bye-laws, declared the dividends, and controlled grants of money above £600, and additions to salary above £200. Latterly the functions of this general court were entirely deliberative, and the vote was by ballot. In 1843 there were 1,880 members of the Court of Proprietors. The meetings in old times were very stormy, and even riotous; the debates virulent. In 1763, Clive, as unscrupulous as he was brave, laid out £100,000 in India stock, to introduce nominees of his own, who would vote at his pleasure. The directors were

then appointed annually; latterly they were elected for four years, six retiring yearly, and the chairman and deputy-chairman, who communicated with the Government, did the greater part of the work.

The Board of Control, established by the Act of 1784, was nominated by the Crown, and (after 1793) consisted of an unlimited number of members, all of whom, except two, were to be of the Privy Council, including the two principal Secretaries of State and the Chancellor of the Exchequer. Three only of the commissioners were paid, and all changed with the Ministry. They had supreme power to keep or send despatches; had access to all books, accounts, papers, and documents in the East India House, orders, or secret despatches; and communicated with the Secret Committee.

In old times "John Company" employed nearly 4,000 men in its warehouses, and, before the trade with India closed, kept more than 400 clerks to transact the business of this greatest company that the world had ever seen. The military department superintended the recruiting and storing of the Indian army. There was a shipping department, a master-attendant's office, an auditor's office, an examiner's office, an accountant's office, a transfer office, and a treasury. The buying office governed the fourteen warehouses, and so worked the home market, having often in store some fifty million pounds weight of tea, 1,200,000 lbs. being sometimes sold in one day, at the annual tea sales. The tea and indigo sales were bear-garden scenes.

The despatches and letters from India poured ceaselessly into the India House. From 1793 to 1813 they made 9,094 large folio volumes; while from 1813 to 1829, the number increased to 14,414 folios. In a debate on East India matters, in 1822, Canning mentioned, in eulogy of the Company's clever and careful clerks, that he had known one military despatch accompanied by 119 papers, and containing altogether 13,511 pages. These were the men who had heard of Clive and Warren Hastings, and remembered that Macaulay had spoken of Indian writers as fallen from their high estate, because then (1840) they could only expect, at forty-five, to return to England with £1,000 a year pension and £30,000 of savings. They never forgot, we may be sure, that India yielded £17,000,000 in taxes.

It must never be forgotten, in describing the old East India House, that that most delightful of all our humourists, Charles Lamb, was a patient, humble, and plodding clerk at its desks for thirty years. "My printed works," he used to say, with his quaint stutter, "were my recreations; my real works may be found on the shelves in Leadenhall

Street, filling some hundred folios." His half painful feelings of pleasure on at last regaining his freedom, he has himself beautifully described; and in one of the best of his essays he has sketched the most fantastic of his fellow-clerks. James Mill, the successor to poor old dead-and-gone "John Company," November 1, 1858. The East India House, in Leadenhall Street, was sold with the furniture in 1861, and pulled down in 1862. The handsome pile of the East India Chambers now

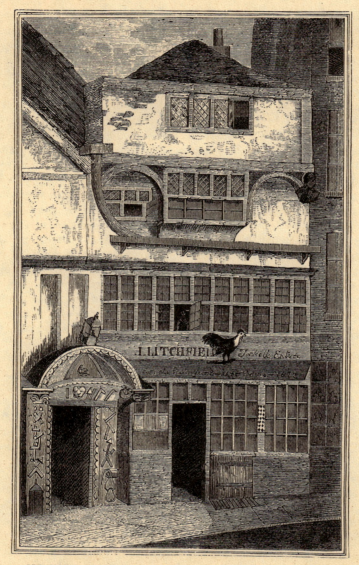

OLD HOUSE FORMERLY IN LEADENHALL STREET. (*See page* 189.)

the author of the "History of India," his son John Stuart Mill, and worthy Hoole, the translator of "Tasso," were also clerks in the India House.

In 1858, in consequence of the break-up occasioned by the mutiny, and the disappearance of the Company's black army, the government of the vast Indian empire was transferred to the Crown; the Board of Control was abolished, and a Council of State for India was instituted. The Queen was proclaimed in all the great Indian cities, as occupies its site, and the museum was transferred to Whitehall.

The Council of India now consists of fifteen members, at £1,200 a year each, payable, together with the salary of the Secretary of State, out of the revenue of India. The old twenty-four directors received £300 a year each, and £500 for their "chairs." At first eight of the council were appointed by the Queen, and seven by the Court of East India Directors from their own body. In

THE FLOWER SERMON IN ST CATHERINE CREE CHURCH. (*See page* 189.)

future, vacancies in the Council will be filled up by the Secretary of State for India.

At the "Two Fans," in Leadenhall Street, Peter Anthony Motteux, a clever but rather unprincipled dramatic writer of the beginning of the eighteenth century, kept an India house, for the sale of Japan wares, fans, tea, pictures, arrack, rich brocades, Dutch silks, Flanders lace and linens. Such houses were then often used by fashionables as places of assignation. Motteux was a Protestant refugee from Rouen. He wrote or translated seventeen plays, including some of Molière's; produced a tragedy called *Beauty in Distress;* translated "Don Quixote" and "Rabelais," and was eventually found murdered on his birthday, 1717–18, in a notorious house in Star Court, Butcher Row, Temple Bar. Steele inserts a letter in the *Spectator*, No. 288, professedly written by Motteux, and calling attention to his shop.

The following fragment of a song of Motteux's, taken from *The Mock Doctor*, a translation of *Le Médécin malgré lui*, has always seemed to us full of spirit and French gaiety :—

> " Man is for woman made,
>   And woman made for man ;
>   As the spur is for the jade,
>   As the scabbard for the blade,
>   As for liquor is the can,
>   So man's for woman made,
>   And woman made for man."

Lime Street, Leadenhall Street, is supposed to have got its name from lime having been once upon a time sold there. It was a street rendered famous, in the time of Pepys, by the great robbery committed by an old rascally Cavalier colonel on his friend Tryan, a rich merchant. Under date of the 8th of January, 1663-4, that omnivorous news-collector, Pepys, records :—" Upon the 'Change, a great talk there was of one Mr. Tryan, an old man, a merchant in Lime Street, robbed last night (his man and maid being gone out after he was a-bed), and gagged and robbed of £1,050 in money, and about £4,000 in jewels, which he had in his house as security for money. It is believed that his man is guilty of confederacy, by their ready going to his secret till, in his desk, wherein the key of his cash-chest lay." On the 10th, which was Sunday, Pepys goes on : "All our discourse to-night was about Mr. Tryan's late being robbed ; and that Colonel Turner (a mad, swearing, confident fellow, well known by all, and by me), one much indebted to this man for his very livelihood, was the man that either did or plotted it ; and the money and things are found in his hand, and he and his wife now in Newgate for it ; of which we are all glad, so very a known rogue he was." On the next day it is added, "The general talk of the town still is of Colonel Turner, about the robbery ; who, it is thought, will be hanged." And so he was. When the old Cavalier was on the ladder he related all his exploits in the wars, and, before he was turned off he kissed his hand to some ladies at a window near.

CHAPTER XXIV.

LEADENHALL STREET (*continued*).

The Old Market—St. Catherine Cree Church—Laud's Folly at the Consecration—The Annual " Flower Sermon"—St. Mary Axe—A Roman Pavement—House of the De Veres—St. Andrew Undershaft—Sawing up the Maypole—Stow's Monument.

THE original Leadenhall Market was a mansion which belonged to Sir Hugh Neville, in 1309, and was converted into a granary, and probably a market for the City, by Sir Simon Eyre, a draper, and Lord Mayor of London in 1445. It appears to have been a large building roofed with lead, and at that time thought, we presume, grand and remarkable.

There was a large chapel on the east side of old Leadenhall Market, dedicated to the Holy Trinity, by Sir Simon Eyre. To this chapel were attached, for daily service of the market people, master, five secular priests, six clerks, two choristers, and three schoolmasters, for whose support Eyre left 3,000 marks. In the reign of Edward IV. a fraternity of sixty priests was established in this chapel. During a scarcity in 1512 (Henry VIII.) a great store of corn was laid up in the Leadenhall granary, and the mayor used to attend the market at four a.m. In the year 1534 it was proposed to make Leadenhall a merchants' Bourse, but the plan dropped through. At Henry VIII.'s death, in 1547, the Bishop of Winchester, the king's almoner, gave alms publicly to the poor at Leadenhall for twelve consecutive days. In Strype's time Leadenhall (now celebrated for its poultry) was a market for meat and fish, a market for raw hides, a wool market, and an herb market.

"The use of Leadenhall, in my youth," says Strype, " was thus :—In a part of the north quadrant, on the east side of the north gate, were the common beams for weighing of wool and other wares, as had been accustomed; on the west side the gate was the scales to weigh meal; the other three sides were reserved (for the most part) to the making and resting of the pageants shewed at Midsummer in the watch. The remnant of the sides and quadrants were employed for the stowage of woolsacks, but not closed up; the lofts above were partly used by the painters in working for the decking of pageants and other devices, for beautifying of the watch and watchmen. The residue of the lofts were letten out to merchants, the woolwinders and packers therein to wind and pack their wools."

Leadenhall Market, says Pennant, "is the wonder of foreigners, who do not duly consider the carnivorous nation to which it belongs." When Don Pedro de Ronquillo, the Spanish ambassador, visited Leadenhall, he told Charles II. with admiration that he believed there was more meat sold in that market than in all the kingdom of Spain in a whole year. In 1730 Leadenhall Market was partly rebuilt, and in 1814 the leather-market was restored, the chapel and other old buildings being removed.

The engraving on page 186 shows an old house formerly standing in Leadenhall Street. The door at the side appears to have been the entrance to an old Jewish synagogue.

St. Catherine Cree (or Christ Church) is the memorable building where Archbishop Laud performed some of those dangerous ceremonials that ultimately contributed to bring him to the scaffold. Between the years 1280 and 1303 this church was built as a chapel for the parish of St. Catherine, in the churchyard of the priory of the Holy Trinity, Christ Church, founded by Matilda, wife of Henry I., who united the parishes of St. Mary Magdalen, St. Michael, St. Catherine, and the Trinity. Of the church of St. Michael, at the angle formed by the junction of Leadenhall and Fenchurch Streets, the crypt existed at the date of Mr. Godwin's writing in 1839, with pointed arched groining and clustered columns, the shafts of which were said to be sunk about fourteen feet deep in the earth.

Henry VIII., at the dissolution, gave the priory and the church to Lord Audley, who bequeathed it to Magdalen College, Cambridge. In Stow's time the high street had been so often raised by pavements round St. Catherine's, that those who entered had to descend seven steps. In the year 1628 the church, all but the tower was pulled down, and the present building commenced. The new building was consecrated by Archbishop Laud, then Bishop of London, Jan. 16, 1630-31. Rushworth gives the following account of the opening :—

"St. Catherine Cree Church being lately repaired, was suspended from all divine service, sermons, and sacraments, till it was consecrated. Wherefore Dr. Laud, Lord Bishop of London, on the 16th January, being the Lord's Day, came thither in the morning to consecrate the same. Now, because great exceptions were taken at the formality thereof, we will briefly relate the manner of the consecration. At the bishop's approach to the west door of the church, some that were prepared for it cried with a loud voice, 'Open, open, ye everlasting doors, that the King of Glory may come in.' And presently the doors were opened, and the bishop, with three doctors, and many other principal men, went in, and immediately falling down upon his knees, with his eyes lifted up, and his arms spread abroad, uttered these words: 'This place is holy, this ground is holy; in the name of the Father, Son, and Holy Ghost, I pronounce it holy.' Then he took up some of the dust, and threw it up into the air several times in his going up towards the church. When they approached near to the rail and communion-table, the bishop bowed towards it several times, and returning they went round the church in procession, saying the Hundredth Psalm, after that the Nineteenth Psalm, and then said a form of prayer, 'Lord Jesus Christ,' &c.; and concluding, 'We consecrate this church, and separate it unto Thee, as holy ground, not to be profaned any more to common use.' After this, the bishop being near the communion-table, and taking a written book in his hand, pronounced curses upon those that should afterwards profane that holy place, by musters of soldiers, or keeping profane law-courts, or carrying burdens through it; and at the end of every curse he bowed towards the east, and said, 'Let all the people say, Amen.' When the curses were ended, he pronounced a number of blessings upon all those that had any hand in framing and building of that sacred church, and those that had given, or should hereafter give, chalices, plate, ornaments, or utensils; and at the end of every blessing he bowed towards the east, saying, 'Let all the people say, Amen.'

"After this followed the sermon, which being ended, the bishop consecrated and administered the sacrament in manner following :—As he approached the communion-table he made several lowly bowings, and coming up to the side of the table where the bread and wine were covered, he bowed seven times; and then, after the reading of many prayers, he came near the bread, and gently lifted up the corner of the napkin wherein the bread were laid; and when he beheld the bread, he laid it down again, flew back a step or two, bowed three several times towards it. Then he drew near again, and opened the napkin and bowed as before. Then he laid his hand on the cup, which was full of wine, with a cover upon it, which he let go again, went back, and bowed thrice towards it; then he came near again, and lifting up the cover of the cup, looked into it, and seeing the wine, he let fall the cover again, retired back, and bowed as before. Then he received the sacrament, and gave it to some principal men; after which, many prayers being said, the solemnity of the consecration ended."

In the Middle Ages morality plays were acted in the churchyard of St. Catherine Cree. In an old parish book, quoted by Malcolm, under the date

an ambassador to France from Queen Elizabeth. The tomb, of marble or alabaster, "now (1839)," says Mr. Godwin, "painted stone-colour, is canopied, and has a recumbent effigy." There is also a small tablet, supported by two figures of monks (beginning of seventeenth century). At the west end is an indifferent bas-relief by the elder Bacon. There is also a man more illustrious than these said to be buried here, and that is the great Holbein. The great painter is said to have died in the parish of St. Andrew Undershaft, and Strype gives this as the place of his interment, adding that the Earl of Arundel had wished to erect a monument to his

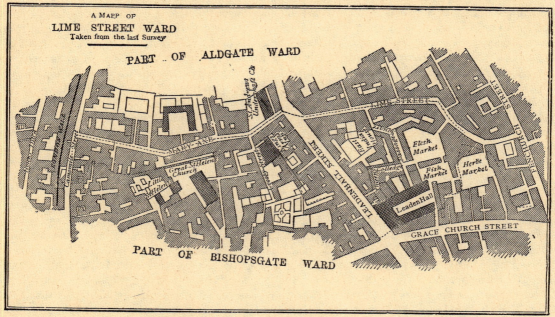

LIME STREET WARD. (*From a Survey made in* 1750.)

1565, there is an entry of certain players, who for licence to play their interludes in the churchyard paid the sum of 27s. 8d.

The most interesting ceremonial to be witnessed in this church is the annual "flower sermon" on Whit-Monday, which is largely attended: the congregation all wear flowers, and a large bouquet is placed on the pulpit before the preacher.

It is generally thought by good authorities that this church was restored under the direction of Inigo Jones. The building displays a strange mixture of Gothic and Greek architecture, yet is still not without a certain picturesqueness. The east window is square-headed; Corinthian columns support a clerestory, and the groined ceiling is coarse and ugly. The chief monument in the church is one to the memory of Sir Nicholas Throgmorton, chief butler of England, a chamberlain, and

memory, but was unable to discover the exact spot of his grave. The close of Holbein's career, however, is wrapped in obscurity. Walpole observes that "the spot of his *interment* is as uncertain as that of his *death*;" and he might have added, that there is quite as much doubt about the time.

St. Mary Axe, so called originally from a shop with the sign of an axe, is a street which runs from Lime Street into Camomile Street, on the line of the old Roman wall, and so named (like Wormwood Street) from the rough herbs that grew among the old Roman stones. The church of St. Mary, long since vanished, was, says Stow, after the union of the parish with that of St. Andrew Undershaft, turned into a warehouse. The Smiths, in one of the best of the "Rejected Addresses," in imitation of Crabbe, play very wittily on the name of St. Mary Axe—

" Jews from St. Mary Axe, for jobs so wary,
 That for old clothes they'd even axe St. Mary."

Near this spot stood, in the reign of Henry V., the London residence of the De Veres, Earls of Oxford. Richard, Earl of Oxford, fought at Agincourt, and died in France, 1417, two years after that great victory.

In Leadenhall Street, opposite the East India House, in 1803 was found the most magnificent Roman tessellated pavement yet discovered in London. It lay at only nine and a half feet below the street, but a third side had been cut away for a sewer. It appeared to have been the floor of a room more than twenty feet square. In the centre was Bacchus upon a tiger, encircled with three borders (inflexions of serpents, cornucopiæ, and squares diagonally concave), with drinking-cups and plants at the angles. Surrounding the whole was a square border of a bandeau of oak, and lozenge figures and true-lover's knots, and a five-feet outer margin of plain red tiles. The pavement was broken in taking up, but the pieces were preserved in the library of the East India Company. A fragment of an urn and a jawbone were found beneath one corner. " In this beautiful specimen of Roman Mosaic," says Mr. Fisher, who published a coloured print of it, "the drawing, colouring, and shadows are all effected by about twenty separate tints, composed of tessellæ of different materials, the major part of which are baked earths; but the more brilliant colours of green and purple, which form the drapery, are of glass. These tessellæ are of different sizes and figures, adapted to the situations they occupy in the design." In connection with this interesting discovery, it may be mentioned that another fine Roman pavement, twenty-eight feet square, was found in 1854 in Old Broad Street, on taking down the Excise Office. It lay about fifteen feet lower than the foundations of Gresham House, on the site of which the Excise Office was built. " It is," if we may accept the statement of Mr. Timbs, in his " Curiosities," "a geometrical pattern of broad blue lines, forming intersections of octagon and lozenge compartments. The octagon figures are bordered with a cable pattern, shaded with grey, and interlaced with a square border shaded with red and yellow. In the centres, within a ring, are expanded flowers, shaded in red, yellow, and grey, the double row of leaves radiating from a figure called a true-love knot, alternately with a figure something like the tiger-lily. Between the octagon figures are square compartments bearing various devices. In the centre of the pavement is Ariadne or a Bacchante, reclining on the back of a panther, but only the fore-paws, one of the hind-paws, and the tail, remain. Over the head of the figure floats a light drapery, forming an arch. Another square contains a two-handled vase. On the demi-octagons, at the sides of the pattern, are lunettes; one contains a fan ornament; another, a bowl crowned with flowers. The lozenge intersections are variously embellished with leaves, shells, true-love knots, chequers, and an ornament shaped like a dice-box. At the corners of the pattern are true-love knots. Surrounding this pattern is a broad cable-like border, broad bands of blue and white alternating, then a floral scroll, and beyond this an edge of demi-lozenges, in alternate blue and white. An outer border composed of plain red tessellæ, surrounds the whole. The ground of the pavement is white, and the other colours are a scale of full red, yellow, and a bluish grey. This pavement is of late workmanship. Various Roman and mediæval articles were turned up in the same excavation; among these were a silver denarius of Hadrian, several copper coins of Constantine, and a small copper coin bearing, on the reverse, the figures of Romulus and Remus suckled by the traditionary wolf; several Roman and mediæval tiles and fragments of pottery; a small glass of a fine blue colour, and coins and tradesmen's tokens were also found.

Perhaps of all the old churches of London there is scarcely one so interesting as St. Andrew Undershaft, Leadenhall Street, nearly opposite the site of the old East India House, the very name itself suggesting some curious and almost forgotten tradition. Stow is peculiarly interesting about this church, which he says derived its singular name from "a high or long shaft or Maypole higher than the church steeple" (hence *under* shaft), which used, early in the morning of May Day, the great spring festival of merry England, to be set up and hung with flowers opposite the south door of St. Andrew's.

This ancient Maypole must have been the very centre of those joyous and innocent May Day revelries sung by Herrick :—

" Come, my Corinna; and a coming, marke
   How each field turns a street, each street a parke
       Made green and trimm'd with trees; see how
       Devotion gives each house a bough,
       Or branch; each porch, each doore, ere this,
       An arke, a tabernacle is,
   Made up of white-thorn neatly interwove;
   As if here were those cooler shades of love.
       Can such delights be in the street
       And open fields, and we not see't?
       Come, we'll abroad, and let's obey
       The proclamation made for May,
   And sin no more, as we have done, by staying
   But, my Corinna, come, let's go a Maying."

The venerable St. Andrew's Maypole was never raised after that fatal "Evil May Day," in the reign of Henry VIII., which we have mentioned in our chapter on Cheapside. It remained dry-rotting on its friendly hooks in Shaft Alley till the third year of Edward VI., when the Reforming preachers, time but between Shrovetide and Easter. The same eccentric reformer used to preach out of a high elm-tree in his churchyard, and sing high mass in English from a tomb, far from the altar. The sermon denouncing the Maypole was preached at Paul's Cross, when Stow himself was present;

STOW'S MONUMENT IN ST. ANDREW UNDERSHAFT. (*See page* 193.)

growing unusually hot and zealous in the sunshine of royal favour, and, as a natural consequence, considerably intolerant, one Sir Stephen, a curate of the neighbouring St. Katherine's Christ Church, Leadenhall Street, preached against the good old Maypole, and called it an "Idol," advising all men to alter the Popish names of churches and the names of the days of the week, to eat fish any day but Friday and Saturday, and to keep Lent any and that same afternoon the good old historian says he saw the Shaft Alley people, "after they had dined, to make themselves strong, gathered more help, and with great labour, raising the shaft from the hooks whereon it had rested two-and-thirty years, they sawed it in pieces, every man taking for his share so much as had lain over his door and stall, the length of his house." Thus was the "idol" mangled and burned. Not long after there was a

Romish riot in Essex, and the bailiff of Romford was hung just by the well at Aldgate, on the pavement in front of Stow's own house. While on the ladder this poor perplexed bailiff said he did not know why he was to be hung, unless it was for telling Sir Stephen (the enemy of the Maypole) that there was heavy news in the country, and many men were up in Essex. After this man's death Sir Stephen stole out of London, to avoid popular reproach, and

divines," for chance readers; and there still is a desk with seven curious old books (mostly black letter), which formerly were chained to open cages. The present church, rebuilt 1520–1532, consists of a nave and two aisles, with a ribbed and flattened perpendicular roof, painted and gilt, with flowers and emblazoned shields. The chancel has also paintings of the heavenly choir, landscapes, and buildings. St. Andrew's boasts much stained glass,

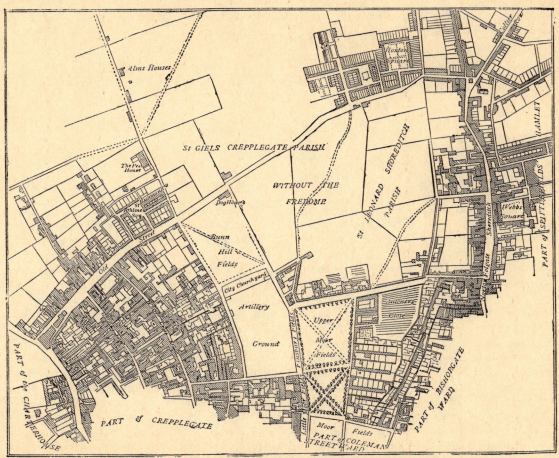

MOORFIELDS AND ITS NEIGHBOURHOOD. (*From a Map of about* 1720.)

was never afterwards heard of by good old Stow. And this is the whole story of St. Andrew's Maypole and the foolish curate of Catherine Cree.

Many eminent citizens were buried in this church. Among them we may name John Kirby, the great Elizabethan merchant tailor, and Stow himself, Stephen Jennings, Mayor of London, another worthy merchant tailor, who, in 1520, rebuilt half the church, but sought a grave in the Grey Friars (Christ's Hospital). An old chronicler mentions "at the lower end of the north ile" of this church "a faire wainscot press full of good books, the works of many learned and reverend

particularly a large painted window at the east end, containing whole-length portraits of Edward VI., Elizabeth, James, Charles I., and Charles II. This church was pewed soon after 1520. It contains many valuable brasses, tablets, and monuments, as might be expected in a celebrated City church lucky enough to escape the Great Fire. The most special and memorable of these is the terra-cotta monument to worthy, indefatigable, honest old Stow. The monument to Stow was erected at the expense of his widow, and the effigy was formerly painted to resemble life. The worthy old chronicler is represented sitting at a table, as he must have spent half his existence, with a book before him an old parish register, no doubt, and he holds a pen in his hand, as was his custom. The figure is squat and stiff, but the portrait is no doubt exact. There was formerly, says Cunningham, a railing before the tomb. That Stow was a tailor, born about 1525, in the parish of St. Michael, Cornhill, we have stated in a previous chapter. That he lived near Aldgate Pump we have also noted. He seems to have written his laborious "Chronicles," "Annals," and "Survey" amidst care and poverty. He was a friend of

Camden, and a *protégé* of Archbishop Parker, yet all he could obtain from James I. was a licence to beg. He died a twelvemonth after this effusion of royal favour, and was buried at St. Andrew's in 1605. In 1732 his body was removed, says Maitland, "to make way for another." His collection for the "Chronicles of England," in sixty quarto volumes, are now in the British Museum. Wonderful *chiffonnier* of topographical facts! Peter Anthony Motteux, the clever translator of "Don Quixote," already mentioned by us, was buried here, but there is no monument to his memory.

CHAPTER XXV.

SHOREDITCH.

The Famous Legend respecting Shoreditch—Sir John de Soerditch—"The Duke of Shoreditch"—Archery Competitions of the Sixteenth Century—St. Leonard's Church—Celebrated Men of Elizabeth's Time—The Fairchild Sermon—Holywell Lane—The "Curtain" Theatre.

THIS ancient and ill-used parish extends from Norton Folgate to Old Street, and from part of Finsbury to Bethnal Green. Originally a village on the old Roman northern road, called by the Saxons Old Street, it is now a continuation of Bishopsgate Street.

The old London tradition is that Shoreditch derived its name from Jane Shore, the beautiful mistress of Edward IV., who, worn out with poverty and hunger, died miserably in a ditch in this unsavoury suburb. This legend, however, is entirely erroneous, as we have shown in a previous chapter. It does not seem to have been popular even so late as 1587. Dr. Percy hit upon quite as erroneous a derivation when he traced the name of the parish to shore (sewer), a common drain. Shoreditch, or, more correctly, Soerdich, really took its name from the old family of the Soerdiches, Lords of the Manor in the time of Edward III. Sir John de Soerdich of that reign, an eminent warrior, lawyer, statesman, and diplomatist, was, on one memorable occasion, sent to Rome to protest before the Pope against the greedy and tyrannical way in which foreign priests were thrust into English benefices, and it was all Sir John could do to get safe back to the little island. The Soerdich family, Mr. Timbs informs us, held the manor of Ickenham, near Uxbridge, and resided there till our own time. The last of the family, an engineer, died in 1865, in the West Indies. In the reign of Richard II. the manor of Shoreditch was granted to Edmund, Duke of York, and his son, the Earl of Rutland,

which accounts for the fact that St. Leonard's Church, Shoreditch, is full of the Manners family. Stow mentions a house in Hackney called Shoreditch Place; and Strype notes the vulgar tradition that Jane Shore once lived there, and was often visited by her royal lover. This was probably the old mansion of Sir John de Soerdich, who rode against the French spears by the side of the Black Prince, and with Manny and Chandos.

In the reign of Henry VIII., when Shoreditch was still a mere waste of fields, dotted with windmills and probably, like Islington (fields, much frequented by archers, for practising at roving marks), the burly king conferred on an archer of Shoreditch, named Barlow, who had pleased him at some wondrous competition at Windsor, the jocular title of Duke of Shoreditch. Happiest and proudest of all London's archers must Barlow have gloried at all civic processions, when, as captain, he strode first to the Hoxton, Islington, or Newington Butts. The duke's companions adopted such titles as the Marquises of Hoxton, Islington, Pancras, and Shacklewell, and other ludicrous appellations of honour. In Elizabeth's reign the archers of London numbered no fewer than 3,000, and on one occasion we hear of one thousand of them, wearing gold chains, going from the Merchant Taylors' Hall to Smithfield, to try their skill, attended by 4,000 billmen, besides pages. In Dryden's time Shoreditch was a disreputable place, frequented by courtesans; and in Lillo's old ballad of "George Barnwell," the apprentice hero of which thrice robbed his master and murdered his uncle in Ludlow, that wicked siren, Mrs. Millwood, lives at Shoreditch, "next door unto the 'Gun.'"

The present St. Leonard's Church, Shoreditch, occupies the site of a church at least as old as the thirteenth century. The old church, which had four gables and a low square tower, was taken down in 1736, and the present ugly church built by the elder Dance, in 1740, with a steeple to imitate that of St. Mary-le-Bow, Cheapside, and a fine peal of twelve bells. The chancel window, the gift of Thomas Awsten, in 1634, and a tablet to the Awstens, are the only relics left of the old church. St. Leonard's is the actor's church of London; for, in the days of Elizabeth and James, the players of distinction from the Curtain, in Holywell Lane, and from "The Theatre," as well as those from the Blackfriars Theatre and Shakespeare's Globe, were fond of residing in this parish. Perhaps nowhere in all London have rooms echoed oftener with Shakespeare's name than those of Shoreditch.

The parish register, within a period of sixty years, says Cunningham, records the interment at St. Leonard's of the following celebrated characters:—"Will. Somers, Henry VIII.'s jester (d. 1560); Richard Tarlton, the famous clown of Queen Elizabeth's time (d. 1588); James Burbage (d. 1596) and his more celebrated son, Richard Burbage (d. 1618–19); Gabriel Spenser, the player, who fell, in 1598, in a duel with Ben Jonson; William Sly and Richard Cowley, two original performers in Shakespeare's plays; the Countess of Rutland, the only child of the famous Sir Philip Sydney; Fortunatus Greene, the *un*fortunate offspring of Robert Greene, the poet and player (d. 1593). Another original performer in Shakespeare's plays, who lived in Holywell Street, in this parish, was Nicholas Wilkinson, *alias* Tooley, whose name is recorded in gilt letters on the north side of the altar, as a yearly benefactor of £6 10s., which sum is still distributed in bread every year to the poor inhabitants of the parish, to whom it was bequeathed.

In the burial register, January 22nd, 1588, is the following entry: "Aged 207 years. Holywell Street. Thomas Cam." The 2 should probably be 1. A correspondent of the *Penny Magazine*, writing in 1833, notices this entry as the most remarkable record of longevity in existence, and adds: "It thus appears that Cam was born in the year 1381, in the fourth of Richard II., living through the reign of that monarch, and through those of the whole of the following sovereigns—

viz., Henry IV., Henry V., Henry VI., Edward IV., Edward V., Richard III., Henry VII., Henry VIII., Edward VI., Mary, and to the thirtieth of Elizabeth. Such an extreme duration of life is, however, contrary to all recorded experience; and unless the fact can be supported by other evidence, it is reasonable to conclude that the entry in the register is inaccurate."

At St. Leonard's, every Whit Tuesday, is preached a sermon on the "Wonderful Works of God in the Creation," or "On the Certainty of the Resurrection of the Dead, proved by certain changes of the Animal and Vegetable Parts of the Creation." The money, £25 in all, left for this purpose to the preacher was bequeathed, in 1728, by Mr. Thomas Fairchild, a gardener, whose gardens (Selby's Gardens) then extended from the west end of Ivy Lane to the New North Road. The sum originally bequeathed was afterwards increased by sundry contributions. It used to be the custom for the President and Fellows of the Royal Society to attend these sermons.

Holywell Lane (west side of Shoreditch) was so called, says Stow, from a sweet, wholesome, and clear well, spoiled, in that writer's time, by the manure-heaps of the nursery gardens. Here formerly, till the dissolution, stood a Benedictine nunnery of St. John the Baptist, founded by some forgotten Bishop of London; and in this street lived and died Richard Burbage, the tragedian, and friend and companion of Shakespeare. Near St. Leonard's Church stood two of the earliest London theatres—the "Curtain" and "The Theatre." The site of the first of these is still marked by Curtain Road.

"The Theatre," on the site of Holywell Priory, was remarkable as being, according to Malone, the first theatre erected in London. It is noticed in a sermon preached at Paul's Cross, in 1578, as the "gorgeous playing-place erected in the Fields." In 1598 this wooden theatre was taken down, and the timber of it was used for enlarging the Globe.

The "Curtain" is mentioned as early as 1577, before Shakespeare came to London, and by Stubbs, in his "Anatomie of Abuses," in 1583. In 1622 it was occupied by Prince Charles's actors. Aubrey, in 1678, calls it the "Green Curtain," and terms it "a kind of nursery, or obscure playhouse." It gradually, like many of the smaller theatres, sank into a sparring-room. Maitland, in his "London" (1772), mentions some remains of the "Curtain" as recently standing. It is supposed to have got its name from having been the first house that used the green curtain.

CHAPTER XXVI.

MOORFIELDS AND FINSBURY.

"This Fen or Moor Field," says Stow, " stretching from the wall of the City betwixt Bishopsgate and the postern called Cripplesgate, to Finsbury, and to Holywell, continued a waste and unprofitable ground a long time, so that the same was all letten for four marks the year in the reign of Edward II. ; but in the year 1415, the 3rd of Henry V., Thomas Falconer, Mayor, caused the wall of the City to be broken toward the said moor, and built the postern called Moorgate, for the ease of the citizens to walk that way upon causeys towards Iseldon and Hoxton."

Fitzstephen the monk, who wrote a curious account of London in the reign of Henry II., describes Moorfields as the general place of amusement for London youth. Especially, he says, was the Fen frequented for sliding in winter-time, when it was frozen. He then mentions a primitive substitute for skates. "Others there are," he says, " still more expert in these amusements ; they place certain bones—the leg-bones of animals—under the soles of their feet, by tying them round their ankles, and then taking a pole shod with iron into their hands, they push themselves forward by striking it against the ice, and are carried on with a velocity equal to the flight of a bird, or a bolt discharged from a cross-bow." The piece of water on which the citizens of London performed their pastimes is spoken of by Fitzstephen as "the great Fen or Moor which watereth the walls of the City on the north side."

The barren region of Moorfields and Finsbury was first drained (no doubt to the great indignation of the London apprentices) in 1527, laid out in pleasant walks in the reign of James I., and first built on after the Great Fire, when all the City was turned topsy-turvy. Moorfields before this must have been a melancholy region, with raised paths and refuse-heaps, deep black ditches, not inodorous, and detestable open sewers ; a walk for thieves and lovers, suicides and philosophers, and as Howes (1631) says, " held impossible to be reformed."

It is described by Peter Cunningham, in a few lines that conceal much research, as a place for cudgel-players and train-band musters, for its madhouse (one of the lions of London), and for its wrestlers, pedestrians, bookstall-keepers, and ballad-sellers. Ben Jonson makes old Knowell follow his son there, when he has the suspicious appointment in the Old Jewry ; and worthy Brainworm has to do his best to screen his young master. In " The Embassy to England in 1626" of Bassompierre, that French ambassador mentions, after dining (the Duke and Earls of Montgomery and Holland having brought him home), taking a fashionable walk in the Moorfields. Sir William Davenant (Charles II.) wittily talks of the laundresses and bleachers of Moorfields, " whose acres of old linen make a show like the fields of Carthagena (the great naval depôt of Spain), when the five months' shifts of the whole fleet are washed and spread." In one of Peter Cunningham's series of admirably-selected extracts bearing on London topography, we find chatty Pepys (June, 1661) going to Moorfields to see the northern and western men wrestle. Then comes a fray in Moorfields between the butchers and weavers, described by the same diarist, very characteristic of the old guild jealousies, not even then quite forgotten —" 26th July, 1664. Great discourse yesterday of the fray in Moorfields ; how the butchers at first did beat the weavers, between whom there hath been ever an old competition for mastery, but at last the weavers rallied, and beat them. At first the butchers knocked down all for weavers that had green or blue aprons, till they were fain to pull them off and put them in their breeches. At last the butchers were fain to pull off their sleeves, that they might not be known, and were soundly beaten out of the field, and some deeply wounded and bruised ; till at last the weavers went out triumphing, calling, ' £100 for a butcher ! ' "

In 1671, Shadwell, a close imitator of Ben Jonson and the old school whom Dryden ridiculed, sneers, in his "Humourist," at a French surgeon, originally a barber, whose chief customers were the cudgel-players of Moorfields, and drawers (waiters) whose heads had been broken with quart-pots. In the " Scowrers" (so called after the predecessors of the Mohocks, those London night-roysterers who made even Swift tremble), the same fat poet makes Lady Maggot, a vulgar pretender, talk with contempt of walking with her husband. "Well," says the insolent parvenu, "I shall never teach a citizen manners. I warrant you think you are in Moorfields, seeing haberdashers walking with their whole fireside." Garth alludes to the cheap book-stalls of Moorfields; and long after Gray refers in a letter to Warton to "a penny history that hangs upon the rails in Moorfields;" while Tom Brown (1709, Queen Anne), to illustrate the insolence and forgetfulness of prosperity, describes how a cutler despises a knife-grinder, and "a well-grown Paul's Churchyard bookseller one of the trade that sells second-hand books under the trees in Moorfields."

Carpenters' Hall, on the southern side of London Wall, was one of the few City Halls which escaped the Great Fire of 1666. It was also, says Timbs, nearly destroyed in a great fire, Oct. 6, 1849, when the end walls and windows were burned out, and the staircase and roof much damaged; while the burning building was only separated from Drapers' Hall by the garden and fore-court. The Hall was originally built in 1429. The walls of old London faced it, and beyond were Moorfields, Finsbury, and open ground. The exterior of the old Hall possessed no trace of antiquity. The court-rooms were built in 1664, and the principal staircase and entrance-hall about 1780; the latter was richly decorated with bas-reliefs of carpentry figures and implements, with heads of Vitruvius, Palladio, Inigo Jones, and Wren. The Hall was rebuilt in 1876–80, and is now a large and imposing edifice, and it stands a little to the east of its predecessor.

The Great Hall of the new building has a rich and beautiful ceiling, supported by marble columns and pilasters. Over the fire-place of the luncheon-room is a series of fresco paintings, which were discovered in 1845 by a workman in repairing the old hall. The groundwork upon which they are executed is composed of laths, with a thick layer of brown earth and clay held well together with straw and a layer of lime. There were originally four, the subjects being:—

1. Noah receiving the commands from the Almighty for the construction of the ark; in another portion of the picture are Noah's three sons at work. 2. King Josiah ordering the repair of the Temple (2 Kings xxii.); mentioning _carpenters_ and builders and masons as having no reckoning of money made with them, "because they dealt faithfully." 3. Joseph at work as a carpenter, the Saviour as a boy gathering the chips;

Mary spinning with the distaff; the figure of Joseph represents that in Albert Durer's woodcut of the same incident, executed in 1511. 4. Christ teaching in the synagogue; "is not this the _carpenter's_ son?" No. 1. has unfortunately been broken and destroyed. The figures are of the school of Holbein; the costumes are _temp_. Henry VIII.

In the board-room is some ancient panelling, which has been brought from the old Hall; and there are also some windows of painted glass, in some of the rooms which have been rescued from the old building.

About the date of the Carpenters' Company's earliest charter there is considerable uncertainty. Their common seal and grant of arms is dated 1466; and a guild of carpentry is noticed in 1421–2. Stow remarks that "amongst many proper houses, possessed for the most part by curriers, is the Carpenter's Hall. The earliest entry in the Company's books is dated 1438; they contain many proofs of their power over the trade. Among the pictures are portraits of William Portington, master carpenter to the Crown, _temp_. Elizabeth and James I.; and John Scott, ordnance carpenter and carriage-maker, _temp_. Charles II. The Company also possess four very curious caps or crowns (the oldest 1561), still used by the master and wardens. Among their plate are three silver-gilt _hanaps_ (1611, 1612, 1628), which are borne in procession round the hall on election-day. Cakes are presented to the members of the court on Twelfth Day, and the ceremony of crowning the master and wardens takes place annually on election-day.

Moorfields was crowded after the Great Fire. "The poor inhabitants," writes Evelyn, "were dispersed about St. George's Fields, and Moorfields, as far as Highgate, and several miles in circle; some under tents, some under miserable huts and hovels; many without a rag or any necessary utensils, bed, or board, who from delicateness, riches, and easy accommodations, in stately and well-furnished houses, were now reduced to extremest poverty and misery. In this calamitous condition, I returned with a sad heart to my house, blessing and adoring the distinguishing mercy of God to me and mine, who, in the midst of all this ruin, was like Lot, in my little Zoar, safe and sound."

"Here in Moorfields," says Strype, "is the new Artillery Ground, so called in distinction from another artillery garden near St. Mary Spittal, where formerly the Artillery Company exercised; who, about the latter end of King James I. his reign, were determined to remove thence, and to hold their trainings and practice of arms here ; being the third great field from Moorgate, next to the six windmills, which field, Mr. Leat, one of the twenty captains, with great pains, was divers years a-preparing to that purpose. The reason of this, their remove, was, because now their meetings and number consisted of many more soldiers than the old ground could well contain, being sometimes 6,000. Though

weight in their ears than the finest oratory. On marching to join the Earl of Essex, this was his speech : "Come, my boys, my brave boys, let us pray heartily and fight heartily ; I will run the same fortune and hazards with you. Remember the cause is for God ; and for yourselves, your wives, and children. Come, my honest brave boys, pray heartily and fight heartily, and God will bless you."

The Tabernacle, in Moorfields, was built in 1752 ; previously to which, in 1741, shortly after White-

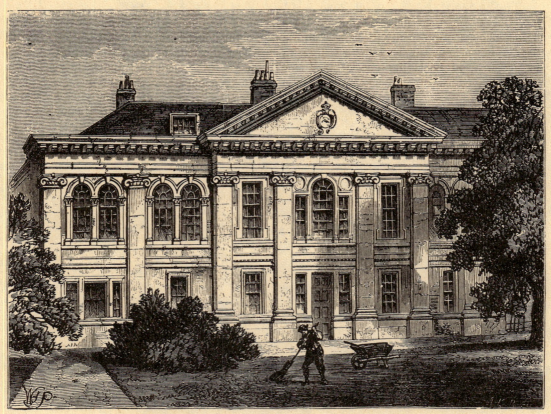

HALL OF THE CARPENTERS' COMPANY, 1870. (*See page* 197.)

sometimes, notwithstanding, they went to the old artillery, and continued so to do in my memory."

It was this company, then known by the name of the Trained-bands, which decided the fate of the great civil war. On every occasion they behaved with the spirit and perseverance of the most veteran troops. They were commanded by Skippon, captain of the Artillery Garden, who had served long in Holland, and raised himself from a common soldier to the rank of captain, and proved himself an excellent officer. From the service he had been in he came over full of prejudice against the Church and State, so was greatly in the confidence of his party. He was totally illiterate, but his speeches to his soldiers had more

field's separation from Wesley, some Calvinistic Dissenters, says Mr. Timbs, raised for Whitefield a large shed near the Foundry, in Moorfields, upon a piece of ground lent for the purpose, until he should return from America. From the temporary nature of the structure it was called the Tabernacle, in allusion to the Tabernacle of the Israelites in the Wilderness ; and the name became the designation of the chapels of the Calvinistic Methodists generally. Whitefield's first pulpit here is said to have been a grocer's sugar hogshead, an eccentricity not improbable. Silas Todd describes the Moorfields Tabernacle, about 1740, as " a ruinous place, with an old pantile covering, a few rough deal boards put together to constitute a temporary pulpit, and

OLD BETHLEM HOSPITAL, MOORFIELDS, ABOUT 1750. (*See page 200.*)

several other decayed timbers, which composed the whole structure." John Wesley also preached here (the Foundry, as it was called), at five in the morning and seven in the evening. The men and women sat apart; and there were no pews, or difference of benches, or appointed place for any person. At this chapel the first Methodist Society was formed in 1740. In 1752, the wooden building was taken down, the site was leased by the City of London, and a new chapel was built, with a lantern roof. This chapel was occupied by the Independents, and would accommodate 4,000 persons. The original wooden chapel was the cradle of Methodism; the preaching-places had hitherto been Moorfields, Mary-le-bone Fields, and Kennington Common. Its successor was pulled down in 1868, and a much smaller edifice now occupies part of the site.

The old Bedlam, one of the chief lions of Moorfields, was a low, dismal-looking pile; enclosed by heavy gates, and surrounded by squalid houses.

"When I remember Moorfields first," says "Aleph" (i.e., Mr. William Harvey), "it was a large open quadrangular space, shut in by the Pavement to the west, the hospital and its outbuildings to the south, and lines of shops without fronts, occupied chiefly by dealers in old furniture, to the east and north. Most of these shops were covered in by screens of canvas or rough boards, so as to form an apology for a piazza; and, if you were bold enough, in wet weather you might take refuge under them, but it was at the imminent risk of your purse or your handkerchief. As Field Lane was the favourite market for wearing apparel, at a low charge, so these stores afforded an endless choice of decayed upholstery to poorer purchasers: a broken-down four-poster or a rickety tent bedstead might be secured at almost any price, 'No reasonable offer was refused.' It was interesting to inspect the articles exposed for sale: here a cracked mirror in a dingy frame, a set of hair-seated chairs, the horse-hair protruding; a tall, stiff, upright easy chair, without a bottom; a cupboard with one shelf left of three, and with half a door; here a black oak chest, groaning to be scraped, so thick with ancient dust that it might have been the den of some unclean animal in Noah's ark; a washhand-stand, with a broken basin; a hall clock-case, with a pendulum, but no dial; and other hopelessly invalided household necessaries, too numerous to mention. These miscellaneous treasures were guarded by swarthy men and women of Israel, who paraded in front of their narrow dominions all the working day; and if you did but pause for an instant, you must expect to be dragged into some hideous Babel of frowsy chattels, and made a purchaser in spite of yourself. Escaping from this uncomfortable mart to the hospital footway, a strange sense of utter desertion came over you; long, gloomy lines of cells, strongly barred, and obscured with the accumulated dust, silent as the grave, unless fancy brought sounds of woe to your ears, rose before you; and there, on each side of the principal entrance, were the wonderful effigies of raving and moping madness, chiselled by the elder Cibber. How those stone faces and eyes glared! How sternly the razor must have swept over those bare heads! How listless and dead were those limbs, bound with inexorable fetters, while the iron of despair had pierced the hearts of the prisoned maniacs! Those terrible presentments of physical anguish were till lately preserved in the entrance of the new hospital, but a rumour went the round of the press that they were about to be removed." This presentiment proved correct, and these two remarkable statues may now (says Mr. Harvey in 1863) be seen in the South Kensington Museum, where they are infinitely less appropriate than in their old home.

"Opposite to Bethlem Hospital, on the north side of Moorfields, stood the hospital of St. Luke, a long plain building, till of late," says Pennant, "appropriated to the same purposes, but totally independent of the former." It was founded on the humane consideration that Bethlem was incapable of receiving all the miserable objects which were offered. A few years before Pennant's writing, in 1790, the patients were removed from the old hospital to a new one, erected under the same name, in Old Street, on the plan of the former, extending in front 493 feet.

In 1753 (says Timbs) pupils were admitted to the hospital; and Dr. Battie, the original physician, allowed medical men to observe his practice. This practice fell into disuse, but was revived in 1843, and an annual course of chemical lectures established, at which pupils selected by the physicians of the different metropolitan hospitals are allowed to attend gratuitously. In 1754 incurable patients were admitted, on payment, to the hospital on Windmill Hill.

"There are few buildings in the metropolis, perhaps in Europe," says Elmes, "that, considering the poverty of the material, common English clamp-bricks, possess such harmony of proportion, with unity and appropriateness of style, as this building. It is as characteristic of its uses as that of Newgate, by the same architect."

This building was commenced in 1782, when green fields could be seen in every direction, and the foundation-stone was laid by the Duke of Montague, July 30 ; the cost, about £50,000, being defrayed by subscriptions. George Dance, junior, was the architect.

Since the first admission of patients on July 30th, 1751, to the same day 1791, 4,421 were admitted, of which 1,936 were discharged cured, and 1,465 uncured. By a very liberal regulation, uncured patients could be taken in again, on the payment of five shillings a week. This was afterwards increased to seven shillings ; so that their friends might, if they pleased, try a second time the force of medicine on their unhappy relations or connections. The number of patients received into the hospital from its opening to April 25, 1809, amounted to 9,042, of whom 3,884 were discharged uncured or as idiots, and 35,911 as cured. The old hospital was at last pulled down and replaced by a row of houses along the north side of London Wall.

The hospital was incorporated in 1838, the end infirmaries added in 1841; a chapel in 1842, and open fire-places set in the galleries ; when also coercion was abolished, padded rooms were provided for violent patients, and an airing ground set apart for them ; wooden doors were substituted for iron gates, and unnecessary guards and bars removed from the windows. In 1843 were added reading-rooms and a library for the patients, with bagatelle and backgammon boards, &c. By Act 9 & 10 Vict., cap. 100, the Commissioners of Lunacy were added to the hospital direction. In 1848, Sir Charles Knightley presented an organ to the chapel, and daily service was first performed. The hospital was next lighted with gas ; the drainage, ventilation, and the supply of water improved, by subscription at the Centenary Festival, June 25, 1851.

"On St. Luke's Day (October 18), a large number of the patients are annually entertained with dancing and singing in the great hall in the centre of the hospital, when the officers, nurses, and attendants join the festival. Balls are also given fortnightly."

Since the year 1684, when Bethlem Hospital admitted into its wards seventy-three lunatic patients, and since the establishment of St. Luke's in 1751, about 40,000 insane persons have been treated in these two institutions. Within comparatively few years insanity in England has more than tripled. During the last forty-five years or so, several large asylums have been built in the metropolitan counties : for example, Hanwell, 1831; Earlswood Asylum for Idiots, founded in 1847 ; and Colney Hatch, 1851. The Lunatic Asylum for the City of London is situated near Dartford. It was erected at the expense of the Corporation of London, and opened in the year 1866, for the reception and treatment of lunatic patients chargeable upon the City of London, and upon the several unions in the City. It contains accommodation for 284 patients.

"Immediately behind this hospital," Pennant remarks, " was Peerless Pool, in name altered from that of Perilous Pond, so called, says old Stow, from the numbers of youths who had been drowned in it in swimming." In our time, says Pennant writing in 1790, it has, at great expense, been converted into the finest and most spacious bathing-place now known ; where persons may enjoy the manly and useful exercise with safety. Here is also an excellent covered bath, with a large pond stocked with fish, a small library, a bowling green, and every innocent and rational amusement ; so that it is not without reason that the proprietor hath bestowed on it the present name."

The parish of St. Luke was taken out of that of St. Giles, Cripplegate, by an Act of George II.'s reign. The same writer directs the reader's attention to the steeple of the church (built in 1732) which terminates most singularly in a fluted obelisk.

From Moorfields we have not far to go to Finsbury. It was in Finsbury Fields, on his return after his exploits in Scotland, that the great Protector, the Duke of Somerset, was met and congratulated by the Lord Mayor, aldermen, and citizens of London. According to the chronicler, Holinshed, " The mayor and aldermen, with certain of the commons, in their liveries and their hoods, hearing of his approach to the City, the 8th of October (1548), met him in Finsbury Fields, where he took each of them by the hand, and thanked them for their good wills. The Lord Mayor did ride with him till they came to the pond in Smithfield, where his grace left them, and rode to his house of Shene that night, and the next day to the king at Hampton Court."

As the old fashionable medical quarter of London, Finsbury has a peculiar interest. The special localities of doctors used to be Finsbury Square, Finsbury Pavement, Finsbury Place, Finsbury Circus, Broad Street, and St. Helen's Place, which, fifty years since, swarmed with doctors and surgeons, who made larger earnings out of the chiefs and prosperous business folk of the City than the West-end faculty made out of the Court and aristocracy. At the same time young surgeons and doctors occupied small houses in the adjacent courts, just as the young barristers and pleaders housed themselves in modest streets and yards near the Inns of Court. William Eccles, formerly surgeon of the Devonshire Square Hospital, and Royal Free Hospital, a notable surgeon thirty or forty years since, had his first house in Union Court, Broad Street. His successor, Edward Chance, lived afterwards in the same house; but was about the only surgeon residing in a street which once housed not less than a score of surgeons and physicians. Broad Street and Union Court are now made up of chambers tenanted by stock-brokers and other City agents. The last pre-eminently great physician to practise in the City was Henry Jeaffreson, M.D. (Senior Physician of St. Bartholomew's), who died some years since in Finsbury Square, where he had long made a larger income than any other doctor of his day. Several eminent doctors still live in Finsbury Square and Finsbury Pavement. St. Helen's Place, Bishopsgate, also still houses a few well-to-do doctors. Charterhouse Square was another great place for East-end doctors.

But the migrations of the eminent doctors is not so much due to mere fashion, as to the centralisation and development of commerce, which have raised the rentals of the residential parts of the quarter so prodigiously, that only very wealthy folk could afford to house themselves there. Such a house as Mr. Eccles had in Broad Street at some £210 a year rent and taxes, is now-a-days let as offices and business chambers for £1,000 a year. Hence, the commercial families have moved westward from economy, as well as from disinclination to live in a socially deserted district. The doctors now swarm in Cavendish Square, Harley Street, Wimpole Street, Henrietta Street, Queen Anne Street, Brook Street, Savile Row, and Spring Gardens; and in these days of circular railways and fast cabs, they are as accessible to their unfashionable visitors in such quarters as the old Finsbury doctors were to their outlying patients.

When the doctors and surgeons thus swarmed in the Finsbury district, the City and its adjacent districts were largely inhabited by wealthy families, that have now also migrated westward, as their doctors naturally have.

That Campo Santo of the Dissenters, the Bunhill Fields burial-ground no longer used for interments, is on the west side of the Artillery Ground, and close to Finsbury Square.

It is generally supposed that the Bunhill Fields Cemetery was the site of the Great Plague pit, so powerfully described, from hearsay, by Defoe. Peter Cunningham, usually so exact, has said so, and every writer since has followed in his wake. That the conjecture is entirely erroneous is ad-

mirably shown in the following accurate account by Mr. J. C. Jeaffreson, who has devoted much time to the study of the question:—The burial-ground in Bunhill Fields, said our authority in 1866, preserves the ashes of Cromwell's favourite minister, Dr. Goodwin, John Owen, the Puritan Vice-Chancellor of Oxford, General Fleetwood, John Bunyan, Daniel Defoe, John Horne Tooke, Isaac Watts, Blake, Stothard, Susannah Wesley (the mother of John Wesley), and many other eminent persons. The "great pit in Finsbury," mentioned by Defoe in his "Journal of the Plague in 1665," occupied ground that abuts on the upper end of Goswell Street; whereas Bunhill Fields Cemetery lies within a step of the Artillery Ground, and a stone's throw of Finsbury Square. The precise locality of Defoe's "Pit" can be pointed out by any person familiar with the novelist's "Journal" and the map of London. In the passage of Defoe which describes how John Hayward, the driver of a dead-cart, was on the point of consigning to the gloomy pit a wretched street-musician, who, whilst in a sound sleep, or perhaps stupefied with drink, had been thrown upon a load of corpses, the writer of the "Journal," says, "Accordingly when John Hayward, with his bell and the cart, came along, finding two dead bodies lie upon the stall, they took them up with the instrument they used and threw them into the cart, and all this while the piper slept soundly. From thence they passed along and took in other dead bodies, till, as honest John Hayward told me, they almost buried him alive in the cart. Yet all this while he slept soundly. At length the cart came to the place where the bodies were to be thrown into the ground; which, as I do remember, was at Mountmill; and as the cart usually stopped some time before they were ready to shoot out the melancholy load they had in it—as soon as the cart stopped the fellow awaked, and struggled a little to get his head out from among the dead bodies; when, raising himself up in the cart, he called out, 'Hey! where am I?'" Of the locality called *Mountmill*, the topographer and historian, William Maitland, writing in 1739, observes, in his "London," "At Mountmill, near the upper end of Goswell Street, was situate one of the forts which were erected by order of Parliament, for the security of the City of London in the year 1643. But the same being rendered useless at the end of the Civil War, a windmill was erected thereon; from which it received its present name." The popular impression that Defoe's "great pit in Finsbury" was on the site of the present Bunhill Fields Cemetery is no matter for surprise, when it is known that the ground of the Dissenters' graveyard was actually set apart and consecrated, in 1665, for the reception of victims of the plague. That the place was not used for the especial purpose for which it was consecrated, we have Maitland's authority.

"Of the ground thus set apart by the Corporation of London for a graveyard the City merely owned a lease. Lying in the centre of a large tract, which the City had held for 350 years under a succession of leases, granted by successive prebendaries of Finsbury, the civic authorities had a limited right over the spot. The fee-simple of the ground was part of the estate attached to the prebend of Finsbury, one of the prebends of St. Paul's Cathedral; and though prebendaries of Finsbury have repeatedly renewed old leases and granted new leases of the land, the freehold of the estate has never passed out of the hands of the Church. The last lease of the Finsbury estate, made by the Church to the City, was executed in 1769, and is a good instance of the nice little arrangements that were formerly made with Church property. Under the authority of a private Act of Parliament, the then Prebendary Wilson gave a lease of the Finsbury estate to the civic Corporation for ninety-nine years, the said lease being renewable at the expiration of seventy-three years, for fourteen years; whereby the term still to expire would become forty years, and afterwards renewable every fourteen years, in like manner for ever. Hence, under this grant, the City, by duly renewing the lease, could hold for ever ground which is now covered by some of the most valuable residential property in London.* By this same private Act," the writer goes on to say, "the City was empowered to keep three-sixths of the net rents, profits, and annual proceeds arising from the estate during the lease. Two-sixths of the same revenue were reserved to Prebendary Wilson and his assigns, and the remaining one-sixth of the income was retained for the prebendary and his successors. This pleasant little arrangement was sanctioned by legislation in the good old times! As holders of the largest single share of the income, the civic authorities took the entire management of the estate, which has, certainly, prospered in their hands. But though the rent-roll has increased prodigiously under civic management, the rulers of the City—

so far as one portion of the estate, *i.e.*, Bunhill Fields Cemetery, is concerned—cannot be said to have acted discreetly, and in one matter affecting the entire property they have been guilty of astounding remissness. Having only a leasehold tenure of the graveyard, they systematically sold the graves in perpetuity, accepting for them money which the buyers of graves would never have thought of paying for ground that might be built upon, or turned into a cattle-market, at the end of a ninety-nine years' lease. Having originally the right to renew the lease on the expiry of seventy-three years, the tenants omitted to renew; and, in consequence, through this omission, their interest in the estate would terminate in 1867.

"It should be observed, that in 1801 the Corporation bought the interest in the estate secured to the Wilson family; consequently, since the date of that purchase, the City has received five-sixths of the annual net income derived from the property. In 1842—in which year, by the terms of the agreement, the Corporation could have renewed the lease—the leaseholders negotiated for the purchase of the freehold of the estate, and the Bishop of London introduced a bill into the Upper House for legalising the sale. Having passed the Lords, this Bill encountered defeat in the Commons, where it was rejected as a money bill that ought to have originated in the Lower Chamber. Occupied with this Parliamentary contest, the civic authorities allowed the time to pass without exercising their right to renew the lease; and, in consequence of this remissness, their interests, in 1867, devolved on the Ecclesiastical Commissioners, in whom the estate of the prebendary of Finsbury vested in 1856, On the termination of the civic interest the Commissioners derived from the property about sixty thousand pounds per annum.

"Not only has the City lost its hold over this magnificent rental, but it finds itself in an awkward discussion with the buyers of graves in Bunhill Fields Cemetery on the one hand, and the Ecclesiastical Commissioners on the other. Apprehensive that the graveyard may be desecrated on the termination of the lease, the Dissenters have, on two occasions, asked the Commissioners to preserve the ground from profanation. On each occasion the Commissioners have expressed a readiness to settle terms. For £10,000 they will make over to trustees the burial-ground—the freehold of which is computed as worth £100,000—on condition that, should it be converted to secular uses, their present rights revive. Moreover, the Commissioners have expressed their readiness to preserve the sacred character of the ground, provided the civic

* This appears to be an error on the part of the writer we are quoting. Mr. Timbs, in his "Curiosities of London," 1868, p. 76, quoting from a communication to the *City Press*, remarks:—"It is said the Act of Parliament authorised the renewal of the lease in perpetuity. . . . This is not the fact. The mistake has arisen from the marginal note saying the lease is renewable; but there is nothing in the Act to warrant the note, and no one at this distance of time can explain how the error has arisen."

authorities pay into the purse of the Commission the sums which they have received for the fee-simple of graves which they had no power to sell. Anyhow, for £10,000 the custody of the cemetery may be purchased; and, if no better terms can be made with the Commissioners, it seems clear that the City is morally bound to supply this sum, for the fulfilment of its engagements to the purchasers of graves.

"There are good reasons to believe that the Commissioners will not stand out for the last

Finsbury estate. The prebendaries, who have received the one-sixth of the revenue reserved to the prebend, by taking a sixth of the money derived from the sale of graves, may be said to have given ecclesiastical sanction to the defective arrangement; and however irregular the arrangement and the sanction may be, it would not be wise in the Ecclesiastical Commissioners to disregard them. The relations of the City and the Commission in this matter involve some delicate questions. However, as a body that has greatly

BUNHILL FIELDS BURIAL GROUND. (*See page 202.*)

farthing of the sum just mentioned. In previous arrangements concerning burial-grounds—the grave-yard, for instance, which contains John Wesley's bones—they acted in a conciliatory and fair manner; and in the present case special considerations counsel them to take a moderate course. In the first place, the ground was actually consecrated; and an Ecclesiastical Commission could not, without indecency, authorise the disturbance of a consecrated burial-ground. Moreover, the Ecclesiastical Commissioners are morally bound by the action of the City. Throughout the stewardship of the municipal authorities the Church has received a portion of the proceeds of the

benefited by the entire transaction, and as a society bound to fulfil its contracts with private persons, the Corporation should effect a settlement of the dispute, even at the sacrifice of £10,000.

"An account of the negotiations for securing Bunhill Fields to the Corporation of London as a place for recreation, and to prevent desecration of the graves of many eminent Englishmen, was eventually presented to the Common Council. The report stated that the Ecclesiastical Commissioners appear to have proposed to accept, for the preservation of the ground, five-sixths of the purchase-money paid for vaults, &c., to the Corporation during its current lease. The total receipts were

THE OLD POST OFFICE IN LOMBARD STREET, ABOUT 1800. (*See page* 210.)

£24,000, *i.e.*, averaging £247 a year. Half this sum had been applied in connection with the prebend of Finsbury; the other was received by the Corporation. Failing agreement about the price to be paid by one of these parties to the other, the negotiations stood over. The latest proposal of the Commissioners was to arbitrate. The committee declined this, and denied the existence of a legal claim on the Corporation on the part of the Commissioners. The report concluded by stating that no useful result would be obtained by further correspondence, and recommended that the Corporation should repeat the offer to preserve the ground for public use and from desecration, plant, and watch it, in failure of performing which the land might revert to the Commissioners; also that they should be authorised to second the efforts of parties who might apply to Parliament or the public for aid to save the graves from speculating builders, and the site for public service. The report was adopted, and referred back to be carried into effect. It was alleged that the Commissioners valued the ground at about £100,000, and asked what the Corporation would give for its preservation. If this be true," said a writer to the *Times*, "the Commissioners, considering that they represented a party which has already received cash for preserving the graves, were hard driven. The Ecclesiastical Commissioners are probably not so black as they are painted. Would it not serve all ends if the Government introduced a Bill to the House of Commons to permit, or, better still, to enjoin the Commissioners to relax their hold on the ground, be content with the half share of profits already received, and that the onus of maintaining the ground should be placed upon the recipients of the other moiety, who are anxious to receive it? It has been stated officially that the Commissioners already receive £50,000 a year on account of the Finsbury prebend. It appears that in 1655, when the estates of that office were sold, the City bought the fee-simple, and for ten years following paid no rent. At the Restoration the property was taken back, rent demanded and paid, to recover which the Corporation farmed part of the land for interments, which began as early as 1665, or the Great Plague. At one time the City received as much as £700 per annum from this source. In 1852 the ground was closed, and the registers removed to Somerset House. This year (1867) the whole estate reverts to the Ecclesiastical Commissioners, who may feel it their duty so far to violate their natural feelings as to let it for building leases. As literary men, if not equally as cosmopolitans, the late and present Chancellors of the

Exchequer ought to unite in exonerating the Ecclesiastical Commissioners from this probably painful sense. It would be disgraceful to the Government if the desecration took place."

This negotiation was eventually completed, and the old cemetery is now a place where meditative men may wander and quietly contemplate the old text, "Dust to dust." The Act for the preservation of the ground as an open space was passed 15th July, 1867, and it was reopened by the Lord Mayor on the 14th of October, 1869. It may be added that a monument to Defoe, the immortal author of "Robinson Crusoe," subscribed by boys and girls, was inaugurated on the 15th of September of the following year.

Lackington, one of the most celebrated of our early cheap booksellers, lived in Chiswell Street, Finsbury, and afterwards at the "Temple of the Muses," Finsbury Place. The shop, into which a coach and six could be driven, was destroyed by fire in 1841. In 1792 Lackington cleared £5,000 by his business, and retired with a fortune in 1798. He was an eccentric and original character, and died in 1815 at Budleigh Salterton, Devonshire.

Finsbury Square dates its erection from the year 1789, and it was built from the designs of George Dance, R.A. Dr. Birkbeck, the founder of Mechanics' Institutes, lived for many years at the south-east corner of the square, and died there in December, 1841.

In South Place, between Finsbury Square and Finsbury Circus, is South Place Chapel and Institute, a large building of Ionic design, erected for a Unitarian congregation. The late Mr. William J. Fox, formerly M.P. for Oldham, a well-known political writer and lecturer, for some time ministered here. The great hall, which is capable of holding 800 persons, is used for public meetings, lectures, concerts, and other entertainments.

The Royal London Ophthalmic Hospital, in Blomfield Street, was founded in 1804, and was the first hospital established in England for the treatment of diseases of the eye. It relieves, on an average, 1,300 in-patients and about 20,000 out-patients annually. The building has recently been enlarged by the addition of a new wing, and its accommodation for in-patients raised to 100 beds, while the out-patient department has been entirely remodelled, and has room for about 400 patients daily. The admission is free to the afflicted poor, whose wants are supplied, including spectacles and artificial eyes, which form a large item of cost. The annual expenditure of the hospital is about £5,000, the greater portion of which is made up by voluntary contributions.

On the north side of Liverpool Street, close by the Ophthalmic Hospital, are the termini of the Great Eastern, the North London, and the London and North-Western Railways; they each cover a large extent of ground, and form conspicuous architectural objects.

On the east side of Blomfield Street are the head-quarters of the London Missionary Society. The building was erected in 1835, and enlarged in 1875. The edifice contains a small museum of curiosities sent home by missionaries abroad.

Finsbury Chapel, at the south-east corner of East Street, which connects Blomfield Street with Finsbury Circus, was erected about half a century ago for the Rev. Alexander Fletcher, D.D., who seceded from one of the branches of the Presbyterians. It is an unsightly building, built after the fashion of a theatre, but will accommodate over 2,000 persons.

At the opposite corner of the street is the Roman Catholic Church of St. Mary, Moorfields, long the pro-cathedral and principal church of the Roman Catholics in London. The first stone of the edifice was laid in 1817, and it was completed in 1820, and consecrated by Dr. Poynter, the Catholic Bishop. The building is in the Italian style of architecture, from the designs of Mr. John Newman; and it was built at a cost of about £26,000. It comprises a centre and north and south aisles, each of which terminates with a chapel. At the back of the high altar is a screen of six marble fluted pillars of the Corinthian order, behind which is a fresco painting of the Crucifixion. This picture, which was executed by Aylio, an Italian, was re-painted by the same artist in 1837; and in 1875, on the formation of the Aldgate extension of the Metropolitan Railway, it was considerably damaged by the subsidence of the walls caused by the railway passing near it, and was again re-painted. The frescoes upon the ceiling were painted by Aylio; but the remainder of the interior decorations have been effected since 1858. In 1852, the edifice having been fixed upon by Cardinal Wiseman as the pro-cathedral of the "diocese" of Westminster, the building was much improved, and the sanctuary arranged according to its present plan. This church is remarkable for the splendour of its plate, all of solid gold. The chalice and paten were given in 1820, by the then Pontiff, Pius VII. The vaults under the church are lofty and spacious, and in some places are formed into catacombs. Three bishops (Poynter, Bramstone, and Gradwell) are buried here, and between thirty and forty priests; and in the small strip of ground adjoining the church, as well as in the vaults, no less than 5,500

Catholics were buried prior to the year 1853, when burials were discontinued there. Here Weber, the celebrated composer, was buried. In this church the remains of Cardinal Wiseman lay in state, previous to interment at Kensal Green Cemetery, in February, 1865. Considerable alterations and repairs have been effected in the interior of this building at different times, particularly since 1858, when the Rev. Dr. Gilbert was appointed head priest.

The first Roman Catholic chapel and presbytery in Little Moorfields stood on the site now occupied by a large chocolate factory at the end of Ropemaker Street. The history of that humble church is intimately connected with the Catholic revival in England; it was from this chapel that Bishop Talbot and two priests were dragged, in 1771, for " daring to offer the Holy Sacrifice ;" and the building was destroyed during the Gordon Riots in 1780. A large house in White Street was shortly afterwards converted into a church for the congregation who had been driven from the chapel in Ropemaker Street; and here they remained till 1820, when they removed to the church of St. Mary, Moorfields. The freehold of the ground on which the church, presbytery, and schools stand was purchased from the Corporation of London.

The London Institution, Finsbury Circus, was established in 1805, and incorporated 1807. A number of gentlemen connected with the City associated together, for the purpose of forming an institution calculated to promote science, literature, and the arts. The number of subscribers was limited to a thousand, and the shares seventy-five guineas each; the subscription-list was soon filled, and the Institution opened with a good library in January, 1806, in a house which formerly belonged to Sir Robert Clayton, in the Old Jewry; the library was afterwards removed to King's Arms Yard, Coleman Street, where it remained until a new and magnificent building was erected for the Institution in Moorfields, under the direction of Mr. Wm. Brooks, the architect. The cost of the building was £31,124, and its annual income is about £3,000 per annum, derived from funded property and six annual payments. The number of volumes is about 65,000, which are available for the holders of a proprietor's share or a nominee of a proprietor, having his medal or ticket. In the winter-time, when the lectures are delivered by leading men of science, the theatre is as full as can well be imagined, and is by no means a quiet resting-place; but the reading-room is a treat, and it is pleasant to get away from the City bustle, and take shelter there. This building is 108 feet in length, with two wings of 16 feet each ; the centre has a handsome portico, with pillars of the Tuscan and Corinthian orders, surmounted by a neat pediment. The interior arrangement is admirable : on the ground floor, in addition to the entrance-halls, there are separate reading-rooms for newspapers, magazines, and reviews, as well as for meetings of the committee, &c., and a noble staircase leads to the library on the first floor, which is 97 feet long by 42 wide ; and the lecture-room is 63 feet by 44. The library consists of a very extensive collection of modern works, and is particularly rich in topography. Richard Porson, the celebrated classical critic, was the first librarian of this institution, and since his time the duties of that office have been filled by, among others, Richard Thomson, author of "Chronicles of London Bridge ;" Professor E. W. Brayley, F.R.S. ; and Mr. J. C. Brough, author of "Fairy Tales of Science."

On the west side of Finsbury Circus, forming a connecting link between Moorgate Street and the City Road, is Finsbury Pavement. "The Pavement—so called, no doubt," wrote "Aleph" in the *City Press*, "as the only firm pathway in the neighbourhood—was formerly edged with some fifty brick houses, to which unpretentious shops were attached—bakers, butchers, ale and spirit stores, and the like, with a chapel in the centre; the whole giving no promise of the gay and tempting shop-windows, blazing with gas,'so soon to be substituted. Yet most of the buildings are unaltered, even now; only the facia has been 'improved and beautified.'

"How, you will ask, was the centre of old Moorfields employed, in its chrysalis state ? Variously.

In the days of Wesley and Whitefield it was the favourite haunt of open-air preachers. Both those remarkable men chose the spot for their London lectures ; and they often gathered audiences of a fabulous number—the prints of the period say, of 20,000, 30,000, and even 50,000. They had begun to preach in the churches, but it was alleged the vast crowds made that practice dangerous, and they extemporised pulpits under the blue vault of heaven. The Tabernacle, not far distant, was the result of this movement.

"In 1812, and long after, carpet-beating was the chief use of the dry or sloppy area (according to the season). Poles with ropes stretched across were placed at intervals, and sturdy arms brandishing stout sticks were incessantly assaulting Turkey, Kidderminster, and Brussels floor-covers, and beating out such clouds of dust that as you passed it was expedient to hold your cambric or bandanna over your mouth and nostrils. Then you had, in fairtime, those humble incentives to gambling which for a penny offer the chance of winning a tin box or a wooden apple. Five uprights are stuck in deep holes ; you stand a few yards off, supplied with short sticks, and if you can knock away box or apple without its lapsing into the hole, it becomes your property, and the gain may be about twopence. Those days are gone ; the open space is filled in with a strange conglomeration of buildings, public and private — the London Institution, a Catholic cathedral, a Scotch church, a seceding ditto, the Ophthalmic Hospital, Finsbury Circus, and dwellings of all sizes, accommodating a mixed population, varying in position from extreme poverty to wealth."

CHAPTER XXVII.

ALDERSGATE STREET AND ST. MARTIN'S-LE-GRAND.

Origin of the Name—History of the Old Gate—Its Demolition—The General Post Office—Origin of the Penny Post—Manley—Bishop—The Duke of York's Monopoly—Murray's Post—Dockwra—Absorption of the Penny Post by the Government—Allen's "Cross Posts"—Postal Reformers—John Palmer, of Bath—Procession of the Mail Coaches on the King's Birthday—The Money Order Office—Rowland Hill's Penny Post—The Post Office Removed to St. Martin's-le-Grand—Statistics and Curiosities of the Post Office—Stamping—Curious Addresses —Report on the Post Office Savings-Bank—Posting the Newspapers—The Site of the Present Post Office—St. Martin's College—Discovery of Antiquities—The New Buildings—The Telegraph Department—Old Houses in Aldersgate Street—The "Bull and Mouth"—Milton's House—Shaftesbury House—Petre House—St. Botolph's Church—The So-called Shakespeare's House—The Barbican and Prince Rupert— The Fortune Theatre—The "Nursery"—Little Britain—The "Albion."

ALDERSGATE was one of the four original gates of London, and formed the extreme corner to the north. Some say it was named after Aldrich, a Saxon, who built it ; others, says Stow, attribute it to the alder trees which grew around it. There is no mention of it previous to the Conquest. Becoming dilapidated and dangerous, it was pulled

down by order of the Lord Mayor and aldermen ; but rebuilt in 1618, the expense (more than £1,000) being defrayed out of a legacy, left for the purpose by one William Parker, a merchant tailor. It was damaged in the Great Fire, but soon after repaired and beautified. Originally, like Temple Bar, it had an arch in the centre for general traffic, and two posterns for pedestrians. Over the arch was a figure in high relief of James I., but the building itself was heavy and inelegant. The imperial arms surmounted the figure, for through this gate the Stuart first entered London when he came to take possession of the Crown. On the eastern side was an effigy of the prophet Jeremiah, and these lines from his prophecies:—" Then shall enter into the gates of this city kings and princes, sitting upon the throne of David, riding in chariots and on horses, they and their princes, the men of Judah, and the inhabitants of Jerusalem; and this city shall remain for ever." In the western niche was an effigy of Samuel, with this inscription :— " And Samuel said unto all Israel, Behold, I have hearkened unto your voice in all that you said unto me, and have made a king over you." On the south was a bas-relief of James in his royal robes.

The City Crier had rooms over the gate, but in Elizabeth's reign they were occupied by John Day, who printed the folio Bible dedicated to Edward VI. in 1549. He also printed the works of Roger Ascham, Latimer's Sermons, and Foxe's "Actes and Monuments." There is a work of his now much sought after by book-collectors on account of the frontispiece, which represents Day with a whip entering the room of his workmen, who are sleeping, the sun shining upon them. He rouses them with these words: "Arise, for it is day." This gate was sold in 1761, and taken down immediately afterwards. The " Castle and Falcon " inn was built near its site.

The General Post Office forms a noble preface to an important street. From two years before the death of Charles II. there has been a Penny Post (one of the greatest blessings of civilisation) established in London. In Cromwell's time, the revenues of the Post Office were farmed to a Mr. John Manley for £10,000 a year, and it was calculated that latterly Manley made £14,000 annually by his bargain. Bishop, his successor, had to pay £21,500 a year for the office (the monopoly of letting post horses being included). In 1675, the fifteenth year of this disgraceful reign, the entire revenue of the Post Office was granted to the Duke of York. About this time Robert Murray, an upholsterer, suggested the idea of a post from one part of London to another, the City having grown too large for messengers. Murray's Post was afterwards assigned to Mr. William Dockwra (or Docwra). By the early regulations, all letters not exceeding a pound in weight were to be charged one penny for the City and suburbs, and twopence for any distance within a ten mile radius. Six large offices were opened in different parts of London, and receiving-houses were established in all the principal streets. The deliveries in the chief streets near the Exchange were as many as six or eight times a day, and in the outskirts there were four daily deliveries.

The moment the Penny Post became a success, the courtiers were all nibbling, and the Duke of York complained that his monopoly was infringed. Titus Oates cried out that the Penny Post was a Jesuit scheme, and useful for transmitting Popish treason. The City porters, too, says Mr. Lewin, in his excellent book, " Her Majesty's Mails," pulled down the placards, " Penny Post Letters taken in here," from the doors of the receiving-houses. The Court of King's Bench, on a trial, decided, of course unjustly, that the new office must be absorbed by the Government. From this time, the London District Post existed as a separate establishment from the General Post, and so continued till 1854. Shortly after this verdict Mr. Dockwra was appointed, under the Duke of York, controller of the District Post. On the accession of the Duke of York the revenues of the Post Office reverted to the Crown. Ten years after the removal of unfortunate Dockwra from the " Penny Post," a Mr. Povey attempted, in vain, to rival the Government by establishing a " Halfpenny Post." In 1720 Pope's friend, Ralph Allen—

> " Let humble Allen, with an awkward shame,
>   Do good by stealth, and blush to find it fame,"

established an improved system of " cross posts," at a rental of £6,000 a year. By this contract Allen is supposed to have made nearly half a million sterling. On the death of this worthy and successful speculator, the cross posts passed under the control of the Postmasters-General. In 1799, when this department was amalgamated, the proceeds, says Mr. Lewin, had reached the enormous yearly sum of £200,000.

The careless post-boy on a slow horse was still the agent employed to carry letters, often requiring to be conveyed with the utmost care and speed. Fifteen years after the death of Allen, a greater reformer arose in the person of Mr. John Palmer, a brewer and theatrical manager at Bath. In 1784, after some successful experiments with coaches and swifter horses, he was at once appointed controller-general of the Post Office, at £1,500 a year, with two and a half per cent. commission upon any excess of net revenue over £240,000, the Post Office's annual revenue for the year of his appointment. The conservative opposition to Palmer's improvements was incessant and untiring, and in 1792 he was compelled to surrender his appointment for a pension of £3,000 a year. After a twenty years' struggle against this unfair removal, Mr. Palmer's son, in 1813, obtained a Parliamentary grant of £50,000. The first year of the introduction of Mr. Palmer's plans the net revenue of the Post Office was about £250,000; thirty years afterwards, the proceeds had increased six-fold—to no less a sum, indeed, than a million and a half sterling.

In 1836 there were fifty four-horse mails, and forty-nine two-horse mails in England, says Mr. Lewis, thirty in Ireland, and ten in Scotland.

and postboys on horseback, arrayed in their new scarlet coats and jackets, proceed from Lombard Street to Millbank, and there dine. At this place the coaches are fresh painted, then the procession, being arranged, begins to move, about five o'clock in the afternoon, headed by the General Post men on horseback. The mails follow them, filled with the wives and children, friends and relations, of coachmen and guards, while the post-boys, sounding their bugles and cracking their whips, bring up the rear. From the commencement of the procession the bells of the different churches ring out

ALDERSGATE. *From a print of* 1670. (*See page* 208.)

The last year of mail coaches, twenty-seven mails left London every night punctually at eight p.m., travelling in the aggregate about 5,500 miles before they reached their several destinations.

The original Post Office, of which a view is given on page 205, stood in Lombard Street,* and one of the most interesting sights of the Post Office in old time was the gay procession of mail coaches thither on the King's birthday. Hone, in 1838, tells us that George IV. changed the annual celebration of his birthday to St. George's Day, April 23rd. "According to annual custom," says he, "the mail coaches went in procession from Millbank to Lombard Street. At about twelve o'clock the horses belonging to the different mails, with new harness, and the postmen

merrily, and continue their rejoicing peals till it arrives at the General Post Office, in Lombard Street, from whence they sparkle abroad to all parts of the kingdom. Great crowds assemble to witness the cavalcade as it passes through the principal streets of the metropolis. . . . The clean and cheerful appearance of the coachmen and guards, each with a large bouquet of flowers in his bright scarlet coat, the beauty of the cattle and the general excellence of the equipment, present a most agreeable spectacle to every eye and mind, that can be gratified by seeing and reflecting on the advantages derived to trade and social intercourse by this magnificent establishment." "Such a splendid display of carriages and four as these mail coaches," says Von Raumer, in 1835, "could not be found or got together in all Berlin. It was

* See Vol. I., p. 525.

ST. MARTIN'S-LE-GRAND IN 1760.   (*See page* 212.)

a real pleasure to see them in all the pride and strength which, in an hour or two later, was to send them in every direction, with incredible rapidity, to every corner of England."

The Money Order Office dates from 1792. No order originally could be issued for more than five guineas, and the charge for that sum amounted to four shillings and sixpence, or nearly five per cent. It was originally a private speculation of three Post Office officials, and so remained till 1838, when it became a branch of the general institution. It began with two small rooms at the north end of St. Martin's-le-Grand, and a staff of three clerks. During the year 1863 the number of orders amounted in round numbers to 7,500,000, representing a money value exceeding £16,000,000, the commission on the whole amounting to more than £144,000.

That great reform of Rowland Hill's, the Penny Postage, was first mooted in 1837, and in 1839 the uniform rate of fourpence a letter was tried. The penny rate for half an ounce commenced in 1840. Telegraph messages were first used to expedite Post Office business in 1847. In 1855, the Duke of Argyll being Postmaster-General, the General Post and the London District Letter-carriers were amalgamated, and the red uniform of the General Post abandoned.

In 1765 four houses in Abchurch Lane were taken for the Post service, and additional offices erected; and from time to time other additions were made, until the whole became a cumbrous and inconvenient mass of buildings, ill adapted to the great increase which had taken place in the business of the Post Office. It was at length determined to erect a building expressly for affording the conveniences and facilities required; and in 1815 an Act was passed authorising certain commissioners to select a site. The situation chosen was at the junction of St. Martin's-le-Grand with Newgate Street, where once stood a monastery which had possessed the privileges of sanctuary. The first stone of the new building was laid in May, 1824. On the 23rd September, 1829, it was completed and opened for the transaction of business. It is about 400 feet long, 130 wide, and 64 feet high. The front is composed of three porticoes of the Ionic order—one of four columns being placed at each end, and one of eight columns forming the centre—and surmounted by a pediment. In the interior is a hall 80 feet long, by about 60 wide, divided into a centre and two aisles by two ranges of six Ionic columns, standing upon pedestals of granite. There is a tunnel underneath the hall by which the letters are conveyed, by

ingenious mechanical means, between the northern and southern divisions of the building.

In 1839, under the old system, the number of letters which passed through the post was 76,000,000. In 1840 came the uniform penny, and for that year the number was 162,000,000, or an increase of 93,000,000, equal to 123 per cent. That was the grand start; afterwards the rate of increase subsided from 36 per cent. in 1841 to 16 per cent. in 1842 and 1843. In 1845, and the three following years, the increase was respectively 39, 37, and 30 per cent. Then succeeded a sudden drop; perhaps the culminating point in the rate of increase had been attained. The Post Office is, however, a thermometer of commerce. During the depressing year 1848 the number of letters increased no more than 9 per cent. But in 1849 337,500,000 epistles passed through the office, being an augmentation of 8,500,000 upon the preceding year, or 11 per cent. of progressive increase.

In 1850 it was estimated that upon an average 300 letters per day passed through the General Post Office totally unfastened, chiefly in consequence of the use of what stationers are pleased to call "adhesive" envelopes. Many were virgin ones, without either seal or direction; and not a few contained money. In Sir Francis Freeling's time the sum of £5,000 in bank-notes was found in a "blank." It was not till after some trouble that the sender was traced, and the cash restored to him. Not long since, a humble postmistress of an obscure Welsh post town, unable to decipher the address on a letter, perceived, on examining it, the folds of several bank-notes protruding from a torn edge of the envelope. She securely re-enclosed it to the secretary of the Post Office in St. Martin's-le-Grand, who found the contents to be £1,500, and the superscription too much even for the hieroglyphic powers of the "blind clerk." Eventually the enclosures found their true destination.

The dead letters of one year alone contained, stowed among other articles, tooth-picks, tooth-files, fishing-flies, an eye-glass, bradawls, portraits, miniatures, a whistle, corkscrews, a silver watch, a pair of spurs, a bridle, a soldier's discharge and sailor's register tickets, samples of hops and corn, a Greek MS., silver spoons, gold thread, dinner, theatre, and pawn tickets, boxes of pills, shirts, nightcaps, razors, all sorts of knitting and lace, "dolls' things," and a vast variety of other articles, that would puzzle ingenuity to conjecture.

The letters formerly were ranged, for stamping the date and hour of despatch, in a long row, like a pack of cards thrown across a table, and so fast did the stamper's hand move, that he could mark 6,000 in an hour. While defacing the Queen's heads, he counted as he thumped, till he enumerated fifty, when he dodged his stamp on one side to put his black mark on a piece of plain paper. All these memoranda were afterwards collected by the president, who, reckoning fifty letters to every black mark, got a near approximation to the number that had passed through the office. This work is now performed by machinery. The total number of letters which passed through the Post Office on Valentine's Day, 1850, was 187,037. To this total are to be added 6,000 "bye" letters—or those which passed from village to village within the suburban limits of the District Post without reaching the chief office—and 100,000, destined for the provinces and places beyond sea, which were transferred to the Inland Department. The grand total for the day, therefore, rose to nearly 300,000. Thus the sacrifices to the fane of St. Valentine, consisting of hearts, darts, Cupids peeping out of paper roses, Hymen embowered in hot-pressed embossing, swains in very blue coats, and nymphs in very opaque muslin, coarse caricatures and tender verses, caused an augmentation to the revenue on this anniversary equal to about 70,000 missives; 123,000 being the usual daily average for district and "byes" during the month of February. This increase, being peculiar to cross and district posts, does not so much affect the Inland Office, for lovers and sweethearts are generally neighbours. The entire correspondence of the three kingdoms it was calculated in 1850 was augmented on each St. Valentine's Day to the extent of about 400,000 letters.

The extraordinary addresses of many of the dead letters are worth noting. Among them we find the following :—

To George Miller, boy on board H.M.S. *Amphitrite,* Voillop a Razzor or ellesaware (the *Amphitrite,* Valparaiso, or elsewhere).

H.M. Steem Freigkt *Vultur,* Uncon or els war (Steam Frigate *Vulture,* at Hong-Kong).

Mr. Weston,
Osburn Cottage,
Ilwait (Isle of Wight).

Mr. Laurence, New Land, I Vicum (High Wycombe).

W. Stratton, commonly ceald teapot (we presume, as a total abstinence man), Weelin (Welwyn).

Thom Hoodless, 3, St. Ann Ct., Searhoo Skur (Soho Square).

Mr. Dick Bishop Caus, ner the Wises (near Devizes).

Peter Robinson, 2 Compney 7 Batilian Rolyl Artirian, Owylige (Woolwich), England.

To Mr. Michl Darcy, in the town of England.

To my Uncle John, in London.

Miss Queen Victoria, of England.

From the report of the Postmaster-General for the year 1880, we gather the following interesting facts :—

The number of Post Offices open in the United Kingdom on the 31st of March, 1880, was 912 head and 13,300 sub-offices, being an increase of 331 offices on the number last reported. The number of letter-boxes in streets, roads, &c., on the same date was 12,541, being an increase of 661. The total number of places of all kinds at which letters may be posted was thus 26,753; and of these 2,012, or about $\frac{1}{13}$ of the whole, are in London.

The number of mails forwarded daily between London and the post towns in England and Wales in the year ending 31st of March, 1880, was 617. The number of letters delivered in the United Kingdom within the year was 1,127,997,500, showing an increase at the rate of 2·8 per cent. upon the previous year. The number of post-cards was 114,458,400, showing an increase of 2·7 per cent. The number of book-packets and circulars was 213,963,000, showing an increase of 8·6 per cent. Taking together the correspondence of all kinds, the number was 1,586,937,300, showing an average of 46 per head of the population, and an increase of 3·3 per cent. over the previous year.

The number of letters registered in the United Kingdom during the year 1879–80 was 8,739,191, being an increase of 21·3 per cent., and more than double the number dealt with in 1877, before the reduction of the registration fee. Of the above number, no fewer than 5,762,853 passed through the chief office. During the year the number of registered letters enclosed in the special envelopes sold by the department received at the chief office averaged 5,000 a day as compared with 4,000 a day in 1878–9.

The registered parcels containing Christmas presents passing through the chief office were 47,000 in number, as compared with 30,000 in 1878.

The Report states that notwithstanding the low charge now made for registration, letters containing coin and articles of value are still frequently posted without being registered, no less than 1,417 such letters having been observed during the year 1879. "Many more," adds the Postmaster-General, "no doubt passed unnoticed; but in every case in which such a letter is detected, it is forwarded to its destination with a registration charge of eightpence to be paid on delivery."

As an instance of the want of care on the part of the public in securing valuable parcels, the Report states that one parcel found open contained a gold watch and many articles of jewellery. . . . Exclusive of postage stamps found loose to the number of 72,000, no less than 27,224 articles of various kinds escaped from their covers and were sent to the Returned Letter Office during the year, this number being about half as large again as in the previous year.

The total number of returned letters in 1879-80 was 5,345,678, of book packets 3,541,103, of postcards 496,446, and of newspapers 374,741. Of the letters, 4,570,743 were returned to the writers; 78,291 were re-issued to corrected addresses; and 170,175 from abroad were sent for disposal to the Post Offices of the countries from which they were received; while in 526,469 cases the writers had given no address to admit of the letters being returned to them. No less than 21,621 letters were posted without any address, among which were 1,141 containing cash and bank notes to the amount of £433, and cheques, bills, &c., for £4,251.

Ten years having now elapsed since the telegraphs were transferred to the State, it may be interesting to learn some particulars of the results which have been achieved.

"At the time of the transfer," the Report tells us, "the Telegraph Companies had 1,992 offices, in addition to 496 railway offices at which telegraph work was performed, making the total number of offices 2,488. At the end of the past year (1879) there were 3,924 post offices and 1,407 railway stations open for telegraph work, making the total number of telegraph offices within the United Kingdom 5,331. . . . On taking over the telegraphs, the Post Office commenced with 5,651 miles of telegraph line, embracing 48,990 miles of wire, and these numbers have been increased to 23,156 miles of line, embracing 100,851 miles of wire. The total length of submarine cables connecting different parts of the United Kingdom was 139 miles in 1869; last year it was 707 miles. . . . The total number of telegraphists employed by the companies was 2,514 (of whom 479 were women), and the number of messengers 1,471. The total number of telegraphists employed by the Post Office last year was 5,611 (of whom 1,556 were women), and of messengers 4,648; but, besides these, many persons are employed in telegraph work who hold no appointment on the establishment, but are paid by the postmasters out of allowances for assistance"

In the course of the year 1879–80 the Post Office Telegraph Department sent an average of 25,697 words a day when Parliament was sitting, and 21,702 when Parliament was not sitting.

In an admirable article in the first volume of *Household Words*, March 30, 1850, the late Mr. Charles Dickens and Mr. W. H. Wills described, in a very animated way, the manner of then closing the evening letter-boxes at St. Martin's-le-Grand. "It was a quarter before six o'clock," they say, "when they crossed the hall, six being the latest hour at which newspapers can be posted without fee. "It was then just drizzling newspapers. The great window of that department being thrown open, the first black fringe of a thunder-cloud of newspapers, impending over the Post Office, was discharging itself fitfully—now in large drops, now in little; now in sudden plumps, now stopping altogether. By degrees it began to rain hard; by fast degrees the storm came on harder and harder, until it blew, rained, hailed, snowed, newspapers. A fountain of newspapers played in at the window. Waterspouts of newspapers broke from enormous sacks, and engulfed the men inside. A prodigious main of newspapers, at the Newspaper River Head, seemed to be turned on, threatening destruction to the miserable Post Office. The Post Office was so full already, that the window foamed at the mouth with newspapers. Newspapers flew out like froth, and were tumbled in again by the bystanders. All the boys in London seemed to have gone mad, and to be besieging the Post Office with newspapers. Now and then there was a girl; now and then a woman; now and then a weak old man; but as the minute hand of the clock crept near to six, such a torrent of boys and such a torrent of newspapers came tumbling in together pell-mell, head over heels, one above another, that the giddy head looking on chiefly wondered why the boys springing over one another's heads, and flying the garter into the Post Office, with the enthusiasm of the corps of acrobats at M. Franconi's, didn't post themselves nightly along with the newspapers, and get delivered all over the world. Suddenly it struck six. Shut, sesame!"

On the site of the General Post Office, in the early days, stood a collegiate church and sanctuary, founded by Withu, King of Kent, in 750, and only enlarged in 1056 by Ingebrian, Earl of Essex, and Girard, his brother, and confirmed by a charter of William the Conqueror, in 1068. The proud Norman also gave to the college all the moor land without Cripplegate, and granted them "soc and sac, dot and sheam," in a chapter confirmed by two cardinals of Pope Alexander. Many of the deans of this college were great people, observes Strype, one being Keeper of the Treasure and Jewels of Edward III., and another Clerk of the Privy Seal. The college was a parish of itself, and claimed great privileges of sanctuary, prisoners from Newgate to Tower Hill sometimes trying to slip from their guards and get through the south gate of St. Martin's. Thus, in 1442 (Henry VI.), a soldier, on his way from Newgate to the Guildhall, was dragged by five of his fellows, who rushed out of Pannier Alley, in at the west door of the sanctuary ; but that same day the two sheriffs came and took out the five men from the sanctuary, and led them fettered to the Compter, and then chained by the necks to Newgate. The Dean and Chapter of St. Martin's, furious at this, complained to the king, who, after hearing the City, who denied the right of sanctuary to the college, returned the five soldiers to their former retreat. In the reign of Henry VII. the right of sanctuary was again violated, and again disputed at law, and this time the sheriffs were "grievously fined" for their pains.

In the reign of Edward II. there was before St. Martin's College a "solar," that is, a large airy room, or chamber, somewhat like the galleries in great houses, being places of entertainment and pleasure. This "solar" was toward the street, and a jetty outward, which was so low that it annoyed the people passing along.

When the college of St. Martin's-le-Grand flourished, the curfew was rung here, as at Bow, St. Giles's, Cripplegate, and Allhallow's, Barking, to warn citizens to keep within doors. Strype also mentions an ordinance of Edward I., at a time when "certain Hectors" infested the streets at night, walking armed, and committing "mischiefs, murders, and robberies," commanding none to wander in the streets after "coverfew" has sounded at St. Martin's-le-Grand.

A crypt was laid open in St. Martin's-le-Grand on clearing for the site of the General Post Office, in 1818. There were then found two ranges of vaults, which had served as cellars to the houses above ; one of these being the crypt of St. Martin's (taken down in 1547) and afterwards the cellar of a large wine-tavern, the "Queen's Head." This was in the pointed style of Edward III., and was most probably the work of William of Wykeham. The second or westernmost range, which must have supported the nave, was of earlier date, and was a square vaulted chamber, divided by piers six feet square. Here was found a coin of Constantine, and a stone coffin containing a skeleton ; and in digging somewhat lower down, Roman remains were met with in abundance. In St. Martin's-le-Grand also, between Aldersgate and St. Anne's Lane end, was the large tavern of the "Mourning Bush," whose vaulted cellars, as they remain from the Great Fire of 1666, disclose the foundation wall of Aldersgate,

and are a remarkably fine specimen of early brick archwork.

The new Post Office buildings, erected from the designs of Mr. James Williams, of H.M. Office of Works and Public Buildings, were opened early in 1874. The building is rectangular, having frontages of 286 feet to St. Martin's-le-Grand and Bath Street, and frontages of 144 feet to Newgate Street and Angel Street, and is 84 feet in height from the paving line. It stands on a base of granite from the De Lank quarries, and the whole of the fronts have been executed in Portland stone of the hardest "Whitbed." The building is four stories in height, exclusive of the basement, and the floors are thus appropriated :—The basement is partly occupied as office-rooms, partly for stores, and partly by the department of the telegraph engineers, the large room in the centre being used as a battery-room. The ground floor is appropriated to the Postmaster-General and the Accountant-General. On the first floor are accommodated the secretaries and their staff; the third and fourth floors being appropriated to the telegraph department. The fourth floor is especially devoted to the telegraph instruments, and the pneumatic tubes are laid on to it, establishing communication with the district offices. The large instrument-room is 125 feet by 80 feet. The central hall is intended for the staff of the Accountant-General. In the north court there are placed four steam-engines, each of 50-horse power, for working the pneumatic tubes. An artesian well has been sunk for the supply of the large quantity of water required, and a small engine is kept at work at pumping to the large tanks (two of 6,000 gallons each) at the top of the building. About three-quarters of a mile of instrument-tables have been fitted up in the telegraph galleries.

The building was commenced in December, 1869, the first block of Portland stone being laid by the Right Hon. A. S. Ayrton, M.P., the First Commissioner of Public Works, on the 16th of that month. The contractor was Mr. William Brass; the clerk of the works, Mr. William Trickett. The contract amounted to £129,718.

The whole of the carving and the sculpture was executed by Mr. Burnie Philip. The site cost in round numbers £300,000.

"In the telegraph department in the new wing," says Mr. Yates, "young ladies are seated at the long rows of tables crossing the room from end to end, and, with few exceptions, each one has before her a single needle or printing instrument, the 'circuit,' or place with which it is in communication, being denoted on a square tablet, something like a headstone in a cemetery, erected immediately in front of her. It may further be remarked of these young ladies, that they talk much less than might be expected, work very quickly, and have generally very nice hands."

The Metropolitan Gallery, consisting of a set of three large rooms, is simply used as a centre for the collection of messages from the metropolitan district. It is arranged upon the plan of the postal districts, with which the public are now familiar, and each division is under the superintendence of a clerk in charge. All messages are brought to the central sorting-table, and there subdivided : those for the

memory a tombstone inscribed "Holborn" has been erected, we find her at fifty-four and a half minutes past three p.m. writing off the last words of a message which had been handed in at the office on Holborn Viaduct at fifty-three minutes past three p.m., and which will thus have been completed and ready for sending out for delivery within two minutes. Here in this south-western division are what are known as the "official circuits," worked by the A B C instrument, with the grinding handle and the alphabetical depressible keys familiar to most of us, which communicate with the War Office, the Foreign Office, the Treasury,

NEW GENERAL POST-OFFICE, ST. MARTIN'S-LE-GRAND. (*See page* 215.)

country being sent to the upper or Provincial Gallery by a lift, those for the City being sorted into different batches, and dispatched by the agency of a pneumatic tube to the delivery station nearest to their destination. These pneumatic tubes, through which the messages are being perpetually shot all day long, have been found of great service, and are now in operation between the office and the principal delivery stations in the City, while they are also used by the Anglo-American, the Indo-European, and the Falmouth and Gibraltar offices, for the transmission of messages to the central station. It should be here noticed that the messages for the Continent received at the office are dealt with entirely by the members of the male staff, a mixed assemblage of foreigners and Englishmen conversant with foreign tongues. Pausing for an instant by the side of the young lady to whose

the Admiralty, the Houses of Parliament, and the "whipper-in." Here, too, is the last specimen left throughout the building of what at one time used to be the favourite telegraphic instrument, the "double needle," which is used for communication with Buckingham Palace. At Windsor, Osborne, and Balmoral there are telegraphic instruments, under the charge of a clerk, who travels with the Court, to which he has been attached for some years ; while Sandringham, Badminton, the seat of Mr. Lowe (now Lord Sherbrooke) at Caterham, and the country-houses of various other noblemen and officials, are similarly furnished.

The work in the Metropolitan Gallery, which is always great, is largely increased on the occasion of any of our great cockney festivals, such as the Derby, or the University Boat Race. A dense fog, too, brings much extra business for them, and the wires, but for the precaution which the department has been able to take against sudden pressure, would be choked with messages explaining the impossibility of keeping appointments already made. All the messages for the tube stations are sorted into different pigeon-holes marked with the name of the superintendent. Some idea of the business done may be guessed, when it is stated that there are already between three and four hundred of these delivery stations in London.

but it is still clamorous for more, and is likely to have its wishes gratified. This is considered rather a dull time in the office. During the busy season, the daily average of messages sent, exclusive of press messages, has been nearly 20,000; now it is about 16,000. We can check these figures, if we like, by the aid of the superintendent of one of the check-tables close by. Her account, she says, stands at this time (quarter to five p.m.) at 6,500 messages; each of these has been sent twice, representing a

THE YARD OF THE "BULL AND MOUTH" ABOUT 1820. (See page 219.)

The Provincial Gallery is more interesting as a show-place for the display of *tours de force* than the Metropolitan. Thus, we are taken to one of the Liverpool circuits, furnished with one of Hughes's instruments, the speciality of which is, that it records the message in actual Roman type, and are invited to communicate with the clerk at the instrument in the Liverpool office. We do so, and in less than a minute and a half we see his printed reply come winding, snake-like, out of the instrument. This Liverpool, by the way, is a very cormorant of telegraphic communication. Already it has eleven direct circuits from the office, and five from the Stock Exchange, making sixteen in all;

total of 13,000, and there is yet plenty of time for the receipt of more.

This extraordinary collection of apparently the brass butt-ends of fishing-rods, with thin coils of wire running around and between them, is one of the most important of the internal arrangements at the office. It is called the testing-box, and, as its name imports, is the place where the trial of the state and efficiency of all the wires is made. When the engineer's attention is called by a clerk to a fault in the wire which he is working, each one of which has a separate number and letter, he proceeds to the test-box, and, by means of the galvanometer in connection therewith, he is able to ascertain at once whether the fault or fracture is at his end of the wire. Finding it is not there, he then proceeds to test the wire in the various sections into which it is divided; thus, supposing it were a north-western wire, he would test the section between the office and Euston, then between Euston and Wolverton, then between Wolverton and Rugby, and so on, until he hit upon the section, and, finally, upon the immediate locality where the fault lay; when the divisional engineer would be instructed as to its whereabouts, and ordered to remedy it. Nearly all the wires radiating from the station are tested at six a.m. every morning, when every terminal station is spoken to and expected to reply, to see if the lines are right throughout. It is calculated that there are nearly sixty miles of wire under the floor of the Provincial Gallery, merely for making local connections with batteries, &c.

Another interesting object is the chronopher, or instrument from which all England is supplied with the correct time. Sixteen of the most important cities in the kingdom are in direct communication with this instrument, which is itself in direct communication with the Observatory at Greenwich. At two minutes before ten every morning all other work is suspended, in order that there may be no interference with what is called the "time current," which, precisely at the striking of the clock, flashes the intelligence to the sixteen stations with which it is in communication. And not merely at these large towns, but at every post-office throughout the kingdom, the clerks at two minutes before ten are on the look-out for the signal which is to be passed along the line, and the clocks are adjusted accordingly. Messrs. Dent, Benson, and all the principal watchmakers in London receive the time every hour from this chronopher. Time-guns at Newcastle and at Shields are also fired at one p.m. by batteries connected with the chronopher at the office, the clock attached to which is regulated for accuracy to the twentieth part of a second.

The principal instruments in use at the office are the single needle, the Morse inker, the Hughes, and the Wheatstone's automatic.

The single-needle instrument conveys its information by the varying vibrations of an indicator or "needle" between two fixed ivory stops. It is read by the eye, and its signals are transitory. It is as though the minute-hand of a small clock, or a large watch, were caused by the electric current to perform rapid calisthenic exercises between the points that indicate eleven and one o'clock. If the minute-hand made two violent efforts to show that it was one o'clock, and after each effort returned exhausted to noon, it would simply indicate the letter M. If panting to go the right way, it made two powerful efforts to go the other way and retired after each effort equally unsuccessful, it would simply indicate the letter I; one such tick to the right would be T, one to the left E. The letters of the alphabet are thus formed by the movements of the indicator to the right and left of some fixed point, and every word is so spelt out letter by letter.

The Morse instrument is different. It depicts its telegraphic language on a long piece of paper that unrolls itself by machinery in tape-like fashion beneath a revolving wheel, one half of which is constantly enjoying a cold bath of ink. While no electric current flows, the paper is free from this circular pen. When the current is caused to speed its lightning career, the paper is pressed against the wheel, and a thin blue line is traced by the ink which the revolving wheel carries with it on the paper with beautiful regularity. If a current of very short duration be sent, there is simply a dot, like a full stop, registered on the paper. If the current be maintained for a little longer period, we have a ——— shown. One dot is the letter E, one dash the letter T, a dot and a dash the letter A, and a dash and a dot the letter N. The letters of the alphabet are thus made up of a series of dots and dashes.

The signals in both instruments are made by the depression of a small lever, which is moved like the key of a piano. The needle instrument has two keys, one for the movements to the right, the other for the movements to the left. The Morse instrument has but one key, which is depressed as though the telegraphic manipulator wished to play crotchets and quavers on one note, the crotchets forming the dots, the quavers the dashes.

The Hughes instrument is most readily appreciated by strangers, as it records the message in actual Roman type.

As regards the Wheatstone instrument, it is only necessary to point out that the speed of the ordinary Morse is dependent upon the rate at which a clerk can manipulate his key. Forty words a minute is very fast sending, and few, if any, clerks can reach forty-five words per minute. But there is no limit to the speed of the electric current, and if the messages are sent mechanically, as in the Wheatstone, that is, if the varying currents required to indicate a despatch are regulated by a machine moving with great speed, we are not only independent of the limited powers of the human hand, but made free from the liability to error in meting out the proper duration of the signal. Thus great accuracy and great speed can be simultaneously attained.

There are instruments, also, that appeal to the ear as well as to the eye. Bright's bell is an instrument which indicates its telegraphic language by sound ; bells of different notes struck by little hammers connected with the right and left movements of the needle, and the dot and dash of the Morse. These little tinkling talkers rattle forth their information with great speed, and many clerks are to be seen writing for their very lives to keep up at the rapid rate at which the bells are speaking.

The staff at present employed by the office consists of between seven and eight hundred clerks, of whom about a third are men, and two-thirds women. Of the latter, some come on duty at eight a.m., and leave at four p.m.; others arrive at twelve noon, and leave at eight p.m. It is noticeable that no women are on duty before eight a.m. or after eight p.m.; but the night duties are performed by a special night male staff, who are employed from eight p.m. to nine a.m., under the superintendence of a clerk in charge. Before the transfer of the office to the Government, the male and female staff were kept rigidly apart, and marriage between any members of either entailed the loss of situation on both the contracting parties. But a paternal Government looks upon these matters with a much more benevolent eye, and so far from forbidding matrimony, is understood to encourage it.

The old sanctuary privileges of St. Martin's-le-Grand led to infinite mischief. There is no doubt that up to the time of the mischievous and abused rights of sanctuary being abolished, St. Martin's-le-Grand was a mere refuge for rogues, ruffians, thieves, and murderers. Any rascal who stabbed his pot-companion, or struck down an innocent traveller in a dark bye-street, any red-handed brawler, could rush through the monastic gates and shelter himself in this den of crime. Here also, says Stow, harboured picklocks, forgers, coiners, makers of sham jewellery, carders, dicers, and other gamblers. After the dissolution a tavern was built where the college church had stood.

In Elizabethan times, when sanctuary privileges were still claimed, French, German, Dutch, and Scotch artificers settled here. Here lived shoemakers, tailors, button-makers, goldsmiths, pursemakers, drapers, and silk-weavers, and the first Flemish silk-throwers settled here. In 1569 the number of inhabitants was 269. There were frequently disorders in this turbulent Liberty, the inhabitants of which often objected to pay taxes, in the Plague-time refused when stricken to close their doors and windows, and often erased the red cross set upon their houses, and even threatened the constable and headboroughs who, according to law, painted them up. " And some," says Stow, " repaired to the court with their wares, a thing dangerous to the queen and nobility ;" and, there being no prison in the Liberty, the Liberty people sent to the Gate House at Westminster frequently brought actions for such illegal imprisonment.

Butler, in " Hudibras," speaks of this district —

" 'Tis not those paltry counterfeits,
  French stones, which in our eyes you set,
  But our right diamonds that inspire,
  And set your am'rous hearts on fire.
  Nor can those false St. Martin's beads,
  Which on our lips you place for reds,
  And make us wear, like Indian dames,
  Add fuel to your scorching flames."

" Round Court, St. Martin's-le-Grand, hath a passage leading into Blowbladder Street, which is taken up," says Strype, " by milliners, sempstresses, and such as sell a sort of copper lace called St. Martin's lace, for which it is of note."

On the west side of Aldersgate Street stood the London residence of the Nevilles, Earls of Westmoreland (still indicated by Westmoreland Buildings), and close on the site of Bull and Mouth Street, stood the mansion of the Percies, Earls of Northumberland. At her house in this street, in 1621, died Mary, Countess of Pembroke, " Sydney's sister, Pembroke's mother," a lady immortalised in Ben Jonson's hyperbolic yet noble epitaph. As an " ancient dame," whom Shakespeare must have seen and honoured, we claim in Aldersgate Street remembrance for her, as well as for Milton, who, according to Philips, had, at one time, " a pretty garden-house in this street, at the end of an entry."

The great coaching-inn of Aldersgate Street, in the old time, was the " Bull and Mouth." The original name of this inn was " Boulogne Mouth," in allusion to the town and harbour of Boulogne, besieged by Henry VIII. But the " gne " being generally pronounced by the Londoners " on," it gradually became " an," and it only required the small addition of " d " to make " and " of it. The first part being before this made a " bull " of, it was ultimately converted into the " Bull and Mouth."

The " Queen's Hotel," St. Martins-le-Grand, rebuilt in 1830, now occupies the site of the old " Bull and Mouth." On the front there is a statuette of a bull, above which are the bust of Edward VI., and the arms of Christ's Hospital, to which the ground belongs. The old inn stood in Bull and Mouth Street, and the south side in Angel Street still retains the name of the old inn, but is merely a luggage depôt of Chaplin and Horne. On the front of the present hotel, much affected by Manchester men, under the turbulent little bull, is a stone tablet probably from the old inn, and on it are deeply cut the following quaint lines :—

> " Milo the Cretonian
> An ox slew with his fist,
> And ate it up at one meal :
> Ye gods, what a glorious twist !"

Howell in his "Londinopolis," 1657, speaking of the spacious and uniform buildings which made Aldersgate Street almost resemble a street in an Italian town, calls Jewin Street "a handsome new street, fairly built by the Company of Goldsmiths."

Jewin Street, Aldersgate, in Stow's time was full of "fair garden plots and summer houses for pleasure." It was anciently called "Leyrestow," and was granted by Edward I. to William de Monteforte, Dean of St. Paul's. For several centuries this spot was the only one allowed the London Jews as a place of interment ; but in the reign of Henry II., after long suits to King and Parliament, they obtained leave to buy local graveyards.

Aldersgate Street, dear to business men for its Post Office, is hallowed to authors by having once, as we have already said, been the residence of Milton. Here the poet came, with bag and baggage, in 1643, the year after Edgehill, removing from St. Bride's Churchyard, the site of the present *Punch* office, where he had kept a small school. This residence is especially interesting to those who honour our great poet, as it was here he became reconciled to Mary Powell, his first wife, the daughter of an Oxfordshire Cavalier. As a first step to their re-union, Milton placed his wife in the house of one Widow Weber, in St. Clement's Churchyard. Mr. Jesse has pointed out very happily the possible reminiscence contained in "Paradise Lost" to this reconciliation. In his beautiful description of Adam's reconciliation with Eve, after their fall, Milton, says Mr. Jesse, had evidently in his mind his own first interview with his repentant wife, after her unhappy estrangement—

> " She, not repulsed, with tears that ceased not flowing,
> And tresses all disordered, at his feet
> Fell humble, and, embracing them, besought
> His peace."

And again—

> " Soon his heart relented
> Towards her, his life so late, and sole delight,
> Now to his feet submissive in distress."

Milton's reconciliation with his wife took place in July, 1645, in which year he removed from Aldersgate Street to a larger house in Barbican. Here he remained till 1647, when he took a smaller house in High Holborn, overlooking Lincoln's Inn Fields. After the Restoration he removed to a house in Jewin Street, where he married his third wife.

On the east side of Aldersgate Street, Nos. 35 to 38 (still distinguished by a series of eight pilasters), stands Shaftesbury or Thanet House, one of Inigo Jones's fine old mansions, formerly the London residence of the Tuftons, Earls of Thanet. From them it passed into the family of that clever and dangerous political intriguer, Anthony Ashley Cooper, Earl of Shaftesbury, the hated "Achitophel" of Dryden, of whom it was said in jest that he hoped to be chosen King of Poland. He was the idol of the anti-Popery apprentices, the hatcher of the Popish plot, the rival of Buckingham for the favour of the Whigs, a man seditious and restless as Wilkes, yet, like that demagogue, a constant striver for constitutional liberty. Sir Walter Scott, in the Notes to his edition of "Dryden," anticipatory of his "Peveril of the Peak," says of Shaftesbury—

"Being heir to a plentiful fortune, a Member of Parliament, and high sheriff of the county of Dorset, he came to Oxford when the Civil War broke out, and though then only twenty-one or twenty-two years of age, presented to the king a digested plan for compromising matters between him and his subjects in arms against him. Charles observed, he was a very young man for so great an undertaking ; to which, with the readiness which marked his character, he answered, that would not be the worse for the king's affairs, provided the business was done. He had, in consequence, a commission from the king to promise indemnity and redress of grievances to such of the Parliamentary garrisons as would lay down their arms. Accordingly, his plan seems to have taken some effect; for Weymouth actually surrended to the king, and Sir Anthony Ashley Cooper, as his style then was, was made governor. Some delays occurred in the course of his obtaining this office ; and whether disgusted with these, and giving scope to the natural instability of his temper, as is intimated by Clarendon, or offended, as Mr. Locke states, at Weymouth having been plundered by Prince Maurice's forces, he made one of those sudden turns, of which his political career furnishes several instances, and went over to the other side. After this, Clarendon says that ' he gave up himself, body and soul, to the Parliament, and became an implacable enemy to the Royal Family.'"

Shaftesbury is thus described by the author of a poem, entitled "The Progress of Honesty ;" or the view of Court and City :—

> "Some call him Hophni, some Achitophel,
> Others chief Advocate for hell ;
> Some cry, he sure a second James is,
> And all things past and present sees ;
> Another, rapt in satire, swears his eyes
> Upon himself are spies ;

And slily do their optics inward roul,
To watch the subtle motions of his soul ;
That they with sharp perspective sight,
And help of intellectual light,
May guide the helm of state aright.
Nay, view what will hereafter be,
By their all-seeing quality."

But Dryden's was the most terrible portrait of this busy politician :—

" For close designs, and crooked counsels fit
Sagacious, bold, and turbulent of wit ;
Restless, unfixed in principles and place,
In power unpleased, impatient of disgrace ;
A fiery soul, which, working out its way,
Fretted the pigmy-body to decay,
And o'er-informed the tenement of clay.
A daring pilot in extremity,
Pleased with the danger when the waves went high,
He sought the storms ; but, for a calm unfit,
Would steer too nigh the sands to boast his wit."

The author of " Hudibras " has sketched Shaftesbury with the etching tool of Gilray.

" 'Mong these there was a politician,
With more heads than a beast in vision,
And more intrigues in every one
Than all the whores of Babylon ;
So politic, as if one eye
Upon the other were a spy,
That, to trepan the one to think
The other blind, both strove to blink ;
And in his dark pragmatic way
As busy as a child at play.
He had seen three governments run down,
And had a hand in every one ;
Was for 'em and against 'em all,
But barb'rous when they came to fall ;
For, by trepanning th' old to ruin,
He made his interest with the new one ;
Play'd true and faithful, though against
His conscience, and was still advanc'd.
Could turn his word, and oath, and faith,
As many ways as in a lath ;
By turning, wriggle, like a screw,
Int' highest trust, and out, for new.
Would strive to raise himself upon
The public ruin, and his own.
So little did he understand
The desperate feats he took in hand,
For, when h' had got himself a name
For fraud and tricks, he spoiled his game ;
Had forc'd his neck into a noose,
To show his play at fast and loose ;
And, when, he chanc'd t' escape, mistook,
For art and subtlety, his luck."

Hudibras, Part III., Canto 2.

Thomas Flatman, that tame poet of Charles II.'s time, whom almost every witling of the period belaboured, was born in Aldersgate Street in 1633.

Almost opposite to Shaftesbury House stood Petre House, the residence of the Petre family in the great Elizabethan times ; and of Henry Pierrepoint, Marquis of Dorchester, in the days of the Commonwealth. It was also used as a state prison in the Commonwealth-times, and subsequently became the temporary abode of the Bishops of London, after the Great Fire had treated their mansion in St. Paul's Churchyard in a Puritanical and remorseless way. In 1688, when the selfish Princess Anne deserted her father, James II., and fled at night from Whitehall, she was conducted by the warlike Bishop Compton to his house in Aldersgate Street in a hackney coach.

The street of which we are taking stock in this chapter contains singularly few churches. St. Anne-in-the-Willows we have already visited (somewhat, perhaps, out of sequence) ; the remaining church, St. Botolph's, at the corner of Little Britain, but for its mean bell-turret and pretty fizzing fountain, singularly resembles a meeting-house. It was erected in 1790 on the site of the old building, which had escaped the Great Fire. An old Jacobean pulpit in the vestibule is the only relic of the old church, except the few uninteresting monuments. There is one to a worthy Dame Anne Packington (died 1563), who founded almshouses near the White Friars' Church, in Fleet Street, which were left under the superintendence of the Clothworkers' Company ; one to Richard Chiswell, an eminent bookseller (died 1711), and another to an Elizabeth Smith, with a cameo bust by Roubiliac.

At the north-east end of this street of noblemen's houses, not far from Shaftesbury House, stood Lauderdale House, the residence of that cruel and unprincipled minister of Charles II. Lauderdale was one of those five "thorough-going" adherents of Charles II. who formed the "cabal" (Clifford, Ashley, Buckingham, Arlington, and Lauderdale), after Clarendon's exile, and the death of Southampton and Monk. It was this same unscrupulous inhabitant of Aldersgate Street whom Charles, in 1669, sent to Edinburgh as High Commissioner to the Scottish Parliament, to put down conventicles with a high hand, to fine Presbyterians, and to hang and shoot field-preachers, severities which eventually led to the rebellion of the Covenanters of 1679. There must have been many a quiet and many a state visit made from Shaftesbury House to Lauderdale House.

An audacious board over two small shops, No. 134, half-way down Aldersgate Street on the west side, used to assert that " This was Shakespeare's House." There is no documentary evidence (the best of all evidence), and not even a tradition, to connect our great poet's name with the house, or even with the street, often as he may have visited good Master Alleyn's "Fortune" Theatre in Golden Lane. The assertion was as impudent as that which claims a small house, opposite Chancery Lane, as the palace of "Wolsey and Henry VIII." An antiquarian of authority has clearly shown that no residence of Shakespeare in London is actually known. There was a house in Blackfriars which he purchased in March, 1612-13, from Henry Walker, "abutting from a street leading down to Puddle Wharf, on the east part, right against the King's Majesty's Wardrobe," and the counterpart of the original conveyance of which (bearing the signature of Shakespeare), is in the library at Guildhall.

subsidy roll of 1598, preserved at the Carlton Ride, in which the name of "William Shakespeare" occurs as the owner of property then to the value of £5, and on which a tax of 13s. 4d. was assessed. But that roll has the memorandum "affid." affixed to his name, and that means that an affidavit had been produced, showing that he did not reside in the parish or district. Shakespeare's name, in respect of that property, does not occur before 1598, nor is it heard of after that date. Besides, we are not to jump to the conclusion that every William

SHAFTESBURY HOUSE. *From a print of* 1810. (*See page* 220.)

That house is of course undoubtedly connected with Shakespeare ; but although he was the owner of it, none of his editors believe he ever lived in it. Mr. Knight and other commentators conjecture that this house was purchased in reference to some object connected with Blackfriars Theatre ; but in addition to that—although we do not positively know when Shakespeare retired from London—all his biographers are of opinion that he left London, and went back to his native Stratford to spend the remainder of his days, about the year 1610 or 1611. The only other place *probably* connected with Shakespeare's name was a property in St. Helen's parish, in the ward of Bishopsgate. There is a

Shakespeare then living in London was *our* William Shakespeare. These are the only two houses in London that can be associated with Shakespeare, and they have long since been improved off the face of the earth. The concocter of the board, says the antiquary we have quoted, finding out that a public-house in that neighbourhood had been mentioned as having been a place of resort of the most celebrated wits of the sixteenth century, at once jumped to the conclusion that this was "the house," and further, that Shakespeare, being a wit of that period, he took it for granted that the poet came there to visit. The house was pulled down in 1879 to make a site for warehouses.

Barbican, an essential tributary of Aldersgate Street, derives its Saracenic-sounding name, according to all old London antiquaries, from the Saxon words, "burgh kennin," or "postern tower," the remains of which existed a little north of the street till towards the end of the last century.

entrusted to Robert Ufford, Earl of Suffolk, no doubt a valiant and stout knight, in whose family it remained hereditary, through the female line, till the reign of Queen Mary. In that cruel reign it is on record that the Barbican (then a mere sinecure, and no longer needed by the City for

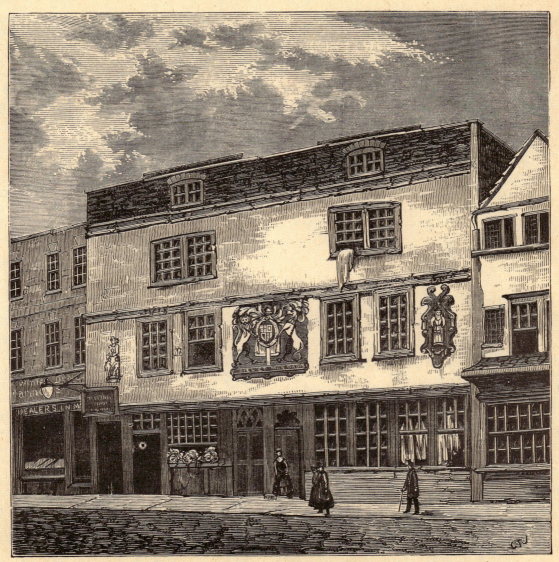

THE "FORTUNE" THEATRE. *From a print published by Wilkinson, 1811.* (*See page 224.*)

According to Bagford, a good old London antiquary, who died in 1716, and who, from being a shoe-maker, turned bookseller, printer, and collector of books for the Earl of Oxford, the Romans kept watch at night in that tower, and gave notice of conflagrations, or an approaching army. At night they lit bonfires on the top of the turret, to guide travellers to the City.

In the reign of Edward III. the Barbican was

defence) was in the keeping of the Baroness Katharine Willoughby d'Eresby, baroness in her own right, and widow of Charles Brandon, Duke of Suffolk, who lived in a lordly mansion near the spot. This was that daring Protestant lady who so narrowly escaped the Smithfield fires for calling her lap-dog Gardiner (after the stern bishop, Bonner's worthy yoke-fellow), and dressing him up in small episcopal rochet and surplice. For this practical joke the jocose lady and Richard Bertie, her second husband, ancestor of the Dukes of Ancaster, had to fly to Poland, where the king, according to Mr. Jesse, installed them in the earldom of Crozan.

On the site of Bridgewater Square resided the Egertons, Earls of Bridgewater, in a mansion famous for its fruitful orchards. The house was burnt down in April, 1687, during the occupancy of John, third earl, " when his two infant heirs," says Mr. Jesse, " Charles, Viscount Brackley, and his second son Thomas, perished in the flames." Hatton, in 1708, calls Bridgewater Square "a new, pleasant, though very small square;" and Strype mentions it as "well inhabited, the middle neatly enclosed with palisado pales, and set round with trees, which renders the place very delightful."

Sir Henry Spelman (born 1562), the learned and laborious author of the " Glossarium," that great archæological work completed by Dugdale, died at his house in Barbican, 1640.

Beech Lane, Barbican, where Prince Rupert resided, and worked on his chemical experiments and his mezzotint plates, was probably so called, says Stow, from Nicholas de la Beech, Lieutenant of the Tower, who was deprived of his office by Edward III. Stow, whose clue we ever follow, describes the lane, in Elizabeth's time, as stretching from Redcross Street to Whitecross Street, and adorned with " beautiful houses of stone, brick, and timber." An old house in Barbican belonging to the Abbot of Ramsey was afterwards called Drury House, from the worshipful owner, Sir Drew Drury, also of Drury Lane. This was the house which Prince Rupert afterwards occupied; parts of the mansion were in existence as late as 1796. Here lived the fiery prince, whom Time had softened into a rough old philosopher, fond of old soldiers, and somewhat of a butt at Whitehall among the scoffing Rochesters of his day, who were all *à la mode de France*. Here Evelyn visited Rupert. In the parish books of St. Giles's, Cripplegate, a guinea is set down as payment to the ringers on the occasion of Charles II. visiting the prince at his Barbican house. In Strype's time the street had lost its gentility, and was inhabited by clothes-salesmen, and on the site of the old watch-tower fronting Redcross Street, stood an ignoble watchhouse for the brawling Mohocks of the day.

The " Fortune," one of the celebrated and one of the earliest Elizabethan theatres, stood between Whitecross Street and Golding Lane. It was opened about 1600 by Philip Henslowe and Edward Alleyn; and here, and at the Bear-garden, Bankside, Southwark, of which he was the proprietor, the latter actor derived the money after-

wards bestowed on God's-gift College, at Dulwich. An adjoining passage still retains the name of Playhouse Yard. Alleyn's theatre was burnt down in 1621, and was shortly afterwards rebuilt, but again destroyed, in 1649, by some rough and fanatical Puritan soldiers. Many of the actors of this theatre, in the last scene of all, when they had shuffled off this mortal coil, were buried at St. Giles's, Cripplegate.

In Golding Lane also stood the Nursery, a seminary for educating children for the profession of the stage, established in the reign of Charles II., under the auspices (says Mr. Jesse) of Colonel William Legge, Groom of the Bedchamber to that monarch, and uncle to the first Lord Dartmouth. Dryden speaks of it in his " Mac Flecknoe ":—

> " Near these a Nursery erects its head,
> Where queens are formed, and future heroes bred;
> Where unfledged actors learn to laugh and cry,
> Where infant punks their tender voices try,
> And little Maximins the gods defy;
> Great Fletcher never treads in buskins here,
> Nor greater Jonson dares in socks appear."

In Pepy's " Diary " are the following notices of the Nursery:—" 2nd Aug., 1664. To the King's Playhouse. . . . . I chanced to sit by Tom Killigrew, who tells me that he is setting up a Nursery; that is, is going to build a house in Moorfields, wherein he will have common plays acted.

" 24th Feb., 1667-8. To the Nursery, where none of us ever were before; the house is better and the music better than we looked for, and the acting not much worse, because I expected as bad as could be; and I was not much mistaken, for it was so. Their play was a bad one, called *Jeronimo is Mad Again*, a tragedy."

According to Stow, the antiquaries of his time believed that Little Britain, without Aldersgate, was so called from the Earls of Brittany lodging there, just as Scotland Yard was where the Kings of Scotland took up their quarters, and Petty Wales, in Thames Street, where Prince Hal held his noisy court. R. B., in Strype, defines Little Britain as stretching from Aldersgate Street, by the corner of St. Botolph's Church, running up to the Pump; then, as it grows wider, turning north up Duck Lane into another passage leading to " the Lame Hospital, or Bartholomew's Hospital." It was full of " old booksellers," especially from the Pump to Duck Lane. Here, especially during the Commonwealth, any hour in the day, might have been found such amiable dozy old antiquaries as still haunt old bookstalls in search after curiosa, all poring over black-letter pamphlets and yellow flying-sheets of the Civil War time, spectacles on nose, and crutch-cane in hand, intent on culling odd learning; and errant 'prentice-boys, their rough hair on end at the wonders of some story-book, which they would have given a month's wages to buy.

"It may not be amiss," says Roger North, in his Life of the Hon. and Rev. Dr. John North, 1740-42, "to step aside to reflect on the vast change in the trade of books between that time (about 1670) and ours. Then Little Britain was a plentiful and perpetual emporium of learned authors; and men went thither as to a market. This drew to the place a mighty trade; the rather because the shops were spacious, and the learned gladly resorted to them, where they seldom failed to meet with agreeable conversation. And the booksellers themselves were knowing and conversable men, with whom, for the sake of bookish knowledge, the greatest wits were pleased to converse. And we may judge the time as well spent there as (in latter days) either in tavern or coffeehouse . . . . but now this emporium is vanished, and the trade contracted into the hands of two or three persons."

Izaak Walton sketches Little Britain in his Life of Dr. Robert Sanderson. "About the time," he says, "of his printing this excellent preface," that is to say, the preface to his last twenty sermons, first printed in 1655, "I met him accidentally in London, in sad-coloured clothes, and, God knows, far from being costly. The place of our meeting was near to Little Britain, where he had been to buy a book, which he then had in his hand. We had no inclination to part presently, and therefore turned to stand in a corner under a penthouse (for it began to rain); and immediately the wind rose, and the rain increased so much, that both became so inconvenient as to force us into a cleanly house, where we had bread, cheese, ale, and a fire for our money."

Here, too, Milton's great work was published, and lay for a time unnoticed on the stalls. "Dr. Tancred Robinson," says Richardson in his "Remarks," "has given permission to use his name, and what I am going to relate he had from Fleet (wood) Shepherd at the Grecian Coffee House, and who often told the story. The Earl of Dorset was in Little Britain, beating about for books to his taste; there was 'Paradise Lost.' He was surprised with some passages he struck upon, dipping here and there, and bought it. The bookseller begged him to speak in its favour if he lik'd it, for that they lay on his hands as waste paper; Jesus-Shepherd was present. My Lord took it home, read it, and sent it to Dryden, who in a short time returned it. 'This man (says Dryden) cuts us all out, and the ancients too.'"

Later still we find that amiable writer, Washington Irving, wandering contemplatively in Little Britain. "In the centre of the great City of London," he says, "lies a small neighbourhood, consisting of a cluster of narrow streets and courts, of very venerable and debilitated houses, which goes by the name of 'Little Britain.' Christ's Hospital and St. Bartholomew's Hospital bound it on the west; Smithfield and Long Lane on the north; Aldersgate Street, like an arm of the sea, divides it from the eastern part of the City; whilst the yawning gulf of Bull-and-Mouth Street separates it from Butcher Lane, and the regions of Newgate. Over this little territory, thus bounded and designated, the great dome of St. Paul's, swelling above the intervening houses of Paternoster Row, Amen Corner, and Ave-Maria Lane, looks down with an air of motherly protection. . . . But though thus fallen into decline, Little Britain still bears traces of its former splendour. There are several houses ready to tumble down, the fronts of which are magnificently enriched with old oak carvings of hideous faces, unknown birds, beasts, and fishes; and fruits and flowers which it would perplex a naturalist to classify. There are also, in Aldersgate Street, certain remains of what were once spacious and lordly family mansions, but which have in latter days been subdivided into several tenements. Here may often be found the family of a petty tradesman, with its trumpery furniture, burrowing among the relics of antiquated finery, in great rambling time-stained apartments, with fretted ceilings, gilded cornices, and enormous marble fireplaces. The lanes and courts also contain many smaller houses, not on so grand a scale, but, like your small ancient gentry, sturdily maintaining their claims to equal antiquity. These have their gable ends to the street; great bow windows, with diamond panes set in lead, grotesque carvings, and low-arched doorways." *

In Aldersgate Street in 1661 (the year after the Restoration), died Brian Walton, Bishop of Chester, a laborious and learned scholar, who edited and in 1657 published the first English Polyglot Bible, in the Hebrew, Syriac, Chaldee, Samaritan, Arabic, Ethiopic, Persian, Greek, and Vulgar Latin languages. Before the war Walton had been rector of St. Martin Orgars and St. Giles-in-the-Fields. He was a good deal hunted about during the Civil Wars for his zeal for tithes; yet the Preface of his Bible contains compliments to Cromwell, which

---

* "It is evident," remarks a note in the complete edition of "The Works of Washington Irving, New York, 1857," vol. ii., p. 308, "that the author has included, in his general title of Little Britain, many of those little lanes and courts that belong immediately to Cloth Fair."

were afterwards altered so as to suit Charles II. "His triumphant return to his see," says an old writer zealously, "was a day not to be forgotten by all the true sons of the Church, though sneered at in private by the most rascally faction and crop-eared whelps of those parts, who did their endeavours to make it a May game, and piece of foppery." This learned prelate, who studied so hard during all the commotions of the Civil Wars, was buried in St. Paul's.

The "Albion," in Aldersgate Street, has long been famed for its good dinners. "Here," says Timbs, "take place the majority of the banquets of the Corporation of London; the sheriffs' inauguration dinners, as well as those of civic companies and committees, and such festivals, public and private, as are usually held at taverns of the highest class.

"The farewell dinners given by the East India Company to the Governors-General of India have often taken place at the 'Albion.' Here likewise (after dinner) the annual trade sales of the principal London publishers take place,' revivifying the olden printing and book glories of Aldersgate and Little Britain.

"The *cuisine* of the 'Albion' has long been celebrated for its *recherché* character. Among the traditions of the tavern, it is told that a dinner was once given here under the auspices of the gourmand alderman Sir William Curtis, which cost the party between thirty and forty pounds apiece. It might as well have cost twice as much, for amongst other acts of extravagance they dispatched a special messenger to Westphalia to choose a ham. There is likewise told a bet as to the comparative merits of the 'Albion' and 'York House' (Bath) dinners, which was to have been formally decided by a dinner of unparalleled munificence, and nearly equal cost at each; but it became a drawn bet, the 'Albion' beating in the first course, and the 'York House' in the second. . . . . Lord Southampton once gave a dinner at the 'Albion' at ten guineas a head."

CHAPTER XXVIII.

ALDERSGATE STREET (continued).

Sir Nicholas Bacon — The Fighting Earl of Peterborough — A Knavish Duke — The Cooks' Company — Noble Street — The "Half-moon Tavern," a house of call for wits — The "Bell Inn" — The City Road — Founding of Bunhill Fields Chapel — The Grecian Saloon — The "Old Milestone," City Road — Northumberland House in the City — The French Protestant Church in St. Martin's-le-Grand.

CLOSE to Shaftesbury House—which, after being a tavern and a lying-in hospital, became in 1848 a general dispensary, and latterly was divided into shops—stood Bacon House, the residence of Sir Nicholas Bacon (Queen Elizabeth's Lord Keeper), an enemy to Mary, Queen of Scots, and the Jesuits, a resolute, honest, unambitious man, and the father of the great philosopher and Lord Chancellor, Francis Bacon. The Lord Chancellor, however, was born at York House in the Strand, of which Buckingham Street marks the site. A popular writer has thus graphically described Bacon's father :—"Huge in person, gouty, asthmatic, high in flesh, Sir Nicholas could not walk from Whitehall to York House without sitting down to rest and blowing for his breath; and this weakness in his legs and chest descended to both his sons by Lady Anne. Queen Elizabeth, laughing, used to say the soul of her lord keeper was well lodged— in fat; but the lusty old knight, who had mother-wit of his own, could have been as brightly sarcastic as the queen. His was a shrewd saying : 'Let us take time, that we may have sooner done.' When Elizabeth, tripping into the hall at Redgrave, cried,

'My lord, what a little house you have gotten!' he adroitly answered, 'Madam, my house is well; but you have made me too great for my house.' When an impudent thief named Hogg asked mercy from him as judge, on the plea of kindred between the Hoggs and Bacons, he replied, 'Ah, you and I cannot be of kin until you have been hanged!'"

Swift's warlike friend, Mordaunt, the Earl of Peterborough, also lived in Aldersgate Street. Many of this energetic general's letters to Swift, are still extant, as well as Swift's pleasantly sarcastic verses to him. In the War of Succession the Earl took Barcelona, and drove the French out of Spain. Swift says of him :—

'Mordanto fills the trump of fame,
The Christian worlds his deeds proclaim,
And prints are crowded with his name.

"In journeys he outrides the post,
Sits up till midnight with his host,
Talks politics and gives the toast ;

"Knows every prince on Europe's face,
Flies like a squib from place to place,
And travels not, but runs a race.

*　　*　　*　　*　　*

"So wonderful his expedition,
    When you have not the least suspicion
    He's with you like an apparition.

"Shines in all climates like a star;
    In senates bold, and fierce in war;
    A land commander, and a tar.

"Heroic actions early bred in,
    Ne'er to be match'd in modern reading,
    But by his namesake, Charles of Sweden."

In "Remarks on the Characters of the Court of Queen Anne" Peterborough is thus described:— "He affects popularity, and loves to preach in coffee-houses and public places; is an open enemy to revealed religion; brave in his person; has a good estate; does not seem expensive, yet always in debt and very poor. A well-shaped, thin man, with a very brisk look, near fifty years old." "*This character,*" observes Swift, "*is for the most part true!*"

Of the famous Duke of Montagu, who also lived in Aldersgate Street, the author of "Remarks on the Characters" says, "Since the queen's accession to the throne, he has been created a duke; and is near sixty years old." "*As arrant a knave,*" is Swift's addition, "*as any in his time.*"

"Opposite to St. Botolph's Church stood the Cooks' Hall, a spacious building," says Aleph, "which escaped the Great Fire, but was consumed by a comparatively insignificant conflagration in 1771, when the worshipful company transferred their business to the Guildhall. The Cooks' Company is a fellowship nearly as ancient as good living; it is thirty-fifth in precedence, was incorporated in 1480 by that luxurious monarch Edward IV., and obtained further privileges from Queen Elizabeth."

In Noble Street, in Shakespearian times, dwelt Mr. Serjeant Fleet, the Recorder of London, and in the same house afterwards resided Robert Tichborne, Lord Mayor in 1657. Tichborne signed the death-warrant of Charles I.; and at the Restoration was tried, with Hugh Peters, Harrison, and others, and executed. The old "Castle and Falcon" inn stood near the old City gate. Nearly opposite Lauderdale House, which was north of Shaftesbury House, stood in 1830 the "Half-moon Tavern," a place of resort for the wits of Charles II.'s time, Wycherley and Congreve being among its *habitués.* The fireplaces were ornamented with curious grotesque carvings in wood.

Higher up than Lauderdale House, two doors only from Barbican, once stood the "Bell" inn, "of a pretty good resort for wagons with meal." From this inn John Taylor, the poetical waterman of the time of James I., set out on his penniless pilgrimage to Scotland. At the west side, a little beyond St. Botolph's, is Trinity Court, so called centuries ago from a brotherhood of the Holy Trinity, first founded in 1377, as a fraternity of St. Fabian and St. Sebastian, licensed by Henry VI., and suppressed by Edward VI. The hall was still standing as late as 1790.

The City Road, an indirect tributary of Aldersgate (opened in 1761), is a continuation of the New Road, and runs from the "Angel" at Islington to Finsbury Square.

In April, 1777, John Wesley laid the first stone of the chapel opposite Bunhill Fields, and remarked, as he laid it, "Probably this will be seen no more by any human eye, but will remain there till the earth and the works thereof are burnt up." This chapel was greatly damaged by fire in December, 1879, but has since been restored.

The theatrical traditions of this neighbourhood demand a few words. The "Eagle" Tavern, now the Grecian Theatre, City Road, when under the management of its originator, Mr. Thomas Rouse, was highly famed for its two comic vocalists, Harry Howell, and Robert Glindon. The first-named was, perhaps, the best buffo singer of his day; and it was for these gardens that Glindon wrote "Biddy the Basket Woman," "The Literary Dustman," and other songs of world-wide repute, singing them himself in the evening, his daytime being fully occupied in painting, with the late Mr. Danson, that marvel of panoramas "London by Day and Night," so many years the main attraction at the Coloseum, Regent's Park. After his voice failed him, he was enlisted in the standing company at the Drury Lane Theatre, assisting in the scene-painting and property department, and doing small parts in the pantomime openings. It was at the Grecian Saloon that Frederick Robson also made his mark with the London playgoers, in the characters of "Jacob Earwig," in *Boots at the Swan,* and "Wormwood" in *The Lottery Ticket.* William Farren, that excellent actor, had seen and admired Robson's wonderful abilities, and wished to secure his services for the Olympic; but fearing the announcement "from the Grecian Saloon" might act detrimentally with public opinion, he got Robson an engagement in Ireland, and then, announcing him "from the Theatre Royal Dublin," launched him on his brilliant career at the little theatre in Wych Street.

The "Old Milestone," City Road, opposite Goswell Street Road, was, in the early part of the present century, much patronised by Cockney tourists, on account of its pretty tea-gardens, and like White Conduit House and Bagnigge Wells, it attracted immense crowds of Sunday ramblers. Concerts were occasionally given here, particularly at holiday times, but its modern reputation was chiefly owing to its Judge and Jury Society, and the forensic ability of its proprietor, Mr. Benjamin Foster, who was afterwards so well-known and respected by literary men as we have shown, over the Gate itself, as the illustrious Cave did at St. John's Gate, Clerkenwell. It afterwards, in Strype's time, was a tavern, the usual end of all celebrated London buildings.

A little north of the "Bull and Mouth," on the

PRINCE RUPERT'S HOUSE IN THE BARBICAN. (*See page 224.*)

as mine host of the "Saint John's Gate," or Gate House, Clerkenwell.

Very near Aldersgate stood Northumberland House, where the fiery Hotspur, who owes all the emblazonment on his escutcheon to Shakespeare, once dwelt. Henry IV. gave the house to Queen Jane, his wife, and it was then called her Wardrobe. In Stow's time it was the house of a printer—not, however, John Day, the celebrated printer of Elizabeth's time, as has been suggested, for he lived, west side of St. Martin's-le-Grand, is the French Protestant Church, opened in 1842, when St. Mary's Chapel, in Threadneedle Street, was taken down. On July 24, 1850, the tercentenary of the Royal Charter to Foreign Protestants granted by Edward VI. was commemorated by special services both at the Dutch Church, Austin Friars, and at St. Martin's-le-Grand, and in the evening the members of the consistories of both churches dined together, and drank to the memory of Edward VI.

CHAPTER XXIX.

CRIPPLEGATE.

Miracles performed by Edmund the Martyr after Death—Cripplegate—The Church of St. Giles—The Tomb of John Speed—The Legend of
Constance Whitney—Sir John Martin Frobisher—Milton's Grave Outraged—The Author of "The Book of Martyrs:" his Fortunate Escape
from Bishop Gardiner—St. Alphage, London Wall—An Old State Funeral—The Barber-Surgeons' Hall: its Famous Picture of Henry VIII.
—Holbein's Death—Treasures in Barber-Surgeons' Hall: its Plate Stolen and Recovered—Another kind of Recovery there—Lambe, the
Benevolent Clothworker—The Perambulation of Cripplegate Parish in Olden Time—Basinghall Street—St. Michael's Bassishaw—William
Lee, the Inventor of the Stocking-loom—Minor City Companies in the Neighbourhood of Basinghall Street—The Bankruptcy Court—
Whitecross Street and its Prison—The Green Yard—The Dissenters' Library in Whitecross Street—A Curious Anecdote about Redcross Street
—Grub Street—The Haunts of Poor Authors—Johnson in Grub Street—Henry Welby, the Grub Street Recluse—General Monk's House—
Whittington's House—Coleman Street and the Puritan Leaders—Venner, the Fanatic—Goodwin—St. Stephen's Church—Armourers' Hall.

STOW, quoting a history of Edmund the Martyr,
King of the East Angles, by Abbo Floriacensis,
says that in 1010, when the Danes approached
Bury St. Edmunds, Bishop Alwyn removed the

rooms over the gate were set apart for the City
Water Bailiff.

The church of St. Giles's, Cripplegate, is the
successor of one founded some twenty-four years

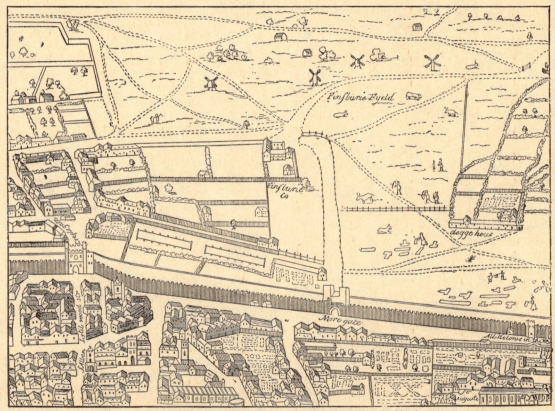

CRIPPLEGATE AND NEIGHBOURHOOD. (*From Aggas's Map.*)

body of the martyred king to St. Gregory's Church,
near St. Paul's; and as it passed through Cripplegate, such was the blessed influence it diffused,
that many lame persons rose upright, and began to
praise God for their miraculous cure. The postern
afterwards became a prison, like the Compter, for
debtors and common trespassers. The gate was
rebuilt, says Fabian, by the Brewers of London, in
1244, and again in 1491, at the cost of 400 marks,
money left by Edmund Shaw, goldsmith and ex-
mayor. It was again repaired and beautified, and
a foot-postern made, in the 15th Charles II. The

after the Conquest. It suffered greatly by fire in
1545 (Henry VIII.) Matilda, queen of Henry I.,
had founded a brotherhood there, dedicated to
St. Mary and St. Giles. The church was repaired,
and perhaps partially rebuilt, after the fire of 1545.
"Since that event," says Mr. Godwin, "it has
undergone miscalled adornments, but has not been
materially changed." The tower was raised fifteen
feet in 1682. St. Giles's had a peal of twelve bells,
besides one in the turret. It boasts one of the
few sets of chimes in London. Those of St. Giles
were, it is said, constructed by a poor working man.

In the north aisle of this interesting and historical church lies a great benefactor to London antiquaries, the learned and laborious John Speed, the great topographical writer, who died 1629. He was a wise tailor, whom Sir Fulke Greville patronised, and who was assisted in his labours by Cotton and Spelman. He had in his time twelve sons and six daughters. His marble monument is adorned with an effigy of Speed (once gilt and painted), holding in one hand a book, and in the other a skull. The long eulogistic Latin inscription describes him as " Civis Londinensis Mercatorum Scissorum Frater. " It is a singular fact that two of the great London antiquaries should have been tailors, yet the sartor's is undoubtedly a contemplative trade, and we owe both worthies much gratitude for laboriously stitching together such a vast patchwork of interesting facts.

Considering that Foxe, the martyrologist (buried, it is believed, on the south side of the chancel) was sheltered by Sir Thomas Lucy, Shakespeare's traditional persecutor—

" At home a poor scarecrow, in London an ass,"

it is singular to find near the centre of the north aisle of St. Giles's a monument to Constance Whitney, eldest daughter of Sir Robert Whitney, and granddaughter of Sir Thomas Lucy, who died at the age of seventeen, excelling " in all noble qualities becoming a virgin of so sweet proportion of beauty and harmonie of parts." From this maiden's grave a lying tradition has sprung like a fungus.

The striking-looking monument represents a female in a shroud rising from a coffin. According to tradition it commemorates the story of a lady who, after having been buried while in a trance, was not only restored to life, but subsequently became the mother of several children, her resuscitation, it is said, having been brought about by the cupidity of a sexton, which induced him to open the coffin, in order to obtain possession of a valuable ring on her finger. This story, however, is entirely fabulous.

A small white marble tablet within the communion-rails also records another Lucy. The inscription is—

" Here lies Margaret Lucy, the second daughter of Sir Thomas Lucy, of Charlcott in the county of Warwicke, Knight (the third by imediate discent of the name of Thomas), by Alice, sole daughter and heire of Thomas Spenser, of Clarenden, in the same county, Esq., and Custos Brevium of the Courte of Comon Pleas at Westminster, who departed this life the 18th day of November, 1634, and aboute the 19th year of her age. For discretion and sweetnesse of conversation not many excelled, and for pietie and patience in her sicknesse and death, few equalled her; which is the comforte of her nearest friendes, to every of whom shee was very dear, but especiallie to her old grandmother, the Lady Constance Lucy, under whose government shee died, who, having long exspected every day to have gone before her, doth now trust, by faith and hope in the precious bloode of Christ Jesus, shortly to follow after, and be partaker, together with her and others, of the unspeakable and eternell joyes in His blessed kingdome ; to whom be all honour, laude, and praise, now and ever. Amen."

In this church, too, after many a voyage and many a battle, rests that old Elizabethan warrior and explorer, Sir Martin Frobisher, who was brought here in February, 1594–5, after receiving his death shot at Brest. His northern discoveries while in search of a north-west passage to China, in a mere fishing-boat of twenty-five tons, his West Indian cruise with Drake, and his noble courage against the Spanish Armada, fully entitle Frobisher to rank as one of the earliest of our naval heroes.

Above all, Milton is buried here. A sacrilegious desecration of his remains, we regret to record, took place in 1790. The object of the search for the sacred body was reasonable, the manner of the search disgraceful. The church being under repair, and £1,350 being spent upon it, the vestry clerk and churchwardens had agreed—as a monument to Milton was contemplated at St. Giles's, and the exact spot of the poet's interment only traditionally known—to dig up the coffin whilst the repairs were still going on. The difficulty was this : the parish tradition had always been that Milton was buried in the chancel, under the clerk's desk, where afterwards the common councilmen's pew stood, in the same grave with his father, the scrivener, of Bread Street. He died fourteen years after the "blessed Restoration," of consumption, say the parish books, not gout, at his house in Bunhill Fields. Aubrey, in 1681, says, " The stone is now removed, for about two years since the two steps to the communion-table were raised." During the repairs of 1682 the pulpit was removed from the second pillar on the north side to the south side of the old chancel, which was then covered with pews. The parish clerks and sextons, forgetting this change, used to show a grave on the south side as Milton's, and Mr. Baskerville, to show his reverence for Milton, was buried in this wrong spot.

The right spot was at last remembered, the ground was searched, and Milton's leaden coffin discovered, directly over the wooden one of his father. The coffin, which was old, and bore no inscription, was five feet ten inches in length. The following ghoulish and disgraceful scene, described by P. Neve, in his " Narrative of the Disinterment of Milton's Coffin," 1790, then took place. The disinterment had been agreed upon after a merry meeting at the house of Mr. Fountain, overseer, in Beech Lane, the night before, Mr. Cole, another overseer, and the journeyman of Mr. Ascough, the parish clerk, who was a coffin-maker, assisting.

"Holmes, the journeyman, having fetched a mallet and a chisel, and cut open the top of the coffin, slantwise from the head, as low as the breast, so that, the top being doubled backward, they could see the corpse, he cut it open also at the foot. Upon first view of the body, it appeared perfect, and completely enveloped in the shroud, which was of many folds, the ribs standing up regularly. When they disturbed the shroud the ribs fell. Mr. Fountain confessed that he pulled hard at the teeth, which resisted, until some one hit them a knock with a stone, when they easily came out. There were but five in the upper jaw, which were all perfectly sound and white, and all taken by Mr. Fountain. He gave one of them to Mr. Laming. Mr. Laming also took one from the lower jaw; and Mr. Taylor took two from it. Mr. Laming said that he had at one time a mind to bring away the whole under-jaw with the teeth in it; he had it in his hand, but tossed it back again. Also, that he lifted up the head, and saw a great quantity of hair, which lay strait and even, behind the head, and in the state of hair which had been combed and tied together before interment; but it was wet, the coffin having considerable corroded holes, both at the head and foot, and a great part of the water with which it had been washed on the Tuesday afternoon having run into it.

"Elizabeth Grant, the gravedigger, and who is servant to Mrs. Hoppy, therefore now took possession of the coffin; and, as its situation under the common councilmen's pew would not admit of its being seen without the help of a candle, she kept a tinder-box in the excavation, and, when any persons came, struck a light, and conducted them under the pew; where, by reversing the part of the lid which had been cut, she exhibited the body, at first for sixpence and afterwards for threepence and twopence each person. The workmen in the church kept the doors locked to all those who would not pay the price of a pot of beer for entrance, and many, to avoid that payment, got in at a window at the west end of the church, near to Mr. Ayscough's counting-house."

The hair torn off the poet's forehead resembled the short locks seen in Faithorne's quarto print of Milton taken in 1670, four years only before the poet's death. In Charles II.'s time, coffin-plates were not generally used, and it was only usual to paint the name, &c., on the outer wooden case. The rascals altogether stole a rib-bone, ten teeth, and several handfuls of hair.

Upon this sacrilege Cowper, horrified, wrote these lines:—

"Ill fare the hands that heaved the stones
　Where Milton's ashes lay,
That trembled not to grasp his bones,
　And steal his dust away.

"O, ill-requited bard! neglect
　Thy living worth repaid,
And blind idolatrous respect
　As much affronts the dead!"

In all fairness, however, it must be added that grave doubts have been raised as to whether the corpse found was really that of the poet. Immediately on the publication of Mr. Neve's Narrative, it was ably answered in the *St. James's Chronicle*, in "Nine Reasons why it is improbable that the coffin lately dug up in the Parish Church of St. Giles, Cripplegate, should contain the reliques of Milton." Mr. Neve, says Todd, one of Milton's biographers, added a postscript to his Narrative, but all his labour appears to have been employed on an imaginary cause. The late Mr. Steevens, who particularly lamented the indignity which the nominal ashes of the poet sustained, has intimated in his manuscript remarks on this Narrative and Postscript that the disinterred corpse was supposed to be that of a *female*, and that the minutest examination of the fragments could not disprove, if it did not confirm, the supposition.

In 1793, Samuel Whitbread, Sheridan's friend, erected a bust to Milton in this church with this inscription:—

"John Milton,
Author of 'Paradise Lost,'
Born Dec., 1608,
Died Nov., 1674.

His father, John Milton, died March, 1646.
They were both interred in this church.

Samuel Whitbread posuit, 1793."

In this most interesting old church were buried many illustrious persons recorded by Stow. Amongst these we may mention Robert Glover, a celebrated Elizabethan herald, who assisted Camden with the pedigrees of his famous "Britannia." John Foxe, the learned and laborious author of that manual of true Protestantism, "The Book of Martyrs," was also interred here, as well as that good old herbalist and physician of Elizabeth's time, Dr. William Bulleyn, author of the "Government of Health" (1558), and a "Book of Simples," works full of old wives' remedies and fantastic beliefs. Foxe the martyrologist was a Lincolnshire man, born in 1517, the year in which Luther first openly opposed Roman dogmas. At Oxford he became famous for writing comedies in especially elegant Latin. For his religious opinions he was expelled Magdalen College, of which he was a Fellow, and, forsaken by his friends, he was reduced to great distress, till he was taken as family tutor by Sir Thomas Lucy, of Warwickshire, the traditional persecutor of Shakespeare. With this worthy knight he remained till his children arrived at mature years, and had no longer need of a tutor. Now commenced a period of want and despair, which closed with what his son calls, in the Life of his father "a marvellous accident and great example of God's mercy."

Foxe was sitting one day in St. Paul's Church, almost spent with long fasting, his countenance wan and pale, and his eyes hollow, when there came to him a person whom he never remembered to have seen before, who, sitting down by him, accosted him very familiarly, and put into his hands an untold sum of money, bidding him to be of good cheer, to be careful of himself, and to use all means to prolong his life, for that in a few days new hopes were at hand, and new means of subsistence. Foxe tried all methods to find out the person by whom he was thus so seasonably relieved, but in vain.

The prediction was fulfilled, for within three days the starving student was taken by the Duchess of Richmond as tutor to her nephews and niece, the children of the poet Earl of Surrey. At the escape of Surrey's father, the Duke of Norfolk, from prison, on the death of that swollen tyrant, Henry VIII., the duke took Foxe under his patronage, but Bishop Gardiner's determination to seize him compelled Foxe to take refuge in Switzerland. On the accession of Elizabeth, Foxe returned to England, and was made Prebendary of Salisbury. Though befriended by Sir Francis Drake, Bishop Grindal, and Sir Thomas Gresham, Foxe never rose high in the church, having Genevese scruples about ecclesiastical vestments, which he was too honest to swallow. Queen Elizabeth used to call the old martyrologist "Father," but she would not spare, at his intercession, two Anabaptists condemned to the flames. Latterly Foxe denounced the extreme Puritans as "new monks," who desired to bring all things contrary to their own discipline and consciences "into Jewish bondage." This worthy man died in 1587, aged seventy years, and was buried in St. Giles's Church.

The parish register of St. Giles's records the marriage of Oliver Cromwell and Elizabeth Bourchier, on the 22nd of August, 1620. The future Protector was then in his twenty-first year.

In 1803 a fine battlemented piece of the London wall of Edward IV.'s time, tufted with wild plants, that stood in the churchyard of St. Giles's, Cripplegate, was taken down, having become dangerous. It joined on to the fine base of the round bastion tower still existing at the south-west corner, and the most perfect portion left.

In 1812 Mr. John T. Smith mentions seeing the workmen remove the wainscoting of the north porch of St. Giles's, when they discovered an old wainscot of Henry IV. or Henry V., its perforated arches beautifully carved, and the vermilion with which it was painted bright as when first put on.

There is little to be said about the Norman church of St. Alphage, London Wall. It was built, remarks Cunningham, "in 1777 (it is said by Dance), on the site of the old Hospital or Priory of St. Mary the Virgin, founded for the sustentation of one hundred blind men in 1532, by William Elsing, mercer, and of which Spittle, the founder, was the first prior. The living is a rectory, and was originally in the gift of the Abbot of St. Martin's-le-Grand. It afterwards came to the Abbot and Convent of Westminster, and was ultimately conferred by Mary I. on the Bishop of London and his successors for ever." The old hospital had become a dwelling-house in Henry VIII.'s reign, and was inhabited by Sir John Williams, Master of the King's Jewels. In 1541 it was destroyed by fire, and many of the jewels were burnt, and more stolen.

The first Barber-Surgeons' Hall, in Monkwell Street, is said to have been of the date of Edward IV. The second hall was built by Inigo Jones, 1636, and was repaired by that distinguished amateur in architecture, the Earl of Burlington. The theatre, one of the finest of Inigo's works, in the opinion of Horace Walpole, was pulled down at the latter end of the last century, and sold for the value of the materials. Hatton describes it temptingly as a theatre fitted with "four degrees of cedar seats," rising one above another, and adorned with the figures of the seven Liberal Sciences, the twelve Signs of the Zodiac, and a bust of King Charles I. The roof was an elliptical cupola. The quaint old wooden doorway, with the deep arched roof, the grotesque goggling head, the monsters, stiff foliage, and heraldry, has been removed, to humour a stuck-up modern set of chambers, and the three razors quartered on the Barber-Surgeons' arms, and the motto, "Trust in God," are gone. The hall, now displaced by warehouses, stood on a bastion of the old Roman wall; and the architect had ingeniously turned it to use, in the erection of the west end of the room. Before the late changes the Barber-Surgeons'

Hall used to be dirty and neglected. The inner hall, now pulled down, was some sixty feet by thirty, and was lighted by an octagonal lantern, enriched with fruit and flowers delicately carved in wood. Many of the pictures are fine, especially one by Holbein, "The Presentation of the Charter by Henry VIII." This picture contains, among eighteen other portraits, that of Sir William Butts, the good-natured physician who saved Cranmer from disgrace, and that of Dr. John Chamber, the doctor who attended Queen Anne Boleyn in her confinement with Elizabeth.

"To this year" (1541), says Mr. Wornum, "also possibly belongs the Barber-Surgeons' picture of Henry granting a charter to the corporation. The Barbers and Surgeons of London, originally constituting one company, had been separated, but were again, in the thirty-second of Henry VIII., combined into a single society, and it was the ceremony of presenting them with a new charter which is commemorated by Holbein's picture, now in their hall in Monkwell Street. In 1745 they were again separated, and the Surgeons constituted a distinct company, and had a hall in the Old Bailey. The date of this picture is not known, but it was necessarily in or after 1541, and as Holbein's life did not extend much beyond this time, there is some probability in the report alluded to by Van Mander, namely, that the painter died without completing the picture. Besides the king's —a seated full-length, crowned, and with the sword of state in his right hand—it contains also portraits of eighteen members of the guild, three kneeling on the right hand of the king, and fifteen on the other, and among them are conspicuous our friends Butts and Chamber on the right. The head of the latter is effective and good, though the portraits generally are unsatisfactory; but Warden Aylef's, the second on the left, is especially good. The rest are indifferent, either owing to the fact of their having been some of them perhaps entirely repainted, or possibly having never had a touch of Holbein in them.

"There is a large engraving of this picture by B. Baron, but reversed. The names of the members of the guild are written in a most offensive manner over the face of the picture, which is a piece of barbarism that belongs, I imagine, to a period long subsequent to the time of Holbein. These names are J. Alsop, W. Butts, J. Chamber, T. Vycary (the master of the guild, who is receiving the charter from the left hand of the king), T. Aylef, N. Symson, E. Harman, J. Monforde, J. Pen, M. Alcoke, R. Fereis, X. Samon, and W. Tylly; five of the second row are without names.

"The king is placed very stiffly, and the face, much repainted, is that we are familiar with in the many ordinary half-lengths of the king, representing him in the last years of his life. The composition is anything but graceful, and there is not an entire hand in the whole piece; the king's hands are good, though slight and sketchy. The principle of the composition is somewhat Egyptian, for the king is made about twice the size of the other figures, though they are in front of him.

"We have an interesting notice of this picture in Pepys' 'Diary,' where, against the date August 29, 1668, that is, two years after the Great Fire, he notes: 'At noon comes, by appointment, Harris to dine with me; and after dinner he and I to Chirurgeons' Hall, where they are building it new, very fine; and there to see their theatre, which stood all the fire, and, which was our business, their great picture of Holbein's, thinking to have bought it, by the help of Mr. Pierce, for a little money. I did think to give £200 for it, it being said to be worth £1,000; but it is so spoiled that I have no mind to it, and is not a pleasant though a good picture.'

"Pepys is very candid about his motive for buying the picture; because it was said to be worth a thousand pounds he was willing to give two hundred for it, not that he wanted the picture for its own sake; however, he did not like it, and he declined the speculation. When we consider the worth of money at that time, the estimated value seems an enormous one. Pepys' own price was not an inconsiderable sum. The picture is on oak, on vertical boards, about six feet high by ten feet three inches in width. The College of Surgeons possesses an old, but smaller, indifferent copy of it, on paper attached to canvas. J. Alsop, on the extreme right, is omitted; and in the place of a tablet with a Latin inscription, which disfigures the Barber-Surgeons' picture, is a window showing the old tower of St. Bride's, indicating, accordingly, the palace of Bridewell as the place of the ceremony.

"There can be no question of the genuineness of this picture in its foundations, but in its present state it is not remarkable that it should cause discussions. I am disposed to believe that Holbein never did finish the picture, and from the great inferiority of the second series of heads on the left hand of the king I think that these must have been added later. There is no trace of Holbein's hand in them; and the fact of five of them being without names is also suggestive of the assumption that these five were not even members of the guild when the picture was painted. Two of this background group are named X. Samson and W. Tilley; these, therefore, may have been Holbein's contemporaries, though not introduced by him into the picture. It is not to be supposed that the king sat to Holbein for this portrait; it is the stock portrait of the time. The king is not looking at the master, Vycary, to whom he is handing the charter, but straight before him. The composition is a mere portrait piece, got up for the sake of the portraits. In the whole group of nineteen only five besides the king wear their beards—Aylef, Symson, Harman, Alcoke, and Fereis. Monforde's, the fifth from the king, is a very expressive face, considerably re-painted, but full of character. The three on the right—Chamber, Butts, and Alsop —are perhaps so separately placed as physicians to the king."

There is a letter of James I. to the Barber-Surgeons still in their possession. It is written from Newmarket, and dated 1617, requesting the loan of this picture, in order that it should be copied. In Mr. Wornum's opinion this copy is the one still to be seen at the College of Surgeons in Lincoln's Inn Fields. It was formerly in the possession of Desenfans, and at his sale in 1786 was purchased by the Surgeons' Company for five guineas. In the Lincoln's Inn picture there is a window at the back instead of the tablet with a long complimentary Latin inscription to Henry VIII. It was probably added after the picture had passed through the Fire of London, where, from what Pepys says, it may have got injured. The Lincoln's Inn picture was cleaned in 1789. The cleaner sent in a bill for £400, but eventually took fifty guineas.

Shortly before this picture of Holbein's was finished, Henry (who was always murdering or mar-

ST. GILES'S, CRIPPLEGATE, SHOWING THE OLD WALL.
(See page 229.)

rying) wedded ugly Anne of Cleves, beheaded Cromwell, and married Lady Katherine Howard. Holbein himself, who lived in the parish of St. Andrew Undershaft, died of the plague in the year 1543, as was proved by Mr. Black's discovery of his hasty will. Before this discovery the date of Holbein's death was generally assigned to 1554.

"Prince Albert," remarks Aleph, "visited this noble Holbein more than once. At his desire it was sent to Buckingham Palace, and remained there a month; but when the directors of the Manchester Exhibition desired the loan of it they were refused. As doubts were entertained that it would be damaged by remaining in the City, a Royal Commission inspected it, and specimens of colours were hung in the hall for several months, with a view to ascertain whether the atmosphere was unfavourable to them, but no change took place, and Dean Milman, with his coadjutors, expressed their conviction that its removal was not desirable. It is pretended that Henry never sat for any other portrait, and that those of him at Hampton Court are merely copies. . . . . The other paintings," continues Aleph, "well deserve notice. Two, certainly, are Vandyke's. 1st. A whole-length of the Countess of Richmond, in a standing position, resting her right hand upon a lamb. This is a beautiful work of art. The face is expressive of unaffected goodness, and the attitude graceful, without stiffness. She is robed in white satin, and so admirably is the fabric imitated that you half believe it may be grasped. There is a copy of this portrait at Hampton Court. 2nd. A likeness of Inigo Jones, very fine, and highly characteristic. Over the entrance to the Hall is a bronzed bust of Jones, which is connected with a

(See page 233.)

THE BARBER-SURGEONS' PICTURE.

rather discreditable story. It seems this bust, not many years since, was found in a lumber-closet. It was of white marble, and the sagacious Master of the day gave orders that it should be bronzed. There is a doubtful sketch of a head, as it is thought, of Linnæus, and by whatever artist painted, its merit is of no common order. Also, portraits of Charles II. and Queen Anne, both benefactors of the Company; of Henry Johnson, a favourite of the Merry Monarch; and of Thomas Lisle, King's barber in 1622—the latter a most solemn and imposing-looking personage, who might well pass for the Prime Minister. Across the principal entrance there stands a very curious two-leaved screen; originally it had four compartments, two are lost or have been destroyed. It exhibits the arms of the Company, and is elaborately wrought over with innumerable artistic emblems, fruit, flowers, fantastic ornaments, and gilding. Its history is a strange one. Once on a time a notable felon was hanged, and his corpse handed over to the Barber-Surgeons for dissection; the operator, fancying the heart still pulsated, used means for resuscitation, and succeeded. The man was kept hidden for a long while, and then sent abroad at the Company's expense. He ultimately became rich, and in gratitude sent them this screen."

"The Company's plate," remarks the same writer, "includes a drinking-cup and cover, in silver gilt, the gift of Henry VIII., very beautifully chased; a similar cup, in silver, still more elaborately worked, the gift of Charles II.; a dish, or bowl, very large, with a flowered edge, not remarkable for elegance, the gift of Queen Anne; an oblong dish, with a well centre, said to have been used for lather when people of rank were shaved; and two velvet caps, in filagree silver bands, worn on state occasions by the Master and his deputy, they being privileged by charter to be covered in the presence of the sovereign."

In the reign of James I. the Company, it appears, nearly lost the whole of their plate, through a successful robbery. "The thieves," says Mr. Jesse, in his "London and its Celebrities," "were four men of the names of Jones, Lyne, Sames, and Foster, of whom the former confessed his guilt, when, in consequence of information which he gave, the plate was recovered. In the books of the Company for November, 1616, is the following matter-of-fact entry recording the fate of the culprits:—'Thomas Jones was taken, who, being brought to Newgate in December following, Jones and Lyne were both executed for this fact. In January following, Sames was taken and executed. In April,

Foster was taken and executed. Now, let's pray God to bless this house from any more of these damages. Amen.'

"The following extract from the Company's papers, under the date of the 13th of July, 1587, is still more curious :—'It is agreed that if any body which shall at any time hereafter happen to be brought to our hall for the intent to be wrought upon by the anatomists of the Company, shall revive or come to life again, *as of late hath been seen*, the charges about the same body so reviving shall be borne, levied, and sustained by such person or persons who shall so happen to bring home the body; and who, further, shall abide such order or fine as this house shall award.' The last instance, it would appear, of recuscitation in a dissecting-room occurred in the latter part of the last century. The case, as used to be related by the late celebrated anatomist, John Hunter, was that of a criminal, whose body had been cut down after execution at Newgate." This case we have already mentioned.

Lambe's Almshouses stood at the upper end of Monkwell Street. The worthy clothworker who built these havens of refuge after life's storms was a gentleman of Henry VIII.'s chapel. These almshouses were on the site of an ancient chapel or hermitage, built in the old City wall, about the time of the early Norman kings, and was partly supported by royal stipend assigned to it in 1275. Soon after 1346 it passed into the hands of the Corporation of London, and after the dissolution it was purchased by Lambe.

This benevolent man also built a conduit at Holborn Bridge, at a cost of £1,500, and gave one hundred and twenty pails for carrying water to such poor women "as were willing," says Strype, "to take pains." Water was not too plentiful in Elizabethan London. As late as the end of the seventeenth century, carriers with yokes and pails perambulated the streets, shouting "Any New River water here?" Lambe also founded a school at Sutton Valence, Kent, the place of his birth, and built almshouses there. He gave £300 to the Shropshire clothiers; gave £15 to Cripplegate parish, for bells, with a bequest of a £6 annuity and £100 ready money to Christ's Hospital; left St. Thomas's Hospital, Southwark, £4 a year, and bequeathed money to the poor prisoners of the London gaols. He provided 10s. each for the marriage of forty poor maids, provided for all his servants, and ordered a hundred and eight frieze gowns to be distributed to the poor at his funeral.

Anthony Munday's account of the perambulation

of Cripplegate parish is so quaint that we cannot refrain from abridging it, as a good specimen of the old parochial anxiety to preserve the parish bounds. The parishioners, says Stow's continuator, first struck down the alley forming part of their churchyard, close by St. Giles's Well (made at the charge of Richard Whittington), and crossing the tower ditch, kept along by the City wall almost to Aldersgate; they then crossed the ditch again, by certain garden-houses near, and came down a little garden alley (formerly leading into Aldersgate), and returned by St. Giles's Well. They then paraded up the west side of Redcross Street and the south side of Barbican, till they came to the "Boar's Head," at the end, and there set up their marks on a great post. From there they crossed over to the north side of the street, through certain garden alleys, on the west side of Willoughby House, a course afterwards denied them. They next passed through Barbican, and turned up Goswell Street; a little beyond the bars they set up their marks, and passed along the right side of the King's highway leading to Islington; then leaving the Mount Mill on the right, they proceeded till they came within three rods of a little bridge at the lower end of a close, over which lay a footpath to Newington Green. They then dug a way over the ditch, and passing south-east by the low grounds and brick-fields, left the footpath leading from the Pest House to Islington on the left. From a boundary-stone in the brick-hill they came south to a bridge, temporarily provided for them, and struck down eastward by the ditch side to the farthest conduit head, where they gave the parish children points (metal tags, used to fasten clothes, in the reign of James I., when Munday lived). This was to fix the boundaries in the children's minds. In some parishes children were whipped at the boundaries, a less agreeable method of mnemonics. From Dame Anne de Clare's famous well, mentioned by Ben Jonson, they pushed on past the Butts, into Holywell Close. Eventually, turning full west over the highway from Moorgate, they came into Little Moorfields; and keeping close to the pales and the Clothworkers' tenters, they reached the Postern, where they put up their final mark, "and so," as Pepys would say, "home."

Basinghall Ward consists of Basinghall Street alone. The present Bankruptcy Court is on the site of the old mansion of the Basings, of whom one, Solomon Basing, was Lord Mayor in the first year of Henry III. To his son, Adam, afterwards mayor, Henry III. gave messuages in Aldermanbury and Milk Street, and the advowson of the church at Basing Hall. According to an old tradition, which

Stow derides, the house had once been a Jewish synagogue. It passed into the hands of the Bakewells, in the reign of Edward III., and in the reign of Richard II. was sold by the king for £50 to the City, who turned it into a cloth exchange, which it continued till 1820, when the present Bankruptcy Court was erected on its site. In old times no foreigner was allowed to sell any woollen cloth but in Bakewell Hall. Part of the tolls or hallage was given by Edward VI. to Christ's Hospital, whose governors superintended the warehouses. It was rebuilt for £2,500 in 1558, destroyed in the Great Fire of 1666, and re-erected about 1672.

St. Michael's Bassishaw, in this ward, was founded about 1140, rebuilt in 1460, destroyed in the Great Fire, and again rebuilt in 1676 by Sir Christopher Wren. Here lies interred Sir John Gresham, uncle to Sir Thomas Gresham.

One of the great benefactors of the church, John Burton, mercer, who died 1460 his (will was dated 1459), bequeathed seven chasubles wrought with gold, in honour of the Passion, to the church of Wadworth, in Yorkshire, and desired his executor to keep the day of his anniversary, otherwise called "yearsmind," for ten years, in the church of St. Michael.

The following is part of an epitaph of an old knight and surgeon, of Henry VIII. and Edward VI.'s reigns:—

> "In chirurgery brought up in youth,
>   A knight here lieth dead;
>   A knight, and eke a surgeon, such
>   As England seld hath bred.
>
> "For which so sovereign gift of God,
>   Wherein he did excel,
>   King Henry VIII. called him to court,
>   Who loved him dearly well.
>
>   *   *   *   *
>
> "King Edward, for his service sake,
>   Bade him rise up a knight,
>   A name of praise; and ever since
>   He Sir John Ailife hight," &c.

No less than four of the smaller City companies pitched their tents in or near Basinghall Street. The Masons' Hall is in Masons' Avenue, between Basinghall Street and Coleman Street. The Masons, with whom are united the Marblers, were incorporated about 1410 as "the Free Masons," they received their arms in 1474, but were not incorporated till 1677. The Weavers' Hall is in Basinghall Street. Cloth and tapestry weavers were the first of the livery companies incorporated, and in the reign of Henry I. paid £16 a year to the Crown for their immunities.

The privileges were confirmed at Winchester by Henry II., in 1184, their charter being sealed by no less an official than Thomas à Becket. The great palladium of the Weavers' Company is their old picture of William Lee, the inventor of the stocking-loom, showing his invention to a female knitter, whose toil it was to spare. Below is this inscription :—

"In the year 1589 the ingenious William Lee, Master of Arts, of St. John's College, Cambridge, devised this profitable art for stockings (but being despised went to France) ; yet of iron to himself, but to us and others of gold, in memory of whom this is here painted."

There is a tradition that Lee invented the machine to facilitate the labour of knitting, in consequence of falling in love with a young country girl, who, during his visits, was more attentive to her knitting than to his proposals.

Lee is named as the inventor in a petition of the Framework-knitters or Stocking-makers of London to Cromwell for a charter, which Charles II. subsequently granted.

In this street also stood Coopers' Hall. The banqueting-hall was large and wainscoted. "The Coopers," says Mr. Timbs, "were incorporated by Henry VII. in 1501, and Henry VIII. empowered them to search and to gauge beer, ale, and soap-vessels in the City and two miles round, at a farthing a cask." At Coopers' Hall the State lotteries were formerly drawn ; and Hone describes, in his "Every-Day Book," the drawing of the last lottery here, October 18, 1826. Coopers' Hall was taken down in 1866 for the enlargement of the site of the Guildhall Offices.

Girdlers' Hall, No. 39, Basinghall Street, was rebuilt after the Great Fire. The Company of Girdle-Makers was incorporated by Henry VI., in 1449, and the charter was confirmed by Elizabeth, and they were subsequently united with the Pinners and Wire-Drawers. In their arms the punning heralds have put a girdle-iron. The Company possesses a document dated 1464, by which Edward IV. confirmed privileges granted to them by Richard II. and Edward III. They had the power to seize all girdles found within the City walls, which were manufactured with spurious silver or copper. The Girdlers still retain one quaint old custom of their craft, and that is, at the annual election the clerk of the Company crowns the new master with a silk crown embroidered in gold with the Girdlers' devices, and the lesser officials wear three ancient caps, after which the master pledges the company in a goblet of Rhenish wine.

The old Bankruptcy Court in Basinghall Street had two judges and five commissioners; the present has only one. The most important changes effected in the bankruptcy laws by the Bankruptcy Act of 1869 are as follow :—

1. Jurisdiction of the London Court confined to the metropolis, and in local cases transferred to the County Court of the district. The abolition of commissioners, official assignees, and messengers. Appointment of a single judge, with registrars, not exceeding four clerks, ushers, and other subordinate officers in substitution.

2. Service of the petition on the debtor.

3. The election of a paid trustee and a committee of creditors to wind up the estate.

4. Debtor's petition abolished.

5. Petition to be presented within six months of act of bankruptcy, and secured creditors only to count for amount unsecured.

6. Debtor's summons extended to non-traders, and judgment summons abolished.

7. Bankrupt not entitled to discharge until 10s. in the pound be paid, or creditors pass a special resolution that bankrupt cannot justly be held responsible.

In Masons' Avenue is Masons' Hall Tavern, where is the chief mart for the sale of public houses. Adjoining are some dining-rooms called after Dr. Butler, once a physician of celebrity. But the proprietor has hung on his wall a portrait apparently of Bishop Butler, the author of the "Analogy !"

In Whitecross Street Henry V. built a house for a branch of the Brotherhood of St. Giles, which Henry VIII., after his manner, eventually suppressed. Sir John Gresham, mayor, afterwards purchased the lands, and gave part of them as a maintenance to a free school which he had founded at Holt, in Norfolk. In this street was a debtor's prison built in 1813–15, from the designs of William Montague. The prison was pulled down in 1877 to make room for a railway goods depôt. Nell Gwynne, in her will, desired her natural son, the Duke of St. Albans, to lay out £20 a year to release poor debtors out of prison, and this sum was distributed every Christmas Day to the inmates of Whitecross Street Prison.

"Whitecross Street Prison," says Mr. H. Dixon, in 1850, in his "London Prisons," "is divided into six distinct divisions, or wards, respectively called—1, the Middlesex Ward ; 2, the Poultry and Giltspur Street Ward ; 3, the Ludgate Ward ; 4, the Dietary Ward ; 5, the Remand Ward ; 6, the Female Ward. These wards are quite separate, and no communication is permitted between the inmates of one and another. Before commencing our rounds, we gain, from conversation with the intelligent governor, an item or two of useful preliminary information. The establishment is capable of holding 500 persons. It is, however, very seldom that half that number is confined at one time within its walls. At this period last year it had 147 inmates; the pressure of the times has since considerably increased the sum-total. There are now 205, of which number eight are females. The population of this prison is, moreover, very migratory. Last year there were no less than 1,143 commitments. This shows an advance upon previous years—the result of the operation of the Small Debts Act—a part of the building having been set apart for persons committed under that Act. Many debtors are now sent hither for a fixed term, mostly ten days, at the expiration of which they are discharged. This punishment is principally inflicted for contempt of court. A woman was recently locked up here for ten days, for contempt, because unable, or unwilling, it was difficult to say which, to discharge a debt of sevenpence! In all such cases a more penal discipline is enforced; the person incarcerated is not allowed to maintain him or herself, but is compelled to accept the county allowance.

"Round the yard are the lofty walls of the prison, and the general pile of the prison buildings, several storeys high. On one side is a large board, containing a list of the benefactors of this portion of the prison. There are similar benefactions to each ward; amongst others, one from Nell Gwynne, still periodically distributed in the shape of so many loaves of bread, attracts attention. These donations are now employed in hiring some of the poorer of the prisoners to make the beds, clean the floors, and do other menial offices for the rest. Passing through a door in the yard, we enter the day-room of this ward. There are benches and tables down the sides, as in some of the cheap coffee-houses in London, and a large fire at the end, at which each man cooks, or has cooked for him, his victuals. On the wall a number of pigeon-holes or small cupboards are placed, each man having the key of one, and keeping therein his bread and butter, tea and coffee, and so forth. These things are all brought in, and no stint is placed upon the quantity consumed. A man *may* exist in the prison who has been accustomed to good living, though he cannot live well. All kinds of luxuries are prohibited, as are also spirituous drinks. Each man may have a pint of wine a day, but not more; and dice, cards, and all other instruments for gaming, are strictly vetoed."

On the demolition of the old prison, at the time of the formation of the Metropolitan Railway, about the year 1865, the site was converted into a goods depôt in connection with the Midland Railway.

The Green Yard, in Little Whitecross Street, close by, has long been used as a kind of "pound" for stray horses or vehicles which may be found in an unprotected condition in the streets of London; and here the Lord Mayor's state coach is kept.

Whitecross Street and Wood Street, it is stated, were the last in the city to surrender their sign-boards; they retained them till 1773.

As Redcross Street derived its name from a cross which stood near the end of Golden Lane, so, also, did Whitecross Street from a stone cross near which ran a watercourse to Moorfields. This cross is mentioned in a "presentment" dated as far back as A.D. 1275. Hughson (1806) calls Whitecross Street "noble, wide, and well built, inhabited by persons of property."

In this street Dr. Williams first established the Free Library, chiefly for the use of Protestant Dissenting ministers, now removed to Grafton Street, Fitzroy Square. Dr. Daniel Williams was a Welsh Nonconformist, in great favour with William III. He was preacher at Hand Alley, Bishopsgate Street, and succeeded Richard Baxter in the lectureship of Pinners' Hall, Broad Street. Opposed by the Antinomians, the Doctor, with Dr. Bates, Dr. Annesley, and others, set up the lectures at Salter's Hall, Cannon Street, already described by us. The richer Dissenters erected a building in Whitecross Street, to contain the Doctor's library, which he generously left for the public use, and employed the building as a place of convocation for their ministers. The building contained two handsome rooms, capable of holding 40,000 volumes, though the original collection contained not many more than 16,000. Dr. Bates and Dr. Williams's libraries formed its basis. There was also a gallery of portraits of celebrated Dissenting ministers. Among its curiosities mentioned in old guide-books of London were the following:—Eighteen volumes of the Bible, written with white ink on black paper, for Mr. Harris, an old linen-draper, in 1745, when he had become nearly blind; portraits of Samuel Annesly, an ejected minister of Cripplegate, and grandfather of Wesley; the preachers at the meeting-house in Little St. Helens, Bishopsgate Street—John Howe, Dr. Watts, Flavell, Baxter, and Jacomb. The library also contains 238 volumes of Civil War tracts and sermons; the manuscripts of Richard Baxter, and the original minutes of the Westminster Assembly of Divines; a folio Shakespeare of the edition of 1623; some original manuscripts of George Herbert, and also of various early Nonconformists; a finely illuminated copy of the Salisbury Liturgy (1530); the Bible in shorthand, written by a zealous Nonconformist in 1686, when the writer feared that

James II. would destroy all the Bibles; a mask of Cartouche, the great robber of Paris; the glass basin in which Queen Elizabeth was christened; a portrait of Colonel John Lilburne, one of the judges of Charles I. The library foundation was, in 1806, under the direction of twenty-three trustees, fourteen ministers, and nine laymen, all Dissenters, with a secretary and steward under them.

Sir Thomas More, in his "Pitiful Life of Edward V.," has a curious anecdote about Redcross Street: "And first," he says, "to show you that by con-

thereof, but of all likelihood he spake it not of ought."

The old Grub Street, the haunt of poor authors, the mosquitoes who tormented Pope, and the humble drudges with whom Dr. Johnson argued and perambulated in his struggling days, has now changed its name to Milton Street. This absurd transition from Lazarus to Dives, from the dunghill to the palace, originated in the illogical remembrance of some dull-headed Government official that Milton died at his house in the Artillery Walk,

BARBER-SURGEONS' HALL, 1800. (*See page* 232.)

jecture he (Richard III.) pretended this thing in his brother's life, you shall understand for a truth that the same night that King Edward dyed, one called Mistlebrooke, long ere the day sprung, came to the house of one Pottier, dwelling in Red Crosse Street, without Cripplegate, of London; and when he was, with hasty rapping, quickly let in, the said Mistlebrooke showed unto Pottier that King Edward was that night deceased. 'By my troth,' quoth Pottier, 'then will my master, the Duke of Gloucester, be king, and that I warrant thee!' What cause he had so to think, hard it is to say, whether he being his servant, knew any such thing pretended, or otherwise had any inkling

Bunhill Fields, adjoining to which place he had removed soon after his third marriage. The direct association of Pope's Grub Street poets was surely better than the very indirect association of Grub Street with the name of Milton; but officials are always the same. Here poor hacks of weak will and mistaken ambition sat up in bed, with blankets skewered round them, and, encouraged by gin, scribbled epics and lampoons, and fulsome dedications to purse-proud patrons. Here poor men of genius, misled by Pleasure's *ignis fatuus*, repented too late their misused hours, and, by the flickering rushlight, desperately endeavoured to retrieve the loss of opportunities by satires on ministers, or ribald attacks on men more successful than themselves. Here poor wretches, like Hogarth's poet, wrestled with the Muses while the milkman dunned them for their score, or the bailiff's man sat sullenly waiting for the guinea bribe that was to close his one malign eye. We have before alluded to Pope's

plied the archers of Finsbury, Moorfields, and Islington, and who were gradually succeeded by keepers of bowling-alleys and diceing-houses, who always favoured the suburbs, where there was little supervision over them. Dr. Johnson, in his Dictionary, defines Grub Street as "the name of a

THE GRUB STREET HERMIT. *From a Picture published by Richardson, 1794.* (*See page 242.*)

attacks on his Grub Street enemies, and shown how he degraded literature by associating poor writers, however industrious or clever, with ribaldry and malice; so that for long Curll's historians, sleeping two in a bed, in Grub Street garrets, were considered the natural kinsmen of all who made literature their profession, and did not earn enormous incomes by the generous but often unremunerative effort of spreading knowledge, exposing error, and discovering truth.

Stow describes Grub Street, in Elizabethan times, as having been inhabited by bowyers, fletchers (arrow-makers), and bow-string makers, who sup-

street in London much inhabited by writers of small histories, dictionaries, and temporary poems; whence any mean production is called Grub Street."

The Memoirs of the Grub Street Society was the title of a publication commenced Jan. 8, 1730. Its object was to satirise unsparingly the personages of the "Dunciad," and the productions of Cibber, Curll, Dennis, &c. It was continued weekly, till the end of 1737. The reputed editors were Dr. Martyn, a Cambridge Professor of Botany, and Dr. Richard Russell, who wrote one of the earliest treatises on the beneficial use of salt water.

Warburton seems prophetically to have anticipated a line of Mr. Disraeli's "Lothair," when, in a note to the "Dunciad," he calls a libeller "nothing but a Grub Street critic run to seed." Pompous Sir John Hawkins, in his "Life of Johnson," says, "During the usurpation a prodigious number of seditious and libellous pamphlets and papers, tending to exasperate the people and increase the confusion in which the nation was involved, were from time to time published. The authors of these were for the most part men whose indigent circumstances compelled them to live in the suburbs and most obscure parts of the town. Grub Street then abounded with mean old houses, which were let out in lodgings, at low rents, to persons of this description, whose occupation was in publishing anonymous treason and slander. One of the original inhabitants of this street was Foxe, the martyrologist." In 1710-11 Swift writes to Stella of a tax on small publications, which, he says, "will utterly ruin Grub Street."

Mr. Hoole, the translator of Tasso, told Dr. Johnson, on one occasion, says Boswell, that "he was born in Moorfields, and had received part of his early instruction in Grub Street. 'Sir,' said Johnson, smiling, 'you have been *regularly* educated.' Having asked who was his instructor, and Mr. Hoole having answered, 'My uncle, sir, who was a tailor,' Johnson, recollecting himself, said, 'Sir, I knew him; we called him the *metaphysical* tailor. He was of a club in Old Street, with me and George Psalmanazar, and some others; but pray, sir, was he a good tailor?' Mr. Hoole having answered that he believed he was too mathematical, and used to draw squares and triangles on his shopboard, so that he did not excel in the cut of a coat. 'I am sorry for it,' said Johnson, 'for I would have every man to be master of his own business.'

"In pleasant reference to himself and Mr. Hoole, as brother authors, Johnson often said to a friend, 'Let you and I, sir, go together, and eat a beef-steak in Grub Street.'"

A remarkable seclusion from the world took place in Grub Street, in the person of Henry Welby, Esq. This gentleman was a native of Lincolnshire, where he had an estate of above £1,000 per annum. He possessed in an eminent degree the qualifications of a gentleman. Having been a competent time at the university and the inns of court, he completed his education by making the tour of Europe. He was happy in the love and esteem of all that knew him, on account of his many acts of humanity, benevolence, and charity. When he was about forty years of age, it is said that his brother (though another account makes it merely a *kinsman*), an abandoned profligate, made an attempt upon his life with a pistol. It missed fire, and Welby, wresting it from the villain's hand, found it charged with bullets. Hence he formed the resolution of retiring from the world; and taking a house in this street, he reserved three rooms for himself—the first for his diet, the second for his lodging, and the third for his study. In these he kept himself so closely retired, that for forty-four years he was never seen by any human creature, except an old female servant that attended him, and who was only permitted to see him in some cases of great necessity. His diet was constantly bread, oatmeal, water-gruel, milk, and vegetables, and as a great indulgence, the yolk of an egg, but no part of the white.

The hermit of Grub Street bought all the new books that were published, most of which, upon a slight examination, he rejected. His time was spent in reading, meditation, and prayer. No Carthusian monk was ever more rigid in his abstinence. His plain garb, his long and silver beard, his mortified and venerable aspect, bespoke him an ancient inhabitant of the desert, rather than a gentleman of fortune in a populous city. He expended a great part of his income in acts of charity, and was very inquisitive after proper objects. He died October 29, 1636, in the eighty-fourth year of his age, and was buried in St. Giles's Church, Cripplegate. The old servant died not above six days before her master. He had a very amiable daughter, who married Sir Christopher Hildyard, a gentleman of Yorkshire; but neither she nor any of her family ever saw her father after his retirement.

A very grand old house in Hanover Yard, near Grub Street, was sketched by J. T. Smith, in 1791. It was called by the neighbours "General Monk's House." On one of the old water-spouts was the date, 1653. The lead on the roof was of enormous thickness, the staircase spacious and heavy. The large rooms had ornamented plaster ceilings, and one of the first-floor wainscotings was richly carved with flowers. But the great feature of the old mansion, after all, was the porch, a deep gable-ended structure, supported by stately Ionic pillars, and in the centre of the pediments a lion looking out. The windows were wide and latticed. There is, however, no proof that General Monk ever resided in the house. When the trimming general returned from Scotland, he took up his head-quarters at Whitehall; and on the refractory citizens refusing the £60,000 demanded by the Parliament, Monk marched into the City, destroyed the portcullises, and drew up his soldiers in Finsbury Fields. When the cowed City advanced the money, chose Monk as the major-general of their forces, and invited the Council of State and the general to reside in London, for their greater safety, it is expressly mentioned that he returned thanks without accepting the offer. If Monk ever resided in Hanover Yard, it must have been after the Restoration. This may have been, as has been suggested by some, the house of Dr. William Bulleyn, that learned physician whom we have mentioned in our chapter on St. Giles's, Cripplegate.

In Sweedon's Passage, Grub Street, Mr. Smith also discovered an extremely old house, which, according to tradition, had been inhabited by both Whittington and Gresham. It formed part of six houses which had occupied the site of an older mansion. The lower portions of the chimneys were of stone, the timber was oak and chestnut, and the ceilings were ornamented. There was a descent of three feet into the parlour from the outer street. This house possessed a great curiosity—an external staircase, which stood out like a rickety tower of timber and plaster, and was covered with a slanting and projecting wooden roof. In an adjacent house was an oriel window, and in the street there ran a long line of lattices, once covered with the relics of a ruined penthouse.

Coleman Street, near London Wall, was so called, says Stow, vaguely, from "Coleman, the first builder and owner thereof," and had the honour to give a name to one of the twenty-six wards of the City of London. From the trial of Hugh Peters, after the Restoration, we gather that the "Star," in Coleman Street, was a place of meeting for Oliver Cromwell and several of his party, in 1648, when Charles I. was in the hands of the Parliament.

Counsel. Mr. Gunter, what can you say concerning meeting and consultation at the "Star," in Coleman Street?

Gunter. My lord, I was a servant at the "Star," in Coleman Street, with one Mr. Hildesley. That house was a house where Oliver Cromwell, and several of that party, did use to meet in consultation. They had several meetings; I do remember very well one amongst the rest, in particular, that Mr. Peters was there; he came in the afternoon, about four o'clock, and was there till ten or eleven at night. I, being but a drawer, could not hear much of their discourse, but the subject was tending towards the king, after he was a prisoner, for they called him by the name of Charles Stuart. I heard not much of the discourse; they were writing, but what I know not, but I guessed it to be something drawn up against the king. I perceived that Mr. Peters was privy to it, and pleasant in the company.

The Court. How old were you at that time?

Gunter. I am now thirty years the last Bartholomew Day, and this was in 1648.

The Court. How long before the king was put to death?

Gunter. A good while. It was suddenly, as I remember, three days before Oliver Cromwell went out of town.

Peters. I was never there but once with Mr. Nathaniel Fiennes.

Counsel. Was Cromwell there?

Gunter. Yes.

Counsel. Was Mr. Peters there oftener than once?

Gunter. I know not, but once I am certain of it; this is the gentleman, for then he wore a great sword.

Peters. I never wore a great sword in my life.

The street had been a loyal street to the Puritan party, for it was here that, in 1642, the five members accused of treason by Charles I. took refuge, when he rashly attempted to arrest them in Parliament.

"And that people might not believe," says Lord Clarendon, "that there was any dejection of mind or sorrow for what was done, the same night the same council caused a proclamation to be prepared for the stopping the ports, that the accused persons might not escape out of the kingdom, and to forbid all persons to receive and harbour them, when it was well known that they were all together in a house in the City, without any fear of their security. And all this was done without the least communication with anybody but the Lord Digby, who advised it, and it is very true, was so willing to take the utmost hazard upon himself, that he did offer the king, when he knew in what house they were together, with a select company of gentlemen who would accompany him, whereof Sir Thomas Lunsford was one, to seize upon them and bring them away alive, or leave them dead in the place; but the king liked not such enterprises.

"That night the persons accused removed themselves into their stronghold, the City; not that they durst not venture themselves at their old lodgings, for no man would have presumed to trouble them, but that the City might see that they relied upon that place for a sanctuary of their privileges against violence and oppression, and so might put on an early concernment for them. And they were not disappointed; for, in spite of all the Lord Mayor could do to compose their distempers (who like a very wise and stout magistrate bestirred himself), the City was that whole night in arms, some people designed to that purpose running from one gate to another, and crying out 'that the Cavaliers were coming to fire the City,' and some saying that 'the king himself was in the head of them.'

"The next morning Charles himself came in search of the five members. He told one of the sheriffs (who was of the two thought less inclined to his service) 'that he would dine with him. He then departed without that applause and cheerfulness which he might have expected from the extraordinary grace he vouchsafed to them; and in his passage, through the City, the rude people flocked together, crying out, 'Privilege of Parliament! privilege of Parliament!' some of them pressing very near his own coach, and amongst the rest one calling out with a very loud voice, 'To your tents, O Israel!' However, the king, though much mortified, continued his resolution, taking little notice of the distempers; and, having dined at the sheriff's, returned in the afternoon to Whitehall, and published the next day a proclamation for the apprehension of all those whom he accused of high treason, forbidding any person to harbour them, the articles of their charge being likewise printed and dispersed."

At No. 14, Great Bell Yard, now Telegraph Street, Robert Bloomfield, the shoemaker poet, followed his calling. The poet's father was a poor tailor in Suffolk, and his mother kept a little school in which her own children were the chief pupils. Being too delicate to follow the plough, Bloomfield was sent to London to his elder brother George, to learn shoemaking. There, penned up in a garret with six or seven other lads, who paid a shilling each for their lodging, Bloomfield wrote "The Farmer's Boy," of which, in three years, 26,000 copies were sold, besides French, German, Italian, and Latin translations. The Duke of Grafton then kindly assigned him a pension of a shilling a day, and gave him a small post in the Seal Office. Compelled by ill-health to resign this situation, Bloomfield returned to the manufacture of ladies' shoes, became involved in debt, and died worn out and nearly insane in 1823. Taylor, the water-poet, describes the Cambridge carriers as lodging in his time at the "Bell," in Coleman Street.

Cowley, in his pleasant comedy of *The Cutter of Coleman Street*, admirably sketches the tricks of the old broken-down Cavaliers after the Restoration, who had to practise all their arts to obtain a dinner, and who, six days out of seven, had to "feast with Duke Humphrey," and flourish a toothpick, while all the time struggling with that unruly member, an empty stomach.

Jolly. (*A gentleman whose estate was confiscated in the late troubles.*) Ye shall no more make monstrous tales from Bruges, to revive your sinking credits in loyal ale-houses, nor inveigle into taverns young foremen of the shop, or little beardless blades of the Inns of Court, to drink to the royal family parabolically, and with bouncing oathes like cannon at every health; nor upon unlucky failing afternoons take melancholy turns in the Temple walks, and when you meet acquaintance cry, "You wonder why your lawyer stays so long, with a hang to him!" . . . .

Worm. (*Cutter's companion, and of much the same character.*) They call him Colonel Cutter, but to deal faithfully with you, madam, he is no more a colonel than you're a major-general.

Cutter. (*A merry, sharking fellow about town*—entering.) Ha! Sure I mistake the rogue!

Wor. He never serv'd his king—not he!—no more than he does his Maker. 'Tis true he's drunk his health as often as any man, upon other men's charges, and he was for a little while, I think, a kind of Hector till he was soundly beaten one day, and dragg'd about the room, like old Hector o' Troy about the town.

Cut. What does this dog mean, trow?

Wor. Once, indeed, he was very low—for almost a twelve-month—and had neither money enough to hire a barber nor buy scissors, and then he wore a beard (he said) for King Charles. He's now in pretty good clothes, but would you saw the furniture of his chamber! Marry, half a chair, an earthen pot without an ear, and the bottom of an ink-horn for a candlestick; the rest is broken foul tobacco-pipes, and a dozen o' gally-pots, with salve in 'em.

Cut. Was there ever such a cursed villain!

Wor. He's been a known cheat about town these twenty years.

It was in a conventicle, hidden away in Swan Alley, on the east side of Coleman Street, that that dangerous fanatic Venner, a wine-cooper and Millenarian (already mentioned in our chapter on Wood Street, Cheapside), preached to "the soldiers of King Jesus," and urged them to commence the Fifth Monarchy. The congregation at once rose in arms, and rushed out into the streets to slay all the followers of Baal. An insurrection followed, which ended in Venner, who had better have been hooping his casks, being hung and quartered in Coleman Street, January 19th, 1660-1.

John Goodwin, a Puritan religious writer who promoted the condemnation of Charles I., was, in 1633, presented to the living of St. Stephen's, Coleman Street. He it was who had intruded himself on the king the day before his execution, and offered to pray with him. The king thanked him, but said he had chosen Dr. Juxon, whom he knew. Fearing the gallows after the Restoration, his pamphlet defending the sentence passed on the king having been burnt by the public hangman, Goodwin fled, but afterwards returned and opened a private conventicle in Coleman Street, where he died in 1665.

Goodwin, whose hand was against every man, was much belaboured by John Vicars, an usher of Christ's Hospital, a man even more violent and intolerant than himself. The title of one of Vicars's works will be sufficient to show his command of theological Billingsgate.

"Coleman Street conclave visited, and that grand impostor, the schismatic's cheater-in-chief (who hath long slily lurked therein), truly and duly discovered; containing a most palpable and plain display of Mr. John Goodwin's self-conviction under his own handwriting), and of the notorious heresies, errors, malice, pride, and hypocrisy of this most huge Garagantua, in falsely-pretended piety, to the lamentable misleading of his too-too credulous soul-murdered proselytes of Coleman Street and elsewhere; collected principally out of his own big—bragadochio and wave-like—swelling, and swaggering writings, full-fraught with six-footed terms, and flashie rhetorical phrases, far more than solid and sacred truths. And may fitly serve (if it be the Lord's will), like Belshazzar's handwriting, on the wall of his conscience, to strike terror and shame into his own soul and shameless face, and to undeceive his most miserably cheated and inchanted or bewitched followers."

St. Stephen's, Coleman Street, can boast some antiquity, if it can boast no beauty; since between the years 1171 and 1181 the Dean and Chapter of St. Paul's granted both this building and St. Olave's, Jewry, to which it was appended as a chapel, to the prior and abbot of Butley in Suffolk. It is said by Stow to have been first a synagogue, then a parish church, and lastly a chapel to St. Olave's, in which vassalage it continued till the 7th of Edward IV., when it was again chosen to reign over a parish of its own. It was destroyed by the Great Fire, and meanly rebuilt by Wren in 1676. The monuments, with few exceptions, are uninteresting. There is one to John Taylor, a haberdasher, who left £200 to be lent to young haberdashers, and 2s. a week in bread to be distributed for ever on Sundays to poor householders; and here lies the only hero of St. Stephen's tombs, good old Anthony Munday, the continuator of Stow, who died in 1633, after much industrious study of the London records, and thirty years' honest labour at City shows and pageants. There is a certain friendly fervour about his epitaph, as if some City laureate had written it to pin to his hearse.

"To the Memory of that ancient Servant to the City, with His Pen, in Divers Imployments, especially the Survey of London, Master Anthony Munday, Citizen and Draper of London:

"He that hath many an ancient tombstone read,
(I' th' labour seeming more among the dead

To live, than with the living), that survaid
Abstruse antiquities, and o'er them laid
Such vive and beauteous colours with his pen,
That (spite of Time) those old are new again.
Under this marble lies interr'd, his tombe
Claiming (as worthily it may) this roome,
Among those many monuments his quill
Has so reviv'd, helping now to fill
A place (with those) in his survey; in which
He has monument, more fair, more rich
Than polisht stones could make him where he lies,
Though dead, still living, and in that ne'er dyes."

The entrance gateway of St. Stephen's has a rude alto-relievo of the Last Judgment; the clouds are as round and heavy as puddings, and the whole is inferior to the treatment of the same subject at St. Giles's-in-the-Fields. Of this parish, according to Defoe's romance, John Hayward was under-sexton during the Great Plague. He carried all the parish dead to the Plague-pit, and drove their bodies in the dead-cart, yet he never caught the disease, and lived twenty years after. Among the modern monuments at St. Stephen's is a marble bas-relief, by E. W. Wyat, erected in 1847, to the Rev. Josiah Pratt, vicar of the parish, whose active missionary labours are personified by an angel addressing an African, a Hindoo, and a New Zealander.

The fine building with a Doric portico situated at the north-east corner of Coleman Street is the Armourers' and Braziers' Hall. It stands on the site of the old hall of the Company, incorporated at the beginning of the reign of Henry VI., in 1422. The Armourers' function is now rather obsolete, but the hall is still decorated with coats of arms, and there is a fine gilt suit at the Tower, which was given by the Company to Charles I., when he was a gay young prince, with his head firm on. In the Banqueting Hall is one of Northcote's vapid but ambitious pictures, "The Entry of Richard II. and Bolingbroke into London," purchased by the Company from Boydell's Shakespeare Gallery, in 1825. How the spiteful, shrewd little painter would writhe could he hear the opinions of critical visitors!

CHAPTER XXX.

ALDGATE, THE MINORIES, AND CRUTCHED FRIARS.

The Aldgate of 1606—Brave Doings at Aldgate—The Conduit—Duke's Place—The Priory of the Holy Trinity—The Jews in Aldgate—The Abbey of St. Clare—Goodman's Fields—The Minories—A fine old London House—Crutched Friars—Sir John Milborne—The Drapers' Almshouses.

"THE gate described by Stow," says Cunningham, "was taken down in 1606, and a new one erected in its stead, the ornaments of which are dwelt on at great length by Stow's continuators. Two Roman soldiers stood on the outer battlements with stone balls in their hands, ready to defend the gate; beneath, in a square, was a statue of James I., and at his feet the royal supporters. On the City side stood a large figure of Fortune, and somewhat lower, so as to grace each side of the gate, gilded figures of

Peace and Charity, copied from the reverses of two Roman coins, discovered whilst digging the new foundations for the gate. The whole structure was two years in erecting."

Ben Jonson, in his *Silent Woman*, says, "Many

1607, were discovered coins of Trajan, Domitian, and Valentinian—the Barons, in 1215, entered London by consent of the citizens, on their way to meet King John. This was one of the most ruinous of the City gates, and the Earl of Essex and

RUINS OF THE CONVENT OF ST. CLARE. *From a View published by J. T. Smith,* 1797. (*See page* 249.)

things that seem foul in the doing, do please done. You see gilders will not work but inclosed. How long did the canvas hang before Aldgate? Were the people suffered to see the City's Love and Charity while they were rude stone, before they were painted and burnished?"

The City's Love and Charity were standing in 1761; the other statues had been long removed.

Through this gate—under which, about the year

Earl of Gloucester repaired it with the stones from monasteries and Jews' houses, that had been ruthlessly pulled down on purpose.

During the reign of Edward IV., Aldgate again felt maces beat at its doors, and clothyard shafts tremble in its tough planks. In 1471 the Bastard Falconbridge, collecting seamen in Essex and Kent, came with his vessels and anchored near the Tower. On hearing of his intention, the mayor and alder-

1. WHITTINGTON'S HOUSE, GRUB STREET. (*Smith*, 1811.)

2. GENERAL MONK'S HOUSE.   3. BLOOMFIELD'S HOUSE (1823).

4. REMAINS OF ALDGATE, BETHNAL GREEN. (*Malcolm*, 1800.)

men fortified the Thames shore, from Baynard Castle to the Tower, and stood to their guns. The Bastard, finding the south side unapproachable, then assailed the east of London, and attacked Aldgate with 5,000 turbulent men; but the citizens, letting the portcullis drop, entrapped and cut off many of their assailants. Elated by this, Robert Bassett, the alderman of Aldgate, ordered the portcullis to be drawn up, in God's name, and, by a brave sortie, drove the enemy back as far as St. Botolph's. At this juncture, Earl Rivers and the Constable of the Tower arriving with reinforcements, drove the rebels back as far as Mile End, Poplar, and Stratford. Many of the assailants of Aldgate were slain in this attack, after which the Bastard fled.

Near this gate, in the reign of Edward I., in a small projecting turret, was a hermitage. Without Aldgate was a conduit, erected in 1535. The water was conveyed from Hackney. The crowd of poor water-bearers, with their tubs, pails, and tankards, proving, however, a nuisance, the conduit was removed into a side court.

Among the records of the City of London is a lease granting the whole of the house above the gate of Aldgate to the poet Chaucer, in 1374.

In Aldgate all the prisoners of the Poultry Compter were lodged after the Great Fire, till the prison could be rebuilt. In the year 1760, when the City gates were taken down to widen the streets, Aldgate was bought by Mr. Mussell, of Bethnal Green, a zealous antiquary, who inhabited a house belonging to Lord Viscount Wentworth, built in the reign of James II. Mr. Mussell rebuilt the gate on the north side of his mansion, to which he henceforth gave the name of Aldgate House. There was on the south front a bas-relief, carved from Wat Tyler's tree, an old oak which once grew on Bow Common, and which the aldermen and council had had carved to adorn the old City gate. A few years ago, as workmen were excavating near Aldgate, some curious arches, resembling the cloisters of an ancient abbey, were discovered.

Duke's Place, Aldgate, was so called from Thomas Howard, Duke of Norfolk, who was beheaded in 1572 for his political intrigues with Mary Queen of Scots, to whose hand the weak and ambitious Catholic nobleman had aspired. "I find," says Strype, "the said duke, anno 1562, with his Duchess, riding thither through Bishopsgate Street to Leadenhall, and so to Cree Church, to his own place, attended with a hundred horse in his livery, with his gentlemen afore, their coats guarded with velvet, and four heralds riding before him, viz., Clarencieux, Somerset, Red Cross, and Blue Mantle." The precinct of the Priory of the Holy Trinity, without Aldgate, was given by Henry VIII. to Sir Thomas Audley, afterwards Lord Chancellor, who lived there, and died there in 1554. Sir Thomas, wishing to rebuild St. Catherine Cree, offered the parish the priory church and its nine bells in exchange for their own. The parish refusing to purchase, Sir Thomas offered the church and steeple to any one who would cart it off, but in vain. He then pulled it down anyhow, breaking half the stones, and sold the bells to Stepney parish and St. Stephen, Coleman Street. The Duke of Norfolk, marrying Sir Thomas's daughter, inherited the estate. The Earl of Suffolk, son of the duke who was beheaded, sold the priory precinct and the mansion-house of his mother to the City. In the year 1622 the inhabitants of Duke's Place, having a quarrel with the parishioners of St. Catherine, obtained leave from King Charles to rebuild the priory church, aided by the donations of Lord Mayor Barkham. The people of Duke's Place claim the priory church as the place of interment of Fitz Alwyn (draper), the first Lord Mayor of London, but their claim is highly doubtful. In 1650, when they were allowed by Cromwell, in his tolerant wisdom, to return to England, many Jews settled in Duke's Place, where, after the Restoration, they still more flourished. The German and Polish Jews built a synagogue here, in 1692, which was rebuilt in 1790. Over the porch of this building is a large hall, once used for the celebration of the weddings of poor Jews. A writer in the *Jewish Chronicle* says:—

"The influx of Jews from Lithuania and Germany became greater and greater towards the end of the seventeenth century. The aristocratic Sephardim, whose ancestors had banqueted with sovereigns, and held the purse-strings of kings, looked, it must be owned, with some disdain on their poorer and humbler brethren—the plebeian Ashkenazim, who had dealt in worn garments or huckstered in petty commodities on the banks of the Vistula, or in German Ghettos. The Portuguese did not allow the Germans to have any share in the management of congregational affairs. The Germans, in point of fact, were treated as belonging to a lower caste, and the only functions that a member of that nationality was permitted to fulfil were the useful, albeit lowly duties of beadle, which were actually entrusted to a German—a certain Benjamin Levy. In time the Germans resolved to establish a synagogue of their own, and in 1692, during the reign of William III., one of their body, a philanthropic and affluent individual, named Moses Hart, built a place of worship in Broad Court, Duke's Place."

In the Minories, lying between Aldgate and Tower Hill, there stood, in the Middle Ages, an abbey of nuns of the order of St. Clare, called the Minories, founded in 1293 by Edmund, Earl of Lancaster, Leicester, and Derby, and brother to Edward I., to receive nuns who were brought from Spain by his wife Blanche, Queen of Navarre. Ribideneira, the Spanish Jesuit, who wrote the "Lives of the Saints," tells us that St. Clare was an Italian saint who, by the advice of St. Francis, ran away from her father's house to take refuge in a convent, where she miraculously multiplied the bread, and rebuked the devil in person. She died in 1253 (Henry III.) During the plague of 1515 twenty-seven of these nuns were carried off, besides lay servants. The nunnery, which spent £418 8s. 5d. a year, was surrendered by Dame Elizabeth Salvage, the last abbess, to Henry VIII., in 1539. After the dissolution the nunnery became the residence of many great people; first of all, of John Clark, Bishop of Bath and Wells, Henry's ambassador, afterwards of officers of the Tower; and early in 1552 Edward VI. gave it to Henry, Duke of Suffolk, father of Lady Jane Grey. In Stow's time, in place of the nunnery were built "divers fair and large storehouses for armour and habiliments of war, with divers workhouses serving the same purpose."

The Church of the Priory of the Holy Trinity, in the Minories, was founded by Matilda, queen of Henry I., in 1108. It escaped the Great Fire, but becoming dangerous was taken down and rebuilt in 1706. In Strype's time this church claimed mischievous privileges, such as marrying without a licence. In the church is the tomb of William Legge, that faithful servant of Charles I., whom the king commended to his son, enjoining him to remember "the faithfullest servant ever prince had." Here, too, was buried the first Earl of Dartmouth, to whose father Charles II. had granted the Minory House; and here is preserved a head, supposed to be that of the Duke of Suffolk, who was executed in the Tower, hard by.

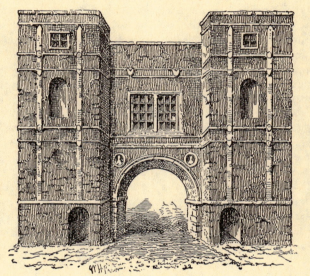

ALDGATE.   (*See page* 245.)

"Here," writes Stow, more autobiographically than usual, "on the south of the abbey, was some time a farm belonging to the said nunnery; at the which farm I myself (in my youth) have fetched many a halfpenny worth of milk, and never had less than three ale-pints for a halfpenny in the summer, nor less than one ale-quart for a halfpenny in the winter, always hot from the cow, as the same was milked and strained. One Trolop, and afterwards Goodman, were the farmers there, and had thirty or forty kine to the pail. Goodman's son being heir thereof, let out the ground, first for grazing of horses, and then for garden plots, and lived like a gentleman thereby. He lieth buried in St. Botolph's Church."

In Strype's time Goodman's Fields were "no longer fields and gardens, but buildings consisting of many fair streets, as Maunsel Street, Pescod or Prescot Street, Leman Street, &c., and tenters for clothworkers, and a large passage for carts and horses out of Whitechapel into Wellclose, besides many other lanes." "On the other side of that street," says Stow, "lieth the ditch without the walls of the City, which of old times was used to lie open, and was always (from time to time) cleansed from filth and mud, as need required; and was of great breadth, and so deep, that drivers watering horses, where they thought it shallowest, were drowned, both horse and man. But now of later time the same ditch is enclosed, and the banks thereof let out for garden plots, and divers houses be thereon builded; whereby the City wall is hidden, the ditch filled up, a small channel left, and made shallow enough."

That miserable and worthless coward, Lord Cobham, who falsely accused Raleigh of a share in his plot, almost died of starvation in the Minories, in the mean lodgings of a poor woman who had been his laundress. Congreve has some verses full of strained wit and gallantry, after his manner, on the Mulcibers of the Minories, who deform themselves in shaping the stays of steel that "give Aurelia's form the power to kill." During the Spa Fields riots of December 2, 1816, when young Watson led on the mob, and Thistlewood tried to persuade the soldiers to surrender the Tower, two gun-shops in the Minories were broken open by the rioters, and many guns and one small brass field-piece stolen. When the cavalry arrived, however, the field-piece was soon deserted.

One of the most extraordinary old houses in London was one sketched by J. T. Smith, in 1792, and taken down in 1801. It stood at the end of a low dark court on the south side of Hart Street, and was universally known in Crutched Friars as Whittington's Palace. The last lodger was a carpenter, who had sunk a saw-pit at the north end of the courtyard. The whole front of the house, which had originally formed three sides of a square, was of carved oak. The tradition was that the cats' heads carved on the ceilings always had their eyes directed on the spectator wherever he stood, and that even the knockers had once been shaped like cats' heads. Two sides of the outer square were nearly all glass lattice, and above and below ran wild-beasts' heads and crouched goblins, that acted as corbels. The doorway panels were richly carved, and above and below each tier of windows were strings of carved shields, including several arms of the City companies. A curious old house which formerly stood in the Minories is shown in page 252. It was once the "Fountain" inn, and when taken down in 1793 the timber-work was so firmly fixed together, that it had to be pulled asunder by horses.

In 1842 a curious group of three figures of Roman goddesses, bearing baskets of fruit in their laps, was discovered in digging a sewer in Hart Street, Crutched Friars. The group is now at the Guildhall.

The House of Crutched Friars, or Friars of the Holy Cross, at the corner of Hart Street, was founded by Ralph Hosiar and William Sabernes, about the year 1298. The founders themselves became friars of the order, and to them Stephen, the tenth prior of the Holy Trinity, granted three tenements for 13s. 8d. In the reign of Henry VIII. the Crutched Friars solicited the City magistrates to take the establishment under their patronage. At the dissolution the emissaries of Cromwell caught the Prior of Crutched Friars, *in flagrante delicto*, and down at once went the king's hammer upon the corrupt little brotherhood. The church was turned into a carpenter's yard and a tennis-court, and the friars' hall eventually became a glass-house. On the 4th of September, 1575, Stow says, a terrible fire burst out there that destroyed all but the stone walls." Turner dedicated his folio "Herbal" (1568) to Queen Elizabeth from this place.

The great benefactor to the Crutched Friars was Sir John Milborne, who was buried in their church. This worthy draper, mayor in the year 1521, was the founder of certain Drapers' Almshouses in the parish of St. Olave's, close to the old priory. The will, given by Strype, is a curious exemplification of the funeral customs of the old religion, and of the superstitions of the reign of Henry VIII. By the last testament of Sir John, his thirteen bedesmen from the adjoining almshouses were required to come daily to the church and hear mass said or sung near the tomb of their benefactor, at eight a.m., at Our Lady's altar in the middle aisle; and before the said mass the thirteen bedesmen, one of them standing right over against the other and encompassing the tomb, were severally, two and two of them together, to say the " De Profundis," and a paternoster, ave, and credo, with the collect thereunto belonging; and those who could not say the " De Profundis" were required to say a paternoster, ave, and credo for the souls of Sir John and Dame Johan, and Margaret, Sir John's first wife, and the souls of their fathers, mothers, children, and friends, and for "all Christian souls." A good and comprehensive benediction, it cannot be denied.

The inmates of the Drapers' Almshouses received 2s. 4d. a month, the first day of every month, for ever. The bedesmen were to be of honest conversation, and not detected in any open crime. They were forbidden to sell ale, beer, or wine, "or any other thing concerning tippling." Over the gate of Milborne's Almshouses, says Strype, there was "a four-square stone, with the figure of the Assumption of our Blessed Lady, supported by six angels in a cloud of glory." Sir Richard Champion, mayor and draper, in Elizabeth's reign gave £19 14s. a year to these same bedesmen. He also desired that every Sunday thirteen penny loaves of white bread should be given to thirteen poor people at the churches of St. Edmund, Lombard Street, and St. Michael's, Cornhill. He also gave the poor of each parish one load of charcoal (thirty sacks) every year; and to carry out these bequests, he left the Drapers' Company twenty-three messuages and eighteen garden-plots in the parish of St. Olave's, Hart Street. But Anthony Munday denies these last bequests, and thinks that Stow unintentionally slandered the Drapers' Company, by asserting that the terms of the will had not been carried out. Lord Lumley's house, built by Sir Thomas Wyat, in the reign of Henry VIII., adjoined these almshouses; and not far off was the house of the prior of Horn-Church, in Essex, afterwards Northumberland House; and Poor Jewry, a small district of Jews.

CHAPTER XXXI.

ISLINGTON.

Etymology of the Word "Islington"—Beauty of the Place in Early Times—The old Northern Roads—Archery at Islington—A Royal Pa ron ot
Archery—The Archers' Marks—The "Robin Hood"—Topham, the Strong Man—Llewellyn and the Welsh Barons—Algernon Percy's
House—Reformers' Meeting at the "Saracen's Head"—Queen Elizabeth and the Islington Beggars—Later Royal Visitors to Islington—
Citizens' Pleasure Parties—Cream and Cake—Outbreak of the Plague—Bunbury and the "New Paradise"—The old "Queen's Head"—
"The London Hospital"—Sir Walter Raleigh's House—The old "Pied Bull"—The "Angel."

No satisfactory etymology of the word "Islington" has yet been given. By some writers the name is supposed to have been derived from the Saxon word *isen* (iron), from certain springs, impregnated with iron, supposed to have their rise in the neighbourhood. Others trace it to the Saxon word *eisel* (a hostage), without ever condescending to explain what hostages had to do with Islington. The more favoured supposition is that the village was originally called "Ishel," an old British word signifying "lower," and "dun," or "don," the usual term for a town or fortress. It might have been so called, Mr. Lewis thinks, to contrast it with Tolentone, a village built on the elevated ground adjoining the woods of Highbury. The germ of the Islington of the Britons, it is generally allowed, must have been along the east side of the Lower Street.

Islington is supposed to have been situated on the great northern Roman road called the Ermin, or Herman Street, which left London by Cripplegate, and passed through Islington, though, as some antiquaries think, the Roman road really intersected Old Street, and, crossing the City Road, passed by Highbury and Hornsey Wood, and continued by way of the green lanes towards Enfield.

Fitzstephen, the friend of Becket, writing between 1170 and 1182, describing the north of London, says, "On the north are fields for pastures, and open meadows, very pleasant, into which the river waters do flow, and mills are turned about with a delightful noise. The arable lands are no hungry pieces of gravel ground, but like the rich fields of Asia, which bring plentiful corn, and fill the barns of the owners with a dainty crop of the fruits of Ceres." Still "beyond them an immense forest extends itself, beautified with woods and groves, and full of the lairs and coverts of beasts and game, stags, bucks, boars, and wild bulls." In later centuries Islington became the pasture-ground of London.

The old highways and roads connected with Islington were very badly kept, and extremely incommodious. Formerly the avenues leading to the village from the metropolis, exclusive of the foot-paths over the fields, were confined to the road from Smithfield, through St. John Street; the Goswell Street road, from Aldersgate; and a bridle way that had once been an old Roman road: all these were frequently impassable in winter. The broad green fields that stretched from Finsbury to Hoxton and Islington seem to have been recognised as the Campus Martius of London as early as the reign of Henry II., for Fitzstephen describes, with more unction than an ascetic monk might be expected to manifest, the scholars of the City going to the northern fields with their teachers, to play at ball, while the old and wealthy citizens came on horseback to watch the merry conflict of the lads. He also mentions the military exercises on horseback, good training for war or the tournament, every Friday in Lent; while other citizens, more intent on their own amusement, he says, carried their hawks on their fists, or took out their dogs there, to have a turn or two after a hare.

Archery was early practised in these pleasant northern fields, and here men shot the shafts that were hereafter to be aimed at Frenchmen's hearts. As early as the reign of Edward III. the royal will was proclaimed that every able-bodied citizen was, in his leisure hours and on all holidays, to practise with bows or crossbows, and not to waste his time in throwing stones, or at football, handball, bandy, or cock-fighting, which were vain and profitless plays; while in the reign of Richard II. an Act was passed to oblige all men-servants to exercise themselves with bows and arrows at all times of leisure, and on all Sundays and holidays.

In the reign of Henry VIII., that manly and warlike king, who was himself an archer, several Acts were passed to promote the practice of archery. Every father was enjoined to provide a bow and two arrows for his son, when he reached his seventh year; and all persons, except the clergy and judges, were obliged to shoot periodically at the butts, which were nowhere more numerous than in the fields towards Islington. Three gentlemen of the Court were constituted overseers of the science of artillery—to wit, of longbows, crossbows, and handguns—and leave was given them, as a body corporate, to practice shooting at all manner of marks and butts, and at fowls, and the game of the popinjay in the City and suburbs, and all other places. And when any member of this society, shooting at well-known and accustomed marks, says the chronicler Hall, the young men of London, finding the fields about Islington, Hoxton, and Shoreditch getting more and more enclosed with hedges and ditches, and that neither the old men could walk for their pleasure, nor lads shoot without

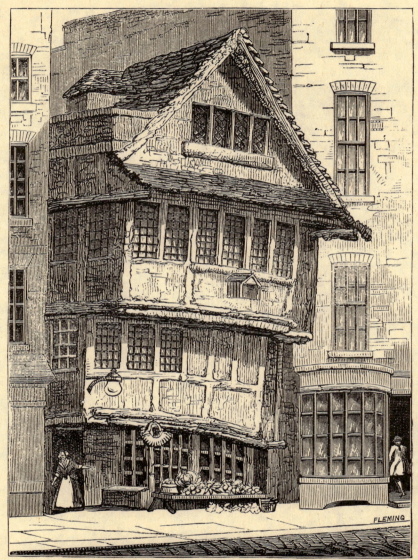

THE OLD "FOUNTAIN," IN THE MINORIES. *From a View by N. Smith*, 1798. *(See page* 256.)

and used the usual caution-word of archers, "Fast," they could not be impeached or troubled by the relations of any passer-by slain at misadventure. It was in these fields the king's favourite archer, Barlow, christened by him "the Duke of Shoreditch," and the Marquis of Islington and the Earl of Pancras, his skilful companions, made their cleverest hits, and in Hoxton Fields took place that great procession of the Duke of Shoreditch and his 3,000 archers and 200 torch-bearers. In the reign of Henry VIII.,

getting their bows and arrows taken away or broken, a riot arose. One morning a turner, dressed as a jester, led a mob through the City shouting "Shovels and spades! shovels and spades!" So many of the people followed, that it was a wonder to behold; and within a short space all the hedges about the City were cast down and the ditches filled up. The rioters then quietly dispersed. "After which," Hall says, with gusto, "those fields were never hedged."

In the reign of Elizabeth archery seems to have

been on the decline, though good old Stow describes the citizens as still frequenting the northern fields, "to walk, shoot, and otherwise recreate and refresh their dulled spirits in the sweet and wholesome air," and mentions that of old it was the custom for the

Stow we gather that the increased enclosures had driven the archers into bowling-alleys and gambling-houses.

James I., in 1605, finding archery still on the decline, though many of his best soldiers preferred

THE OLD "QUEEN'S HEAD" TAVERN.   (*See page* 260.)

officers of the City—namely, the sheriffs, the porters of the Weigh House, and all others—to be challengers of all men in the suburbs to wrestle, "shoot the standard, broad arrow and flight," for games, at Clerkenwell and in Finsbury Fields.   In 1570, however, we find the London bowyers, fletchers, stringers, and arrow-head makers petitioning the Lord Treasurer concerning their decayed condition, by reason of the discontinuance of archery, and the practice of unlawful games; and from

bows to guns, still issued letters patent to several distinguished persons, and among them to Sir Thomas Fowler, of Islington, to survey all the open grounds within two miles of the City, and to see that they were put in proper order for the exercise of the City, as in the reign of Henry VIII.   Charles I. published a similar edict, ordering all mounds to be lowered that obstructed the archers' view from one mark to another.   There were indeed at this time, or a little later, no less than 160 marks set up in the Finsbury Fields, each duly registered by name. These marks, placed at varying distances, to accustom the archers to judge the distance, are all named in a curious old tract, entitled " Ayme for Finsbury Archers," published at the "Swan" in Grub Street, in 1594, and several times reprinted. Among them we find the following quaint titles, suggestive of old nicknames, lucky shots, and bowmen's jokes :—Sir Rowland, Lurching, Nelson, Martin's Mayflower, Dunstan's Darling, Beswick's Stake, Lambert's Goodwill, Lee's Leopard, Thief in the Hedge, Mildmay's Rose, Silkworm, Lee's Lion. Goodly shots, no doubt, these marks had recorded, and pleasant halts they had been for the Finsbury bowmen of old time.

The dainty archers of the present day can scarcely believe the strength of the old yew bows, or the length of the arrows, and are apt to be incredulous of the pith of their ancestors' shafts. Nevertheless, the statute of the thirty-third year of Henry VIII. distinctly lays down that men of the age of twenty-four were prohibited from shooting at any mark under two hundred and twenty yards ; and the longest distance of that stalwart epoch seems to have been nineteen score, or three hundred and eighty yards.

During the Cromwell time archery seems to have been deemed unpractical, and was not much enforced. The old ways, however, revived with Charles II., and in 1682 there was a great cavalcade to the Finsbury Fields, at which the king himself was present, and the old titles of the Duke of Shoreditch and Marquis of Islington were bestowed on the best shots. On a Finsbury archer's ticket for the shooting of 1676, all lovers of archery are invited to meet at Drapers' Hall, in Throgmorton Street ; and it is noted that the eleven score targets would be set up in the new Artillery Ground. It was in this year that the great archer, "Sir" William Wood, was presented with a silver badge. This stout bowman was eventually buried in Clerkenwell Church, with archers' honours. Sir William Davenant, in his playful poem of "The Long Vacation in London," describes the attorneys shooting against the proctors, and thus sketches the citizen archer of those days—

> " Each with solemn oath agree
> To meet in fields of Finsburie ;
> With loynes in canvas bow-case tyde,
> Where arrows stick with mickle pride ;
> With hats pin'd up, and bow in hand,
> All day most fiercely there they stand,
> Like ghosts of ADAM BELL and Clymme,
> Sol sets, for fear they'll shoot at him."

Up to the last edition of the Map of Archers' Marks in 1738, the fields from Peerless Pool to northward of the " Rosemary Branch " are studded with "roving" marks, generally wooden pillars, crowned by some emblem, such as a bird or a circle. The last great meeting of Islington archers was in 1791, at Blackheath, when the archers' company of the Honourable Artillery Company contended with the Surrey and Kentish bowmen, the Hainault Foresters, the Woodmen of Arden, the Robin Hood Society, &c. Several times in the last century the Artillery Company asserted their old archer privileges, and replaced the marks which had been removed by encroachers. In 1782 they forced the gate of a large field in which stood one of their stone marks, close to Balls Pond ; and in 1786 they ordered obstructions to be removed between Peerless Pool, south, Baume's Pond, north, Hoxton, east, and Islington, west. In the same year they threatened to pull down part of a wall erected by the proprietors of a white-lead mill, between the marks of Bob Peak and the Levant. One of the partners of the works, however, induced them to desist ; but a member of the archers' division shot an arrow over the enclosure, to assert the Company's right. In 1791, when the long butts at Islington Common were destroyed by gravel-diggers, the Artillery Company also required the marks to be replaced. In 1842, of all the old open ground there only remained a few acres to the north of the City Road.

An old public-house fronting the fields at Hoxton, and called the "Robin Hood," was still existing in Nelson's time (1811). It had been a great place of resort for the Finsbury archers, and under the sign was the following inscription :—

> "Ye archers bold and yeomen good,
> Stop and drink with Robin Hood ;
> If Robin Hood is not at home,
> Stop and drink with Little John."

There is a traditional story that Topham, the strong man of Islington, was once challenged by some Finsbury archers whom he had ridiculed to draw an arrow two-thirds of its length. The bet was a bowl of punch ; but Topham, though he drew the shaft towards his breast, instead of his ear, after many fruitless efforts, lost the wager.

The historical recollections of Islington are not numerous. One of the earliest is connected with the visit of Llewellyn and his Welsh barons, who in the reign of Edward I. came to London to pay homage to the king. They were quartered at Islington, but they disliked our wine, ale, and bread, and could not obtain milk enough. Moreover, their Welsh pride was disgusted at being so stared at by the Londoners, on account of their uncommon dress. "We will never visit Islington again except as conquerors," they cried, and from that instant resolved to take up arms. In 1465, Henry VI., who had been captured in Lancashire, was brought to London with his legs bound to his horse's stirrups. At Islington he was met by his great enemy, the Earl of Warwick, who removed his gilt spurs contemptuously, and hurried him to the Tower. Edward IV., on the occasion of his accession to the throne, was welcomed between Islington and Shoreditch by the Lord Mayor and aldermen of London, some of whom he knighted. In the same manner the crafty King Henry VII., on his return from the overthrow of Lambert Simnel, was met in Hornsey Park by the mayor, aldermen, sheriffs, and principal commoners, all on horseback in one livery, when he dubbed the mayor, Sir William Horn, knight, and between Islington and London knighted Alderman Sir John Percivall.

Henry VIII. frequently visited Islington, to call on noblemen of his court, for Dudley, Earl of Warwick, held the manor of Stoke Newington ; and Algernon Percy, Earl of Northumberland, occupied a mansion on Newington Green. From this house we find the earl writing in an alarmed way to Secretary Cromwell, vowing that he had never proposed marriage to Anne Boleyn. The earl, who died the year after, is supposed to have left the house in which he lived, and one on the south side of Newington Green, to the king, who resided for some time in the first, and employed the other for the use of his household. From this country palace of Henry VIII. a pathway leading from the corner of Newington Green, to the turnpike road at Ball's Pond, became known as "King Harry's Walk." Game was plentiful about Islington, and by a proclamation dated 1546 the king prohibited all hunting and hawking of hares, partridges, pheasants, and heron, from "Westminster to St. Giles-in-the-Fields, and from thence to Islington, to Our Lady of the Oak, to Highgate, to Hornsey Park, and to Hampstead Heath."

In 1557, during Queen Mary's hunting down of Protestants, a small congregation of Reformers, who had assembled at the " Saracen's Head," Islington, under pretext of attending a play, were betrayed by a treacherous tailor, arrested by the Queen's vice-chamberlain, and thrown into prison. The most eminent of these persecuted men was John Rough, who had been a preacher among the Black Friars at Stirling, chaplain to the Earl of Arran, and the means of persuading John Knox to enter the ministry. He was burnt at the stake at Smithfield, and four of the others perished praising God in one fire at Islington. But there is the old saying, "The blood of martyrs is the seed of the Church."

Only the next year forty "godly and innocent persons," who had assembled in " a back close in the field by the town of Islington " to pray and meditate, were apprehended by the constables, bowmen, and billmen. All but twenty-seven escaped, and of these twenty-two lay in Newgate seven weeks before they were examined, though offered pardon if they would consent to hear a mass. "Eventually," says Foxe, in his "Acts and Monuments," " seven were burnt in Smithfield and six at Brentford."

Queen Elizabeth seems to have been partial to Islington, paying frequent visits to Sir Thomas Fowler and to Sir John Spencer of Canonbury House. In 1561 she made a grand tour of the east of London which took several days. From the Tower she first visited Houndsditch and Spitalfields, thence went through the fields to Charterhouse, and in a few days continued her route back to the Savoy and thence to Enfield. On her return to St. James's as she passed through Islington, hedges were cut down and ditches filled up to quicken her progress across the fields.

In 1581, the queen, riding by Aldersgate Bars towards the Islington Fields to take the air, was environed by a crowd of sturdy beggars, which gave the queen much disturbance. That same evening Fleetwood, the Recorder, had the fields scoured, and apprehended seventy-four rogues, some blind, " yet great usurers, and very rich." The strongest of the seventy-four " they bestowed in the milne and the lighters."

In the great entertainment given at Kenilworth by the Earl of Leicester to Queen Elizabeth in 1575, a minstrel discoursed with tiresome minuteness on the Islington dairies, that supplied London bridal parties with furmenty, not over-sodden, for porridge, unchalked milk for " flawnery," unadulterated cream for custards, and pure fresh butter for pasties. The arms of Islington, it was proposed, should be three milk tankards proper on a field of clouted cream, three green cheeses upon a shelf of cake bread, a furmenty bowl, stuck with horn spoons, and, for supporters, a grey mare (used to carry the milk tankards) and her silly foal ; the motto, " Lac caseus infans," or " Fresh cheese and cream," the milkwives cry in London streets.

The ill-starred Earl of Essex, on his way to Ireland, where he was to sweep away rebellion by a wave of his hand, passed through Islington with his gay and hopeful train of noblemen and gentlemen, returning only to become himself a rebel, and to end his days on the Tower Hill block.

In 1603, when James I., with all his hungry Scotch courtiers, rode into London, he was met at Stamford Hill by the Lord Mayor, aldermen, and 500 of the principal citizens, who escorted him through the Islington Fields to the Charterhouse. He passed along the Upper Street, which was for a short time after known as King Street.

Charles I., on his return from Scotland in 1641, passed through Islington, accompanied by his queen, the Prince of Wales, and the Duke of York. In the following year the Committee of the London Militia gave orders to fortify the approaches to the City, and in 1643 the entrenchment began in earnest, the Trained Band citizens, and even their wives and children, toiling at the work. The trades volunteered by turns. One day there were 5,000 felt-makers and cappers, and nearly 3,000 porters; another day, 4,000 or 5,000 shoemakers; and a third day, 6,000 tailors. Several of the works were in the neighbourhood of Islington. There was a breastwork and battery at Mount Mill, in the Goswell Street Road, another at the end of St. John Street, a large fort, with four half bulwarks, at the New River Upper Pond, and a small redoubt near Islington Pound.

When the great plot to assassinate Cromwell was detected, in 1653, Vowell, an Islington schoolmaster, one of the plotters, was hung at Charing Cross. He died bravely, crying out for Church, King, and Restoration, and warning the soldiers of their dangerous principles. Colonel Okey, whom Cromwell compelled to sit as one of King Charles's judges, was in early life a drayman and stoker at an Islington brewery. He was seized in Holland, after the Restoration, and executed in 1662. A curious story is told of the famous Parliamentary general, Skippon, in connection with Islington. This tough old soldier was being brought from Naseby, where he had been desperately wounded. As his horse litter was passing through Islington, a mastiff sprang at one of the horses, and worried him, nor would he let go till a soldier ran him through with his sword. Skippon, however, on getting to London, had a piece of his waistcoat drawn from his bullet-wound, and soon recovered.

For many ages Islington, especially in summer, was a favourite resort for London citizens, who delighted to saunter there to drink creams and eat cakes, or to hunt the ducks of the suburban ponds with their water-dogs. As early as 1628, George Wither, the poet, in his "Britannia's Remembrances," describing holiday-making, says—

"Some by the banks of Thames their pleasure taking
Some sillibubs among the milkmaids making,
With music some upon the waters rowing,
Some to the next adjoining hamlets going;
And Hogsdone, Islington and Tothnam Court
For cakes and cream had there no small resort."

Davenant describes very pleasantly in rough verse the setting out of a citizen's party for Islington :—

"Now damsel young, that dwells in Cheap,
For very joy begins to leap;
Her elbow small she oft doth rub,
Tickled with hope of syllabub,
For mother (who does gold maintaine
On thumb, and keys in silver chaine),
In snow-white clout, wrapt nook of pye,
Fat capon's wing, and rabbit's thigh;
And said to Hackney coachman, go,
Take shillings six—say, I or no;
Whither? (says he)—quoth she, thy teame
Shall drive to place where groweth creame.
　　But husband grey, now comes to stall,
For 'prentice notch'd he strait doth call.
Where's dame? (quoth he)—quoth son of shop,
She's gone her cake in milke to sop.
Ho! ho!—to Islington—enough—
Fetch Job my son, and our dog *Ruffe*;
For there, in pond, through mire and muck,
We'll cry, hay, duck—there *Ruffe*—hay, duck," &c.

In the *Merry Milkmaid of Islington,* 1681, the prices noted down are highly curious.

SCENE—*Lovechange, Sir Jeffery Jolt, Artezhim* (the Lady Jolt), *and Tapster.*

Love. What is the reckoning?

Tap. Nine and elevenpence.

Jeff. How's that? Let's have the particulars. Mr. Lovechange shall know how he parts with his money.

Tap. Why, sir, cakes two shillings, ale as much; a quart of mortified claret eighteen pence, stewed prunes a shilling.

Art. That's too dear.

Tap. Truly, they cost a penny a pound of the one-handed costermonger, out of his wife's fish-basket. A quart of cream half-a-crown.

Art. That's excessive.

Tap. Not if you consider how many carriers' eggs miscarried in the making of it, and the charge of isinglass, and other ingredients, to make cream of the sour milk.

Art. All this does not amount to what you demand.

Tap. I can make more. Two threepenny papers of sugar a shilling; then you had bread, sir—

Jeff. Yes, and drink too, sir—my head takes notice of that.

Tap. 'Tis granted, sir—a pound of sausages, and forty other things, make it right. Our bar never errs.

The Ducking-ponds were on Islington Green, near White Conduit House in the Back Road, and in East Lane, the spot where the Reservoir of the New River Head afterwards stood. Thomas Jordan, in a coarse comedy called *The Walks of Islington and Hogsden, with the Humours of Wood Street Compter*, 1641, the scene of which is laid at the "Saracen's Head," Islington, and his Prologue speaks of the diet of the place, and the sort of persons who went there for amusement.

"Though the scene be Islington, we swear
We will not blow ye up with bottle beer,

> Cram ye with creams and fools which sweetly please
> Ladies of fortune and young 'prentices,
> Who (when the supervisors come to find 'um)
> Quake like the custard, which they leave behind 'um."

Browne, in his "New Academy," 1658, alludes to the "Cream and Cake Boys" who took their lasses to Islington or Hogsden to feast on white pots, puddings, pies, stewed prunes, and tansies.

The plague seems to have raged at Islington in the years 1577, 1578, and 1592. In 1665 593 persons died of the plague. The story of the first outbreak is told graphically in the "City Remembrancer." A citizen had broken out of his house in Aldersgate Street, and had applied in vain for admission at the "Angel" and the "White Horse," in Islington. At the "Pied Horse" he pretended to be entirely free from infection, and on his way to Lincolnshire, and that he only required lodgings for one night. They had but a garret bed empty, and that but for one night, expecting drovers with cattle next day. A servant showed him the room, which he gladly accepted. He was well dressed, and with a sigh said he had seldom lain in such a lodging, but would make a shift, as it was but for one night, and in a dreadful time. He sat down on the bed, desiring a pint of warm ale, which was forgot. Next morning one asked what had become of the gentleman. The maid, starting, said she had never thought more of him. "He bespoke warm ale, but I forgot it." A person going up, found him dead across the bed, in a most frightful posture. His clothes were pulled off, his jaw fallen, his eyes open, and the rug of the bed clasped hard in one hand. The alarm was great, the place having been free from the distemper, which spread immediately to the houses round about. Fourteen died of the plague that week in Islington.

Cromwell is said to have resided in a house (afterwards the "Crown" public house) on the north side of the road at Upper Holloway, but there is no proof of the fact. He probably, however, often visited Islington to call on his friend Sir Arthur Haselrigge, colonel of a regiment of cuirassiers, called the "Lobster" regiment, who had a house there. In May, 1664-5, Sir Arthur complained to Parliament that as he was riding from the House of Commons in the road leading from Perpoole Lane to Clerkenwell, returning to his house at Islington, the Earl of Stamford and his two servants had struck at him with a drawn sword and "other offensive instruments," upon which he was enjoined to keep the peace, and neither send nor receive any challenge.

In later times Islington still remained renowned for its tea-gardens and places of rustic amusement, and in the *Spleen*, or *Islington Spa*, a comic piece, written by George Colman, and acted at Drury Lane in 1756, the author sketches pleasantly enough the bustle occasioned by a citizen's family preparing to start for their country house at Islington. The neats' tongues and cold chickens have to be packed up preparatory to the party starting in the coach and three from the end of Cheapside. It was here and at Highbury that Goldsmith spent many of his "shoemaker's holidays," and Bonnell Thornton has sketched in the *Connoisseur* the Sunday excursions of the citizens of his times, in which he had no doubt shared.

Bunbury, that clever but slovenly draftsman, produced, in 1772, a caricature of a London citizen in his country villa, and called it "The delights of Islington." Above it he has written the following series of fierce threats :—

" Whereas my new pagoda has been clandestinely carried off, and a new pair of dolphins taken from the top of my *gazebo* by some bloodthirsty villains, and whereas a great deal of *timber* has been cut down and carried away from the *Old Grove*, that was planted last spring, and *Pluto* and *Proserpine* thrown into my basin, from henceforth steel traps and spring-guns will be constantly set for the better extirpation of such a nest of villains.

" By me,
" JEREMIAH SAGO."

On a garden notice-board, in another print after Bunbury, of the same date, is this inscription :—

"THE NEW PARADISE.

"No gentlemen or ladies to be admitted with nails in their shoes."

Danger lent a certain dignity to these excursions. In 1739 the roads and footpaths of Islington seem to have been infested by highwaymen and footpads, the hornets and mosquitoes of those days. In the year above mentioned, the Islington Vestry agreed to pay a reward of £10 to any person who apprehended a robber. It was customary at this time for persons walking from the City to Islington after dark to wait at the end of St. John Street till a sufficient number had collected, and then to be escorted by an armed patrol. Even in 1742 the *London Magazine* observed that scarcely a night passed without some one being robbed between the "Turk's Head," near Wood's Close, Islington, and the road leading to Goswell Street. In 1771 the inhabitants of Islington subscribed a sum of money for rewarding persons apprehending robbers, as many dwellings had been broken open, and the Islington stage was frequently stopped. In 1780, in consequence of riots and depredations, the inhabitants furnished themselves with arms and equipments, and formed a military society for general protection. In spite of this, robberies and murders in the by-roads constantly took place. In 1782 Mr. Herd, a clerk in the Custom House, was murdered in the fields near the "Shepherd and Shepherdess." Mr. Herd, a friend of Woodfall, the publisher of "Junius," was returning from town

One of the celebrities of old Islington was Alexander Aubert, Esq., who first organised the corps of Loyal Islington Volunteers. In 1797 the loyal inhabitants of Islington formed themselves into a corps, to defend the country against its revolutionary enemies. It consisted of

SIR WALTER RALEIGH'S HOUSE.   (*See page* 260.)

with a friend and two servants well armed, when he was attacked by footpads armed with cutlasses and firearms, one of whom (who was afterwards hanged) shot him with a blunderbuss as he was resisting. In 1797 Mr. Fryer, an attorney of Southampton Buildings, was attacked by three footpads and shot through the head. Two men were hung for this murder, but a third man afterwards confessed on the gallows that he was the murderer.

a regiment of infantry and one of cavalry. Mr. Aubert became lieutenant-colonel commandant of the corps. The uniform consisted of a blue jacket with white facings, scarlet cuffs, collar, and epaulets, and trimmed with silver lace; white kerseymere pantaloons, short gaiters, helmets, and cross-belts. The corps was broken up in 1801, when a superb silver vase, valued at 300 guineas, was presented to Mr. Aubert. This

ISLINGTON IN 1780.

gentleman, who was an eminent amateur astronomer, assisted Smeaton in the construction of Ramsgate Harbour. He died in 1805, from a cold caught when inspecting a glass house in Wales. A portrait of him, in uniform, holding his charger, by Mather Brown, used to be hung in the first floor parlour of the "Angel and Crown" at Islington.

In 1803, the old fears of French invasion again filling the minds of citizens, a volunteer corps of infantry was organised at Islington. It consisted of about 300 members. They wore as uniform a scarlet jacket turned up with black, light-blue pantaloons, short gaiters, and beaver caps. This second Islington Volunteer Corps broke up in 1806 from want of funds. The adjutant, Mr. Dickson, joined the 82nd Regiment, and was killed near Roeskilde, in the island of Zealand, in 1807.

Nelson, writing in 1811, explains the great disproportion that there appeared in the Islington parish registers between the burials and baptisms, from the fact of the great number of invalids who resorted to a district then often called "The London Hospital." Dr. Hunter used to relate a story of a lady, who, in an advanced age, and declining state of health, went, by the advice of her physician, to take lodgings in Islington. She agreed for a suite of rooms, and, coming down stairs, observed that the banisters were much out of repair. "These," she said, "must be mended before she could think of coming to live there." "Madam," replied the landlady, "that will answer no purpose, as the undertaker's men, in bringing down the coffins, are continually breaking the banisters." The old lady was so shocked at this funereal intelligence, that she immediately declined occupying the apartments.

The most interesting hostelry in old Islington was the old "Queen's Head," at the corner of Queen's Head Lane. It was pulled down, to the regret of all antiquaries, in 1829.

"It was," says Lewis, "a strong wood and plaister building of three lofty storeys, projecting over each other in front, and forming bay windows, supported by brackets and carved figures. The centre, which projected several feet beyond the other part of the building, and formed a commodious porch, to which there was a descent of several steps, was supported in front by caryatides of carved oak, standing on either side of the entrance, and crowned with Ionic scrolls. The house is said to have been once entered by an *ascent* of several steps, but, at the time it was pulled down, the floor of its front parlour was four feet below the level of the highway; and this alteration is easily accounted for, when the antiquity of the building, the vast accumulation of matter upon the road, in the course of many centuries, and the fact of an arch having been thrown over the New River, in front of the house, are considered."

"The interior of the house was constructed in a similar manner to that of most of the old buildings in the parish, having oak-panelled wainscots and stuccoed ceilings. The principal room was the parlour already alluded to, the ceiling of which was ornamented with dolphins, cherubs, acorns, &c., surrounded by a wreathed border of fruit and foliage, and had, near the centre, a medallion, of a character apparently Roman, crowned with bays, and a small shield containing the initials 'I. M.' surrounded by cherubim and glory. The chimney-piece was supported by two figures carved in stone, hung with festoons, &c., and the stone slab, immediately over the fireplace, exhibited the stories of Danaë and Actæon in relief, with mutilated figures of Venus, Bacchus, and Plenty."

Tradition had long connected this house with the name of Sir Walter Raleigh, though with no sufficient reason. In the thirtieth year of Elizabeth, Sir Walter obtained a patent "to make licences for keeping of taverns and retailing of wines throughout England." This house may be one of those to which Raleigh granted licences, and the sign then marked the reign in which it was granted. There is also a tradition that Lord Treasurer Burleigh once resided here, and a topographical writer mentions the fact that two lions carved in wood, the supporters of the Cecil arms, formerly stood in an adjoining yard, and appeared to have once belonged to the old "Queen's Head." Another story is that Queen Elizabeth's saddler resided here; while others assert that it was the summer residence of the Earl of Essex, and the resort of Elizabeth. Early in the last century, this occasional house belonged to a family named Roome, one of whom left the estate to Lady Edwards. The oak parlour of the old building was preserved in the new one. In a house adjoining the "Queen's Head" resided John Rivington, the well-known bookseller, who died in 1792.

Behind Frederick Place we reach the site of the old "Pied Bull" Inn, pulled down about the year 1830, which was originally either the property or the residence of Sir Walter Raleigh. In the parlour window, looking into the garden, was some curious stained glass, containing the arms of Sir John Miller, Knight, of Islington and Devon. These arms bear date eight years after Sir Walter was beheaded, and were, it is supposed, substituted by Miller when he came to reside here. The sea-horses, parrots in the window, and the leaves, supposed to represent tobacco, seem to have been chosen as emblems of his career by Raleigh himself.

"The arms in the parlour window," says Nelson, "are enclosed within an ornamental border, consisting of two mermaids, each crested with a globe, as many sea-horses supporting a bunch of green leaves over the shield, and the lower part contains a green and a grey parrot, the former eating fruit. Adjoining to this is another compartment in the window, representing a green parrot perched on a wreath, under a pediment, within a border of figures and flowers, but which does not seem to have been intended for any armorial ensign." The ceiling of this room is enriched with a personification of the Five Senses, in stucco, with Latin mottoes underneath; the chimney-piece contains figures of Faith, Hope, and Charity, with their usual insignia in niches.

That corner stone of Islington, the "Angel," has been now an established inn for considerably more than 200 years. In old days it was a great halting-place for travellers in the first night out of London. "The ancient house," says Lewis, "which was pulled down in 1819 to make way for the present one, presented the usual features of a large old country inn, having a long front with an overhanging tiled roof, and two rows of windows, twelve in each row, independently of those on the basement storey. The principal entrance was beneath a projection, which extended along a portion of the front, and had a wooden gallery at the top."

The inn-yard, approached by a gateway, was a quadrangle with double galleries. In 1880 the character of the "Angel" was changed, the inn being converted into a modern "Restaurant."

There is a tradition that the whole of the ground from the corner of the Back Road to the "Angel" was forfeited by the parish of Islington, and united to that of Clerkenwell, in consequence of the refusal of the Islingtonians to bury a pauper who was found dead at the corner of the Back Road. The corpse being taken to Clerkenwell, the district above described was claimed, and retained by that parish.

On the north side of the High Street, and extending back to Liverpool Road, is the Agricultural Hall, which was built in 1861-2, at a cost of £53,000. The building, designed by Mr. F. Peck, covers about three acres of ground. The principal entrance, in Liverpool Road, is beneath a lofty arch, flanked by towers, with cupolas, 95 feet high. The main hall, 384 feet long by 217 feet wide, has an iron arched roof, glazed, 130 feet span, and is surrounded by galleries 30 feet wide. There is also a minor hall, 100 feet square, and an entrance arcade, 150 feet long, from Islington Green. The Hall was originally established by members of the Smithfield Club, and the first cattle-show was held here in December, 1862. Horse-shows have been held here annually since 1864. The Hall is also occasionally used for Industrial Exhibitions, equestrian performances, concerts, and other entertainments.

CHAPTER XXXII.

ISLINGTON (continued).

The old Parish Church of Islington—Scaffolding superseded—A sadly-interesting Grave—Fisher House—George Morland, the Artist—A great Islington Family—Celebrities of Cross Street—John Quick, the Comedian—The Abduction of a Child—Laycock's Dairy Farm—Alexander Cruden, the Author of the Concordance—William Hawes, the Founder of the Royal Humane Society—Charles Lamb at Islington—William Woodfall and Colley Cibber—Baron D'Aguilar, the Miser—St. Peter's Church, Islington—Irvingites at Islington—The New River and Sir Hugh Myddelton—The Opening Ceremony—Collins, the Poet—The "Crown" Inn—Hunsdon House—Islington Celebrities—Mrs. Barbauld—The Duke's Head—Topham, the "Strong Man."

THE old parish church of Islington, dedicated to the Virgin Mary, was a strange rambling structure, entered through a gable-ended school-room which blocked up the west end. It had an old flint tower, with six bells, a clock, and a sun-dial. The date of the building was not much earlier than 1483. In 1751, the church becoming ruinous, it was pulled down and rebuilt by Mr. Steemson, under the direction of Mr. Dowbiggin, one of the unsuccessful competitors for the erection of Blackfriars Bridge. It cost £7,340. In 1787 the church was repaired and the tower strengthened.

"Thomas Birch, a basket-maker," says Nelson,

"undertook, for the sum of £20, to erect a scaffold of wicker-work round the spire, and which he formed entirely of willow, hazel, and other sticks. It had a flight of stairs within, ascending in a spiral line from the octagonal balustrade to the vane, by which the ascent was as easy and safe as the stairs of a dwelling-house. This ingenious contrivance entirely superseded the use of a scaffold, which would have been more expensive, and is frequently attended with danger in works of this kind. The spire on this occasion presented a very curious appearance, being entirely enveloped, as it were, in a huge basket, within which the workmen were performing the necessary repairs in perfect safety. The late Alderman Staines is said to have been the first person who contrived this kind of scaffolding, in some repairs done to the spire of St. Bride's Church, London, which was damaged by lightning in the year 1764, after having his scaffold-poles, &c., which had been erected in the usual way, carried away by a violent storm."

In Islington Church were buried, in 1609, Sir George Wharton, son of Lord Wharton, and James Steward, son of Lord Blantyre, and godson of James I. These young gallants quarrelled at the gaming-table, and fought at Islington with sword and dagger, and in their shirts, for fear of either wearing concealed armour. They both fell dead on the field, and, by the king's desire, were buried in one grave. In the church vault are two iron coffins, and one of cedar, the last containing the body of Justice Palmer, train-bearer to Onslow, the Speaker. The object of the cedar was to resist the attack of the worms, and the cover was shaped like the gable roof of a house to prevent any other coffin being put upon it. Here, also, is buried a great-grandson of the eminent navigator, Magelhaens, and Osborne, the Gray's Inn bookseller, whom Dr. Johnson knocked down with a folio. Osborne gave £13,000 for the Earl of Oxford's library, the binding of which alone had cost £18,000. In 1808 the body of a young woman named Thomas was disinterred here, there being a suspicion that she had been murdered, as a large wire was formerly thrust through her heart. It was, however, found that this had been done by the doctor, at her dying request, to prevent the possibility of her being buried alive.

One of the celebrated buildings of Islington was Fisher House, in the Lower Street, and nearly opposite the east end of Cross Street. It was probably built about the beginning of the seventeenth century. In the interior the arms of Fowler and Fisher were to be seen. Ezekiel Tongue, an old writer against the Papists, is supposed to have kept a school here about 1660 for teaching young ladies Greek and Latin. It was afterwards a lodging-house, and then a lunatic asylum. Here Brothers, the prophet, was confined, till Lord Chancellor Erskine liberated him in 1806.

At the south end of Frog Lane was formerly a public-house called "Frog Hall;" the sign, a plough drawn by frogs. At the "Barley Mow" public-house, in Frog Lane, George Morland, the painter, resided for several months, about the year 1800. Morland would frequently apply to a farm-house opposite for harness, to sketch, and if he saw a suitable rustic for a model pass by, would induce him

to sit, by the offer of money and beer. Here he drank and painted alternately. Close by, at No. 8, Popham Terrace, resided that useful old writer, John Thomas Smith (he was a pupil of Nollekens), "Rainy Day Smith," to whose works on London we have been much indebted. He became Keeper of the Print-Room of the British Museum, and died in 1833.

Opposite Rufford's Buildings there stood, till 1812, an old Elizabethan house of wood and plaster, with curious ceilings, and a granite mantel-piece representing the Garden of Eden and the Tree of Knowledge. The new house became Shield's school, where Dr. Hawes and John Nichols, the antiquary, were educated. In a house which formerly stood in the Upper Street, opposite Cross Street, resided Dr. William Pitcairn, elected physician, in 1750, to St. Bartholomew's Hospital. He commenced a botanical garden of five acres behind the house, but it does not now exist.

One of the celebrated houses of old Islington was No. 41, Cross Street, and formerly the mansion of the Fowler family, lords of the manor of Barnesbury. The Fowlers were great people in their swords and ruffs, in the days of Elizabeth and James; and Sir Thomas Fowler appears to have been one of the jurors upon the trial of Sir Walter Raleigh, at Winchester, in 1603. The house is wood and plaster, with a modern brick front. It appears to be of the age of Elizabeth.

"The ceiling of a back room on the first floor," says Lewis, "is decorated with the arms of England in the reign of that princess, with her initials, and the date (1595) in stucco; also the initials of Thomas and Jane Fowler, $_{T.I.}^{F.}$ with *fleur de lis*, medallions, &c., in the same style as the ceilings at Canonbury House. The rooms are wainscoted with oak in panels, and till the year 1788, when they were removed, the windows contained some arms in stained glass, among which were those of Fowler, with the date (1588), and those of Herne, or Heron. In pulling down some old houses for the formation of Halton Street, at the east end of this house, some remains of the ancient stabling and offices were taken away. In these stables a fire broke out on the 17th February, 1655, but it does not appear to have done any injury to the dwelling-house.

"At the extremity of the garden which belonged to the mansion is a small building, originally about fifteen feet square, and presenting an exterior of brick, absurdly called Queen Elizabeth's Lodge. It appears to have afforded access to the house through the grounds, and was probably built as a summer-house or porter's lodge, at the entrance of the garden, about the time the mansion-house was erected. The arms of Fowler, bearing an esquire's helmet, are cut in stone on the west side of the building, near the top, which proves that the time of its erection was before the honour of knighthood had been conferred upon its owner."

The name attached to the lodge may have arisen from some visit paid by Elizabeth to Sir Thomas Fowler or Sir John Spencer.

A house near the old charity school at the top of Cross Street was partly demolished by the London rioters in 1780, when it was occupied by the obnoxious Justice Hyde, who had ordered out the troops, and whose goods the true Protestants with the blue cockade burnt in the street.

In Cross Street, in 1817, died Mrs. Hester Milner, the youngest of ten daughters of the Dr. John Milner in whose school Dr. John Hawkesworth and Oliver Goldsmith were assistants. At the "Old Parr's Head," at the corner of Cross Street, John Henderson, the best Falstaff ever known on the stage, made his first appearance in public, by reciting Garrick's ode to Shakespeare, with close imitations of the actor's manner. He appeared as Hamlet at the Bath Theatre in 1772.

John Quick, a celebrated comedian, resided at Hornsey Row. He was the son of a Whitechapel brewer, and was the original Tony Lumpkin, Bob Acres, and Isaac Mendosa; he was one of the last of the Garrick school, and was a great favourite of George III. He retired in 1798, after thirty-six years on the boards, with £10,000, and died in 1831, aged eighty-three, another proof of the longevity of successful actors. Up to the last of his life Quick frequented a club at the "King's Head," opposite the old church, and officiated as president. Mrs. Davenport was Quick's daughter.

In the year 1818 great interest was excited by the abduction of the child of a shipbroker, named Horsley, who resided at 3, Canonbury Lane. It had been stolen by a man named Rennett, who had conceived a hatred for the boy's grandfather, Charles Dignum, the singer, and also for the sake of the reward. The man was tracked, taken, and eventually transported for seven years.

Laycock's dairy farm faced Union Chapel, built by Mr. Leroux, at the beginning of the century. Laycock, an enterprising man, who died in 1834, erected sheds for cattle on their way to Smithfield. Laycock and a Mr. Rhodes had gradually absorbed the smaller grass farms (once the great feature of Islington), and which were common seventy or eighty years ago, says Mr. Lewis, writing in 1842. The stocks varied from twenty to a hundred cows. "One of these was on the site of Elliot's Place,

Lower Street; another where Bray's Buildings now stand, and others in the Upper Street, and at Holloway."

At a house in Camden Passage, near the west end of Camden Street, and also in the Upper Street and at Paradise Row, lived that extraordinary man, Alexander Cruden, the compiler of the laborious Concordance to the Bible. Cruden, the son of an Aberdeen merchant, was born in 1701. After being a private tutor and a corrector of the press, he opened a bookseller's shop under the Royal Exchange, London, and there wrote his Concordance. His mind becoming disordered at the bad reception of the Concordance, he was sent to an asylum at Bethnal Green, the practices at which he afterwards attacked, bringing an unsuccessful action against the celebrated Dr. Munro. In 1754, on his release, he applied for the honour of knighthood, put himself in nomination for the City of London, and assumed the title of "Alexander the Corrector," believing himself divinely inspired to reform a corrupt age. One of his harmless eccentricities was going about with a sponge, erasing the number forty-five from the walls, to show his aversion for John Wilkes, against whom he published a pamphlet. Eventually he became corrector for the press on Mr. Woodfall's paper, the *Public Advertiser*, and devoted his spare time to teaching the felons in Newgate, and other works of charity. He dedicated the second edition of his Concordance to George III., and presented him a copy in person. He died in 1770, being found dead on his knees, in the attitude of prayer. He was buried in a Dissenting burial-ground, in Deadman's Place, Southwark.

That excellent man, Dr. William Hawes, the founder of the Royal Humane Society, was born in 1736, in "Job's House," or the "Old Thatched House" Tavern, in Cross Street, and was the son of the landlord. In 1773 he began to call attention to the means of resuscitating persons apparently drowned, a subject which the *Gentleman's Magazine* had been urging for thirty years. At first he encountered much ridicule and opposition, but, in 1774, Dr. Hawes and Dr. Cogan brought each fifteen friends to a meeting at the "Chapter" Coffee House, and the Humane Society was at once formed, and the "Thatched House" Tavern became one of the first houses of reception. This same year Dr. Hawes wrote a pamphlet on the death of Goldsmith, to show the dangers of violent medicine. In 1793 this good man was the chief means of saving 1,200 families of Spitalfields weavers from starvation, at a time when cotton had begun to supersede silk. Dr. Hawes died in

LONDON FROM CLERKENWELL (CITY AND EAST END). *From a View by Canaletto, published in 1753.* (See page 287.)

LONDON FROM CLERKENWELL (WEST END). *From a View by Canaletto, published in 1753. (See page 287.)*

1808, and was buried in the cemetery attached to the churchyard at Islington.

Colebrooke Row was built in 1768. Six acres at the back formed at first a nursery and then a brick-field. Here that delightful humourist, Charles Lamb, resided, with his sister, from about 1823 to 1826, immediately after his retirement from the India House.

Lamb describes his place of abode at Islington, in a letter to Bernard Barton, dated September 2, 1823:—"When you come Londonward, you will find me no longer in Covent Garden ; I have a cottage in Colebrooke Row, Islington—a cottage, for it is detached—a white house, with six good rooms in it. The New River (rather elderly by this time) runs (if a moderate walking-pace can be so termed) close to the foot of the house ; and behind is a spacious garden, with vines (I assure you), pears, strawberries, parsnips, leeks, carrots, cabbages, to delight the heart of old Alcinous. You enter without passage into a cheerful dining-room, all studded over and rough with old books ; and above is a lightsome drawing-room, three windows, full of choice prints. I feel like a great lord, never having had a house before." And again, in the November following, in a letter to Robert Southey, he informs the bard, who had promised him a call, that he is " at Colebrooke Cottage, left hand coming from Saddler's Wells." It was here that that amiable bookworm, George Dyer, editor of the Delphin classics, walked quietly into the New River from Charles Lamb's door, but was soon recovered, thanks to the kind care of Miss Lamb.

A small house at the back of Colebrooke Row was the residence of that great Parliamentary reporter, William Woodfall, the friend of Garrick, Goldsmith, and Savage. In lodgings at a house near the " Castle Tavern " and Tea Gardens, old Colley Cibber, the best fop that ever appeared on the stage, died in 1757, aged eighty-six. As one of Pope's most recalcitrant butts, as the author of the *Careless Husband*, and as poet laureate, Cibber occupied a prominent place among the lesser lights of the long Georgian era. Cibber's reprobate daughter, Charlotte Charke, among other eccentricities in her reckless life, kept a public-house at Islington, where she died in 1760.

At the close of the last century the Baron D'Aguilar, a half-crazed miser, lived in Camden Street, and kept a small farm on the west bank of the New River, near the north end of Colebrooke Row. He beat his wife and starved his cattle, which were occasionally in the habit of devouring each other. He died in 1802, leaving jewels worth £30,000. The total bulk of his property is supposed to have been worth upwards of £200,000, which he left to two daughters, one of whom he cursed on his dying bed.

St. Peter's Church, Islington, consecrated in 1835, was erected at an expense of £3,407. The Irvingite church, in Duncan Road, was erected in 1834, the year of Irving's death. After his expulsion from the Presbytery, Irving frequently preached in Britannia Fields, Islington, till his admirers rented for him West's Picture Gallery, in Newman Street.

And here we may, as well as anywhere else, sketch the history of the New River, which passes along Colebrooke Row, but was some years ago covered over. In the reign of Elizabeth, the London conduits being found quite inadequate to the demands of the growing City, the Queen granted the citizens leave to convey a stream to London, from any part of Middlesex or Hertfordshire. Nothing, however, was done, nor was even a second Act, passed by King James, ever carried into effect. What all London could not do, a single public-spirited man accomplished. In 1609, Mr. Hugh Myddelton, a Welsh goldsmith, who had enriched himself by mines in Cardiganshire, persuaded the Common Council to transfer to him the power granted them by the above-mentioned Acts, and offered, in four years, at his own risk and charge, to bring the Chadwell and Amwell springs from Hertfordshire to London, by a route more than thirty-eight miles long. Endless vexations, however, befell the enterprising man. The greedy landholders of Middlesex and Herts did all they could to thwart him. Eventually he had to petition the City for an extension of the time for the fulfilment of his contract to nine years, and at last, when the water had been brought as far as Enfield, Myddelton was so completely drained that he had to apply to the City for aid. On their ungenerous refusal, he resorted to the King, who, tempted by a moiety of the concern, paid half the expenses. The scheme then progressed fast, and on the 29th of September, 1613, the water was at last let into the New River Head, at Clerkenwell. Hugh Myddelton's brother (the Lord Mayor of London) and many aldermen and gentlemen were present at the ceremony, which repaid the worthy goldsmith for his years of patient toil.

Stow gives us an account of the way in which the ceremony was performed. "A troop of labourers," he says, " to the number of sixty or more, well apparelled, and wearing green *Monmouth caps*, all alike, carryed spades, shovels, pickaxes, and such like instruments of laborious employment marching after drummes, twice or thrice about the cisterne, presented themselves before the mount, where the

Lord Maior, aldermen, and a worthy company beside, stood to behold them; and one man in behalf of all the rest, delivered this speech :—

' Long have we labour'd, long desir'd, and pray'd
  For this great work's perfection ; and by th' aid
  Of Heaven and good men's wishes, 'tis at length
  Happily conquered, by cost, art, and strength.
  And after five yeeres deare expence, in dayes,
  Travaile, and paines, beside the infinite wayes
  Of malice, envy, false suggestions,
  Able to daunt the spirits of mighty ones
  In wealth and courage.   This, a work so rare,
  Onely by one man's industry, cost, and care,
  Is brought to blest effect ; so much withstood,
  His onely ayme, the Citie's generall good.
  And where (before) many unjust complaints,
  Enviously seated, caused oft restraints,
  Stops and great crosses, to our master's charge,
  And the work's hindrance ; Favour, now at large,
  Spreads herself open to him, and commends
  To admiration, both his paines and ends
  (The King's most gracious love).

        *   *   *   *   *

  Now for the fruits then ; flow forth precious spring
  So long and dearly sought for, and now bring
  Comfort to all that love thee ; loudly sing,
  And with thy chrystal murmurs strook together,
  Bid all thy true *well-wishers* welcome hither.'

At which words the flood-gates flew open, the streame ran gallantly into the cisterne, drummes and trumpets sounding in triumphall manner, and a brave peale of chambers gave full issue to the intended entertainment."

It was a considerable time before the New River water came into full use, and for the first nineteen years the annual profit scarcely amounted to twelve shillings a share.   The following figures will give the best idea of the improvement of value in this property :—1634 (the second), £3 4s. 2d. ; 1680, £145 1s. 8d. ; 1720, £214 15s. 7d. ; and 1794, £431 8s. 8d.   The shares in 1811 were considered worth £11,500, and an adventurer's share has been sold for as much as £17,000.   The undertaking cost the first projectors half a million sterling.   There were originally seventy-two shares, and thirty-six of these were vested in the projector, whose descendants, however, became impoverished, and were obliged to part with the property.   The mother of the last Sir Hugh indeed received a pension of twenty pounds per annum from the Goldsmiths' Company.

Sir Hugh died in 1631 a prosperous man, though there is an old Islington tradition that he became pensioner in a Shropshire village, applied in vain for relief to the City, and died in obscurity.

The last Sir Hugh was a poor drunken fellow who strived hard to die young, and boarded with an Essex farmer.   Even as late as 1828 a female descendant of the Welsh goldsmith obtained a small annuity from the Corporation.

The New River is mentioned by Nelson in 1811 as having between 200 and 300 bridges over it, and upwards of forty sluices.   Lewis, writing in 1842, speaks of it as having in his day "one hundred and fifty-four bridges over it, and four large sluices in its course, and in various parts, both over and under its stream, numerous currents of land-waters, and brooks, and rivulets."   It was formerly conducted over the valley near Highbury, in a huge wooden trough 462 feet long, supported by brick piers, and called the Boarded River.   This was, however, removed in 1776.

Dr. Johnson describes going to Islington to see poor Collins, the poet, when his mind was beginning to fail.   It was after Collins had returned from France, and had come to Islington, directing his sister to meet him there.   "There was then," says the Doctor, "nothing of disorder discernible in his mind by any but himself; but he had withdrawn from study, and travelled with no other book than an English Testament, such as children carry to the school."   When his friend took it in his hand, out of curiosity, to see what companion a man of letters had chosen, "I have but one book," said Collins, "but that is the best."

On the east side of the Lower Street was formerly a very old public-house called "The Crown." "It contained," says Lewis, "several fragments of antiquity, in the form of carved work, stained glass, &c., and had been probably once the residence of some opulent merchant or person of distinction.   In the window of a room on the ground-floor were the arms of England, the City of London, the Mercers' Company, and another coat ; also the red and white roses united, with other ornaments, indicative of its having been erected about the time of Henry VII. or Henry VIII.   Many years previous to the pulling down of the building, it had been converted into a public-house, the common fate of most of the old respectable dwellings in this parish, and was latterly kept by a person named Pressey, who frequently accommodated strolling players with a large room in the house for the exhibition of dramatic performances."

Between Lower Chapel Street and Paradise Place stood an old mansion generally known as Hunsdon House, which was pulled down in 1800.   It was supposed to have been the residence of Queen Elizabeth's favourite cousin, Henry Carey, created by her Lord Hunsdon.   The front, abutting on Lower Street, was inscribed King John's Place, as that king was said to have had a hunting-lodge there.   Sir Thomas Lovell rebuilt the house.   It was supposed, from the armorial bearings in one of the stained glass windows, that this chosen residence had been at one time the abode of the great Earl of Leicester, the most favoured of all Elizabeth's suitors. It afterwards became the property of Sir Robert Ducy, Bart., the banker of Charles I. The memorable mansion was celebrated for its rich windows, illustrating the subjects of the Faithful Steward and the Prodigal Son, and crowded besides with prophets and saints. There was also a magnificent chimney-piece, containing the arms of the City of London, with those of Lovell quartering Muswell or Mosell, the arms of St. John's Priory, always potent in this neighbourhood, besides those of Gardeners of London, grocer, and the Company of Merchant Adventurers.

Among the celebrities of Islington we may notice the following, in addition to those already given :—Sir Henry Yelverton, a judge of Common Pleas in the reign of Charles I., who was baptised at St. Mary's. He got entangled in opposition to the imperious Duke of Buckingham, and paid for it by an imprisonment in the Tower and a heavy fine.

Robert Brown, the founder of the sect of Brownists, was a lecturer at Islington. After flying to Holland, and being excommunicated on his return to England by a bishop, he went back to the Establishment about 1590, and accepted a living in Northamptonshire, where he lived a somewhat discreditable life. For striking a constable who had demanded a rate from him Brown was sent to Northampton gaol, where he boasted that he had been in thirty-two prisons. He died in 1630, aged eighty-one.

Defoe was educated at a Nonconformist seminary at Islington, and four years there was all the education the clever son of a butcher in St. Giles's seems ever to have had. Edmund Halley, the celebrated astronomer royal, fitted up an observatory at Islington; and resided there from 1682 till 1696. It was Halley who urged Newton to write the "Principia," and superintended its publication. He is accused of gross unfairness to his two great contemporaries, Leibnitz and Flamsteed, breaking open a sealed catalogue of fixed stars drawn up by the latter, and printing them with his own name. Halley's greatest work was the first prediction of the return of a comet, and a discovery of inequalities in the motion of Jupiter and Saturn, which confirmed Newton's great discovery of the law of gravitation.

Mrs. Foster, the granddaughter of Milton, kept a chandler's shop at Lower Holloway for some years, and died at Islington in 1754. In her the family of Milton became extinct. She was poor and infirm, and in 1750 *Comus* was represented at Drury Lane Theatre for her benefit, Dr. Johnson writing the prologue, which was spoken by Garrick. She used to say that her grandfather was harsh to his daughters, and refused to allow them to be taught to write; but we must allow perhaps something for the perpetual irritation of gout, which would sour the temper of an archangel. At Newington Green resided Dr. Richard Price, a Nonconformist minister, celebrated for his financial calculations in connection with assurance societies. He was a friend of Howard, Priestley, and Franklin, and was consulted by Pitt as to the adoption of the Sinking Fund. He died in 1791. Mary Woolstonecroft, the wife of William Godwin, and the mother of Mrs. Shelley, in early life conducted a day-school at Newington Green. She was one of the first advocates of the rights of women, and died in 1797.

That excellent woman, Mrs. Barbauld, was wife of Mr. Barbauld, a minister at a Unitarian chapel on Newington Green. Amongst the vicars of St. Mary's we should not forget Daniel Wilson, Heber's successor as Bishop of Calcutta. He succeeded the good Cecil at St. John's, Bedford Row. Nelson, the best of the Islington historians, lived and died, says Mr. W. Howitt, at his house at the corner of Cumberland Street, Islington Green. Rogers, the banker-poet, was born in 1763 at Newington Green, "the first house that presents itself on the west side, proceeding from Ball's Pond." On his mother's side Rogers was descended from Philip Henry, the father of Matthew Henry, the pious author of the well-known exposition of the Bible. In one of the detached houses opposite Lorraine Place lived that pushing publisher and projector, Sir Richard Phillips. We have described this active minded compiler elsewhere. Dr. Jackson, Bishop of London, was for a time head-master of the Islington Proprietary School.

The "Duke's Head," at the south-east corner of Cadd's Row, near the Green, was, in the middle of the last century, kept by Thomas Topham, the celebrated "Strong Man" of Islington. His most celebrated feats were pulling against a horse at a wall in Moorfields; and, finally, in 1741, in Coldbath Fields, lifting three hogsheads of water, weighing 1,831 pounds, to commemorate the taking of Porto Bello by Admiral Vernon. He once hoisted a sleeping watchman in his box, and dropped both box and watchman over the wall into Bunhill Fields Burying Ground. Towards the close of his life this unhappy Samson took a public-house in Hog Lane, Shoreditch, and there, in 1749, in a paroxysm of just jealousy, he stabbed his unfortunate wife and killed himself.

CHAPTER XXXIII.

CANONBURY.

The Manor of Canonbury—The Rich Spencer—Sweet Tyranny—Canonbury House—Precautions against another Flood—A Literary Retreat—The Special Glory of a Famous House—The Decorative Taste of a Former Age.

THE manor of Canonbury, so called from a mansion of the Prior of the Canons of St. Bartholomew, was given to the priory by Ralph de Berners, not long after the Conquest. At the dissolution it fell into the receptive hands of Cromwell, the Lord Privy Seal, and at his execution an annuity from the manor was bestowed on ill-favoured Anne of Cleves. In 1547 Canonbury was granted by Edward VI. to John Dudley, Earl of Warwick, from whom it passed to the ill-starred Duke of Northumberland, only a few months before his beheadal. In 1570 Lord Wentworth, to whom Queen Mary had granted the manor, alienated it to Sir John Spencer, "the rich Spencer" who figures so often in the civic history of Elizabeth's reign.

Sir John was an alderman and clothworker of London, sheriff in 1583–4, and Lord Mayor in 1594. He appears to have been a public-spirited honest man, and often stood forward boldly in defence of the Privileges of the City. On one occasion we find him protesting against the great Bridge House granaries of London being taken as storehouses for the navy ; and on another, resisting an attempt to force a new recorder on the City. He also helped actively to suppress a riot of London apprentices, five of whom were hung on Tower Hill. The wealth of Sir John was so notorious, that it is said a Dunkirk pirate once contrived a plot, with twelve of his men, to carry him off, in hopes of obtaining £50,000 as ransom. The men came in a shallop to Barking Creek, and hid themselves in ditches near a field-path leading to Sir John's house, but luckily for Sir John he was detained in London that night, and so the plot was frustrated. The residence of this citizen at Crosby House, where, in 1603, he entertained the French ambassador, the Marquis of Rosny, afterwards better known as the Duke of Sully, we have alluded to in a former chapter. Sir John's only daughter, Elizabeth, tradition says, was carried off from Canonbury House in a baker's basket, by the contrivance of her lover, young Lord Compton, and Mr. Lewis says this story is confirmed by a picture representing the fact preserved among the family paintings at Castle Ashby, a seat of the Comptons, in Northampton-

shire. An old Islington vestry-clerk has preserved an anecdote about this curious elopement. Sir John, incensed at the stratagem, discarded his daughter, till Queen Elizabeth's kind interference effected a reconciliation. The wily queen, watching her opportunity, requested the knight to stand sponsor to the first offspring of a young discarded couple. Sir John complied, honoured and pleased at the gracious request, and her Majesty dictated his own surname for the Christian name of the child. The ceremony over, Sir John declared, as he had discarded his undutiful daughter, he would adopt the boy as his son. The queen then told him the truth, and the old knight, to his surprise, discovered that he had adopted his own grandson, who ultimately succeeded " his father in his honour, his grandfather in his wealth." Sir John died in 1609, and in St. Helen's there is still his monument, with his daughter kneeling at the feet of his effigy. At his funeral about a thousand persons, clad in black gowns, attended, and 320 poor men had each a basket given them, containing a black gown, four pounds of beef, two loaves of bread, a little bottle of wine, a candlestick, a pound of candles, two saucers, two spoons, a black pudding, a pair of gloves, a dozen points, two red herrings, four white herrings, six sprats, and two eggs.

Lord Compton's mind was so shaken by the vast wealth he inherited at his father-in-law's death, that he became for a time insane. He died in 1630, of a fit produced by bathing in the Thames, after supping at Whitehall. A curiously imperious letter of his wife to her lord was published in the *European Magazine* of 1782. It begins with loving tyranny, and demands the most ample pin-money :

"MY SWEET LIFE — Now I have declared to you my mind for the settling of your state, I suppose that it were best for me to bethink or consider with myself what allowance were meetest for me. For considering what care I have had of your estate, and how respectfully I dealt with those which both by the laws of God, of nature, and of civil polity, wit, religion, government, and honesty, you, my dear, are bound to, I pray and beseech you to grant me £1,600 per annum, quarterly to be paid."

She then calmly requires £600 additional for charitable works, three horses for her own saddle, two mounted gentlewomen, six or eight gentlemen, two four-horse coaches lined with velvet and cloth, and laced with gold and silver, two coachmen, a horse for her gentleman usher, and two footmen, twenty gowns a year, a purse of £2,220 to pay her debts, £10,000 to buy jewels, and as she is so reasonable, schooling and apparel for her children, and wages for her servants, furniture for all her houses, and when he is an earl, £1,000 more and double attendance. In truth these citizens'

Well's Row. The original house covered the whole of what is now Canonbury Place, and had a small park, with garden and offices. Prior Bolton either built or repaired the priory and church of St. Bartholomew, and, according to tradition, as Hall says, in his chronicle, fearing another flood, he built a tower on Harrow Hill, and victualled it for two months. Stow, however, redeems the prior from ridicule, by telling us that the supposed tower proved to be only a dove-house.

THE NEW RIVER HEAD. *From a View published in* 1753. (*See page* 266.)

daughters knew their rights, and exacted them. Lord Compton was created an earl in 1618. The second earl, a brave soldier, was killed during the Civil War, at the battle of Hopton Heath, in 1642–3.

Canonbury House is generally supposed to have been built in 1362, ten years after Edward III. had exempted the priory of St. Bartholomew from the payment of subsidies, in consequence of their great outlay in charity. Stow says that William Bolton (prior from 1509 to 1532) rebuilt the house, and probably erected the well-known brick tower, as Nichols, in his "History of Canonbury," mentions that his rebus, a bolt in a tun, was still to be seen cut in stone, in two places, on the outside facing

The mansion was much altered by Sir John Spencer, who came to reside there, in splendour, about 1599, and it is now divided into several houses, Canonbury Place having absorbed the grand old residence, and portioned out its relics of bygone grandeur. A long range of tiled buildings, supposed to have been the stables of the old mansion, but which had become an appendage to the "Canonbury" Tavern, was pulled down in 1840. A tradition once prevailed at Islington that the monks of St. Bartholomew had a subterranean communication from Canonbury to the priory at Smithfield. This notion had arisen from the discovery of brick archways in Canonbury, which seem to have been only conduit heads, and had really served to lead water to the priory.

After the Spencers, the Lord-Keeper Coventry rented this house. In 1635 we find the Earl of Derby detained here, and prevented from reaching St. James's by a deep snow; and in 1685 the Earl work, in 1737. This Humphreys was a second-rate poet, who sang the glories of the Duke of Chandos's seat at Canons, and whose verse Handel praised for its harmony. Ephraim Chambers, the author of one of the earliest cyclopædias, also died here, in 1740. Among other lodgers at Canonbury

CANONBURY TOWER, ABOUT 1800.

of Denbigh died here. About 1719 it seems to have been let as lodgings. In 1780 it was advertised as a suitable resort for invalids, on account of the purity of the air of Canonbury, and the convenience of a sixpenny stage every hour to the City. It then became a resort for literary men, who craved for quiet and country air. Amongst those who lodged there was Samuel Humphreys, who died here from consumption, produced by over-

House were Onslow, the Speaker; Woodfall, who printed "Junius;" Deputy Harrison, many years printer of the *London Gazette;* and Mr. Robert Horsfield, successor to Messrs. Knapton, Pope's booksellers.

But the special glory of the old house is the fact that here Oliver Goldsmith for a time lodged and wrote, and also came here to visit his worthy friend and employer, Mr. John Newbury, the good-natured publisher of children's books, who resided here, having under his protection the mad poet, Christopher Smart. We know for certain that at the close of 1762, Goldsmith lodged at Islington, at the house of a Mrs. Elizabeth Fleming, to whom he paid £50 a year. This choleric and strictly just landlady had her portrait taken by Hogarth, as tradition says, when he paid a visit to Goldsmith. Goldsmith frequently mentions Islington in his writings, and his jovial "shoemaker's holidays" were frequently made in this neighbourhood. The poet and three or four of his favourite friends used to breakfast at his Temple chambers about ten a.m., and at eleven they proceeded by the City Road and through the fields to dinner at Highbury Barn. About six in the evening they adjourned to White Conduit House to tea, and concluded the evening by a merry supper at the Grecian or the Globe.

"The two principal rooms," says Lewis, "which are in the first and second storeys of the plaister part of the building facing Canonbury Square, and appear to have been fitted up by Sir John Spencer, are each about twenty feet square and twelve feet high, and wainscoted with oak from the floor to the ceiling in complete preservation, and uncovered with paint. The lower room is divided into small panels, with fluted pilasters and a handsome cornice ; and over the fireplace are two compartments containing lions' heads, escalop shells, &c., in finely carved oak, as represented in the engraving. The other room, which is over this, is yet more highly ornamented in the Grecian taste, with carved wainscot in panels, intersected with beautifully wrought pilasters. A handsome cornice runs round the top, composed of wreathed foliage and escalop shells, and over the fireplace are two female figures carved in oak, representing 'Faith' and 'Hope,' with the mottoes, 'Fides · Via · Deus · Mea,' and 'Spes certa supra.' These are surmounted by a handsome cornice of pomegranates, with other fruit and foliage, having in the centre the arms of Sir John Spencer. The floors of both rooms are of very large fir boards, the ceilings are of plain plaister, and the windows are modern glazed sashes, opening towards Canonbury Square.

"The other apartments are smaller in size, and contain nothing worthy of remark. On the white wall of the staircase, near the top of the tower, are some Latin hexameter verses, comprising the abbreviated names of the Kings of England, from William the Conqueror to Charles I., painted in Roman characters an inch in length, but almost obliterated. The lines were most probably the effusion of some poetical inhabitant of an upper apartment in the building, during the time of the monarch last named, such persons having frequently been residents of the place.

"The adjoining house contains many specimens of the taste for ornamental carving and stucco work that prevailed about the time of Queen Elizabeth. At the top of the first flight of stairs are two male caryatide figures in armour, and a female carved in wood, fixed as ornaments in the corners of a doorway ; and the ceilings of a fine set of rooms on the first floor are elaborately embellished with a variety of devices in stucco, consisting of ships, flowers, foliage, &c., with medallions of Alexander the Great, Julius Cæsar, Titus Vespasian, &c. The arms of Queen Elizabeth are also given in several places, one of which bears also her initials 'E.R.,' and the date 1599, at which time the premises were fitted up by Sir John Spencer. The chimney-pieces in this house are very handsome, and in their original state must have had a rich and grand appearance, but they are now covered with white paint, although in other respects they have not sustained any material injury. One of them exhibits a very elaborate piece of workmanship in carved oak, containing figures of the Christian and cardinal virtues, and the arms of the City of London, with those of Sir John Spencer and the Clothworkers' Company, of which he was a member. There is also a monogram or device, apparently intended for his name, with the date 1601, and the whole is supported by caryatides of a very elegant form. In another room is a chimney-piece divided into three compartments, and intersected by handsome columns with Corinthian capitals, and containing a male and female figure in long robes, with the arms of Sir John Spencer in the centre, surrounded by curious carved work. The Spencer arms and the crest (an eagle volant) also occur in other parts of the sculpture, and the whole is supported by two caryatides bearing on their heads baskets of fruit. The rooms of this house still retain the ancient wainscoting of oak in square and lozenge panels, but covered with white paint; and the old oak staircase also remains, together with several ponderous doors of the same wood, having massive bolts, hinges, and fastenings of iron.

"In another adjoining house is a handsome chimney-piece of carved oak, covered with white paint. In the passage of the house, placed over a door, is an arch having a blank escutcheon, and another charged with the rebus of Prior Bolton. There are also over another doorway the arms of Sir Walter Dennys, who was knighted (fifth Henry VII.) on Prince Arthur being created Prince of

Wales. These are cut on a stone about a yard square, formerly fixed over a fireplace in another part of the old house, but since placed in its present situation, with the following inscription underneath :—

"'These were the arms of Sir Walter Dennys, of Gloucestershire, who was made a knight by bathing at the creation of Arthur Prince of Wales, in November, 1489, and died September 1, 21 Henry VII., 1505, and was buried in the church of Olviston, in Gloucestershire. He married Margaret, daughter of Sir Richard Weston, Knt.,

to which family Canonbury House formerly belonged. The carving is therefore above 280 years old.'" But the latter part of this inscription is probably erroneous.

"The old mansion, when in its perfect state, was ornamented with a turret, &c., and surrounded by a highly picturesque neighbourhood, as shown in a scarce print published by Boydell about 1760."

The house has been for some years the head-quarters of a Church of England Young Men's Association.

CHAPTER XXXIV.

HIGHBURY—UPPER HOLLOWAY—KING'S CROSS.

Jack Straw's Castle—A Famous Hunt—A Celebrity of Highbury Place—Highbury Barn and the Highbury Society—Cream Hall—Highbury Independent College—"The Mother Redcap"—The Blount Family—Hornsey Road and "The Devil's House" therein—Turpin, the Highwayman—The Corporation of Stroud Green—Copenhagen Fields—The Corresponding Society—Horne Tooke—Maiden Lane—Battle Bridge—The "King's Cross" Dustheaps and Cinder-sifters—Small-pox Hospital—The Great Northern Railway Station.

IN 1271 the prior of the convent of Knights Hospitallers of St. John of Jerusalem, at Clerkenwell, purchased an old manor house here, as a summer residence, and it was afterwards rebuilt higher to the eastward, changing its name from Tolentone to Highbury In the reign of Richard II., when Wat Tyler and his bold Kentish men poured down on London, a detachment under Jack Straw, Wat's lieutenant, who had previously plundered and burnt the Clerkenwell convent, pulled down the house at Highbury. The ruins afterwards became known as "Jack Straw's Castle." It is thought by antiquaries that the prior's moated house had been the prætorium of the summer camp of the Roman garrison of London.

Many of the old conduit heads belonging to the City were at Highbury and its vicinity, one of these supplied the parish of St. Giles's, Cripplegate ; and Mr. Lewis mentions another remaining in 1842, in a field opposite No. 14, Highbury Place. It might have been from Highbury that the hunt took place, noted by Strype as occurring in 1562, when the Lord Mayor, aldermen, and many worshipful persons rode to the Conduit Heads, then hunted and killed a hare, and, after dining at the Conduit Head, hunted a fox and killed it, at the end of St. Giles's, Cripplegate, with a great hallooing and blowing of horns at his death ; and thence the Lord Mayor, with all his company, rode through London to his place in Lombard Street.

One of the former celebrities of Highbury Place was that well-known chief cashier of the Bank of England, honest old Abraham Newland. For

twenty-five years this faithful servant had never slept out of the Bank of England, and his Highbury house was only a pleasant spot where he could rest for a few hours. He resigned his situation in 1807, on which occasion he declined an annuity offered by the Company, but accepted a service of plate, valued at a thousand guineas. He left £200,000, besides £1,000 a year, arising from estates. He made his money chiefly by shares of loans to Government, in which he could safely speculate. He was the son of a Southwark baker.

Another distinguished inhabitant of Highbury was John Nichols, for nearly half a century editor of the *Gentleman's Magazine*, and partner of William Bowyer, the celebrated printer. His "Anecdotes of Hogarth," and his "History of Leicestershire," were his chief works. He was a friend of Dr. Johnson, and seems to have been an amiable, industrious man, much beloved by his friends. He died suddenly, while going up-stairs to bed, in 1826.

Highbury Barn (built on the site of the barn of the prior's old mansion) was originally a small ale and cake house. It was the old rendezvous of the Highbury Society as far back as the year 1740. This society was established to commemorate the dropping of a Schism Act, cruelly severe on Protestant Dissenters, and which was to have received the Royal sanction the day Queen Anne died.

"The party," says a chronicler of the society, "who walked together from London had a rendezvous in Moorfields at one o'clock, and at Dettingen Bridge (where the house known by the name of the 'Shepherd and Shepherdess' now stands), they chalked the initials of their names on a post, for the information of such as might follow. They then proceeded to Highbury; and, to beguile their way, it was their custom in turn to bowl a ball of ivory at objects in their path. This ball has lately been presented to the society by Mr. William Field. After a slight refreshment, they proceeded to the field for exercise; but in those days of greater economy and simplicity, neither wine, punch, nor tea was introduced, and eightpence was generally the whole individual expense incurred. A particular game, denominated *hop-ball*, has from time immemorial formed the recreation of the members of this society at their meetings. On a board, which is dated 1734, which they use for the purpose of marking the game, the following motto is engraven:—'Play justly; play moderately; play cheerfully; so shall ye play to a rational purpose.' It is a game not in use elsewhere in the neighbourhood of London, but one something resembling it is practised in the West of England. The ball used in this game, consisting of a ball of worsted stitched over with silk or pack-thread, has from time immemorial been gratuitously furnished by one or another of the members of the society. The following toast has been always given at their annual dinner in August, viz.:—'The glorious 1st of August, with the immortal memory of King William and his good Queen Mary, not forgetting Corporal John; and a fig for the Bishop of Cork, that bottle-stopper.' John, Duke of Marlborough, was probably intended as the person designated Corporal John." The Highbury Society, says an authority on such subjects, was dissolved about the year 1833.

At a little distance northward of Highbury Barn was another dairy-farm called Cream Hall, where Londoners came, hot and dusty, on shiny summer afternoons, to drink new milk and to eat custards, smoking sillabubs, or cakes dipped in frothing cream. Gradually Highbury farm grew into a tavern and tea-gardens, and the barn was added to the premises, and fitted up as the principal room of the tavern, and there the court baron for the manor was held. Mr. Willoughby, an enterprising proprietor who died in 1785, increased the business, and his successors added a bowling-green, a trap ball-ground, and more gardens. A hop-garden and a brewery were also started, and charity and club dinners became frequent here. The barn could accommodate nearly 2,000 persons at once, and 800 people have been seen dining together, with seventy geese roasting for them at one fire. In 1808, the Ancient Freemasons sat down, 500 in number, to dinner; and in 1841, 3,000 licensed victuallers. There is now a theatre and a dancing-room, and all the features of a modern Ranelagh. The Sluice House, Eel Pie House, and Hornsey-wood House were old haunts of anglers and holiday-makers in this neighbourhood.

Highbury Independent College was removed from Hoxton in 1826. The institution began in a house at Mile End, rented, in 1783, by Dr. Addington, for a few students to be trained for the ministry. The present site was purchased for £2,100, by the treasurer, Mr. Wilson, and given to the charity. The building cost upwards of £15,000. "The Congregationalist College at Highbury, an offshoot from the one at Homerton," says Mr. Howitt, "was built in 1825, and opened in September, 1826, under the superintendence of Drs. Harris, Burder, and Halley, for the education of ministers of that persuasion. Amongst the distinguished men whom this college produced are the popular minister of Rowland Hill's Chapel, Blackfriars Road, the Rev. Newman Hall, and Mr. George Macdonald, the distinguished poet, lecturer, and novelist. Mr. Macdonald, however, had previously graduated at the University of Aberdeen, and had there taken his degree of M.A. In 1850 the buildings and property of the College of Highbury were disposed of to the Metropolitan Church of England Training Institution, and the business of the college transferred to New College, St. John's Wood, into which the three Dissenting colleges of Homerton, Coward, and Highbury, were consolidated."

A well-known public-house the "Mother Redcap," at Upper Holloway, is celebrated by Drunken Barnaby in his noted doggerel. The "Half Moon," a house especially celebrated, was once famous for its cheesecakes, which were sold in London by a man on horseback, who shouted "Holloway cheesecakes!"

In an old comedy, called *Jacke Drum's Entertainment* (4to, 1601), on the introduction of a Whitsun morris-dance, the following song is given:—

" Skip it and trip it nimbly, nimbly,
　Tickle it, tickle it lustily,
Strike up the tabor for the wenches favour,
　Tickle it, tickle it, lustily.

" Let us be seene on Hygate Greene
　To dance for the honour of Holloway.
Since we are come hither, let's spare for no leather,
　To dance for the honour of Holloway."

Upper Holloway was the residence of the ancient and honourable Blount family, during a considerable part of the seventeenth century. Sir Henry Blount, who went to the Levant in 1634, wrote a curious book of travels, and helped to introduce coffee into England. He is said to have guarded the sons of Charles I. during the battle of Edgehill. His two sons both became authors. Thomas wrote "Remarks on Poetry," and Charles was a Deist, who defended Dryden, attacked every one else, and wrote the life of Apollonius Tyaneus. He shot himself in 1693, in despair at being refused ecclesiastical permission to marry the sister of his deceased wife. The old manor house of the Blounts was standing a few years ago.

Hornsey Road, which in Camden's time was a "sloughy lane" to Whetstone, by way of Crouch End, eighty years ago had only three houses, and no side paths, and was impassable for carriages. It was formerly called Devil's, or Du Val's, Lane, and further back still Tollington Lane. There formerly stood on the east side of this road, near the junction with the Seven Sisters' Road, an old wooden moated house, called "The Devil's House," but really the site of old Tollington House. Tradition fixed this lonely place as the retreat of Duval, the famous French highwayman in the reign of Charles II. After he was hung in 1669, he lay in state at a low tavern in St. Giles's, and was buried in the middle aisle of St. Paul's, Covent Garden, by torchlight. The tradition is evidently erroneous, as the Devil's House in Devil's Lane is mentioned in a survey of Highbury taken in 1611 (James I.) Duval may, however, have affected the neighbourhood, as near a great northern road. The moat used to be crossed by a bridge, and the house in 1767 was a public-house, where Londoners went to fish, and enjoy hot loaves, and milk fresh from the cow. In 1737, after Turpin had shot one of his pursuers near a cave which he haunted in Epping Forest, he seems to have taken to stopping coaches and chaises at Holloway, and in the back lanes round Islington. A gentleman telling him audaciously he had reigned long, Dick replied gaily, "'Tis, no matter for that, I'm not afraid of being taken by you; so don't stand hesitating, but stump up the cole." Nevertheless, Dick came at last to the gallows.

Stroud Green (formerly a common in Highbury Manor) boasts an old house which once belonged to the Stapleton family, with the date 1609. It was afterwards converted into a public-house, and a hundred and thirty years ago had in front the following inscription—

> "Ye are welcome all
>   To Stapleton Hall."

About a century ago a society from the "Queen's Arms" Tavern, Newgate Street, used to meet annually in the summer time at Stroud Green, to regale themselves in the open air. They styled themselves "The Lord Mayor, Aldermen, and Corporation of Stroud Green," and the crowd that joined them made the place resemble a fair.

Copenhagen Fields were, it is said, the site of a public-house opened by a Dane, about the time when the King of Denmark paid his visit to his brother-in-law, James I. In Camden's map, 1695, it is called "Coopen Hagen," for the Danes who were then frequenting it had kept up the Danish pronunciation. Eventually, after the Restoration, it became a great tea-house, and a resort for players at skittles and Dutch pins.

The house was much frequented for its tea-gardens, its fine view of the Hampstead and Highgate heights, and the opportunities it afforded for recreation. Hone was told by a young woman who had been the landlady's assistant that in 1780 a body of the Lord George Gordon rioters passed Copenhagen House with blue banners flying, on their way to attack Caen Wood, the seat of Lord Mansfield, and that the proprietor was so alarmed at this, that at her request Justice Hyde sent a party of soldiers to protect the establishment. Soon after this a robbery at the house was so much talked of that the visitors began to increase, and additional rooms had to be built. The place then became famous for fives-playing, and here Cavanagh, the famous Irish player, immortalised in a vigorous essay by Hazlitt, won his laurels. In 1819 Hazlitt, who was an enthusiast about this lively game, writes, "Cavanagh used frequently to play matches at Copenhagen House for wagers and dinners. The wall against which they play is the same that supports the kitchen chimney; and when the ball resounded louder than usual, the cooks exclaimed, 'Those are the Irishman's balls,' and the joints trembled on the spit." The next landlord encouraged dog-fighting and bull-baiting, especially on Sunday mornings, and his licence was in consequence refused in 1816.

In the early days of the French Revolution, when the Tories trembled with fear and rage, the fields near Copenhagen House were the scene of those meetings of the London Corresponding Society, which so alarmed the Government. The most threatening of these was held on October 26, 1795, when Thelwall, and other sympathisers with France and liberty, addressed 40,000, and threw out hints that the mob should surround Westminster on the 29th, when the king would go to the House. The hint was attended to, and on that day the king was shot at, but escaped unhurt. In 1794 many members of the Corresponding Society, including Hardy, Thelwall, Holcroft, and Horne Tooke, had been tried for treason in connection with the doings of the society, but were all acquitted.

After Horne Tooke's acquittal, he is reported to have remarked to a friend, that if a certain song, exhibited at the trial of Hardy, had been produced against him, he should have sung it to the jury; that, as there was no treason in the words, they might judge if there was any in the music.

hall, to present an address to his Majesty (which, however, Lord Melbourne rejected), signed by 260,000 unionists, on behalf of some of their colleagues who had been convicted at Dorchester for administering illegal oaths. Among the leaders appeared prominently Robert Owen, the socialist, and a Radical clergyman in full canonicals, black silk gown and crimson Oxford hood.

Maiden Lane (perhaps Midden or Dunghill Lane), an ancient way leading from Battle Bridge

COPENHAGEN HOUSE. *From a View taken about* 1800. (*See page* 275.)

As he was returning from the Old Bailey to Newgate, one cold night, a lady placed a silk handkerchief round his neck, upon which he gaily said, "Take care, madam, what you are about, for I am rather ticklish in that place just now." During his trial for high treason, Tooke is said to have expressed a wish to speak in his own defence, and to have sent a message to Erskine to that effect, saying, "I'll be hanged if I don't!" to which Erskine wrote back, "You'll be hanged if you do."

In April, 1834, an immense number of persons of the trades' unions assembled in the Fields, to form part of a procession of 40,000 men to White-

to Highgate, and avoiding the hill, was once the chief road for northern travellers. At present, bone-stores, chemical works, and potteries render it peculiarly unsavoury.

Battle Bridge is so called for two reasons. In the first place, because there was formerly a brick bridge over the Fleet at this spot; and, secondly, because, as London tradition has steadily affirmed, here was fought the great battle between Suetonius Paulinus, the Roman general, and Boadicea, the Queen of the Iceni. It is still doubtful whether the scene of the great battle was so near London, but there is still much to be said in its favour.

The arguments pro and con are worth a brief discussion. Tacitus describes the spot, with his usual sharp, clear brevity. "Suetonius," he says, "chose a place with narrow jaws, backed by a forest." Now the valley of the Fleet, between Pentonville and Gray's Inn Lane, backed by the great northern forest of Middlesex, undoubtedly corresponds with this description; but then Tacitus, always clear and vivid, makes no mention of the river Fleet, which would have been most important as a defence for the front and flank of the Roman army, and this raises up serious doubts. The Roman summer camp near Barnsbury Park, opposite Minerva Terrace, in the Thornhill Road, we have already mentioned. There was a prætorium there, a raised breastwork, long visible from the Caledonian Road, a well, and a trench. In 1825 arrow-heads and red-tiled pavements were discovered in this spot.

In 1680 John Conyers, an antiquarian apothecary of Fleet Street, discovered in a gravel-pit near the "Sir John Oldcastle," in Coldbath Fields, the skeleton of an elephant, and the shaft and flint head of a British spear. Now it is certain that the Romans in Britain employed elephants, as Poly-bius expressly tells us, when Julius Cæsar forced the passage of the Thames, near Chertsey, an elephant, with archers in a houdah on its back, led the way, and drove the astonished Britons to flight. Another important proof also exists. In 1842 a fragment of a Roman monumental inscription was found built into a cottage on the east side of Maiden Lane. It was part of the tomb of an officer of the twentieth legion, which had been dug up in a field on the west side of the road leading to the Cale-

KING'S CROSS. *From a View taken during its demolition in* 1845. (*See page* 278.)

donian Asylum. This legion formed part of the army of Claudius which Paulinus led against Boadicea. Mr. Tomlins, however, is inclined to think that a fight took place at Battle Bridge during the early Danish invasions.

The great battle with the Romans, wherever it took place, was an eventful one, and was one of the last great efforts of the Britons. Suetonius, with nearly 10,000 soldiers, waited for the rush of the wild 200,000 half-savage men, who had already sacked and destroyed Colchester, St. Albans, and London. His two legions were in the centre, his light-armed troops at hand, while his cavalry formed his right and left wings. Boadicea and her two daughters, in a war-chariot, was haranguing her troops, while the wives of her soldiers were placed in wagons at the rear end of the army, to view the battle. The Britons rushed to the attack with savage shouts, and songs of victory; the Romans received their charge with showers of javelins, and then advanced in the form of a wedge, the Britons eagerly opening their ranks, to surround and devour them up. The British chariots, armed with scythes, made great havoc among the Romans, till Suetonius ordered his legionaries to aim only at the charioteers. The Britons, however, after a stubborn fight, gave way before the close ranks of disciplined warriors, leaving some 80,000 men upon the field, while the Romans, shoulder to shoulder, are reported to have lost only 400 men. The line of wagons with the women proved a fatal obstruction to the flight of the Britons. The last fact to be recorded about the Romans at Battle Bridge is the discovery, in 1845, under the foundation of a house in Maiden Lane, of an iron urn, full of gold and silver coins of the reign of Constantine.

Gossiping Aubrey mentions that in the spring after the Great Fire of London the ruins were all overgrown with the Neapolitan cress, "which plant," says he, "Thomas Willis (the famous physician) told me he knew before but in one place about town, and that was at Battle Bridge, by the 'Pinder of Wakefield,' and that in no great quantity." In the reign of Edward VI., says Stow, a miller of Battle Bridge was set in the pillory in Chepe, and had his ears cut off, for uttering seditious words against the Duke of Somerset. In 1731, John Everett, a highwayman, was hung at Tyburn, for stopping a coach and robbing some ladies at Battle Bridge. The man had served in Flanders as a sergeant, and had since kept an ale-house in the Old Bailey.

In 1830 Battle Bridge assumed the name of King's Cross, from a ridiculous octagonal structure crowned by an absurd statue of George IV., which was erected at the centre of six roads which there united. The building, ornamented by eight Doric columns, was sixty feet high, and was crowned by a statue of the king eleven feet high. Pugin, in that bantering book, "The Contrasts," ridiculed this effort of art, and contrasted it with the beautiful Gothic market cross at Chichester. The Gothic revival was only just then beginning, and the dark age was still dark enough. The basement was first a police-station, then a public-house with a camera-obscura in the upper storey. The hideous monstrosity was removed in 1845. Battle Bridge, which had been a haunt of thieves and murderers, was first built upon by Mr. Bray and others, on the accession of George IV., when sixty-three houses were erected in Liverpool Street, Derby Street, &c. The locality being notorious, it was proposed to call it St. George's Cross, or Boadicea's Cross, but Mr. Bray at last decreed that King's Cross was to be the name.

Early in the century the great dust-heaps of London (where now stand Argyle, Liverpool, and Manchester Streets) were some of the disgraces of London; and when the present Caledonian Road was fields, near Battle Bridge were heaped hillocks of horse-bones. The Battle Bridge dustmen and cinder-sifters were the pariahs of the metropolis. The mountains of cinders and filth were the *débris* of years, and were the haunts of innumerable pigs. The Russians, says the late Mr. Pinks, in his excellent "History of Clerkenwell," bought all these ash-heaps, to help to rebuild Moscow after the French invasion. The cinder-ground was eventually sold, in 1826, to the Pandemonium Company for £15,000, who walled in the whole and built the Royal Clarence Theatre at the corner of Liverpool Street. Somewhere near this Golgotha was a piece of waste ground, where half the brewers of the metropolis shot their grains and hop-husks. It became a great resort for young acrobats and clowns (especially on Sunday mornings), who could here tumble and throw "flip-flaps" to their hearts' content, without fear of fracture or sprain.

In 1864 Mr. Grove, an advertising tailor of Battle Bridge, bought Garrick's villa, at Hampton, for £10,800. In 1826, opposite the great cinder-mountain of Battle Bridge, was St. Chad's Well, a chalybeate spring supposed to be useful in cases of liver attacks, dropsy, and scrofula. About the middle of the last century 800 or 900 persons a morning used to come and drink these waters, and the gardens were laid out for invalids to promenade.

The Great Northern Railway Terminus at King's Cross occupies more than forty-five acres of land. For the site of the passenger station, the Small-pox and Fever Hospital was cleared away. The front towards Euston Road has two main arches, each 71 feet span, separated by a clock tower 120 feet high. The clock has dials 9 feet in diameter, and the principal bell weighs 29 cwt. Each shed is 800 feet long, 105 feet wide, and 71 feet high to the crown of the semicircular roof, without a tie. The roof is formed of laminated ribs 20 feet apart, and of inch-and-a-half planks screwed to each other. The granary has six storeys, and will hold 60,000 sacks of corn. On the last storey are water-tanks, holding 150,000 gallons; and the grain is hoisted by hydraulic apparatus. The goods shed is 600 feet in length, and 80 feet wide ; and the roof is glazed with cast glass in sheets, 8 feet by 2 feet 6 inches. Under the goods platform is stabling for 300 horses. The shed adjoins the Regent's Canal, which, passing eastwards, enters the Thames at Limehouse. The coal stores will contain 15,200 tons. The buildings are by Lewis and Joseph Cubitt. The railway passes under the Regent's Canal and Maiden Lane, beneath Copenhagen Fields, over the Holloway Road, through tunnels at Hornsey and elsewhere, and forms the chief line of communication with York and Edinburgh.

CHAPTER XXXV.

PENTONVILLE.

Origin of the Name—The " Belvidere " Tavern—The Society of Bull Feathers' Hall—Penton Street—Joe Grimaldi—Christ Church—" White Conduit House :" Oliver Goldsmith a Visitor there—Ancient Conduits at Pentonville—Christopher Bartholomew's Reverses of Fortune—The Pentonville Model Prison.—The Islington Cattle Market—A Daring Scheme—Celebrated Inhabitants of Hermes Hill—Dr. de Valangin—Sinner-Saved Huntington—Joe Grimaldi and the Dreadful Accident at Sadler's Wells—King's Row and Happy Man's Place—Thomas Cooke, the Miser—St. James's Chapel, Pentonville—A Blind Man's favourite Amusement—Clerkenwell in 1789—Pentonville Chapel—Prospect House— " Dobney's "—The Female Penitentiary—A Terrible Tragedy.

THE site of Pentonville was once an outlying possession of the priory of St. John, Clerkenwell, and called the " Commandry Mantels," from its having belonged to Geoffrey de Mandeville—*vulgo*, Mantell. Eventually the fields were given to the Hospitallers. There were springs and conduit-heads in the meadows ; and Gerard, the Elizabethan herbalist, specially mentions the white saxifrage as growing abundantly there.

The district of Pentonville, once a mere nameless vassal of Clerkenwell and Islington (the latter itself a comparative parvenu), received its present name from Henry Penton, Esq., member for Winchester, and a Lord of the Admiralty, who died in 1812, and on whose estate the first buildings in Penton Street were erected, according to Mr. Pinks, about the year 1773.

The " Belvidere " Tavern, at the corner of Penton Street, was at an early period the site of a house known as " Busby's Folly," probably from Christopher Busby, who was landlord of the " Whyte Lyon," at Islington, in 1668. In 1664 (four years after the Restoration), the members of the quaint Society of Bull Feathers' Hall met at the Folly before marching to Islington, to claim the toll of all gravel carried up Highgate Hill. Their thirty pioneers, with spades and pickaxes, were preceded in the hall procession by trumpeters and horn-blowers. Their standard was a large pair of horns fixed to a pole, and with pennants hanging to each tip. Next came the flag of the society, attended by the master of the ceremonies. After the flag came the mace-bearers and the herald-at-arms of the society. The supporters of the arms were a woman with a whip, and the motto, " Ut volo, sic jubeo ; " on the other side, a rueful man, and the motto, " Patientia patimur."

This singular club met in Chequer Yard, White-chapel, the president wearing a crimson satin gown, and a furred cap surmounted by a pair of antlers, while his sceptre and crown were both horned. The brethren of this great and solemn fraternity drank out of horn cups, and were sworn as members on a blank horn-book. Busby's house retained its name as late as 1710, but was afterwards called " Penny's Folly." It had fourteen windows in front ; and here men with learned horses, musical glasses, and sham philosophical performances, gave evening entertainments. The " Belvidere " Tavern was in existence as early as 1780, and was famous for its racket-court. At No. 37, Penton Street, that emperor of English clowns, Joe Grimaldi, lived in 1797, after his marriage with Miss Hughes, the pretty daughter of the manager of Sadler's Wells. Penton Street was then the St. James's or Regent's Park of the City Road quarter.

On the west side of Penton Street is a new church, opened in 1863. It contains sittings for 1,259 persons, and with the site cost about £8,600. The first incumbent was Dr. Courtenay, formerly curate of St. James's, Pentonville. St. James's was made a district, assigned out of the parish of St. James's, Clerkenwell, in 1854. On the east side of Penton Street formerly stood that celebrated Cockney place of amusement, "White Conduit House." The original tavern was erected in the reign of Charles I., and the curious tradition was that the workmen were said to have been regaling themselves after the completion of the building the very hour that King Charles's head fell at the Whitehall scaffold. In 1754 " White Conduit House" was advertised as having for its fresh attractions a long walk, a circular fish-pond, a number of pleasant shady arbours, enclosed with a fence seven feet high, hot loaves and butter, milk direct from the cow, coffee, tea, and other liquors, a cricket-field, unadulterated cream, and a handsome long room, with "copious prospects, and airy situation." In 1760 the following spirited verses describing the place, by William Woty, author of the "Shrubs of Parnassus," appeared in the *Gentleman's Magazine* :—

"Wish'd Sunday's come—mirth brightens every face,
And paints the rose upon the house-maid's cheek,
Harriott, or Moll more ruddy.　Now the heart
Of prentice, resident in ample street,
Or alley, kennel-wash'd, Cheapside, Cornhill,
Or Cranborne, thee for calcuments renown'd,
With joy distends—his meal meridian o'er,
With switch in hand, he to *White Conduit House*
Hies merry-hearted.　Human beings here,
In couples multitudinous, assemble,
Forming the drollest groupe that ever trod
Fair Islingtonian plains.　Male after male,
Dog after dog succeeding—husbands, wives,
Fathers and mothers, brothers, sisters, friends,
And pretty little boys and girls.　Around,
Across, along the garden's shrubby maze
They walk, they sit, they stand.　What crowds press on
Eager to mount the stairs, eager to catch
First vacant bench, or chair, in long room plac'd !
Here prig with prig holds conference polite,
And indiscriminate the gaudy beau
And sloven mix.　Here, he who all the week
Took bearded mortals by the nose, or sat
Weaving dead hairs, and whistling wretched strain,
And eke the sturdy youth, whose trade it is
Stout oxen to contund, with gold-bound hat
And silken stocking strut.　The red-armed belle
Here shews her tasty gown, proud to be thought
The butterfly of fashion ; and, forsooth,
Her haughty mistress deigns for once to tread
The same unhallowed floor.　'Tis hurry all,
And rattling cups and saucers.　Waiter here,
And Waiter there, and Waiter here and there,
At once is called, Joe, Joe, Joe, Joe, Joe !
Joe on the right, and Joe upon the left,
For every vocal pipe re-echoes Joe !

"Alas ! poor Joe ! like Francis in the play,
He stands confounded, anxious how to please
The many-headed throng.　But should I paint
The language, humours, custom of the place,
Together with all curtseys, lowly bows,
And compliments extern, 'twould swell my page
Beyond its limits due.　Suffice it then
For my prophetic muse to say, 'So long
'As Fashion rides upon the wing of Time,
While tea and cream, and butter'd rolls, can please,
While rival beaux and jealous belles exist,
So long, White Conduit House shall be thy fame.'"

About this time the house and its customers were mentioned by Oliver Goldsmith.　He says, " After having surveyed the curiosities of this fair and beautiful town (Islington), I proceeded forward, leaving a fair stone building on my right.　Here the inhabitants of London often assemble to celebrate a feast of hot rolls and butter.　Seeing

such numbers, each with their little tables before them, employed on this occasion, must no doubt be a very amusing sight to the looker-on, but still more so to those who perform in the solemnity."

"White Conduit Loaves," says Mr. Timbs, " was one of the common London street-cries, before the French war raised the price of bread."

Washington Irving, in his " Life of Goldsmith," says :—" Oliver Goldsmith, towards the close of 1762, removed to 'Merry Islington,' then a country village, though now swallowed up in omnivorous London.　In this neighbourhood he used to take his solitary rambles, sometimes extending his walks to the gardens of the 'White Conduit House,' so famous among the essayists of the last century. While strolling one day in these gardens he met three daughters of the family of a respectable tradesman, to whom he was under some obligation. With his prompt disposition to oblige, he conducted them about the garden, treated them to tea, and ran up a bill in the most open-handed manner imaginable.　It was only when he came to pay that he found himself in one of his old dilemmas.　He had not the wherewithal in his pocket.　A scene of perplexity now took place between him and the waiter, in the midst of which came up some of his acquaintances, in whose eyes he wished to stand particularly well.　When, however, they had enjoyed their banter, the waiter was paid, and poor Goldsmith enabled to carry off the ladies with flying colours."

This popular place of amusement derives its name from an old stone conduit, removed in 1831, and used to repair part of the New Road.　It bore the date 1641, and beneath, the arms of Sutton, the founder of the Charterhouse, with initials and monograms probably of past masters.　The conduit, repaired by Sutton, was built in the reign of Henry VI., and it supplied the Carthusian friars.　The water-house was used by the school till about 1654, when the supply fell short, and a New River supply was decided on.　The site of the conduit was at the back of No. 10, Penton Street, at the corner of Edward Street.　There was a smaller conduit at the back of White Conduit Gardens, close to where Warren Street now stands.　Huntington (Sinner Saved) the preacher cleansed the spring, but his enemies choked it with mud to spite him. Latterly, however, the Conduit House fell to ruins, and the upper floors became a mighty refuge for tramps and street pariahs.

An old drawing of 1731 represents White Conduit House as a mere tall building, with four front windows, a gable roof, a side shed, and on the other side the conduit itself. On either hand stretched bare sloping fields and hedge-rows.

The anonymous writer of the " Sunday Ramble," 1774, describes the place as having boxes for tea, cut into the hedges and adorned with pictures; pleasant garden walks, a round fish-pond, and two handsome tea-rooms. Later the fish-pond was filled up, and an Apollo dancing-room erected. In 1826 a " Minor Vauxhall " was established here, and the place became somewhat disreputable. Mr. Chabert, the fire-eater, after a collation of phosphorus, arsenic, and oxalic acid, with a sauce of boiling oil and molten lead, walked into an oven, preceded by a leg of lamb and a rump-steak, and eventually emerged with them completely baked, after which the spectators dined with him. Graham also ascended from these gardens in his balloon. In this year Hone talks of the gardens as "just above the very lowest," though the fireworks were as good as usual.

About 1827 archery was much practised ; and in 1828 the house was rebuilt with a great ball-room and many architectural vagaries. A writer in the *Mirror* of 1833 says :—" Never mind Pentonville, it is not now what it was, a place of some rural beauty. The fields behind it were, in my time, as wild and picturesque, with their deep-green lanes, richly hedged and studded with flowers, which have taken fright and moved off miles away— and their ' stately elms and hillocks green,' as they are now melancholy and cut up with unfurnished, and, of course, unoccupied rows of houses, run up during the paroxysm of the brick and mortar mania of times past, and now tumbling in ruins, with the foolish fortunes of the speculators. The march of town innovation upon the suburbs has driven before it all that was green, silent, and fitted for meditation. Here, too, is that paradise of apprentice boys, ' White Cundick Couse,' as it is cacophoniously pronounced by its visitors, which has done much to expel the decencies of the district. Thirty years ago this place was better frequented—that is, there was a larger number of respectable adults ; fathers and mothers, with their children, and a smaller moiety of shop-lads, and such-like Sunday bucks, who were awed into decency by their elders. The manners, perhaps, are much upon a par with what they were. The ball-room gentlemen then went through country dances with their hats on and their coats off. Hats are now taken off, but coats are still unfashionable on these gala nights. The belles of that day wore long trains to their gowns. It was a favourite mode of introduction to a lady there to tread on the train, and then apologising handsomely, acquaintance was begun, and soon ripened into an invitation to tea

and the hot loaves for which these gardens were once celebrated. Being now a popular haunt, those who hang on the rear of the march of human nature, the sutlers, camp-followers, and plunderers, know that where large numbers of men or boys are in pursuit of pleasure, there is a sprinkling of the number to whom vice and debauchery are ever welcome; they have, therefore, supplied what these wanted, and Pentonville may now hold up its head, and boast of its depravities before any other part of London."

The place grew worse and worse, till, in 1849, the house was pulled down and streets built on its site. The present "White Conduit" Tavern covers a portion of the original gardens. Mr. George Cruikshank has been heard to confess that some of his early knowledge of Cockney character, and, indeed, of City human nature, was derived from observing evenings at "White Conduit House."

An old proprietor of the gardens, who died in 1811, Mr. Christopher Bartholomew, was believed to have realised property to the amount of £50,000. The " Angel," at Islington, was also his ; and he used to boast that he had more haystacks than any one round London. He, however, became a prey to the vice of gambling, and is said at last to have sometimes spent more than 2,000 guineas in a single day in insuring numbers at the lottery. By degrees he sank into extreme poverty, but a friend giving him half of a sixteenth of a favourite number, that turned up a £20,000 prize, he again became affluent, only to finally sink into what proved this time irreparable ruin.

The Pentonville Model Prison was the result of a Government Commission sent over to America in 1832, to inquire into the system of isolation so much belauded on the other side of the Atlantic. "Many people," says Mr. Dixon in his "London Prisons," published in 1850, "were seduced by the report issued in 1834, into a favourable impression of the Philadelphian system ; and, amongst these, Lord John Russell, who, being secretary for the Home Department, got an Act introduced into Parliament in 1839 (2 & 3 Vict. c. 56), containing a clause rendering separate confinement legal in this country. A model prison on this plan was resolved upon. Major Jebb was set to prepare a scheme of details. The first stone was laid on the 10th of April, 1840, and the works were completed in the autumn of 1842, at a cost of more than £90,000. The building so erected consists of five wings or galleries, radiating from a point, the view from which is very striking, and at the same time very unprison-like. On the sides of four of these galleries the cells are situate, and numbered. There are 520 of them, but not more than 500 are ever occupied. If we divide £90,000 by 500, we shall find that the accommodation for each criminal costs the country £180 for cell-room as original outlay.

"Last year the expenses of mere management at Pentonville were £16,392 1s. 7d.; the daily average of prisoners for the year was 457; consequently, the cost per head for victualling and management was nearly £36.

Embankment, projected by Martin, the painter, and others, and the Holborn Viaduct, projected by Mr. Charles Pearson) was planned out nearly half a century ago, by active London minds. In 1833 John Perkins, Esq., of Bletchingley, in Surrey, struck with the dirt and cruelty of Smithfield, and the intolerable danger and mischief produced by driving vast and half-wild flocks and herds of cattle through the narrow and crowded London streets, projected a new market in the fine grazing dis-

BATTLE BRIDGE IN 1810. (see page 277.)

"This flourishing institution, then, stands thus in account with the nation yearly:—The land given for nothing, i.e., not set down in the account; taxes, ditto; interest of outlay, £100,000 at 5 per cent., £5,000; cost of maintenance, £15,000; repairs, &c. (for 1847 this item is nearly £3,000). If we take the three items here left blank at an average of £2,000, a very moderate estimate for the yearly drain, we shall have a prison capable of accommodating 450 prisoners, at a charge upon county rates of £22,000 per annum; or, in another form, at about £50 per head for each prisoner yearly. Compare this with the cost of the maintenance of the poor in workhouses, ye disciples of economy!"

The Islington Cattle Market (like the Thames

trict north of the metropolis. The place was built at an expense of £100,000, and opened under an Act of Parliament, April 18th, 1836. So strong, however, was the popular and Conservative interest in old abuses, that the excellent new market proved a total failure, and was soon closed. The area for cattle at Islington was nearly fifteen acres, abutting on the road leading from the Lower Street to Ball's Pond. It was enclosed by a brick wall, ten feet high, and had vast sheds on all the four sides. A road ran entirely round the market, which was quadrated by paths crossing it at right angles, and there was to have been a central circus, to be used as an exchange for the greasy graziers and bustling salesmen, with offices for the money-takers and clerks of the market. The market was capable of accommodating 7,000 head of cattle, 500 calves, 40,000 sheep, and 1,000 pigs. The principal entrance from the Lower Road had an arched gateway, and two arched footways. Poor Mr. Perkins, he was before his age. The spot was excellently chosen, lying as it does near the great roads from the northern and eastern counties, the great centres of cattle, and communicating easily with the town by means of the City Road,

Copenhagen Fields." It was calculated that the undertaking would pay the subscribers $12\frac{1}{2}$ per cent. on the capital embarked, which was to be £200,000; but the proposition met with little encouragement, and was soon abandoned.

The present Metropolitan Cattle Market occupies seventy-five acres of ground. The market-place is an irregular quadrangle, with a lofty clock-tower in the centre, and four taverns at the four corners, the open area being set off into divisions for the dif-

WHITE CONDUIT HOUSE, ABOUT 1820.   (*See page* 281.)

which was also convenient for the western part of London. Twenty years later, in 1852, the nuisance of Smithfield (thanks, perhaps, to "Oliver Twist") became unbearable, even to the long-suffering abuse-preservers; so Smithfield was condemned to be removed, and a new cattle-market was opened in Copenhagen Fields in 1855, and that enriched district now rejoices in many cattle and all the attending delights of knackers' yards, slaughterhouses, tripe-dressers, cats'-meat-boilers, catgut-spinners, bone-boilers, glue-makers, and tallow-melters.

It was proposed by a company of projectors, in the year 1812, to establish a sea-water bathing-place at Copenhagen Fields, by bringing water through iron pipes "from the coast of Essex to

ferent kinds of live stock. No less than £400,000 have been expended upon the land and buildings. In the parts of the market appropriated for the reception of the different cattle, each central rail is decorated with characteristic casts of heads of oxen, sheep, pigs, &c.; these were designed and modelled by Bell, the sculptor. The open space of the market will accommodate at one time about 7,000 cattle and 42,000 sheep, with a proportionate number of calves and pigs. The calf and pig markets are covered, the roofs being supported by iron columns, which act at the same time as water-drains. In the centre of the whole area is a twelve-sided structure, called "Bank Buildings," surmounted by an elegant campanile, or bell tower,

The twelve sides give entrance to twelve sets of offices, occupied by bankers, salesmen, railway companies, and electric telegraph companies. In one year (1862) the returns were 304,741 bullocks, 1,498,500 sheep, 27,951 calves, and 29,470 pigs. The great Christmas sale, in the closing year of old Smithfield, ranged from 6,000 to 7,000 bullocks, and between 20,000 and 25,000 sheep. On December 15, 1862, the bullocks were 8,340, being a greater number than ever before known at any metropolitan market. The market-days for cattle, sheep, and pigs are Mondays and Thursdays. There is a miscellaneous market for horses, asses, and goats on Fridays. (Timbs.)

At a large house on Hermes Hill, afterwards (in 1811) occupied by "Sinner-saved Huntington," the converted coal-heaver, a useful man in his generation, resided, in the last century, from 1772 till his death in 1805, Dr. de Valangin, an eminent Swiss physician, who had been a pupil of Boerhaave. He called this hill "Hermes," from Hermes Trismegistus, the fabled Egyptian king, and discoverer of chemistry, to whom fawning Lord Bacon compared James I., because, forsooth, that slobbering, drunken monarch was king, priest, and philosopher. De Valangin—the inventor of several useful and useless medicines, including the "balsam of life," which he presented to Apothecaries' Hall—was the author of a sensible book on diet, and "the four non-naturals." The doctor, who was a man of taste and benevolence, married as his second wife the widow of an eminent surveyor and builder, who, says Mr. Pinks, had recovered £1,000 for a breach of promise, from a lover who had jilted her. He buried one of his daughters in his garden, but the body was afterwards removed to the vaults of Cripplegate Church. In his book (1768) De Valangin particularly mentions the increased use of brandy-and-water by English people. His house was remarkable for a singular brick tower or observatory, which was taken down by the next tenant.

That eccentric preacher, William Huntington, was an illegitimate son, whose reputed father was a day-labourer in Kent. In youth he was alternately an errand-boy, gardener, cobbler, and coal-heaver. He seems, even when a child, to have been endowed with an extraordinary deep sensibility to religious impressions, and early in life he began to exhort men to save their souls, and flee the wrath to come, and, we fully believe, in all sincerity, though his manner was vulgar. His original name was Hunt, but flying the country to escape the charge of an illegitimate child, he took for safety the name of Huntington; and, unable to pay for a Dissenting title of D.D., he christened himself S.S. (sinner saved). Huntington seems to have had a profound belief in the efficacy of faith and prayer. Whether it was tea, a horse, a pulpit, or a hod of lime, he prayed for it, he tells us, and it came. Even a pair of leather breeches was thus supplied, as he mentions in his John Bunyan way.

"I often," he says, "made very free in my prayers with my invaluable Master for this favour; but he still kept me so amazingly poor, that I could not get them, at any rate. At last I was determined to go to a friend of mine at Kingston, who is of that branch of business, to bespeak a pair, and to get him to trust me until my Master sent me money to pay him. I was that day going to London, fully determined to bespeak them as I rode through the town. However, when I passed the shop, I forgot it; but when I came to London I called on Mr. Croucher, a shoemaker in Shepherds' Market, who told me a parcel was left there for me, but what it was he knew not. I opened it, and behold, there was a pair of *leather breeches* with a note in them, the substance of which was to the best of my remembrance as follows :—'Sir,— I have sent you a pair of breeches, and I hope they will fit. I beg your acceptance of them; and if they want any alteration, leave in a note what the alteration is, and I will call in a few days and alter them.—J. S.' I tried them on, and they fitted as well as if I had been measured for them; at which I was amazed, having never been measured by any leather breeches maker in London."

S. S. had strong belief in eternal perdition, and attacked the mad prophet Brothers, for his wild prophecies of the sudden fall of the Turkish, German, and Russian empires. When Huntington's chapel, in Tichfield Street was burnt, his congregation erected a new one on the east side of Gray's Inn Lane, at a cost of £9,000, of which he craftily obtained the personal freehold. By his first wife S. S. had thirteen children; he then married the widow of Sir James Sanderson, who came one day to his chapel to ridicule him, but "remained to pray," and to fall in love. He died in 1813, and was buried in a garden in the rear of Jireh Chapel, on the cliff at Lewes. A few hours before his death, at Tunbridge Wells, he dictated the following epitaph for himself :—

"Here lies the coal-heaver, who departed this life July 1, 1813, in the 69th year of his age, beloved of his God, but abhorred of men. The omniscient Judge, at the grand assize, shall ratify and confirm this, to the confusion of many thousands; for England and its metropolis shall know that there hath been a prophet among them.—W. H., S. S."

At the sale of his goods at Pentonville, which realised £1,800, a humble admirer bought a barrel of ale, as a souvenir of his pastor.

"When," says Huntington, "I first began to open my mouth for the Lord, the master for whom I carried coals was rather displeased; at which I do not wonder, as he was an Arminian of the Arminians, or a Pharisee of the Pharisees. I told him, however, that I should prophesy to thousands before I died; and soon after the doors began to be opened to receive my message. When this appeared, and I had left the slavish employment of coal-carrying, others objected to my master against such a fellow as me taking up the office of a minister. His answer was, 'Let him alone. I once heard him say that he should prophecy to thousands before he died; let us see whether this prophecy comes to pass or not.'"

"Huntington is described as having been, towards the close of his career, a fat burly man with a red face, which rose just above the cushion, and a thick, guttural and rather indistinct voice."

"His pulpit prayers," writes a contemporary, "are remarkable for omitting the king or his country. He excels in extempore eloquence. Having formally announced his text, he lays his Bible at once aside, and never refers to it again. He has every possible text and quotation at his finger's end. He proceeds directly to his object, and, except such incidental digressions as 'Take care of your pockets!' 'Wake that snoring sinner!' 'Silence that noisy numskull!' 'Turn out that drunken dog!' he never deviates from his course. Nothing can exceed his dictatorial dogmatism. Believe him—none but him—that's enough. When he wishes to bind the faith of his congregation, he will say, over and over, 'As sure as I am born, 'tis so;' or, 'I believe this,' or 'I know this,' or 'I am sure of it,' or 'I believe the plain English of it to be this.' And then he will add, by way of clenching his point, 'Now you can't help it;' or, 'It must be so, in spite of you.' He does this with a most significant shake of the head, and with a sort of Bedlam hauteur, with all the dignity of defiance. He will then sometimes observe, softening his deportment, 'I don't know whether I make you understand these things, but I understand them well.' He rambles sadly, and strays so completely from his text, that you often lose sight of it. The divisions of his subject are so numerous, that one of his sermons might be divided into three. Preaching is with him talking; his discourses, story-telling. Action he has none, except that of shifting his handkerchief from hand to hand, and hugging his cushion. Nature has bestowed on him a vigorous, original mind, and he employs it in everything. Survey him when you will, he seems to have rubbed off none of his native rudeness or blackness. All his notions are his own, as well as his mode of imparting them. Religion has not been discovered by him through the telescopes of commentators."

"Huntington's portrait," says Mr. Pinks, "is in the National Portrait Gallery, in Great George Street, Westminster. He 'might pass, as far as appearances go, for a convict, but that he looks too conceited. The vitality and strength of his constitution are fearful to behold, and it is certain that he looks better fitted for coal-heaving than for religious oratory.'"

Penton Place, leading to what was once called Bagnigge Wash, used to be frequently overflowed, when the Fleet Sewer was swollen by heavy rains or rapid thaws. The street was made about the year 1776. In 1794 Grimaldi lived here, and took in brother actors as lodgers. He removed to Penton Street in 1797. This wonderful clown was the son of a celebrated Genoese clown and dancer, who came to England in 1760, in the capacity of dentist to Queen Charlotte. He played at Drury Lane, under Garrick's management, and was generally known on the boards, from his great strength, as "Iron Legs." At one performance the agile comic dancer is said to have jumped so high that he actually broke a chandelier which hung over the side stage-door, and kicked one of the glass drops into the face of the Turkish ambassador, who was gravely sitting in a stage-box. Joe was born in 1778, in Stanhope Street, Clare Market, and his first appearance was at Sadler's Wells, in 1781, before he was three years old. Grimaldi's amusements, in his leisure time, were innocent enough; he was devoted to the breeding of pigeons and collecting of insects, which latter amusement he pursued with such success, as to form a cabinet containing no fewer than 4,000 specimens of butterflies, "collected," he says, "at the expense of a great deal of time, a great deal of money, and a great deal of vast and actual labour;" for all of which, no doubt, the entomologist will deem him sufficiently rewarded. He appears, in old age, to have entertained a peculiar relish for these pursuits, and would call to mind a part of Surrey where there was a very famous sort, and a part of Kent where there was another famous species. One of these was called the "Camberwell Beauty" (which, he adds, was very ugly); and another, the "Dartford Blue," by which Dartford Blue he seems to have set great store.

At a dreadful accident at Sadler's Wells, in 1807, during the run of *Mother Goose*, when twenty-three people were trodden to death, during a false alarm of fire, Grimaldi met with a singular adventure. On running back to the theatre that night he found the crowd of people collected round it so dense, as to render approach by the usual path impossible. " Filled with anxiety," says his " Memoirs," " and determined to ascertain the real state of the case, he ran round to the opposite bank of the New River, plunged in, swam across, and, finding the parlour window open and a light at the other end of the room, threw up the sash and jumped in, *à la* Harlequin. What was his horror, on looking round, to discover that there lay stretched in the apartment no fewer than nine dead bodies! Yes; there lay the remains of nine human beings, lifeless, and scarcely yet cold, whom a few hours back he had been himself exciting to shouts of laughter."

Grimaldi died in 1837. For many years he had been a nightly frequenter of the coffee-room of the " Marquis of Cornwallis" Tavern, in Southampton Street, Pentonville. Mr. George Cook, the proprietor, used to carry poor half-paralysed Joe out and home on his back.

King's Row, on the north side of Pentonville Road, was erected, says Mr. Pinks, prior to 1774. It formerly bore the odd name of " Happy Man's Row," from a public-house which bore the sign of the " Happy Man."

In Pentonville Road resided Mr. James Pascall, a much-respected public-spirited man, who laboured forty years for the interests of Clerkenwell parish, and helped to detect a fraudulent guardian named Scott, who defrauded the parish, in 1834, of more than £16,000. He also urged forward the covering up the noisome Fleet Ditch, and wrote a useful work on the Clerkenwell charity estates.

At No. 16, Winchester Place, now No. 61, Pentonville Road, lived for fifteen wretched years the celebrated miser, Thomas Cooke. This miserable wretch was the son of an itinerant fiddler near Windsor. Early in life he was a common porter, but by a stratagem obtained the hand of the rich widow of a paper-maker at Tottenham, and then bought a sugar-baker's business at Puddle Dock. Here his miserable life as a miser began. He would often feign fits near a respectable house, to obtain a glass of wine. His ink he begged at offices, and his paper he stole from the Bank counters. It is said that he collected with his own hands manure for his garden. His horse he kept in his kitchen, and his chaise he stored up in his bedroom. His one annual treat was the Epsom Races. Turned out of this house at last, Cooke betook himself to No. 85, White Lion Street, Pentonville, and died in 1811, aged eighty-six. He was buried at St. Mary's, Islington, the mob attending throwing cabbage-stalks on his dishonoured coffin. He

left (and here was his pride) £127,705 in the Three per Cents. chiefly to the Shoreditch and Tottenham Almshouses ; such is the inconsistency of human nature. In an old portrait Cooke is represented with an enormous broad-brimmed hat, a shade over his eyes, knee breeches, buckle shoes, an immense coat with a cape, while a stiff curled wig and huge cable pigtail completed the strange-looking figure.

St. James's Chapel, Pentonville, was first projected by Mr. Penton, in 1777, to benefit his estate ; but the incumbent of St. James's refusing to sign a bond to the Bishop of London for the regular payment of the minister, closed the matter for ten years. In 1787, however, a chapel was begun by subscription, and was opened in 1788. The first minister was Mr. Joel Abraham Knight, from the Spa Fields Chapel. The church trustees of St. James's purchased the chapel in 1789 for £5,000. Mr. Hurst, the architect of the chapel, who died in 1799, lies in a vault beneath the building. The chapel and cemetery were consecrated for the use of the Church of England in 1791.

" Mr. Francis Linley, organist of Pentonville Chapel," says Caulfield, in his " Portraits," " was blind from his birth. His greatest amusement was to explore churchyards, and with his fingers trace out memorials of the dead from tombstones ; indeed, the fineness of his touch would lead him to know a book from the lettering on the back of a volume ; and he could, without a guide, make his way throughout the bustling streets of London."

In 1789 Clerkenwell pickpockets had grown so daring, that one day, as the society of " Sols" were going into this chapel, a gentleman looking on had his pocket picked, and was knocked down, and the person who informed the gentleman he was robbed was also knocked down and dragged about the road by his hair, no one interfering, although hundreds of honest persons were present.

Pentonville Chapel is built chiefly of brick, with a stone façade. The building stands north and south, instead of east and west. The altar-piece, " The Raising of Jairus's Daughter," in West's feeble manner, was painted by Mr. John Frearson, an amateur artist. At the death of a Mr. Faulkner, in 1856, the Bishop of London ordered the church-wardens of Clerkenwell to sequestrate at once all the " fruits, tithes, profits, oblations, and obventions," for the benefit of the next incumbent, but the Rev. Dr. A. L. Courteney, the curate, claimed the profit, as having by the incumbent's death become perpetual curate of the district chapelry erected in 1854. The case, however, never came on for trial, as the trustees dreaded litigation.

In 1863 Dr. Courteney opened his new church at the corner of John Street. The incumbent of St. James's, Clerkenwell, presents to the living of St James's, Pentonville.

Prospect House, in Winchester Place, now Pentonville Road, was one of those old houses of half rural entertainment once common in this part of London. It derived its attractive name from the fine view it commanded northward—a great point with the Cockney holiday-maker. From Islington Hill, as the vicinity was called, there really was a fine *coup d'œil* of busy, moody London; and Canaletto sketched London from here, when he visited England. Prospect House is mentioned as early as 1669, and is noted in Morden and Lee's Survey and Map of 1700. The tavern was famous, like many other suburban taverns, for its bowling-greens. Subsequently it was re-christened from its proprietor, and was generally known as "Dobney's," or D'Aubigney's. In 1760 Mr. Johnson, a new landlord, turned the old bowling-green into a circus, and engaged one Price, from the "Three Hats," a rival house near, to exhibit feats of horsemanship, as he had done before the Royal Family. Price, the desultory man, eventually cleared £14,000 by his breakneck tricks. The time of performance was six p.m. In 1766, newspapers record, a bricklayer beat his wife to death, in a field near Dobney's, in presence of several frightened people. In 1770 Prospect House was taken for a school, but soon re-opened as the "Jubilee Tea Gardens." The interior of the bowers were painted with scenes from Shakespeare. It was the year of the Jubilee, remember. In 1772 an extraordinary man, a bee-tamer, named Wildman (perhaps from America), exhibited here. His advertisement ran—"Exhibition of Bees on Horseback.—June 20th, 1772. At the Jubilee Gardens, late Dobney's, this evening, and every evening until further notice (wet evenings excepted), the celebrated Mr. Daniel Wildman will exhibit several new and amazing experiments, never attempted by any man in this or any other kingdom before. He rides standing upright, one foot on the saddle and the other on the horse's neck, with a curious mask of bees on his head and face. He also rides standing upright on the saddle, with the bridle in his mouth, and, by firing a pistol, makes one part of the bees march over a table, and the other part swarm in the air, and return to their proper hive again. With other performances. The doors open at six, begins at a quarter before seven. Admittance in the boxes and gallery, two shillings; other seats, one shilling." This Wildman seems to have sold swarms of bees.

In 1774 the gardens were fast getting into the "sere and yellow leaf" that awaits, sooner or later, all such fools' paradises. A verse-writer in the *London Evening Post*, 1776, says—

"On Sabbath day who has not seen,
    In colours of the rainbow dizened,
The 'prentice beaux and belles, I ween,
    Fatigued with heat, with dust half poisoned,
To Dobney's strolling, or Pantheon,
    Their tea to sip, or else regale,
As on the way they shall agree on,
    With syllabubs or bottled ale?"

In 1780 the worn-out house became a lecture and discussion room; but about 1790 the ground was cleared, and Winchester Place built. The gardens, however, struggled on till 1810, when they disappeared, leaving as a slight memorial a mean court in Penton Street known as Dobney's Court. Until the building of Pentonville, says Mr. Pinks, the only carriage-way leading to Dobney's was one leading from High Street, Islington, under the gateway of the "White Lion," and from thence to the bowling-green.

The London Female Penitentiary, at No. 166, Pentonville Road, was formerly a convent school. This excellent charity, intended to save those whom vanity, idleness, and the treachery of man have led astray—poor creatures, against whom even woman hardens her heart—started here in 1807. The house was fitted for about thirty-five inmates, but was in a few years enlarged, so as to hold one hundred women. The path of penitence is up-hill everywhere, but especially in London. The inmates are trained for service, and their earnings at needlework and washing go far to maintain the institution. If the peace-makers were expressly blessed by our Saviour, how much more blessed must be those who step forward to rescue poor women like these who are willing to repent, but who are by poverty drifted irresistibly down the black river to the inevitable grave. The report, a few years ago, showed good results. There were 171 then in the house, thirty-one had been placed out in service, and eight reconciled to their friends. From 1807 to 1863 there were 1,401 poor women sent to service, 941 reconciled and restored to their friends, thirteen married, and forty-eight who have emigrated. Altogether in that time charity and kindness had been held out to 4,172 of the most miserable outcasts of the metropolis.

In 1834 a terrible and wholesale tragedy was enacted at No. 17, Southampton Street, by a German whip-maker named Steinberg. On a September night this wretch, from no known reason, but perhaps jealousy, murdered his mistress and her four children, the youngest a baby, and then cut his own throat. It was with difficulty the mob

SADLER'S WELLS IN 1756. (See page 293.)

was prevented from dragging the murderer's body through the streets. His victims were buried in St. James's Churchyard, and he himself in the paupers' burial-ground in Ray Street, the corpse being shaken out of the shell into a pit. No stake was driven through the body, as usual formerly with suicides, but one of the grave-diggers broke in the skull with an iron mallet. There was afterwards a shameful exhibition opened at Steinberg's house, a sham bloody knife being shown, and wax figures of the woman and her children placed in the various rooms, in the postures in which they had been found. The victims' clothes were bought for £25, and nearly £50 was taken for admission in one day. And yet this was not in the Ashantee country, but in civilised England, only a few years ago.

SADLER'S WELLS. (*From a View taken in* 1750.)

CHAPTER XXXVI.

SADLER'S WELLS.

Discovery of a Holy Well—Fashion patronises it—The Early Days of Sadler's Wells Theatre—A Fatal Panic—Sadler's Wells Visitors—A Grub Street Eulogy—Eighteenth Century Acrobats—Joe Grimaldi's Father—Dogs that Deserved a Good Name—Theatrical Celebrities at Sadler's Wells—Belzoni, the Patagonian Samson—"Hot Codlins"—Advent of T. P. Cooke—Samuel Phelps becomes Lessee of Sadler's Wells—The Original House of Correction—The "Sir Hugh Myddelton" Tavern—A Sadler's Wells Theatrical Company—Spencer's Breakfasting House —George Alexander Stevens' Lectures on Heads.

WHILE we treat of the places of amusement in the north of London near Islington, we must not forget Sadler's Wells (Islington Spa), or New Tunbridge Wells, as it used to be called. The chalybeate spring was discovered in 1683 by a Mr. Sadler, a surveyor of the highways, in a pleasant, retired, and well-wooded garden of a music-house he had just opened. The discovery was trumpeted in a pamphlet, detailing the virtues of the water. It was, the writer asserted, a holy well, famed, before the Reformation, for its healing power, which the priests attributed to their prayers. It had been, in consequence, looked on as a place venerated by superstition, but arched over at the Reformation, it had been since forgotten.

The Wells soon became famous with hypochondriacs. Burlesque poems (one probably by Ned Ward*) were written on the humours of the place,

---

* "Islington Wells; or, The Threepenny Academy, 1654."

as well as treatises on the cure of invalids by drinking the water ; and finally, in 1776, George Colman produced a farce, called *The Spleen; or, Islington Spa.*

In the summer of 1700 Sadler's Wells became in high favour with the public. Gout hobbled there ; Rheumatism groaned over his ferruginous water ; severe coughs went arm-in-arm, chuckling as they hobbled ; as for Hypochondria, he cracked jokes, he was in such high spirits at the thought of the new remedy. At this time dancers were admitted during the whole of the day on Mondays and Tuesdays, says Malcolm, provided they did not come in masks.

In 1733 the Wells were so fashionable that the Princesses Amelia and Caroline frequented the gardens in the June of that year daily, and drank the waters, the nobility coming in such numbers that the proprietor took above £30 a morning. Feathers flaunted, silks rustled, fans fluttered, and lovers sighed, partly with nausea and partly with love, as they sipped the bitter waters of Æsculapius. On the birthday of one of the princesses, the ladies were saluted as they passed through Spa Fields (then full of carriages) by a discharge of twenty-one guns—a compliment always paid to them on their arrival—and in the evening there was a great bonfire, and more powder was burnt in their honour. On ceasing to visit the gardens, the Princess Amelia presented the master with twenty-five guineas, each of the water-servers with three guineas, and the other attendants with one guinea each.

From 1683 till after 1811 these gardens were famous. Nervous, hypochondriac, hysteric affections, asthmas, indigestions, swellings, and eruptions, all took their doleful pleasure in them, and drank the waters with infinite belief. In 1811 the Wells were still frequented. The subscription for the water was a guinea the season ; to non-subscribers, and with capillaire, it cost sixpence a glass. The spring was then enclosed by an artificial grotto of flints and shells, which was entered by a rustic gate ; there was a lodging-house, to board invalids, and in the garden a breakfast-room, about forty feet long, with a small orchestra. In the room was hung up a comparative analysis of the water, and there were testimonials of its efficacy from gentlemen who had been ill for quarters of centuries, and had drunk all other mineral waters in vain.

On the bark of one of the trees (before 1811) were cut the two following lines : *—

" Obstructum recreat ; durum terit ; humidum siccat ;
 Debile fortificat—si tamen arte bibas."

—— * Nelson's "Islington," 1st edit., p. 212.

The following lines were written in a room of the lodging-house, just as a votive tablet might have been hung up on the walls of a Greek temple :—

" For three times ten years I travell'd the globe,
 Consulted whole tribes of the physical robe ;
 Drank the waters of Tunbridge, Bath, Harrogate, Dulwich,
 Spa, Epsom (and all by advice of the College) ;
 But in vain, till to Islington waters I came,
 To try if my cure would add to their fame.
 In less than six weeks they produc'd a belief
 This would be the place of my long-sought relief ;
 Before six weeks more had finished their course,
 Full of spirits and strength, I mounted my horse,
 Gave praise to my God, and rode cheerfully home,
 Overjoy'd with the thoughts of sweet hours to come.
 May Thou, great Jehovah give equal success
 To all who resort to this place for redress !"

Amusements resembling those of Vauxhall—music, fireworks, &c.—were resorted to at New Tunbridge Wells, in 1809-1810, but without much success.

On the death of Sadler, his music-house passed to Francis Forcer, whose son exhibited rope-dancing and tumbling till 1730, when he died.

The place was then taken by Mr. Rosoman, a builder, and the wooden house was, about the year 1765, replaced by a brick building. A painting, introducing Rosoman and some of his actors, was in 1811, to be seen in the bar of the " Sir Hugh Myddelton," the inn introduced by Hogarth in his print of " Evening," published in 1738. There was a club, at this time, at the " Sir Hugh Myddelton," of actors, who, in 1753, formed a regular company, at what had now become a theatre. The amusements here were originally in the open air, the tickets to spectators including refreshments. The *Connoisseur*, of 1756, notes the feats of activity exhibited here. After that time this suburban theatre became famous for burlettas, musical interludes, and pantomimes. Here Grimaldi cracked his drollest jokes, and here the celebrated Richer exhibited on the tight rope. The New River was also taken advantage of, and introduced into a tank the size of the stage, to represent more effectively naval victories and French defeats. After Rosoman, Mr. Thomas King, the comedian, and Mr. Wroughton, of Drury Lane, became proprietors ; and at one time Mr. Charles Dibdin, jun., was stage-manager.

A most fatal panic took place at this theatre on the 15th of October, 1807. The cry, " A fight !" was mistaken for " A fire !" and a rush took place from the gallery. The manager, shouting to the people through speaking-trumpets, entreated them to keep their seats ; but in vain, for many threw themselves down into the pit, and eighteen were crushed to death on the gallery stairs. The proceeds of two benefits were divided among the children and widows of the sufferers.

Sadler's Musical House, which, tradition affirms, was a place of public entertainment even as early as the reign of Elizabeth, seems early to have affected a theatrical air. In May, 1698, we find a vocal and instrumental concert advertised here, the instrumental part being "composed of violins, hautboys, trumpets, and kettle-drums." It was to continue from ten to one, every Monday and Thursday, during the drinking of the waters. In 1699 the Wells were called "Miles's Music House;" and in that year Ned Ward, always coarse and always lively, describes going with a crowd of Inns of Court beaux to see a wretch, disguised in a fool's cap, and with a smutty face like a hangman, eat a live fowl, feathers and all.

"The state of things described by Ned Ward," says Mr. Pinks, "is abundantly confirmed by the reminiscences of Edward Macklin, the actor, who remembered the time when the admission here was but threepence, except to a few places scuttled off at the sides of the stage at sixpence, which were reserved for people of fashion, who occasionally came to see the fun. 'Here we smoked and drank porter and rum-and-water, as much as we could pay for.' Of the audience Macklin says, 'Though we had a mixture of very odd company, there was little or no rioting; there was a public then that kept one another in awe.'"

Ned Ward, who was a quick observer, describes the dress-circle gallery here as painted with stories of Apollo and Daphne, Jupiter and Europa, &c. In his poem, "A Walk to Islington," Ned Ward is not complimentary to the Sadler's Wells visitors. In the pit, he says, were butchers, bailiffs, housebreakers, footpads, prizefighters, thief-takers, deerstealers, and bullies, who drank, and smoked, and lied, and swore. They ate cheesecakes and drank ale, and one of the buffoons was also a waiter. The female vocalist was followed by a fiddler in scarlet. Then came a child, who danced a sword-dance, and after her

> "A young babe of grace,
> With mercury in his heels, and a gallows in his face;
> In dancing a jig lies the chief of whose graces,
> And making strange music-house, monkey-like faces."

About 1711 the Wells seems to have become still more disreputable, and in 1712 a lieutenant of the navy was run through the body there by a Mr. French, of the Temple, in a drunken quarrel.

Macklin says there were four or five exhibitions in a day, and that the duration of each performance depended upon circumstances. The proprietors had always a fellow outside to calculate how many persons were collected for a second exhibition, and when he thought there were enough, he came to the back of the upper seats and cried out, "Is Hiram Fisteman here?" This was a cant word between the parties, to know the state of the people without, upon which they concluded the entertainment, and dismissed the audience with a song, and prepared for a second representation.

In a poem called "The New River," written about 1725, by William Garbott, the author thus describes the Wells, with advertising enthusiasm:—

> "There you may sit under the shady trees,
> And drink and smoak fann'd by a gentle breeze;
> Behold the fish, how wantonly they play,
> And catch them also, if you please, you may."

Forcer, a barrister, the proprietor in the early part of the eighteenth century, improved the pantomimes, rope-dancing, and ladder-dancing, tumbling, and musical interludes. Acrobats threw summersaults from the upper gallery, and Black Scaramouch struggled with Harlequin on the stage. The old well was accidentally discovered in Macklin's time, between the New River and the stage-door. It was encircled with stone, and you descended to it by several steps. Cromwell, writing in 1828, says that it was known that springs existed under the orchestra, and under the stage, and that the old fountain of health might hopefully be sought for there. In 1738, in his "Evening," not one of his most successful works, Hogarth introduced a bourgeois holiday-maker and his wife, with Sadler's Wells in the background. In "The Gentlemen's and Ladies' Social Companion," a book of songs published in 1745-6, we find a song on Sadler's Wells, which contained several characteristic verses. Rope-dancing and harlequinade, with scenery, feats of strength, and singing, seem to have been the usual entertainment about this period. In 1744 the place was presented by the grand jury of the county as a scene of great extravagance, luxurious idleness, and ill-fame, but it led to no good results. In 1746 any person was admitted to the Wells, "and the diversions of the place," on taking a ticket for a pint of wine. This same year a ballet on the Battle of Culloden, a most undanceable subject, one would think, was very popular; and Hogarth's terrible "Harlot's Progress" was turned into a drama, with songs, by Lampe.

The Grub Street poets, in the meantime, belauded the Wells, not without reward, and not always inelegantly, as the following verses show:—

> "Ye cheerful souls, who would regale
> On honest home-brewed British ale,
> To Sadler's Wells in troops repair,
> And find the wished-for cordial there;

Strength, colour, elegance of taste,
Combine to bless the rich repast ;
And I assure ye, to my knowledge,
'T has been approved by all the Colledge,
More efficacious and prevailing
Than all the recipes of Galen.
Words scarce are able to disclose
The various blessings it bestows.
It helps the younger sort to think,
And wit flows faster as they drink ;
It puts the ancient a new fleece on,
Just as Medea did to Eson ;
The fair with bloom it does adorn,
Fragrant and fresh as April morn.
Haste hither, then, and take your fill,
Let parsons say whatever they will ;
The ale that every ale excels
Is only found at Sadler's Wells."

A writer in the *Connoisseur* of 1756 praises a dexterous performer at the Wells, who, with bells on his feet, head, and hands, jangled out a variety of tunes, by dint of various nods and jerks. The same year a wonderful balancer named Maddox performed on the slack wire, tossing balls, and kicking straws into a wine-glass which he held in his mouth. Maddox, the equilibrist, entertained the public for several seasons by his "balances on the wire," and his fame was celebrated by a song set to music, entitled "Balance a Straw," which for a time was very popular. A similar feat was afterwards performed at the Wells by a Dutchman, with a peacock's feather, which he blew into the air and caught as it fell, on different parts of a wire, at the same time preserving his due equilibrium. The same performer used to balance a wheel upon his shoulder, his forehead, and his chin, and afterwards, to show his skill as an equilibrist, he poised two wheels, with a boy standing on one of them.

The road home from the Wells seems to have been peculiarly dangerous about 1757, as the manager announces in the *Public Advertiser* that on the night of a certain charitable performance a horse-patrol would be sent by Mr. Fielding (the blind magistrate, and kinsman of the novelist) for the protection of nobility and gentry who came from the squares. The road to the City was, as he promised, also to be properly guarded. A year later an armed patrol was advertised as stationed on the New Road, between Sadler's Wells and Grosvenor Square. Foote wrote, about the same time :—

" If at Sadler's Wells the wine should be thick,
   The cheesecakes be sour, or Miss Wilkinson sick ;
If the fumes of the pipes should prove powerful in June,
Or the tumblers be lame, or the bells out of tune,
We hope that you'll call at our warehouse at Drury,
We've a good assortment of goods, I assure you."

In 1765 the old wooden theatre at the Wells was pulled down and a new one built, at an expense of £4,225. A three-shilling ticket for the boxes, in 1773, entitled the bearer to a pint of port, mountain, Lisbon, or punch. A second pint cost one shilling.

In 1763 Signor Grimaldi, Joe Grimaldi's father, first appeared as chief dancer and ballet-master. He continued there till the close of 1767. In 1775 James Byrne, the famous harlequin of Drury Lane, and the father of Oscar Byrne, was employed at Sadler's Wells as a dancer, and a Signor Rossignol gave imitations of birds, like Herr Joel, and accompanied the orchestra on a fiddle without strings. About this time, too, Charles Dibdin the elder wrote some clever and fanciful pieces for this theatre, entitled " Intelligence from Sadler's Wells."

In 1772 Rosomon surrendered the management to King, the famous comedian, who held it till 1782, when Sheridan gave him up the sovereignty of Drury Lane. King had been an attorney, but had thrown up his parchments to join theatres and play under Garrick. He excelled in *Sir Peter Teazle, Lord Ogleby, Puff*, and *Dr. Cantwell*. His *Touchstone* and *Ranger*, says Dr. Doran, were only equalled by Garrick and Elliston. He was arch, easy, and versatile, and the last time he played *Sir Peter*, in 1802, the fascinating Mrs. Jordan was the young wife. King remained an inveterate gambler to the last, in spite of Garrick's urgent entreaties. King sold the Wells, says Mr. Pinks, for £12,000. Joe Grimaldi appeared at Sadler's Wells first in 1781, in the character of a monkey. In 1783 egg-dancers and performing dogs were the rage, the dogs alone clearing for the managers, in one season, £10,000. The saying at the theatre at that time was, that if the dogs had not come to the theatre, the theatre must have gone to the dogs. Horse-patrols still paraded the roads to the City at night.

In 1786 Miss Romanzini (afterwards the celebrated ballad vocalist, Mrs. Bland) appeared at the Wells, and also Pietro Bologna, father of the celebrated clown, Jack Bologna. In 1788 Braham, then a boy, who had first appeared in 1787, at the Royalty Theatre, Wells Street, near Goodman's Fields, made his first appearance at the Wells. " Two Frenchmen," says Mr. Pinks, " named Duranie and Bois-Maison, as pantomimists, eclipsed all their predecessors on that stage. Boyce, a distinguished engraver, was the harlequin, and, from all accounts, was the most finished actor of the motley hero, either in his own day or since. On the benefit-night of Joseph Dortor, clown to the rope, and Richer, the rope-dancer, Miss Richer made her first appearance on two slack wires, passing through a hoop, with a pyramid of glasses on her head, and Master Richer performed on the tight rope, with a skipping-rope. Joseph Dortor, among other almost incredible feats, drank a glass of wine backwards from the stage floor, beating a drum at the same time. Lawrence threw a somersault over twelve men's heads, and Paul Redigé, the 'Little Devil,' on October 1st, threw a somersault over two men on horseback, the riders having each a lighted candle on his head. Dubois, as clown, had no superior in his time, and the troop of voltigeurs were pre-eminent for their agility, skill, and daring."

After Wroughton's time, Mr. Siddons (husband of the great actress) became one of the proprietors of the Wells, where, in 1801, a young tragedian, Master Carey, the "Pupil of Nature," otherwise known as Edmund Kean, recited Rollo's speech from *Pizarro*. His great-grandfather, Henry Carey, the illegitimate son of the Marquis of Halifax, and the author of the delightful ballad, "Sally in our Alley," had written and composed many of the ballad operas and ballad farces which were very successful at Sadler's Wells.

In 1802, Charles Dibdin, jun., and Thomas Dibdin, his brother, were busy at the Wells.

In 1803 appeared Signor Belzoni, afterwards the great Egyptian traveller, as the "Patagonian Samson," in which character, says Mr. Pinks, "he performed prodigious feats of strength, one of which was to adjust an iron frame to his body, weighing 127 lbs., on which he carried eleven persons. The frame had steps or branches projecting from its sides, on which he placed eleven men in a pyramidical form, the uppermost of whom reached to the border of the proscenium. With this immense weight he walked round the stage, to the astonishment and delight of his audience. On one occasion a serio-comic accident occurred, which might have proved fatal not only to the mighty Hercules, but also to his pyramidical group. As he was walking round the stage with the vast load attached to his body, the floor gave way, and plunged him and his companions into the water beneath. A group of assistants soon came to the rescue, and the whole party marched to the front of the stage, made their bows, and retired. On Belzoni's benefit-night he attempted to carry thirteen men, but as that number could not hold on, it was abandoned. His stature, as registered in the books of the Alien Office, was six feet six inches. He was of good figure, gentlemanly manners, and great mind. He was an Italian by birth, but early in life he quitted his native land to seek his fortune."

In 1804 Sadler's Wells first began to assume the character of an aquatic theatre. An immense tank was constructed under the stage, and a communication opened with the New River. The first aquatic piece was a *Siege of Gibraltar*, in which real vessels bombarded the fortress. A variety of pieces were subsequently produced, concluding with a grand scene for the *finale*, on "real water." Thomas Greenwood, a scene-painter at the Wells, thus records the water successes in his "Rhyming Reminiscences :"—

> "Attraction was needed the town to engage,
>   So Dick emptied the river that year on the stage;
>   The house overflowed, and became quite the *ton*,
>   And the Wells for some seasons went swimmingly on."

"Among the apparently perilous and appalling incidents exhibited," says a writer to whom we have already been much indebted, "were those of a female falling from the rocks into the water, and being rescued by her hero-lover; a naval battle, with sailors escaping by plunging into the sea from a vessel on fire; and a child thrown into the water by a nurse, who was bribed to drown it, being rescued by a Newfoundland dog."

In 1819 Grimaldi sang for the first time his immortal song of "Hot Codlins," the very night a boy was crushed to death in the rush at entering. "Sadler's Wells was let at Easter, 1821, for the ensuing three seasons, to Mr. Egerton, of Covent Garden Theatre; in which year it was honoured by the presence of Queen Caroline, the wife of George IV., and her Majesty's box and its appointments were exhibited daily to the public for a week afterwards. In 1822, in a piece called *Tom and Jerry*, pony races were introduced, a course having been formed by laying a platform on the stage and pit. Upon the expiration of Egerton's term the Wells were let to Mr. Williams, of the Surrey Theatre, the son of the proprietor of the once-famous boiled beef house in the Old Bailey. He employed one half of his company, in the earlier part of the evening, at Sadler's Wells, and thence transferred them to the Surrey, to finish there; and at that theatre he adopted the same course, the performers being conveyed between the two houses by special carriages. Williams's speculation, however, turned out a complete failure."

In 1823 the use of water for scenic purposes was discontinued for a time at Sadler's Wells, and in 1825 the old manager's house, next the New River Head, was turned into wine-rooms and a saloon; the season, in consequence of the immense growth of the neighbourhood, was extended from six to twelve months, and Tom Dibdin was engaged as acting manager. The year 1826 being very hot, the manager got up some pony-races in the grounds, which drew large audiences. On

March 17, 1828, Grimaldi took his farewell benefit at Sadler's Wells.

Subsequently Mr. T. Dibdin became manager at the Wells, and produced a variety of ballets, pantomimes, burlettas, and melodramas. In 1832 that best of all stage sailors, Mr. T. P. Cooke, made his first appearance at this theatre as William, in *Black-Eyed Susan*, a piece which ran one

At the west end of a paved avenue on the south side of Sadler's Wells Theatre, on the opposite side of the now buried New River, just where a row of lofty poplars once fringed the left bank, stands the "Sir Hugh Myddelton" Tavern, erected in 1831, on the site of the "Myddelton's Head," which was built as early as 1614. This was the favourite house for the actors and authors of the Wells, and

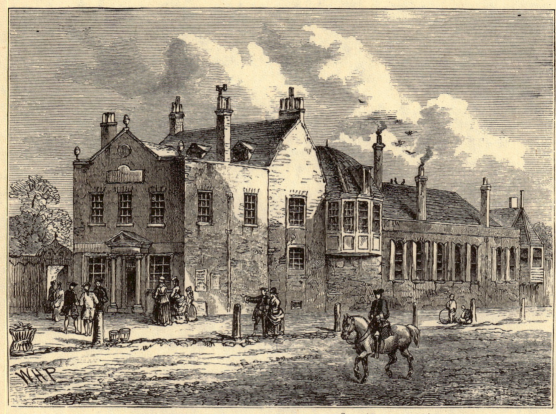

THE EXTERIOR OF BAGNIGGE WELLS IN 1780. (*See page* 296.)

hundred nights. In 1833, during a serio-romantic lyric drama called *The Island*, and founded on the mutiny of the *Bounty*, the stage and its scenery was drawn up bodily to the roof of the house, to avoid the tediousness of a "wait." The *Russian Mountains* were also a great success.

But a great epoch was now about to commence. In 1844 Mr. Samuel Phelps appeared, aided by Mrs. Warner. In 1846 Mr. Phelps resolved to produce all Shakespeare's plays, and actually did represent thirty of them. These thirty, under Mr. Phelps's management, occupied about 4,000 nights, *Hamlet* alone running for 400.

Having been closed for some years, the theatre was rebuilt, and opened in 1879 by Miss Bateman.

here sturdy Macklin, the best of Shylocks, Rosoman, the manager, Dibdin, and Grimaldi used to fill their churchwarden's pipes, and merrily stir their glasses. In Hogarth's "Evening," published in 1738, we have a glimpse of the old signboard, and of a gable end and primitive weather-boarding, against which a vine spreads itself, and displays its clustering fruit. At an open window honest citizens are carousing, while the fat and sour City dame, of by no means unimpeachable virtue, as the painter implies, is pettishly fanning herself, attended by her obsequious Jerry Sneak of a husband, who toils along, carrying the ugly baby. Malcolm, in 1803, describes the tavern as facing the river, which was "adorned with tall poplars, graceful willows, and sloping banks and flowers." In the bar of the "Sir Hugh Myddelton" is a curious old picture of Manager Rosoman, surrounded by his select friends and members of his company; and of this picture Mr. Mark Lonsdale, a once manager of the theatre, drew up the following account:—

"The portrait of Mr. Rosoman, the then manager of Sadler's Wells, forms the centre. Then proceeding to the gentleman on his left hand, and so round the table as they sit. The seven gentlemen who are standing up are taken the last, beginning in Cow Cross. The name of the next gentleman, who is pointing his finger to his nose, is forgotten; he was a dancer at Sadler's Wells, and went by an unpleasant nickname, from the circumstance of his nose being much troubled with warts. The gentleman at his right hand, having his hand upon the neck of a bottle, is Mr. Smith, a well-known carcase butcher in Cow Cross. The next, who has his fingers upon a glass of wine, is Mr. Ripley, of Red Lion Street. Mr. Cracraft, a barber in the

COLDBATH HOUSE. *From a View published in* 1811. (*See page* 299.)

with Mr. Maddox, the wire-dancer, and so on, with the remaining six in the order they stand. The gentleman with one hand upon the pug-dog is Mr. Rosoman, manager of Sadler's Wells. On his left hand is Mr. Justice Keeling, a brewer. Mr. Romaine, a pipe-maker, is distinguished by his having a handful of pipes, and is in the act of delivering one to Mr. Justice Keeling. Mr. Copeland, the tobacconist, is also distinguished by his having a paper of tobacco in his hand, on which is written 'Copeland's best Virginia.' The gentleman with his hand upon the greyhound is Mr. Angier, a carver in Long Acre; on his left is Mr. Cowland, a butcher in Fleet Street. At Mr. Cowland's right hand is Mr. Seabrook, a glazier same street, sits at his right hand, and is filling his pipe out of a paper of tobacco. At his right hand is Mr. Holtham, scene-painter at Sadler's Wells. The gentleman who sits higher than the rest of the company, and who is in the attitude of singing, having a bottle under his arm, is Mr. Ranson, a tailor at Sadler's Wells, known by the name of Tailor Dick. Mr. Bass, a plasterer in Cow Cross, sits at his right hand, and is in the attitude of putting a punch ladle into the bowl. At his right hand Mr. Chalkill, a poulterer in Whitecross Street. At Mr. Chalkill's right hand is Mr. Norris, a salesman in the sheep-skin market. When he died he left £2,000 in hard cash in his chest. At his right hand is Mr. Davis, a walksman at the New River

Head. The name of the gentleman at Mr. Davis's right hand is forgotten. Mr. George, a tallow-chandler in Islington, sits at the right hand of the unknown gentleman. He married the late Alderman Hart's mother. The gentleman next to him is Mr. Davenport, ballet master at Sadler's Wells, and was master to Charles Matthews. Next to him is Mr. Greenwood, painter, father of the scene-painter. The gentleman at Mr. Rosoman's right hand is Mr. Hough, his partner. The gentleman in a blue and gold theatrical dress, with one hand upon Mr. Davis's shoulder, is Mr. Maddox, the wire-dancer, who was drowned. The one standing by in a cocked hat is Mr. Thomas Banks, a carver and arts' master in Bridewall ; also harlequin and clown at Sadler's Wells. Billy Williams, a tumbler, is standing between Tailor Dick and Mr. Bass. Peter Garman, a rope-dancer and tumbler at Sadler's Wells, is between Mr. Holtman and Tailor Dick, and is in the attitude of blowing the smoke from his pipe into Tailor Dick's face. The next standing figure is Mr. John Collier, a watch finisher in Red Lion Street. A cheesemonger (name forgot) is at the left hand. Mr. Talmash, vestry clerk of St. James's, Clerkenwell (a mighty great man in Red Lion Street), is at the back of the chair of the gentleman before-mentioned with the vulgar nick-name."

In the days when clover grew round Islington, and the cows of that region waded knee-deep in golden buttercups—when the skylark could be heard in Pentonville, the Cockney pedestrian, after his early summer walk, expected to fall upon a good honest breakfast at some such suburban tavern as the "Sir Hugh Myddelton." About 1745,

Spencer's Breakfasting House, a mere hut with benches outside, at the end of Myddelton Place, supplied this want—tea at threepence per head, and coffee at three halfpence per dish, fine Hyson tea at sixpence per head, "a cat with two legs, to be seen gratis." On Sunday mornings Spencer's hut was filled with 'prentices and their sweethearts. The house had a cow-lair and a wooden fence that almost surrounded it. Here, in July, 1765, the celebrated mimic and adventurer, George Alexander Stevens, delivered his "Lectures on Heads," which the celebrated comedians of the day attempted in vain to rival. In the *Public Advertiser*, July 24th, 1765, is the following advertisement :—

"This evening, and every evening during the summer season, at the Long Room opposite to Sadler's Wells, will be delivered the celebrated 'Lectures on Heads,' by Mr. Geo. Alex. Stevens.

"Part I. Introduction :—Alexander the Great—Cherokee Chief — Quack Doctor — Cuckold — Lawyer, humourous Oration in Praise of the Law, Daniel against Dishclout—Horse Jockeys—Nobody's, Somebody's, Anybody's, and Everybody's Coats of Arms—Family of Nobody—Architecture — Painting — Poetry — Astronomy — Music—Statues of Honesty and Flattery.

"Part II. Ladies' Heads—Riding Hood—Ranelagh Hood—Billingsgate—Laughing and Crying Philosophers—Venus's Girdle—Cleopatra—French Nightcap—Face Painting—Old Maid—Young Married Lady—Old Batchelor—Lass of the Spirit—Quaker—Two Hats Contrasted—Spitalfields Weaver.

"Part III. Physical Wig—Dissertation on Sneezing and Snuff-taking—Life of a Blood—Woman of the Town—Tea-table Critic—Learned Critic—City Politician, humourously described—Gambler's Three Faces—Gambler's Funeral and Monument—Life and Death of a Wit—Head of a well-known Methodist Parson, with Tabernacle Harangue.

"The doors to be opened at five, begin exactly at six. Front seats, 1s. 6d.; Back seats 1s."

CHAPTER XXXVII.

BAGNIGGE WELLS.

Nell Gwynne at Bagnigge Wells—Bagnigge House—"Black Mary's Hole"—The Royal Bagnigge Wells—"The 'Prentice to his Mistress"—"A Bagnigge Well's Scene."—Mr. Deputy Dumpling—Curious Print of Bagnigge Wells.

BAGNIGGE WELLS HOUSE was originally the summer residence of Nell Gwynne. Here, near the Fleet and amid fields, she entertained Charles and his saturnine brother with concerts and merry break-fasts, in the careless Bohemian way in which the noble specimen of divine right delighted. The ground where the house stood was then called Bagnigge Vale.

Bagnigge House, "near the 'Pindar of Wake-field,'" became a place of entertainment for rus-

ticating Londoners as early as 1680. It stood on the site of the present Phœnix Brewery. The garden entrance was a little south-west of the Clerkenwell Police Court. The gate and an inscription remained in Coppice Row, on the left, going from Clerkenwell towards the New Road, as late as 1847. In the memory of man the garden still possessed fruit-trees ; and at the north side stood a picturesque gable-ended house, the front luxuriously covered with vines. At the back stood a small brewery. The "Pinder of Wake-field" was an old public-house in the Gray's Inn Road, near Chad's Well, formerly much frequented by the wagoners of the great north road. The Pinder of Wakefield was a jolly Yorkshireman, it will be remembered, who once thrashed Robin Hood himself.

About 1760 Bagnigge House became famous, from the discovery in the garden of two mineral springs. Dr. Bevis, who wrote a pamphlet on Bag-nigge Wells, describes them as near Coppice Row and Spa Fields, and about a quarter of a mile from Battle Bridge Turnpike, and the great new road from Paddington to Islington, and near a footpath which led from Southampton Row and Russell Square to Pentonville. The doctor also mentions that over one of the chimney-pieces was the garter of St. George, the Royal arms, and a bust of "Eleanor Gwynne, a favourite of Charles II.'s." Cromwell says that a black woman named Woolaston lived near one of the fountains, and sold the water, and that, therefore, it was called "Black Mary's Hole." The spring was situated, says Mr. Pinks, in the garden of No. 3, Spring Place. Close by there used to be a low public-house called "The Fox at Bay," a resort, about 1730, of footpads and highwaymen.

In the "Shrubs of Parnassus," poems on several occasions, by W. Woty, otherwise "John Copywell," published in 1760, there are some lines entitled "Bagnigge Wells," wherein the following allusion is made to these springs :—

> ` . . . . . . "And stil'd the place
> Black Mary's Hole—there stands a dome superb,
> Hight Bagnigge ; where from our forefathers hid,
> Long have two springs in dull stagnation slept ;
> But taught at length by subtle art to flow,
> They rise, forth from oblivion's bed they rise,
> And manifest their virtues to mankind."

In the *Daily Advertisement* for July, 1775, we find the following :—

"The Royal Bagnigge Wells, between the Foundling Hospital and Islington.—Mr. Davis, the proprietor, takes this method to inform the publick, that both the chalybeate and purging waters are in the greatest perfection ever known, and may be drank at 3d. each person, or delivered at the pump-room at 8d. per gallon. They are recommended by the most eminent physicians for various disorders, as specified in the handbills. Likewise in a treatise written on those waters by the late Dr. Bevis, dedicated to the Royal Society, and may be had at the bar, price 1s., where ladies and gentlemen may depend upon having the best tea, coffee, hot loaves, &c."

The prologue to Colman's *Bon Ton*, published in 1775, notices Bagnigge Wells as a place of low fashion :—

> "Ah, I loves life and all the joy it yields,
> Says Madam Fupock, warm from Spittlefields,

> Bon Ton's the space 'twixt Saturday and Monday,
> And riding in a one-horse chair on Sunday,
> 'Tis drinking tea on summer's afternoons
> At Bagnigge Wells, with china and gilt spoons."

In the opening lines of a satirical poem, attributed to Churchill, entitled "Bagnigge Wells," published in 1779, the kind of persons then resorting to the gardens are described :—

> "Thy arbours, Bagnigge, and the gay alcove
> Where the frail nymphs in amourous dalliance rove ;
> Where 'prenticed youths enjoy the Sunday feast,
> And City matrons boast their Sabbath rest ;
> Where unfledged Templars first as fops parade,
> And new-made ensigns sport their first cockade."

"In later days," says Mr. Pinks, "Miss Edge-worth, in one of her tales, alludes to this place as one of vulgar resort :—

> "The City to Bagnigge Wells repair,
> To swallow dust, and call it air."

We have seen an old engraving of Bagnigge Wells Gardens, bearing the following inscription :—

"Frontispiece—A view taken from the centre bridge in the gardens of Bagnigge Wells. Published as the Act directs."

We do not know whether the engraving appeared in a magazine or in a book giving an account of the gardens. The "centre bridge" was, we think, the one crossing the Fleet. The engraving represents on the left a round, railed pond, in the middle of which is the figure of a boy clasping a swan, from the mouth of which issue six jets of water. Round the garden are plain-looking wooden drinking bowers or boxes ; and on the right are trees with tall stems and closely-cut for-mal foliage at the top ; and also two large figures representing a pastoral-looking man with a scythe, and a pastoral-looking woman with a hay-rake in one hand and a bird's nest in the other.

In the old song of "The 'Prentice to his Mis-tress" are the following lines :—

"Come, prithee make it up, miss, and be as lovers be,
We'll go to Bagnigge Wells, miss, and there we'll have some tea ;
It's there you'll see the ladybirds perch'd on the stinging nettles,
The chrystal water fountain, and the copper shining kettles,
It's there you'll see the fishes, more curious they than whales,
And they're made of gold and silver, miss, and wags their little tails,
O ! they wags their little tails, they wags their little tails,
O ! they're made of gold and silver, miss, and they wags their little tails.
O dear ! O la ! O dear ! O la ! O dear ! O la ! how funny !"

Another engraving, published by the famous print-seller, Carrington Bowles, of St. Paul's Church-yard, represents "A Bagnigge Wells Scene ; or, No Resisting Temptation." The scene is laid in the gardens, close by the boy and swan fountain ; and a young lady, in an elaborate old-fashioned head-dress, and a gaily-trimmed petticoat and long skirt, is plucking a rose from one of the flower-beds, while another damsel of corresponding elegance looks on.

A mezzotint, also published by Bowles, in 1772, shows "The Bread and Butter Manufactory; or, the Humours of Bagnigge Wells." This plate, which is in size fourteen inches by ten, and repre-sents several parties of anciently-dressed ladies and gentlemen, and a boy-waiter with a tray of cups and saucers, was hung up, framed and glazed, in the bar of Old Bagnigge Wells House.

Another engraving, issued by the same publisher, shows "Mr. Deputy Dumpling and Family, enjoy-ing a Summer Afternoon." One of the lower pro-jecting windows of "Bagnigge Wells" Tavern, with the western side-entrance to the gardens, is repre-sented. Over the gate, on a board, are the words "Bagnigge Wells." Mr. Deputy Dumpling is a very short, fat man, wearing a wig, perspiring freely, and carrying a child. His wife, who is also short and fat, is walking behind him, with an open fan

and his walking-stick. Beside them is a boy, dragging a perambulator of the period, in which is a girl with a doll.

In 1772, a curious aquatinta print of Bagnigge Wells, from a painting by Saunders, was pub-lished by J. R. Smith. It represents the interior of the long room, filled with a gay and numerous company, attired in the fashion of the period. Some are promenading, others are seated at tables partaking of tea. The room is lighted by brazen sconces of wax lights, hanging from the ceiling, and the organ is visible at the distant end. The artist has, after the manner of Hogarth, well de-picted the humours of the motley company who are quizzing one another, and being ogled in turn. The prominent feature of the sketch is a richly-bedizened madam on the arm of a gallant, who is receiving a polite salute from an officer, by whom she is recognised, at which her companion seems to be somewhat chagrined.

In 1813, Bagnigge Wells boasted a central temple, a grotto stuck with sea-shells, &c. It ceased to be a place of amusement many years ago.

CHAPTER XXXVIII.

COLDBATH FIELDS AND SPA FIELDS.

Coldbath Field's Prison—Thistlewood and his Co-conspirators there—John Hunt there—Mr. Hepworth Dixon's Account of Coldbath Fields Prison—The Cold Bath—Budgell, the Author—An Eccentric Centenarian's Street Dress—Spa Fields—Rude Sports—Gooseberry Fair—An Ox Roasted whole—Ducking-pond Fields—Clerkenwell Fields—Spa Fields—Pipe Fields—Spa Fields Chapel—The Countess of Huntingdon—Great Bath Street, Coldbath Fields—Topham, the Strong Man—Swedenborg—Spa Fields Burial-ground—Crawford's Passage, or Pickled Egg Walk.

THE original House of Correction here was built in the reign of James I., the City Bridewell being then no longer large enough to hold the teeming vagabonds of London.

The oldest portion of the Coldbath Fields Prison now standing was built on a swamp, in 1794, at an expense of £65,650, and large additions have from time to time been made. For a long time after it was rebuilt, Coldbath Fields had a reputa-tion for severity. In 1799 Gilbert Wakefield, the classic, expressed a morbid horror of it; and Coleridge and Southey, many years later, in "The Devil's Walk," published their opinion that it ex-ceeded hell itself, as a place of punishment:—

"As he went through Coldbath Fields he saw
  A solitary cell;
And the Devil was pleased, for it gave him a hint
  For improving his prisons in hell."

In 1820 Thistlewood and the other Cato Street conspirators were lodged here, before being sent to

the Tower. At present the prison has proper ac-commodation for about 1,250 prisoners, though many more are sometimes thrust into it, causing great confusion.

The prison, built on a plan of the benevolent Howard's, soon became a scene of great abuses. Men, women, and boys were herded together in this chief county prison, and smoking and drink-ing were permitted. The governor of the day strove vigorously to reform the hydra abuses, and especially the tyranny and greediness of the turn-keys. Five years later he introduced stern silence into his domain. "On the 29th of December, 1834, a population of 914 prisoners were suddenly apprised that all intercommunication, by word, gesture, or sign, was prohibited." "This is what is called the Silent Associated System. The tread-mill had been introduced at Coldbath Fields several years before. This apparatus, the inven-tion of Mr. Cubitt, an engineer at Lowestoft, was first set up," says Mr. Pinks, "at Brixton Prison, in 1817. At first, the allowance was 12,000 feet of ascent, but was soon reduced to 1,200."

This desolate prison has made a solitude of the immediate neighbourhood, but not far off brass-founders, grocers' canister makers, and such like abound.

The dismal Bastille has frequently been enlarged. In 1830 a vagrants' ward for 150 prisoners was added, and shortly afterwards a female ward for 300 inmates. Coldbath Fields is now devoted to male prisoners alone, the females having been removed from it to Westminster Prison in 1850. The tread-mill finds labour for 160 prisoners at a time, and grinds flour. The ordinary annual charge for each prisoner is estimated at £21 19s. 4d. The Report of the Inspector of Prisons for 1861 speaks of the Coldbath Fields cells as too crowded and badly ventilated, the prisoners being sometimes 700 or 800 in excess of the number of cells, and sleeping either in hammocks slung too close together in dormitories, or, still worse, on the floors of work-shops, only a short time before emptied of the working inmates.

John Hunt, Leigh Hunt's brother, was im-prisoned here for a libel, in the *Examiner*, on the Prince Regent, the "fat Adonis," afterwards George IV. Mr. Cyrus Redding, Campbell's friend, used to come and chat and play chess with him. He had a lofty and comfortable, though small apartment at the top of the prison. Townsend, the old Bow Street runner, the terror of highway-men, was the governor at the time. Hunt had the privilege from the kind, shrewd old officer, of walk-ing for a couple of hours daily in the governor's gardens.

"Leaving the oakum room," says Mr. H. Dixon, writing about this prison in 1850, "we enter the body of the original building. It consists of four long galleries, forming a parallelogram by their junction, on the sides of which are ranged the cells. If the system on which the prison is ostensibly conducted were rigorously carried out, all the prisoners would be separated at night; but the number of separate cells is only 550, while the inmates often amount to upwards of 1,300. The surplus is, therefore, to be provided for in general dormitories, in which officers are obliged to remain all night to prevent intercourse or disorder. . . . .

"It is in the midst of passions like these, seething in the hearts of 1,200 criminals, not separately con-fined as at Pentonville, that the administration of this vast prison has to be conducted. The official staff consists of the governor, 2 chaplains, 1 surgeon, 3 trade instructors, and 134 assistant officers; in all 141 persons: a corps rather too small than too large, considering the nature of the duties devolving upon it. Without system, or without a system rigorously administered, it would be impossible to maintain order in such a place, unless each indi-vidual was kept under lock and key, as in the neighbouring House of Detention. . . . . . .

"Passing through an inner gate to the left, we come upon a yard in which we find a number of prisoners taking walking exercise, marching in regular order and perfect *silence*. All of these are habited in the prison uniform, a good warm dress of coarse woollen cloth; the misdemeanants in blue, the felons in dark grey. Each prisoner wears a large number on his back, which number con-stitutes his prison name and designation, proper names not being used in this gaol. Every kind of personality that can possibly be sunk is sunk. The subordinate officers of the prison seldom know anything of the real name, station, crime, connections, or antecedents of the person who is placed under their charge; and this kind of know-ledge, except in rare cases indeed, never comes to the ears of fellow-culprits while within the walls of the prison. Some of the men, it will also be noticed, bear stars upon their arms; these are marks of good conduct, of great value to the wearer when in the gaol, and entitling him to a certain allowance on discharge, varying according to cir-cumstances from five shillings to a pound. These allowances are often the salvation of offenders."

Coldbath Square derives its chief name, says Mr. Pinks, from a celebrated cold bath, the best known in London, fed by a spring which was dis-covered by a Mr. Baynes, in 1697. The active discoverer declared the water had great power in nervous diseases, and equalled those of St. Magnus and St. Winifred. In Mr. Baynes's advertisement in the *Post Bag* he asserts that his cold bath "prevents and cures cold, creates appetite, helps digestion, and makes hardy the tenderest con-stitution. The coach-way is by Hockley-in-the-Hole." The bath is described as "in Sir John Oldcastle's field, near the north end of Gray's Inn Lane." The bathing-hours were from five a.m. to one, the charge two shillings, unless the visitor was so infirm as to need to be let down into this Cockney Pool of Bethesda in a chair. Mr. Baynes died in 1745, and was buried in the old church of St. James's. He was originally a student of the Middle Temple, and was for fifteen years treasurer of St. James's Charity School. The old bath-house was a building with three gables, and had a large garden with four turret summer-houses. In 1811 the trustees of the London Fever Hospital bought the property for £3,830, but, being driven away by the frightened inhabitants, the ground was sold for building, the bath remaining.

In Coldbath Square, near the Cold Bath, Eustace Budgell, a relation of Addison, resided in 1733. Budgell, who wrote many articles in the *Spectator*, was pushed into good Government work by his kinsman, Addison, but eventually ruined himself by the South Sea Bubble and litigation. Budgell having helped Dr. Tindal in the publication of

> " But ill the motion with the music suits ;
>   So Orpheus fiddled, and so danced the brutes."

In this same square, for ninety monotonous years, also lived Mrs. Lewson, or Lady Lewson, as she was generally called, who died in 1816, aged, as was asserted, one hundred and sixteen years. She seldom went out, and still more seldom saw visitors. In one changeless stagnant stream her wretched life flowed on. "She always," says Mr. Pinks, "wore powder, with a large *tache*, made of

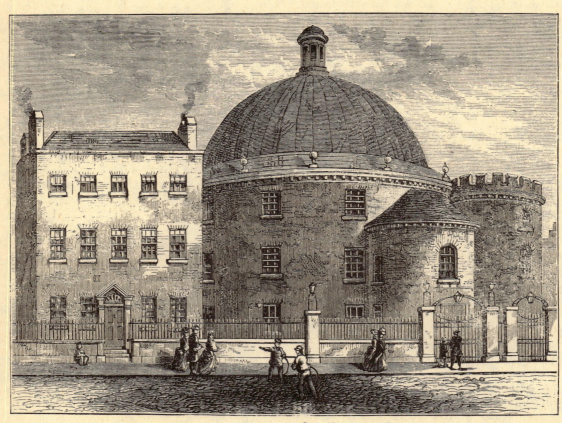

SPA FIELDS CHAPEL IN 1781.   (*See page* 303.)

one of his infidel works, was in consequence left by the doctor £2,000. There arose, however, a suspicion of fraud, and the will was set aside. Pope did not forget the scandal, in attacking his enemies—

> " Let Budgell charge even Grub Street on my bill,
>   And write whate'er he please, except my will."

This disgrace seems to have turned Budgell's brain. He took a boat, one May-day, at Somerset Stairs, having first filled his pockets with stones, and vainly tried to decoy his little daughter with him. While the boat was shooting London Bridge Budgell leaped out, and was drowned. Budgell's best epigram was on some persons who danced detestably to good music—

horsehair, upon her head, over which the hair was turned up, and a cap was placed, which was tied under her chin, and three or four curls hung down her neck. She generally wore silk gowns, with the train long, a deep flounce all round, and a very long waist. Her gown was very tightly laced up to her neck, round which was a kind of ruff, or frill. The sleeves came down below the elbows, and to each of them four or five large cuffs were attached. A large bonnet, quite flat, high-heeled shoes, a large black silk cloak trimmed round with lace, and a gold-headed cane, completed her everyday costume for the last eighty years, in which dress she walked round the square. She never washed herself, because she thought those people who did so were always taking cold, or laying the foundation of some dreadful disorder. Her method was to besmear her face and neck all over with hog's-lard, because that was soft and lubricating; and then, because she wanted a little colour on her cheeks, she bedaubed them with rose-pink. Her manner of living was so

reigns, and was supposed to have been the most faithful living historian of her time, events of the year 1715 being fresh in her recollection. The sudden death of an old lady who was a near neighbour made a deep impression on Mrs. Lewson. Believing her own time had come she became

RAY STREET, CLERKENWELL, ABOUT 1860. (*See page* 306.)

methodical, that she would not drink tea out of any other than a favourite cup. At breakfast she arranged in a particular way the paraphernalia of the tea-table, and dinner the same. She observed a general rule, and always sat in her favourite chair. She enjoyed good health, and entertained the greatest aversion to medicine. At the age of eighty-seven she cut two new teeth, and she was never troubled with the toothache. She lived in five

weak, took to her bed, refused medical aid, and on Tuesday, the 28th May, 1816, died at her house in Coldbath Square, at the advanced age of one hundred and sixteen. She was buried in Bunhill Fields Burying Ground."

"In former times," says Mr. Pinks, "the district around the chapel known as Spa Fields, or the Ducking-pond Fields, now intersected by streets of well-built houses, was the summer's evening resort of the townspeople, who came hither to witness the rude sports that were in vogue a century ago, such as duck-hunting, prize-fighting, bull-baiting, and others of an equally demoralising character. We are informed by an old newspaper that in 1768 'Two women fought for a new shift, valued at half-a-crown, in the Spaw Fields, near Islington. The battle was won by a woman called "Bruising Peg," who beat her antagonist in a terrible manner.' In the summer of the same year 'an extraordinary battle was fought in the Spa Fields by two women against two taylors, for a guinea a head, which was won by the ladies, who beat the taylors in a severe manner.' On Saturday, the 28th August, 1779, 'a scene of fun and business intermixed took place in Spa Fields, to which no language can do justice. Bills had been stuck up and otherwise circulated, that an ox would be roasted whole, and beer given to the friends of their king and country, who were invited to enlist; that two gold-laced hats should be the reward of the two best cudgel-players; that a gown, a shift, and a pair of shoes and stockings should be run for by four old women; and that three pounds of tobacco, three bottles of gin, and a silver-laced hat, should be grinned for by three old men, the frightfullest grinner to be the winner.'

"About the middle of the last century it was dangerous to cross these fields in the dusk of evening, robberies being frequent, and the persons filched were often grievously maltreated by the villains who waylaid them."

About 1733—1748 Spa Fields seem to have been much infected by sneaking footpads, who knocked down pedestrians passing to and from London, and despoiled them of hats, wigs, silver buckles, and money. It was about this dangerous time that link-boys were in constant attendance at the door of Sadler's Wells, to light persons home returning by the lonely fields to the streets of Islington, Clerkenwell, or Holborn. The lessees of the theatre constantly put at the foot of their bills, "There will be moonlight," as a special inducement to timid people. "I have seen two or three link-men," Mr. Britton says, in his Autobiography, "thus traverse the fields from the Wells towards Queen's Square."

At Whitsuntide there was annually held in these fields a fair generally known in London as "the Welsh" or "Gooseberry Fair." A field on which the south side of Myddelton Street is built was from this reason distinguished in old maps as "the Welsh Field." The grand course for horse and donkey racing was where Exmouth Street and Cobham Row are now built. The fair is mentioned as early as 1744, about which time it was removed to Barnet.

In 1779 appeared in the *Clerkenwell Chronicle* the following notice of sports which took place in Spa Fields:—"On Friday, some bricklayers enclosed a piece of ground ten feet by six, for roasting the ox; and so substantial was the brickwork that several persons sat up all night to watch that it did not fall to pieces before the morning. An hour before sunrising the fire was lighted for roasting the ox, which was brought in a cart from St. James's Market. At seven o'clock the ox was laid over the fire in remembrance of the cruelty of the Spaniards in their conquest of Mexico. By nine o'clock one of the legs was ready to drop off, but no satire on the American colonies was intended; for if it had fallen there were numbers ready to have swallowed it. At seven o'clock came a sergeant and a number of deputy Sons of the Sword. The sergeant made an elegant speech, at which every one gaped in astonishment, because no one could understand it. At half-past two the beef was taken up, slices cut up and thrown among the crowd, and many and many a one catched his hat full to fill his belly.

"Instead of four old women to run for the gown, &c., there were only three girls, and the race was won without running; for two of the adventurers gave out before half the contest was over, and even the winner was a loser, for she tore off the sleeve of her gown in attempting to get it on. Only one man grinned for the tobacco, gin, &c. But it was enough. Ugliness is no word to express the diabolicality of his phiz. If the king had ten such subjects he might fear they would grin for the crown. Addison tells us of a famous grinner who threw his face into the shape of the head of a base viol, of a hat, of the mouth of a coffee-pot, and the nozzle of a pair of bellows; but Addison's grinner was nothing to the present, who must have been born grinning. His mother must have studied geometry, have longed for curves and angles, and stamped them all on the face of the boy. The mob was so immense that, though the tide was constantly ebbing and flowing, it was supposed the average number was 4,000 from nine in the morning till eight at night; and as this account is not exaggerated, 44,000 people must have been present. All the ale-houses for half a mile round were crowded, the windows were lined, and the tops and gutters of the houses filled. The place was at once a market and a fair; curds and whey were turned sour, ripe filberts were hardened, and extempore oysters baked in the sun. The bread intended for the loyal was thrown about the fields by the malcontents. The beer was drunk out of pots without measure and without number; but one man who could not get liquor swore he would eat if he could not drink His Majesty's health; and observing an officer with a piece of beef on the point of his sword, he made prize of it, and ate it in the true cannibal taste.

"The feast, on the whole, was conducted with great regularity; for if one got meat another got bread only, and the whole was consumed; but to add to the farce a person threw a basket of onions among the bread-eaters. Some men were enlisted as soldiers, but more were impressed, for the blood-hounds were on the scent, and ran breast-high. If not spring-guns, it might fairly be said that men-traps had been fixed in the Spa Fields. The beef was good of its kind, but like the constitution of Old England, more than half spoiled by bad cooks."

The Ducking-pond Fields, Clerkenwell Fields, Spa Fields, and Pipe Fields, were one and the same place, under different names. The oldest of these names was the first, which applied especially to the district surrounding Spa Fields Chapel, and extending to the northward. The Pipe Fields were so called from the wooden pipes (merely elm-trees perforated) of the New River Company mentioned by Britton about the close of last century.

The building, afterwards Spa Fields Chapel, on the south side of Exmouth Street, was originally opened in 1770, as a place of public amusement. The "Pantheon," as it was called, soon became disreputable. It is described by a contemporary as a large round building crowned by a statue of Fame. In the inside were two galleries. There was a garden with fancy walks, classical statues, and boxes for tea-parties, wine-drinkers, and negus-sippers. The company, as might be supposed, consisted chiefly of small tradesmen, apprentices, dressmakers, servant-girls, and disreputable women. This building had been preceded by a small country inn, with swinging sign, and a long railed-in pond, where citizens used to come and send in their water-dogs to chase ducks. In this ducking-pond six children were drowned in 1683, while playing on the ice. The Spa Fields Pantheon proprietor became bankrupt in 1774, and the house and gardens, which had cost the speculator £6,000, were sold.

In 1776 Selina, the zealous Countess of Huntingdon, consulted Toplady as to purchasing the Pantheon for a chapel, but was dissuaded from the attempt. It was then taken by a company, and opened as a Church of England chapel, in 1777,

but the Rev. William Sellon, incumbent of St. James's, Clerkenwell, being refused the pew-rents, compelled the proprietors to close it. Eventually the Countess of Huntingdon purchased it, but Mr. Sellon again obtained a verdict in a law-court, and stopped all further services. The countess then turned it into a Dissenting chapel, and two of her curates seceded from the Established Church, and took the oath of allegiance as Dissenting ministers. The Gordon rioters of 1780 threatened to destroy it, but did not, when they heard it belonged to the good countess. Shrubsole, the organist of the Spa Fields Chapel, was the composer of that beautiful hymn, "All hail the power of Jesu's name." The Rev. T. E. Thoresby accepted the pastorate in 1846. The fine building will hold more than 2,000 persons, and was for many years one of the wealthiest and most influential Dissenting chapels in London.

The Spa Fields Charity School was established in 1782 by the good countess before mentioned, and new school-rooms were built in 1855 on the site of the countess's garden.

The Countess of Huntingdon herself lived in a large house covered with jasmine, once a part of the old Pantheon tea-gardens, and standing on the east side of the chapel. This lady, who did so much to benefit a godless age, was born in 1707 (Queen Anne), and died in 1791 (George III.) She married the Earl of Huntingdon in 1728. Both by birth and marriage she was connected, says her chaplain, Dr. Haweis, with English kings. Her profound impressions of religion seem to have commenced in early infancy, at the funeral of a child of her own age. A severe illness in later life, and conversation with her sister-in-law, Lady Margaret Hastings, a convert to Methodism, still more affected her. She went to court, but soon married a serious nobleman, and devoted herself to her true profession—not the mere encouragement of milliners, but the study of doing good.

"Bishop Benson," says Mr. Pinks, "was sent for by her husband to reason with her ladyship on her changed religious views, but she pressed upon him so hard with articles and homilies, and so urged upon him the awful responsibility of his station, that his temper was ruffled, and he rose up in haste to depart, bitterly lamenting that he had ever laid his hands on George Whitefield, to whom he imputed the change. She called him back, saying, 'My lord, when you come to your dying bed that will be one of the few ordinations you will reflect upon with complacence.' The Prince of Wales one day at court asked a lady of fashion where my Lady Huntingdon was, that she seldom visited the city. Lady Charlotte E—— replied, with a sneer, 'I suppose praying with her beggars.' The Prince shook his head, and said, 'When I am dying I shall be happy to seize the skirt of Lady Huntingdon's mantle to lift me up with her to heaven.' We cannot help remarking the prejudice of Lady Mary Wortley Montagu, who says, in one of her letters, 'I have seen very little of Lady Huntingdon, so I am not able to judge of her merit; if I wanted to paint a fanatic, I should desire her to sit for the picture. I hope she means well, but she makes herself ridiculous to the profane, and dangerous to the good.'"

The countess having opened her house in Park Street for religious services, Whitefield and Romaine preached in her drawing-room to the great and fashionable. She began to build chapels at Brighton, Bath, Tunbridge Wells, and elsewhere, and also established a training-college in South Wales. Altogether, she either built or helped to build sixty-four chapels, and is supposed to have expended £100,000 in charity, though for many years she lived on a small jointure of £1,200 a year. The countess seems to have been a truly excellent and sensible woman, but with a warm-tempered prejudice, and with a true aristocratic dislike to opposition. "I believe," says her chaplain, "that during the many years I was honoured with her friendship, she often possessed no more than the gown she wore. I have often said she was one of the poor who lived on her own bounty."

Great Bath Street, Coldbath Fields, where Topham, the Strong Man of Islington, exhibited his feats of strength in 1741, was built about 1725. On the sale of the Jervoise estate, in 1811, this property was sold for £8,560. At No. 26 in this street that extraordinary man of science and divine, Emanuel Swedenborg, resided towards the end of his life, and died there in 1772. A short sketch of this philosopher will not be uninteresting.

This great "seer" was the son of a Swedish bishop, and was born in 1688. As a child his thoughts turned chiefly on religion. At the University of Upsala the lad steadily studied the classical languages, mathematics and natural philosophy, and at the age of twenty-two took his degree as a doctor of philosophy, and published his first essay. In 1710 the young student came to London, when the plague prevailed in Sweden, and narrowly escaped being hung for breaking the quarantine laws. He spent some time at Oxford, and then went abroad for three years, living chiefly in Utrecht, Paris, and Griefswalde. He returned to Sweden in 1714 through Stralsund, which that valiant madman, Charles XII., was just then besieging. Introduced to the chivalrous king in 1716, he was made Assessor to the Board of Mines. During the siege of Frederickshall Swedenborg "rendered important service by transporting over mountains and valleys, on rolling machines of his own invention, two galleys, five large boats, and a sloop, from Strömstadt to Iderfjol, a distance of fourteen miles. Under cover of these vessels the king brought his artillery (which it would have been impossible to have conveyed by land) under the very walls of Frederickshall" He now devoted years to the production of works on mathematics, astronomy, chemistry, and mineralogy. He retired from his office of assessor in 1747, and probably then returned to his theological contemplations and writings. It appears that Swedenborg came from Amsterdam to London in 1771, and resided at Shearsmith's, a peruke-maker's, No. 26, Great Bath Street, Coldbath Fields, where he finished his "True Christian Religion." Towards the end of the year Dr. Hartley and Mr. Cookworthy visited him in Clerkenwell. "The details of the the interview," says Mr. Pinks, "are not given, but we gather enough to show his innocence and simplicity, for on their inviting him to dine with them he politely excused himself, adding that his dinner was already prepared, which dinner proved to be a meal of bread and milk. On Christmas Eve, 1771, a stroke of apoplexy deprived him for a time of speech. Towards the end of February, 1772, the Rev. John Wesley was in conclave with some of his preachers, when a Latin note was put into his hand. It caused him evident astonishment, for the substance of it was as follows:

'Great Bath Street, Coldbath Fields, 1772.

'SIR,—I have been informed in the world of spirits that you have a desire to converse with me. I shall be happy to see you if you will favour me with a visit.

'I am, Sir, your humble servant,

'E. SWEDENBORG.'

"Wesley frankly acknowledged that he had been strongly impressed with a desire to see him, but that he had not mentioned that desire to any one. He wrote an answer that he was then preparing for a six-months' journey, but he would wait upon Swedenborg on his return to London. Swedenborg wrote in reply that he should go into the world of spirits on the 29th of the then next month, never more to return. The consequence was that these two remarkable persons never met."

Swedenborg professed to the last the entire truth of all his strange revelations of heaven and hell, and died on the day he had predicted to Wesley.

After lying in state for several days at the undertaker's, he was buried in the Lutheran Chapel, Princes' Square, Ratcliff Highway, and his coffin lies by the side of that of Captain Cook's friend, Dr. Solander, the naturalist.

"In person," says Mr. Pinks, "Swedenborg was about five feet nine inches in height, rather thin, and of brown complexion; his eyes were of a brownish-grey, nearly hazel, and rather small; he had always a cheerful smile upon his countenance. His suit, according to Shearsmith, was made after an old fashion; he wore a full-bottomed wig, a pair of long ruffles, and a curious-hilted sword and he carried a gold-headed cane. In diet he was a vegetarian, and he abstained from alcoholic liquors. He paid little attention to times and seasons for sleep, and he often laboured through the night, and sometimes continued in bed several days together, while enjoying his spiritual trances. He desired Shearsmith never to disturb him at such times, an injunction which was necessary, for the look of his face was so peculiar on those occasions, that Shearsmith thought he was dead."

Soon after Spa Fields Chapel was opened, in 1777, some speculators leased from the Earl of Northampton the two acres of ground in the rear of the building, and converted it into a general burying-ground. The new cemetery, embedded among houses, was intended to bring in a pretty penny, as it was calculated to have room for 2,722 adults, but it soon began to fill at the rate of 1,500 bodies annually, there being sometimes thirty-six burials a day. In fifty years it was carefully computed that 80,000 interments had taken place in this pestilential graveyard! in 1842 some terrible disclosures began to ooze out, proving the shameless greediness of the human ghouls who farmed the Spa Fields burial-ground. It was found that it was now the nightly custom to exhume bodies and burn the coffins, to make room for fresh arrivals. To make the new grave seven or eight bodies were actually chopped up, and corpses recently interred were frequently dragged up by ropes, so that the coffin might be removed and split up for struts to prop up the new-made graves. Bodies were sometimes destroyed after only two days' burial. A grave-digger who, being discharged, insisted on removing the body of his child, which had been recently interred, declared that he and his mates had buried as many as forty-five bodies in one day, besides still-borns. In one year they had had 2,017 funerals, and the stones of families who had purchased graves in perpetuity were frequently displaced and destroyed. The inhabitants of the neighbourhood then petitioned Parliament, complaining of the infectious smells from the burial-ground, and of the shameful scandal generally.

"The lessees of the ground," says the historian of Clerkenwell, "sought to allay the general excitement by repudiating the charges brought against their underlings, but there was no mitigation of the evil complained of; nightly burnings still took place. On the night of the 14th December, 1843, an alarm was raised that the bone-house of Spa Fields ground was on fire, and the engine-keeper stated he saw in the grate a rib-bone and other bones, partly burnt, and a quantity of coffin-wood in different stages of decay. By the exertions of Mr. G. A. Walker, M.D., of the Society for the Abolition of Burials in Towns, seconded by several of the principal inhabitants, this disgraceful state of things was brought again under the attention of the magistrates, and the lessees, managers, and others were summoned to appear at the Clerkenwell Police Court, when other revolting statements were made and confirmed. At length these disgusting and loathsome practices were suppressed by law."

Dorrington Street was erected, says Mr. Pinks, in 1720, and was famous for its old public-house, the "Apple Tree," at the south-east corner. It was a favourite resort of prisoners discharged from the neighbouring House of Correction. Topham, the Strong Man, already mentioned by us in our chapter on Islington, once kept the "Apple Tree." The favourite tap-room joke was, that the bell-pulls were handcuffs; and when a guest wished a friend to ring the bell for the barman, he shouted, "Agitate the conductors!"

Crawford's Passage—or, as it was formerly called, Pickled Egg Walk—is a small lane, leading from Baker's Row into Ray Street. Half-way up stood till recently a public-house known as the "Pickled Egg," from a Dorsetshire or Hampshire man, who here introduced to his customers a local delicacy. It is said that Charles I., during one of his suburban journeys, once stopped here to taste a pickled egg, which is said to be a good companion to cold meat. There was a well-known cockpit here in 1775. There were two kinds of this ancient but cruel amusement, which is now only carried on by thieves and low sporting men in sly nooks of London; one was called the "battle royal," and the other the "Welsh main." In the former a certain number of cocks were let loose to fight, the survivor of the contest being accounted the victor, and obtaining the prize; in the latter, which was more cruel, the conquerors fought again and again, till there was only one survivor, and he became "the shakebag" or pet of the pit.

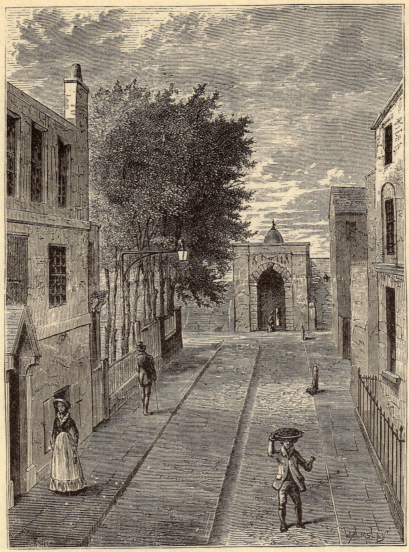

THE OLD HOUSE OF DETENTION, CLERKENWELL.   (*See page* 309.)

CHAPTER XXXIX.

HOCKLEY-IN-THE-HOLE.

Ray Street—Bear Garden of Hockley-in-the-Hole—Amusements at Hockley—Bear-baiting—Christopher Preston Killed—Indian Kings at
Hockley—Bill of the Bear Garden—Dick Turpin.

THIS place was formerly one of those infamous localities equalled only by Tothill Fields, at Westminster, and Saffron Hill, in the valley of the Fleet. It was the resort of thieves, highwaymen, and bull-baiters. Its site was marked by Ray Street, itself almost demolished by the Clerkenwell improvements of 1856-7. The ill-omened name of Hockley-in-the-Hole seems to have been derived from the frequent overflows of the Fleet. Hockley, in Saxon, says Camden, means a "muddy field:" there is a Hockley-in-the-Hole in Bedfordshire; and Fielding makes that terrible thief-taker, Jonathan Wild, the son of a lady who lived in Scragg Hollow, Hockley-in-the-Hole. In 1756 this wretched locality was narrow, and surrounded by ruinous houses, but the road was soon after widened, raised, and drained. In 1855 the navvies came upon an old pavement near Ray Street, and oak piles, black and slimy, the site of a City mill.

The upper portion of the thoroughfare in con-

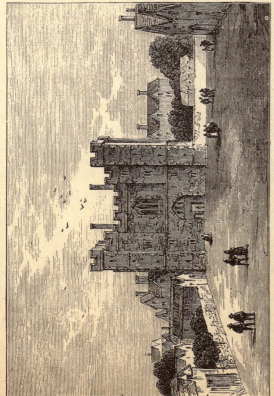

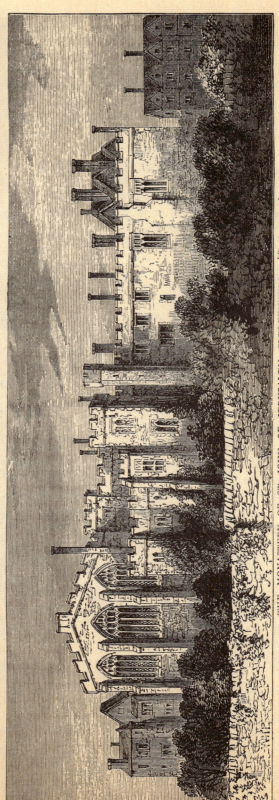

THE MONASTERY OF ST. JOHN OF JERUSALEM, CLERKENWELL. (*See page* 310.)

THE GATE FROM THE WEST.   GENERAL VIEW FROM THE NORTH-EAST.   THE CHAPEL FROM THE SOUTH.

tinuation of Coppice Row was, says Mr. Pinks, formerly called Rag Street, in allusion, it may be, to the number of marine-store shops. In 1774 the notorious and polluted name of Hockley-in-the-Hole was formally changed to that of Ray Street.

On the site of the "Coach and Horses," in Ray Street, once stood the Bear Garden of Hockley-in-the-Hole, which, in Queen Anne's time, rivalled the Southwark Bear Garden of Elizabethan days. Here, in 1700, the masters of "the noble science of self-defence" held their combats.

The earliest advertisement of the amusements at Hockley occurs in the *Daily Post* of the 10th July, 1700. In the spring of the following year it was announced that four men were "to fight at sword for a bet of half-a-guinea, and six to wrestle for three pairs of gloves, at half-a-crown each pair. The entertainment to begin exactly at three o'clock." The same year a presentment of the grand jury for the county of Middlesex, dated the 4th June, 1701, complained of this place as a public nuisance, and prayed for its suppression. "We having observed the late boldness of a sort of men that stile themselves masters of the noble science of defence, passing through this city with beat of drums, colours displayed, swords drawn, with a numerous company of people following them, dispersing their printed bills, thereby inviting persons to be spectators of those inhuman sights which are directly contrary to the practice and profession of the Christian religion, whereby barbarous principles are instilled in the minds of men; we think ourselves obliged to represent this matter, that some method may be speedily taken to prevent their passage through the city in such a tumultuous manner, on so unwarrantable a design."

"You must go to Hockley-in-the-Hole and Marybone, child, to learn valour," says Mrs. Peachum to Filch, in Gay's *Beggar's Opera*. On Mondays and Thursdays, the days of the bull and bear baitings at this delectable locality, the animals were paraded solemnly through the streets.

In 1709 a most tragical occurrence took place at Hockley-in-the-Hole. Christopher Preston, the proprietor of the Bear Garden, was attacked by one of his own bears, and almost devoured, before his friends were aware of his danger. A sermon upon this sad event was preached in the church of St. James's by the Rev. Dr. Pead, the then incumbent of Clerkenwell.

When the bulls and bears were paraded in the street, or swordsmen were to fight, bills such as the following were distributed among the crowd:—

"A trial of skill to be performed between two profound masters of the noble science of self-defence, on Wednesday next, the 13th of July, 1709, at two o'clock precisely. I, George Gray, born in the city of Norwich, who has fought in most parts of the West Indies—viz., Jamaica, Barbadoes, and several other parts of the world, in all twenty-five times upon the stage, and was never yet worsted, and am now lately come to London, do invite James Harris to meet and exercise at the following weapons: back-sword, sword and dagger, sword and buckler, single falchion, and case of falchions. I, James Harris, master of the said noble science of defence, who formerly *rid* in the Horse Guards, and hath fought 110 prizes, and never left a stage to any man, will not fail (God willing) to meet this brave and bold inviter at the time and place appointed, desiring sharp swords, and from him no favour. No person to be upon the stage but the seconds.

"VIVAT REGINA."

"At his Majesty's Bear Garden, in Hockley-in-the-Hole, a trial of skill is to be performed to-morrow, being the 9th instant (without beat of drum), between these following masters:—I, John Terrewest, of Oundle, in Northamptonshire, master of the noble science of defence, do invite you, William King, who lately fought Mr. Joseph Thomas, once more to meet me and exercise at the usual weapons.—I, William King, will not fail to meet this fair inviter, desiring a clear stage, and, from him, no favour. Note. There is lately built a pleasant cool gallery for gentlemen." (Advertisement in the *Postboy* for July 8th, 1701.)

"At the Bear Garden, Hockley-in-the-Hole, 1710.—This is to give notice to all gentlemen gamesters, and others, that on this present Monday is a match to be fought by two dogs, one from Newgate Market against one from Hony Lane Market, at a bull, for a guinea, to be spent. Five let-goes out of hand; which goes fairest and farthest in wins all. Likewise a *green bull* to be baited, which was never baited before, and a bull to be turned loose, with fireworks all over him; also a mad ass to be baited. With a variety of bull-baiting and bear-baiting, and a dog to be drawn up with fireworks. To begin exactly at three of the clock."

In 1710 the four Indian kings mentioned by Addison came to Hockley-in-the-Hole, to see the rough playing at backsword, dagger, single falchion, and quarter-staff. In 1712 Steele described a combat here, in the *Spectator*. The result of these fights was, it appears, often arranged beforehand, and the losing man often undertook to receive the cuts, provided they were not too many or too deep. About this time the proprietor of the Bear Garden left Hockley, and started a new garden at Marylebone, and for a time Hockley-in-the-Hole fell into disrepute with "the fancy." In 1715, however, there was a great backsword player here, who boasted he had cut down all the swordsmen of the West, and was ready to fight the best in London. In 1716 a wild bull was baited with fireworks here, and bears were baited to death; and, in 1721, people came to Hockley to see sparring and eat furmenty and hasty pudding.

In 1735 we find swordsmen having nine bouts with single sword, their left hands being tied down. When a favourite dog was tossed by a Hockley-in-the-Hole bull, his master and his friends used to run and try to catch him on their shoulders, for fear he should be hurt in the fall. Good sensitive creatures ! It was also the custom to stick ribbon crosses on the foreheads of favourite bull-dogs, and when these were removed and stuck on the bull's forehead, the dog was cheered on till he had recovered his treasured decoration. Cowardly dogs stole under the bull's legs, and often got trampled to death. The really "plucky" dog pinned the bull by the nose, and held on till his teeth broke out or he was gored to death. There was cock-fighting here too, and, in 1744, says Mr. Pinks, the prize was a large sow and ten pigs. No game-cock was to exceed four pounds and an ounce in weight.

The old dwelling-house that adjoined the Bear Garden was, in later years, the "Coach and Horses" public-house. The place is so old that the present large room over the bar was originally on the second storey, and the beer-cellars were habitable apartments. Many years ago a small valise, with wooden ends, and marked on the lid "R. Turpin" (perhaps the famous Dick Turpin, the highwayman) was found here, and also several old blank keys, such as thieves wax over to get impressions of locks they wish to open. For the use of such "minions of the moon," there used to be a vaulted passage, now closed, that communicated with the banks of the Fleet.

CHAPTER XL.

CLERKENWELL.

House of Detention—Explosion and Attempted Rescue of Fenian Prisoners—St. John's Gate—Knights Hospitallers and Knights Templars—Rules and Privileges of the Knights of St. John—Revival of the Order—Change of Dress—The Priors of Clerkenwell and the Priory Church—Its Destruction—Henry II.'s Council—Royal Visitors at the Priory—The Present Church—The Cock Lane Ghost—St. John's Gate—The Jerusalem Tavern—Cave and the *Gentleman's Magazine*—Relics of Johnson—The Urban Club—Hicks's Hall—Red Lion Street and its Associations—St. John's Square and its Noble Inhabitants—Wilkes's Birthplace—Modern Industries in Clerkenwell—Burnet House and its Inmates—Bishop Burnet—Clarke the Commentator—An Unjust Judge—Poole of the *Synopsis*—Jesuits' College Discovered.

THE House of Detention, Clerkenwell, a place of imprisonment as old as 1775, was rebuilt in 1818, and also in 1845. This prison was the scene, in December, 1867, of that daring attempt to rescue the Fenian prisoners, Burke and Casey, which for a day or two scared London.

"In the course of the day," says a writer in the *Annual Register*, "a policeman on duty outside the prison had his suspicions so strongly aroused, by seeing a woman named Justice and a man frequently conversing together, that he communicated with one of the prison authorities, who, in consequence, made arrangements for giving an alarm, if it should become necessary. During the day, a warder on duty inside had his attention directed to a man at a window in the upper part of a house in Woodbridge Street, overlooking the prison-yard. He went to bring another warder, and on their return the man had vanished, but was shortly afterwards seen talking to the woman Justice near the entrance to the prison, and to the man who had been seen loitering with her. Later in the day, the warder had his attention called to the same window in the opposite house in Woodbridge Street, overlooking the prison-yard; and there he saw a woman leaning out, and several men inside the room. He distinctly counted five men; but there seemed to him to be more, and they were all looking anxiously in the direction of the

place where the explosion occurred almost immediately afterwards.

"The explosion, which sounded like a discharge of artillery, occurred at exactly a quarter to four o'clock in the afternoon, when there was still some daylight, and was heard for miles round. In the immediate neighbourhood it produced the greatest consternation; for it blew down houses, and shattered the windows of others' in all directions. A considerable length of the outer wall of the prison was levelled with the ground. The windows of the prison, of coarse glass more than a quarter of an inch thick, were, to a large extent, broken, and the side of the building immediately facing the outer wall in which the breach was made, and about 150 feet from it, showed the marks of the bricks which were hurled against it by the explosion. The wall surrounding the prison was about twenty-five feet high, two feet three inches thick at the bottom, and about fourteen inches thick at the top.

"The result of the explosion upon the unfortunate inmates of the houses in Corporation Lane and other adjoining buildings was most disastrous. Upwards of forty innocent people—men, women, and children of all ages, some of whom happened to be passing at the time—were injured more or less severely; one was killed on the spot, and three more died shortly afterwards."

Several persons were arrested as having been

implicated in the crime, and tried at the Central Criminal Court. At their trial a boy, who was the only eye-witness of the attempt, deposed that about a quarter to four o'clock he was standing at Mr. Young's door, No. 5, when he saw a large barrel close to the wall of the prison, and a man leave the barrel and cross the road. Shortly afterwards the man returned with a long squib in each hand. One of these he gave to some boys who were playing in the street, and the other he thrust into the barrel. One of the boys was smoking, and he handed the man a light, which the man applied to the squib. The man stayed a short time, until he saw the squib begin to burn, and then he ran away. A policeman ran after him; and when he arrived opposite No. 5 "the thing went off." The boy saw no more after that, as he himself was covered with bricks and mortar. "There was a white cloth over the barrel, which was black; and when the man returned with the squib he partly uncovered the barrel, but did not wholly remove the cloth. There were several men and women in the street at the time, and children playing. Three little boys were standing near the barrel all the time. Some of the people ran after the man who lighted the squib."

The legends and traditions of this most ancient and interesting district of London all cluster round St. John's Gate (the old south gate of the priory of St. John of Jerusalem), and the old crypt of St. John's Church, relics of old religion and of ancient glory.

For upwards of four hundred years the Knights Hospitallers flourished in Clerkenwell, and a brief note of their origin here becomes indispensable. The order seems to have had its rise in the middle of the eleventh century, when some pious merchants of Amalfi obtained leave of the Mohammedans to build a refuge for sick and needy Christian pilgrims, near the church of the Holy Sepulchre at Jerusalem. The hospital was dedicated to St. John the Cypriote, Patriarch of Alexandria, a good man, who, in the seventh century, when the Saracens first took Jerusalem, had generously sent money and food to the afflicted Christians of Syria. Subsequently the order renounced John the Patriarch, and took as their patron St. John the Baptist instead.

In the first crusade, when the overwhelming forces of Christian Europe forced their way into the Holy City, and the streets which Christ had trodden, scattering blessings, floated in infidel blood, the hospital of St. John was filled with wounded Crusaders, many of whom, on their recovery, doffed their mail and put on the robes of the holy and charitable brotherhood. The real founder of the order was Gerard, who, when Godfrey de Bouillon was chosen King of Jerusalem, in 1099, proposed to the brethren a regular costume, and became the first rector or master of the order. The dress formally adopted, in 1104, was a black robe and white cross. Raymond de Pay, who succeeded Gerard, took a bolder step. Tired of merely feeding and nursing sick and hungry pilgrims, he proposed to his brethren to make the order a military one. By 1130 this section of the church militant had whipped off hundreds of shaven heads, and covered themselves with glory.

In 1187, when Saladin retook Jerusalem, he was gracious to the Hospitallers, who had been kind to the wounded and the prisoners, and he allowed ten of the order to remain and complete their cures. Still indefatigable against the unbelievers, the men of the black robe and white cross fought bravely at the taking of Ptolemais, in 1191, and from them this strong seaport town, which they held for nearly two centuries, derived its new name of St. Jean d'Acre.

Siege and battle, desert march and hill fights, had, however, now thinned the black mantles, and more men had to be sent out to recruit the little army of muscular Christians. The departure of the reinforcement from Clerkenwell Priory is thus picturesquely described by the old monkish chronicler, Matthew Paris:—"In 1237 the Hospitallers sent their prior, Theodoric, a German by birth, and a most clever knight, with a body of other knights and stipendiary attendants, and a large sum of money, to the assistance of the Holy Land. They having made all arrangements, set out from their house at Clerkenwell, and proceeded in good order, with about thirty shields uncovered, with spears raised, and preceded by their banner, through the midst of the City, towards the bridge, that they might obtain the blessings of the spectators, and, bowing their heads with their cowls lowered, commended themselves to the prayers of all."

"It is said," says one writer, "that on the return of the English Crusaders to their native country, the Knights Hospitallers and Knights Templars, on the 3rd of October, 1247, presented King Henry III. with a beautiful crystalline vase, containing a portion of the blood of our Saviour that He had shed on the cross for the salvation of mankind, the genuineness of the relic being attested by the seals of the Patriarch of Jerusalem, and the archbishops, bishops, abbots, and other prelates of the Holy Land."

In 1292, at the desperate siege of Acre, the fighting of straight sword against sabre was so hot, and such were the falls from roof and battlement, that only seven of the Syrian detachment escaped to Cyprus. In 1310 the Hospitallers conquered Rhodes and seven other islands from the Infidel, and commenced privateering against all Mohammedan vessels. In 1344 these stalwart Christians took Smyrna, which post they held for fifty-six years, till they were forced out of the stronghold by Tamerlane. Rhodes becoming an unbearable thorn in the flesh to turbaned mariners, in 1444, an army of 18,000 Turks besieged the island for forty days, but in vain. In 1492 Mahomet II. was repulsed, after a siege of eighty-nine days, leaving 9,000 shaven Infidels dead around the ramparts. In 1502 cautious Henry VII. of England was chosen Protector of the order, and promised men and money against the scorners of Christianity, but supplied neither. But the end came at last; in 1522 Solyman the Magnificent besieged Rhodes with 300,000 men, and eventually, after a stubborn four months' siege, and the loss of 80,000 men by violence, and as many by disease, the brave grand master, L'Isle Adam, after his honourable capitulation, came to England to appeal to Henry VIII., whose fat, greedy hand was already stretched out towards the Clerkenwell Priory. The order had done its duty, and Henry was touched by the venerable old warrior's appeal: he confirmed the privileges of the knights, and gave L'Isle Adam a golden basin and ewer, set with jewels, and artillery to the value of 20,000 crowns. The recovery of Rhodes was not, however, attempted by the Hospitallers, as the Emperor Charles V. ceded Malta to them on the annual payment of a falcon to the reigning King of Spain.

The generous concessions of Henry VIII. lasted only as long as the tyrant's purse was full. Having little to say against the Clerkenwell knights, he suppressed the order because it "maliciously and traitorously upheld the 'Bishop of Rome' to be Supreme Head of Christ's Church," intending thereby to subvert "the good and godly laws and statues of this realm." William Weston, the last prior, and other officers of the order, were bought off by small annuities. Fuller particularly mentions that the Knights Hospitallers, "being gentlemen and soldiers of ancient families and high spirits," would not present the king with puling petitions, but stood bravely on their rights. They judged it best, however, to submit. Some of the knights retired to Malta. Two who remained were beheaded as traitors to King Henry, and a third was hanged and quartered. Queen Mary restored the order to their possessions, but Elizabeth again drove off the knights to Malta.

"The rules and privileges of the order of the Knights of St. John," says Mr. Pinks, "were as follows. Raymond de Pay made the following rules, which were confirmed by Pope Boniface, in the sixth year of his pontificate:—Poverty, chastity, and obedience; to expect but bread and water and a coarse garment. The clerks to serve in white surplices at the altar. The priests in their surplices to convey the Host to the sick, with a deacon or clerk preceding them bearing a lantern, and a sponge filled with holy water. The brethren to go abroad by the appointment of the master, but never singly; and, to avoid giving offence, no females to be employed for or about their persons. When soliciting alms, to visit churches, or people of reputation, and ask their food for charity; if they received none, to buy enough for subsistence. To account for all their receipts to the master, and he to give them to the poor, retaining only one-third part for provisions, the overplus to the poor. The brethren to go soliciting only by permission, to carry candles with them, to wear no skins of wild beasts, or clothes degrading to the order. To eat but twice a day on Wednesday and Saturday, and no flesh from Septuagesima until Easter, except when aged or indisposed. To sleep covered. If incontinent in private, to repent in privacy, and do penance. If the brother was discovered, he was to be deprived of his robe in the church of the town after mass, severely whipped, and expelled from the order, but if truly penitent, he might be again received, but not without penance, and a year's expulsion. If two of the brethren quarrelled, they were to eat only bread and water on Wednesday and Friday, and off the bare ground for seven days. If blows passed, and to those who went abroad without permission, this discipline was extended to forty days. No conversation when eating, or after retiring to the dormitory, and nothing to be drunk after the ringing of the compline. If a brother offended, and did not amend after the third admonition, he was compelled to walk to the master for correction. No brother was to strike a servant. The twenty-second rule of this monastic code was both revolting and disgraceful to any community. It ordered that if a brother died without revealing what he possessed, his money should be tied about the body's neck, and it was to be severely whipped in the presence of the members of the house. Masses were sung thirty days for deceased brethren and alms given in the house. In all decisions they were to give just judgment. They sung the epistle and gospel on Sundays, made a procession, and sprinkled holy water. If a brother embezzled money appropriated to the poor, or excited opposition to the master, he was expelled. When a brother's conduct was found to be too bad, another was to reprove him, but not to publish his faults. If amendment did not follow, the reprover was to call the assistance of others, and ultimately report his crimes to the master in writing; but those accusations were to be supported by proof. The brothers were universally to wear the cross on their breasts.

"The order was that of St. Augustine. He who man, that he would live and die under the superior whom God should place over him, to be chaste and poor, and a servant to the sick. He who received the new brother then promised him bread and water, and coarse garments, and a participation in all the good works of the order.

"Whoever wished to be received into the brotherhood was required to prove his nobility for four descents, on his mother's as well as his father's side; to be of legitimate birth (an exception being

THE ORIGINAL PRIORY CHURCH OF ST. JOHN, CLERKENWELL. (*See page* 310.)

wished for admission came before the Chapter on Sunday, and humbly expressed his hope that he might be received. If no objection was made, a brother informed him that numbers of men of consequence had preceded him, but that he would be entirely deceived in supposing that he should live luxuriously; for that instead of sleeping he would be required to wake, and fast when desirous to eat, to visit places he would rather have avoided, and, in short, have no will of his own. The exordium concluded with a demand whether he was willing to do these things. Upon answering in the affirmative, an oath was administered, by which he bound himself never to enter any other order, declared himself a bachelor without having promised marriage, that he was free from debt, and a free-

made only in favour of the natural sons of kings and princes); to be not less than twenty years of age, and of blameless life and character.

"The following ceremonies were performed at the creation of a knight:—' 1. A sword was given to the novice, in order to show that he must be valiant. 2. A cross hilt, as his valour must defend religion. 3. He was struck three times over the shoulder with the sword, to teach him patiently to suffer for Christ. 4. He had to wipe the sword, as his life must be undefiled. 5. Gilt spurs were put on, because he was to spurn wealth at his heels. 6. He took a taper in his hand, as it was his duty to enlighten others by his exemplary conduct. 7. He had to go and hear mass, where we will leave him.'

"In the season of its prosperity this renowned order included in its fraternity men of eight different nations, of which the English were the sixth in rank. The languages were those of Provence, Auvergne, France, Italy, Arragon, England, and Germany. The Anglo-Bavarian was afterwards substituted for that of England, and that of Castile was added to the number. Cowardice on the battle-field involved the severest of all penalties—degradation and expulsion from the order. 'We

"the Langue of England," as an independent corporation existing under the royal letters patent of Philip and Mary, but it proved hard to galvanise the corpse of chivalry. In 1831 Sir Robert Peat was installed into the office of grand prior; and in 1834, by proceedings in the Court of King's Bench, the corporation of the sixth Langue was formally revived. Sir Robert Peat was succeeded in 1837 by Sir Henry Dymoke, seventeenth hereditary champion of the Crown; and he in 1847 by Sir

COFFEE-ROOM AT ST. JOHN'S GATE.   (*See page* 318.)

place this cross on your breast, my brother,' says the ritual of admission, 'that you may love it with all your heart; and may your right hand ever fight in its defence and for its preservation. Should it ever happen that, in combating against the enemies of the faith, you should retreat and desert the standard of the cross, and take flight, you will be stripped of the truly holy sign, according to the customs and statutes of the order, and you will be cut off from our body, as an unsound and corrupt member.' A knight, when degraded, had his habit torn from off him, and the spurs which he received at his investiture were hacked off."

Between the years 1826 and 1831 an attempt was made in London by a body of gentlemen to revive

C. Lamb. The revived order, now under the headship of the Duke of Manchester, still holds the meetings at St. John's Gate, devoting their funds to feeding convalescent patients from the London Hospitals, and founding Ambulance Associations.

About 1278 the knights adopted a red cassock, and a white cross as their military dress, reserving the black mantle worn in imitation of the Baptist's garment in the wilderness for hospital use. Their standard was red, with a white cross. The Hospitallers' churches were all sanctuaries, and lights were kept perpetually burning in them. The knights had the right of burying even felons who had given them alms during life.

The Hospitallers had also the privilege of administering the sacrament to interdicted persons, and even in interdicted towns; and they were also allowed to bury the interdicted in the churchyards of any of their commanderies.

The order began, like the Templars, in poverty, and ended in luxury and corruption. The governor was entitled, at first, "The Servant to the Poor Serviteurs of the Hospital of Jerusalem." The knights ended by growing so rich, that about the year of our Lord 1240, says Weever, they held in Christendom 19,000 lordships and manors. They are known to have lent Edward III. money. In 1211 Lady Joan Grey, of Hampton, left her manor and manor-house of Hampton (several thousand acres) to the Knights Hospitallers of St. John of Jerusalem, an estate of which Cardinal Wolsey procured a lease for ninety-nine years from Sir Thomas Docwra, the last prior, who lost the election for the grand mastership by only three votes, when contesting it with his kinsman, L'Isle Adam.

Brave as the Hospitallers of Clerkenwell always remained, they soon, we fear, grew proud, avaricious, and selfish. Edward III. had to reprove the brotherhood for its proud insolence. When Henry III. threatened to take away their charter, the prior told him that a king who was unjust did not deserve the name of monarch. In 1338 the English prior, Thomas l'Archer, raised £1,000 by cutting down woods round all the commanderies; he also sold leases and pensions for any terms of ready money, and by bribes to the judges, he procured for the order forfeited lands of the Templars.

Every preceptory of the Hospitallers paid its own expenses, except that of Clerkenwell, where the grand prior resided, and had many pensioners to support, and many courtly and noble guests to entertain. In the year 1337 this priory spent more than its entire revenue, which was at least £8,000.

"The consumption," says Mr. Pinks, "of the good things of the earth in the preceptory of Clerkenwell by the brotherhood, the pensioners, guests, and servitors was enormous. In one year, besides fish and fowl from its demesnes, it expended 430 quarters of wheat, 413 quarters of barley, 60 quarters of mixed corn (draget), 225 quarters of oats for brewing, 300 quarters of oats for horse-feed. They used eight quarters of oats and four quarters of peas for pottage, and laid out in expensis coquinæ (in the expenses of the kitchen) £121 6s. 8d. The next item shows that in the midst of all their excesses they had not forgotten to be hospitable. 'For twenty quarters of beans distributed among the poor on St. John

the Baptist's Day, according to custom, at 3s. per quarter, 60s.'"

The prior of St. John of Jerusalem ranked as the first baron of England, "a kind of otter," says Selden, "a knight half-spiritual, half-temporal." His proud motto was "Sane Baro"—a baron indeed.

Sir William Weston, the last prior but one of St. John, distinguished himself during the siege of Rhodes. His father's two brothers were also knights of the order, and one of them had been Lord Prior of England and General of the Galleys. At the dissolution King Henry awarded Sir William a pension of £1,000 a year; but the suppression of the order in England broke his brave heart soon after. Sir Thomas Tresham, the last prior, died a year or two after his investiture. A Sir William Tresham was residing at Clerkenwell Green in 1619. He was of the same family as Sir Francis Tresham, whose mysterious letter to his friend Lord Monteagle led to the fortunate discovery of the Gunpowder Plot. It will not be forgotten by our readers that a Protestant band of the Knights Hospitallers still exists in Prussia, rich and numerous.

The Priory of St. John of Jerusalem, at Clerkenwell, was founded by Lord Jordan Briset, in the reign of Henry I. He founded also the Nuns' house at Clerkenwell. In 1185 the church was consecrated by Heraclius, Patriarch of Jerusalem. In the reign of Edward I. further additions were made to the priory; the preceptory was burned by Wat Tyler's rabble, and it was not till 1504 that the hospital was restored to its full grandeur, and the grand south gate erected by Sir Thomas Docwra. Camden says of the second building, admiringly, that it resembled a palace, and had in it a very fair church, and a tower-steeple raised to a great height, with so fine workmanship that it was a singular beauty and ornament to the city.

At the dissolution Henry VIII. gave the priory church to John Dudley, Viscount Lisle, Lord High Admiral of England for £1,000; and the church and priory were used by the unscrupulous Henry, as a storehouse for his toils and hunting-tents. Edward VI., as careless of confiscating sacred things as his tyrannical father, gave away the remaining land.

"But in the third year of Edward VI.," says Stow, "the church for the most part, to wit, the body and side aisles, with the great bell-tower (a most curious piece of workmanship, graven, gilt, and inameled, to the great beautifying of the city, and passing all other that I have seen), was undermined and blown up with gunpowder; the stone thereof was employed in building of the Lord

Protector's house in the Strand (old Somerset House)."

The curse of sacrilege, in Spelman's opinion, fell on the Protector. He never finished his Strand house, nor did his son inherit it, and he himself perished on the scaffold. The stones of St. John's Priory went to build the porch of the church of Allhallows, in Gracechurch Street. The choir, in Fuller's time, was in "a pitiful plight," the walls having been shattered by the Protector's gunpowder.

On Mary's succession, Cardinal Pole, on the revival of the order, built a west front to the priory church, and repaired the side chapels. We find on the day of the decollation of St. John the Baptist, that the Merchant Taylors came to celebrate mass at the priory church, when the choir was hung with arras, and every one made offerings at the altar.

Many remarkable historical scenes took place at the priory of Clerkenwell. One of the most remarkable of these was the aulic council held by Henry II. and his barons, when the patriarch Heraclius and the grand master of the Hospitallers, came to England to urge Henry to a new crusade. Heraclius brought with him the keys of David's Tower and the Holy Sepulchre, and an offer of the crown of Jerusalem. When the barons agreed that the king should not lead the crusaders in person, the patriarch flew into an inappeasable rage. "Here is my head," he cried; "here is my head; treat me, if you like, as you did my brother Thomas," meaning A'Becket. "It is a matter of indifference to me whether I die by your orders or in Syria by the hands of the infidels; for you are worse than a Saracen." The master of the Hospitallers was extremely hurt at the behaviour of the patriarch Heraclius, but the king took no notice of his insolence.

In 1212 King John, that dark and malign usurper, spent a whole month at the Priory of St. John, feasted by the prior, and on Easter Sunday, at table, he knighted Alexander, the son of the King of Scotland, a ceremony which cost young Sandy £14 4s. 8d. In 1265 Prince Edward and his loving wife, Eleanor of Castile, were entertained here. The prince had married his wife when she was only ten years of age, and on claiming her, at twenty, came to St. John's Priory for their honeymoon. In 1399 we find Henry IV., not yet crowned, coming down Chepe to St. Paul's, and, after lodging with the bishop for five or six days, staying a fortnight at the priory. In 1413 King Henry V., that chivalrous king, says the Grey Friars' chronicler, was "lyvinge at Sent Jones."

In the year 1485 a royal council was held at St. John's. Public indignation was aroused by a well-founded rumour of the intended espousal by Richard III. of Elizabeth of York, his niece, his queen, Anne, being then lately dead. "Richard, perceiving the public disgust, gave up the idea of marrying Elizabeth, and immediately after the funeral of his wife was over, called a meeting of the civic authorities in the great hall of St. John's, Clerkenwell, just before Easter, and in their presence distinctly disavowed any intention of espousing his niece, and forbade the circulation of the report, as false and scandalous in a high degree." The chronicler relates that a convocation of twelve doctors of divinity had sat on a case of marriage of uncle and niece, and declared that the kindred was too near for the Pope's bull to sanction.

The Princess Mary lived at the priory in much pomp, sometimes visiting her brother, Edward VI., in great state. Machyn, in his curious diary, describes her riding from St. John's to Westminster, attended by Catholic lords, knights, and gentlemen, in coats of velvet and chains of gold, and on another day returning to St. John's, followed by fourscore Catholic gentlemen and ladies, each with an ostentatious set of black beads, "to make a profession of their devotion to the mass." In 1540 ten newly-made serjeants-at-law gave a great banquet at St. John's, to all the Lords and Commons, and the mayor and aldermen. Rings were given to the guests, and, according to Stow, at one of these feasts, in 1531, thirty-four great beeves were consumed, besides thirty-seven dozen pigeons and fourteen dozen swans.

In Elizabeth's reign, when great changes frequently took place, Tylney, the queen's Master of the Revels, resided at St. John's, with all his tailors, embroiderers, painters, and carpenters, and all artificers required to arrange court plays and masques. In this reign Master Tylney licensed all plays, regulated the stage for thirty-one years, and passed no less than thirty of Shakespeare's dramas, commencing with *Henry IV.* and ending with *Antony and Cleopatra;* he might have told us one or two things about the "great unknown," but he died in 1610, and left no diary or autobiography. The court revels were all rehearsed in the great hall at St. John's. In 1612 James I. gave the priory to Lord Aubigny, and the Revels' Office was removed to St. Peter's Hill. The house afterwards came into the possession of Sir William Cecil, grandson of the famous Lord Treasurer Burleigh. The repaired choir was reopened in 1623, by Dr. Joseph Hall, afterwards Bishop of

Exeter and Norwich. In the reign of Charles I. the church served as private chapel to the Earl of Elgin, who occupied the house, and it was called Aylesbury Chapel. It became a Presbyterian meeting-house till 1710.

During the absurd Sacheverell riots, when a High Church mob turned out to destroy Dissenting chapels, St. John's Chapel happening to be near the house of the obnoxious Bishop Burnet, the fanatics gutted the building, and burnt the pews, &c., before Burnet's door. Sacheverell was a High Church clergyman, who, in a public sermon at St. Paul's, had proclaimed the doctrine of passive obedience, and was, in consequence, sent for trial to Westminster Hall, where the Tories triumphantly acquitted him. The chapel was enlarged in 1721, and in 1723 was bought for £3,000 by the commissioners for building fifty new churches.

In the present church, which was restored and improved by Mr. Griffith, in 1845, one of the large painted windows at the east end remains in its old state. In the south and east walls are remains of Prior Docwra's perpendicular work, and the pews stand upon capitals and rib mouldings of the former church. There are some few traces of early English architecture. An old gabled wooden building near the south side of the church, as seen in Hollar's view of the priory (1661), is still standing, says Mr. Pinks, and is occupied by St. John's Sunday Schools. Stones of the old church were discovered in 1862, forming sides of the main sewer through St. John's Square. The arms of Prior Botyler (1439–1469), a chevron between three combs, are still to be seen in the central east window. The head of the beadle's staff, a Knight Hospitaller in silver, was in use in the time of James II., and belonged to the old church of St. James. The portable baptismal bowl is antique, and once supplied the place of a font. Langhorne, the poet, was curate and lecturer at St. John's, Clerkenwell, in 1764. He defended the Scotch against Churchill's satire, and helped his brother to translate Plutarch's "Lives." A poem of Langhorne's moved Burns to tears, the only night Sir Walter Scott, then a child, ever saw him.

In the vaults of this church the celebrated "Cock Lane Ghost" promised to manifest itself to credulous Dr. Johnson and others. The great bibliopole and his friends were thus ridiculed by Churchill for their visit to St. John's :—

> " Through the dull deep surrounding gloom,
>   In close array, t'wards Fanny's tomb
>   Adventured forth. Caution before,
>   With heedful step, a lanthorn bore,

> Pointing at graves ; and in the rear,
>   Trembling and talking loud, went Fear.
>   *   *   *   *   *
>   At length they reach the place of death.
>   A vault it was, long time apply'd
>   To hold the last remains of pride.
>   *   *   *   *   *
>   Thrice each the pond'rous key apply'd,
>   And thrice to turn it vainly try'd,
>   'Till, taught by Prudence to unite,
>   And straining with collected might,
>   The stubborn wards resist no more,
>   But open flies the growling door.
>   Three paces back they fell, amazed,
>   Like statues stood, like madmen gazed.
>   *   *   *   *   *
>   How would the wicked ones rejoice,
>   And infidels exalt their voice,
>   If M——e and Plausible were found,
>   By shadows aw'd, to quit their ground ?
>   How would fools laugh should it appear
>   Pomposo was the slave of fear?
>   *   *   *   *   *
>   Silent all three went in ; about
>   All three turn'd silent, and came out."

The church is, in fact, chiefly remarkable for its crypt, the descent to which is at the north-east angle, under the vestry. It seems originally, by Hollar's view of the east end of the church, in 1661, to have been then above ground. Though 700 years old, the crypt of St. John's is in good preservation. The chief portion consists of four bays, two semi-Norman and two early English, the ribs of the latter bays springing from triple clustered columns, with moulded capitals and bases. From each keystone hangs an iron ring. On each side of the two western bays are pointed window openings, now blocked up. The central avenue of the crypt is sixteen feet wide, and twelve feet high, and there are corresponding side-aisles. At the entrance of the vault is a place where the gardener used to keep his tools, and where, for many years, stood a coffin said to have been arrested for debt. The coffins used to stand in rows, four or five deep, covered with dust and shreds of black cloth. The ends of some had fallen out, and the bony feet had protruded. In 1800 a committee of gentlemen reporting on repairs found a sheet of cobweb hanging from the upper coffins ten to fifteen feet long, and in parts nearly as broad. In 1862 the coffins were piled up in the aisles, that of "Scratching Fanny," the Cock Lane Ghost, among them, and all the side passages bricked up.

Many years ago workmen making a sewer beneath the square, nearly in a line with Jerusalem Passage, came on a chalk and flint wall seven feet thick, and Mr. Cromwell decided that this was part of the foundation of the stately tower described by Stow. It is supposed that the church was 300 feet long, and that its transepts stood in a direct line with St. John's Gate. The enclosure walls can still partially be traced, and the modern buildings in St. John's Square, says Mr. Griffiths,"are mostly built on the old rubble walls of the hospital." The foundations of the cellars under No. 19, and the basements of Nos. 21 and 22 on the north side of St. John's Square, formed the foundations of the old priory walls. Between No. 19 and No. 20 a wall was found seven feet thick : some of the stones had been used for windows, and showed the action of fire. The north postern of the priory was taken down in 1780 : here were then sixty-seven feet of old wall westward of St. John's Gate. There were also remains of the priory in Ledbury Place, which formed the west garden-wall of Bishop Burnet's house, and also in the west garden-wall of Dr. Adam Clarke's house, which adjoined Burnet's house.

That fine specimen of Sir Thomas Docwra's architecture, St. John's Gate, is built of brick and freestone. The walls are about three feet thick, and are built of brick, faced with Rye-gate stone, the same as used for Henry VII.'s Chapel. The famous gate and its flanking towers, formerly much higher than they are now since the soil has risen around them, are pierced with numerous windows, the principal one being a wide Tudor arch, with three mullions and many coats of arms. Beneath this window are several shields, set in Gothic niches. In the centre are the arms of France and England, surmounted by a crown ; on each side are the arms of the priory. Outside these are two shields, one bearing the founders' arms impaling the arms of England, the other emblazoning the insignia of Sir Thomas Docwra. Underneath these last shields were formerly the initials "T. D.," separated by a Maltese cross and the word "Prior." On the north side of the gate, facing the square, are three other shields, and, in low relief, the words " Ano.-Dni., 1504."

The entrance to the west tower, says Mr. Pinks, from the north side of the gate, now no longer used, once led to a staircase, the entrance to Cave's printing-office. The carvings on the spandrils of the doorcase, now decayed, are described in 1788 as representing a hawk and a cock, a hen and a lion, supporting the shield of the priory, and that of Sir Thomas Docwra. The old stone floor is three feet below the present surface. The round tower internally contains remains of the old well staircase (half stone, half oak) which led to the top of the gateway. The upper part was made of blocks of oak six inches thick. The east tower had probably a similar staircase. The stone stair-

case in the north-west tower was removed in 1814. The entrance to the east tower, on the north side the gate, has been long ago blocked up.

In 1661 Hollar draws the gate as blocked up with a wooden structure, beneath which were two distinct passages. This was removed in 1771. The roof of the now dwarfed archway is, says an able historian of Clerkenwell, " a beautiful example of the groining of the fifteenth century, adorned with shields, bosses, and moulded ribs, springing from angular columns with moulded capitals." On the keystone is carved the paschal lamb, kneeling on a clasped copy of the Gospels, and supporting a flag. In a line with the lamb are coloured shields of the priory, and of Docwra.

On the east side of the archway Mr. Foster, the keeper of the " Jerusalem" Tavern, and a great lover of ancient architecture, placed a large oil-painting, by Mr. John Wright, representing the Knights of St. John starting for a joust. For the " Jerusalem" Tavern, on the east basement, a south side-entrance was ruthlessly cut through the angle of the projecting gate-tower.

The basement on the west side was, in 1813, converted into a watch-house, and was afterwards turned into a dispensary hospital by the modern Knights of St. John, which in its first year benefited 2,062 persons. It had previously been used as a coal-shed and a book-store. In many of the gate-house rooms there are still oak-panelled ceilings. The "grand hall," the memorable room over the arch, is approached by an Elizabethan staircase, and in the hall are two dull figures in armour, supposed, by courtesy, to represent Prior Weston and Prior Docwra ; and a handsome bust of Mr. Till, the numismatist, adorns the mantel-piece. It was this Mr. Till who cast from old Greek and Roman coins the bronze armorial bearings of the priory and of Docwra, which adorn the parlour and hall.

It was here Dr. Johnson toiled for Cave, the editor of the *Gentleman's Magazine*, and here Garrick made his first theatrical *début* in London.

Between 1737—1741, says Mr. Percy Fitzgerald, in his " Life of Garrick," Garrick's friend Johnson —"now working out a miserable 'per-sheetage' from the very humblest hack-work, and almost depending for his crust on some little article that he could now and again get into the *Gentleman's Magazine*—was by this time intimate with Mr. Cave, of St. John's Gate, the publisher of that journal. Johnson mentioned his companion, and speaking of his gay dramatic talents, inspired this plain and practical bookseller with some curiosity, and it was agreed that an amateur performance should take place in a room over the archway, with Mr. Garrick in a leading comic character. It was duly arranged; the piece fixed on was Fielding's *Mock Doctor*. Several of the printers were called in, parts were given to them to read, and there is an epilogue to the *Mock Doctor*, by Garrick, which, as it was

The delightful traditions that encrust, as with many-coloured lichens, the old gate, cluster thickest around the old room over the arch, for there Johnson, Garrick, and Goldsmith spent many pleasant hours, and it is good to sit there among the club, and muse over the great men's memories.

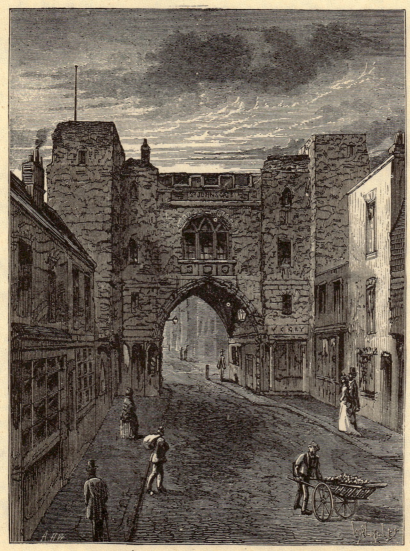

ST. JOHN'S GATE, CLERKENWELL. (*See page* 317.)

inserted shortly afterwards in the *Gentleman's Magazine* would seem to have been spoken on this occasion. This shows how absorbing was his taste for the stage, sure to break out when there was the slightest promise of an opening. The performance gave great amusement, and satisfied the sober Cave; and presently, perhaps as a mark of the publisher's satisfaction, some of Mr. Garrick's short love verses were admitted into the poetical department of the magazine."

In the coffee-room on the first floor is an old-fashioned wide wooden chair, which, tradition asserts, was the favourite chair of Dr. Johnson. On the top rail is boldly painted the date of the doctor's birth and death. The chair was, however, it is hinted, merely an old chair found in an upper room by Mr. Benjamin Foster, when he took the tavern, and labelled "Dr. Johnson's," as an attraction to the gullible public. The stone Tudor mantelpiece in the coffee-room is an old one discovered on the pulling down of a modern fireplace. In the wall (three feet four inches thick) in the side of this fireplace was found the entrance to a secret passage opening at the archway of the gate. It is doubtful whether this tavern was opened before or after Cave's death, but it is supposed £108, the Society of Antiquaries refusing to assist. The original gate was no doubt burned by Wat Tyler's men, but Mr. Griffith, F.S.A., during these restorations, discovered a fragment of the first gate, carved with scallop-shells and foliage, in a ceiling in Berkeley Street, Clerkenwell, on the site of the

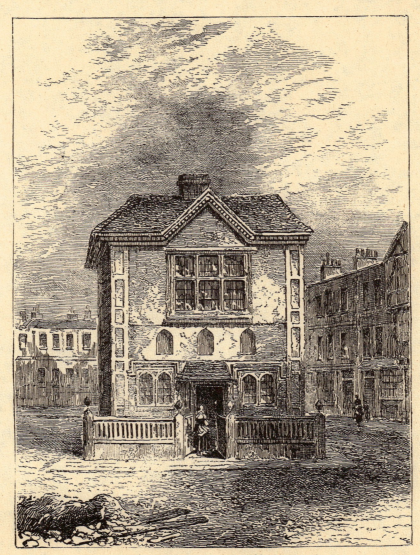

HICKS'S HALL, ABOUT 1750. (*See page* 321.)

that it was first called the "Jerusalem" Tavern; this name being assumed from the "Jerusalem" Tavern in Red Lion Street. In 1845 the terms of the Metropolitan Building Act compelled the parish to repair the gate, when the Freemasons of the Church, a useful architectural society, at once generously undertook its restoration, and saved it from being daubed up with cement. The upper portions of the towers were then re-cased with rough stone, the windows new mullioned, at a cost of residence of Sir Maurice Berkeley, standard-bearer to Henry VIII., Edward VI., and Elizabeth. He also, in 1855, discovered near the gate a stone boss, sculptured with foliage, and a carved stone window-head, from the old priory, with the priory arms in the spandril of the arch. Both interesting fragments are preserved at the South Kensington Museum. In the reign of James I. this great south gate was given to Sir Roger Wilbraham, who resided here.

In 1731 the gate became dignified by its connection with literature. Cave, the printer, careful, shrewd, and industrious, set up his presses in the hall over the gateway, and started the *Gentleman's Magazine*, January, 1731, displaying the gate in a rude woodcut on the exterior of the periodical, and very soon drew public attention to his magazine.

With St. John's Gate is connected Dr. Johnson's first struggles towards the daylight. Here, after hungry walks with Savage round St. James's Square, and long controversies in Grub Street cook-shops, he came to toil for Cave, who employed him to edit the contributions, and to translate from Latin, French, and Italian. About the year 1738 he produced his "London," a grand imitation of the third satire of Juvenal. In 1740, like a loyal vassal of his editor, Johnson gratified an insatiable public curiosity, by giving himself a monthly sketch of the debates in both Houses of Parliament, a scheme projected by a man named Guthrie. "These productions were characterised by remarkable vigour, for they were written at those seasons, says Hawkins, when Johnson was able to raise his imagination to such a pitch of fervour as bordered upon enthusiasm. We can almost picture the doctor in his lone room in the gate, declaiming aloud on some public grievance. For the session of 1740–41 he undertook to write the debates entirely himself, and did so for the whole of three sessions. He began with a debate in the House of Commons on the bill for prohibiting exportation of corn, on the 19th November, 1740, and ended with one in the Lords, on the bill for restraining the sale of spirituous liquors, on the 23rd February, 1742-3. Such was the goodness of Johnson's heart, that a few days before his death he solemnly declared to Mr. Nichols, whom he had requested to visit him, " that the only part of his writings which then gave him any compunction was his account of the debates in the *Gentleman's Magazine*, but that at the time he wrote them he did not think he was imposing on the world. The mode of preparing them which he adopted, he said, was to fix upon a speaker's name, then to make an argument for him, and to conjure up an answer." He wrote these debates with more velocity than any of his other productions ; he sometimes produced three columns of the magazine within an hour. He once wrote ten pages in one day, and that not a long one, beginning, perhaps, at noon, and ending early in the evening. Of the "Life of Savage" he wrote forty-eight octavo pages in one day, but that day included the night, for he sat up all night to do it.

"The memoranda for the debates," continues Mr. Pinks, "which were published in the *Gentleman's Magazine* were obtained sometimes by stealth, and at others from members of the House who were favourable to their publication, and who furnished Cave with notes of what they had themselves said or heard, through the medium of the post, and frequently by *vivâ voce* communication. Cave, when examined at the bar of the House of Lords on the charge of printing an account of the trial of Lord Lovat, in 1747, being asked, says Nichols, in his 'Literary Anecdotes,' how he came by the speeches which he printed in the *Gentleman's Magazine*, replied that he got into the House and heard them, and made use of black-lead pencil, and took notes of only some remarkable passages, and from his memory he put them together himself. He also observed that sometimes he had speeches sent him by very eminent persons, as well as from the members themselves."

When working for Cave, at St. John's Gate, Johnson was still dependent. "We are told," remarks Mr. Pinks, "by Boswell that soon after his 'Life of Richard Savage' was anonymously published, Walter Harte, author of the 'Life of Gustavus Adolphus,' dined with Cave at the gate, and in the course of conversation highly commended Johnson's book. Soon after this Cave met him, and told him that he had made a man very happy the other day at his (Cave's) house. ' How could that be?' said Harte ; ' nobody was there but ourselves.' Cave answered by reminding him that a plate of victuals had been sent behind a screen at the dinner-time, and informed him that Johnson, who was dressed so shabbily that he did not choose to appear, had emptied that plate, and had heard with great delight Harte's encomiums on his book.

"From that spoilt child of genius, Richard Savage, Cave had many communications before he knew Johnson. The misfortunes and misconduct of this darling of the Muses reduced him to the lowest state of wretchedness as a writer for bread ; and his occasional visits to St. John's Gate brought him and Johnson together, poverty and genius making them akin.

"The amiable and accomplished authoress, Mrs. Elizabeth Carter, whom Johnson, from an appreciation of her talents, highly esteemed, and who was a frequent contributor to the *Magazine*, under the name of Eliza, during the interval of her occasional visits to London, lodged at St. John's Gate. Hither also came Richard Lauder, Milton's detractor ; Dr. Hawkesworth, the author of ' Belisarius ;' and a shoal of the small-fry of literature, who shared the patronage of Cave.

"Jedediah Buxton, a mental calculator of extraordinary powers, resided for several weeks in 1754 at St. John's Gate. This man, although he was the son of a schoolmaster (William Buxton), and the grandson of a vicar of his native parish (John Buxton), Elmton, in Derbyshire, had never learned to write, but he could conduct the most intricate calculations by his memory alone; and such was his power of abstraction, that no noise could disturb him. One who had heard of his astonishing ability as a calculator, proposed to him for solution the following question :—In a body whose three sides measure 23,145,789 yards, 5,642,732 yards, and 54,965 yards, how many cubical eighths of an inch are there? This obtuse reckoning he made in a comparatively short time, although pursuing the while, with many others, his labours in the fields."

In 1746 some small cannon were mounted on the battlements of St. John's Gate, but for what purpose is not known. About 1750 one of the lightning-conductors recommended by Dr. Franklin was erected on one of the eastern towers of St. John's Gate, for electrical experiments, which were the rage of the day.

After Cave's death, in 1754, the *Magazine* was printed and published at the gate by Cave's brother-in-law and nephew. On the nephew's death Mr. David Bond became the publisher for the family, and continued so till the end of 1778. Mr. Nichols then purchased a large share of the *Magazine*, and in 1781 the property was transferred to Red Lion Passage, Fleet Street, and forty years after to Parliament Street. It was subsequently published by Messrs. Parker, of the Strand, and by Messrs. Bradbury and Evans, in Whitefriars.

A short biographical notice of the worthy Cave, Johnson's earliest patron, is indispensable to a full history of that interesting relic of old London, St. John's Gate. The enterprising printer and publisher, born in 1691, was the son of a man reduced in fortune, who had turned shoemaker, and was educated at Rugby. In youth he was alternately clerk to an excise collector, and a Southwark timber-merchant. After being bound apprentice to a London printer, he was sent to manage an office and publish a weekly newspaper at Norwich. He was subsequently employed at the printing-office of Alderman Barber (a friend of Swift), and wrote Tory articles in *Mist's Journal*. Obtaining a small place in the Post Office, he began to supply the London papers with provincial intelligence, and the country printers with surreptitious reports of Parliamentary debates, for which, in 1728, he was imprisoned for several days.

From the Post Office he was moved to the Frank Office, where he was dismissed for stopping a letter—as he considered legally—being a frank given to the terrible old Duchess of Marlborough by Mr. Walter Plummer. Putting by, at last, a sum of money (in spite of endless unsuccessful projects), Cave started the *Gentleman's Magazine*, and for the last twenty years of his industrious life was an affluent, thrifty man. His prizes for poems and epigrams brought forward but few poets, and his chief prize-takers, after all, turned out to be Moses Browne, a Clerkenwell pen-cutter, and Mr. John Duick, another pen-cutter, in St. John's Lane, with whom Cave used to play at shuttlecock in the old gate-house.

In 1751 the death of his wife hastened Cave's end. One of his last acts was to fondly press the hand of his great contributor, and the main prop and stay of the *Gentleman's Magazine*, Dr. Samuel Johnson. Cave died at the old gate-house in 1754, and was buried (probably without memorial) in the old church of St. James, Clerkenwell. An epitaph was, however, written by Dr. Hawkesworth for Rugby Church, where all Cave's relations were buried.

An old three-quarter length portrait of Cave was found by Mr. Foster in a room on the south side of the great chamber over St. John's gateway, and, in his usual imaginative yet business-like way, Mr. Foster labelled it "Hogarth." This gentleman, it is said, originally kept the "Old Milestone" house, in the City Road, near the "Angel," and in 1848 removed to St. John's Gate, where, by energy and urbanity, he soon hunted up traditions of the place, and, indeed, where they were thin, invented them. He was chairman of the Licensed Victuallers' Asylum, and was active in the cause of benevolence. He died in 1863, of apoplexy, after speaking at a Clerkenwell vestry-meeting.

The Urban Club, a pleasant literary society, well supported, was started at St. John's Gate during Mr. Foster's reign, under the name of "The Friday Knights," but soon changed its name, in compliment to that abstract yet famous personage, Sylvanus Urban. It annually celebrated the birth of Shakespeare in an intellectual and yet convivial way.

The once famous "Hicks's Hall," whence one of the milestone distances from London was computed, "stood," says the indefatigable Mr. Pinks, "about 200 yards from Smithfield, in the widest part of St. John's Street, near the entrance to St. John's Lane." Hicks's Hall was a stately house, built in 1612, as a sessions house for Clerkenwell, by that great citizen, Sir Baptist Hicks, silk mercer, in Soper Lane, in the reign of James I. During the reigns of Edward VI., Mary, and Elizabeth the Middlesex magistrates had generally met in a scrambling and indecorous fashion, at some chance inn, frequently the "Windmill" or the "Castle," in St. John Street, by Smithfield Bars. The noise of the carriers' wagons vexing the grave Justice Shallows of those days, James I. granted, in 1610, to Sir Thomas Lake and fourteen other knights and esquires of Middlesex, a piece of ground, 128 feet long and 32 feet broad, with 20 feet of carriage-way on each side. Sir Baptist, having built the new sessions hall at his own proper charge, feasted, on the day of opening, twenty-six justices of the county, who then, standing up with raised goblets, with one consent christened the new building Hicks's Hall. Sir Baptist seems to have been a most wealthy and influential citizen, and to have lent King James, who was careless and extravagant enough, vast sums of money, besides supplying the court with stuffs and cloths, of tissue and gold, and silks, satins, and velvets, the courtiers getting very much entangled with the rich mercer's bills and bonds. In 1614 the Earl of Somerset borrowed Sir Baptist's house at Kensington, and it is certain that he lived with all the splendour of a nobleman. In 1628 Sir Baptist Hicks was advanced to the peerage as Viscount Campden. He died in the year 1629, and was buried at Campden, in his native county of Gloucestershire. Of his daughters, one married Lord Noel, the other Sir Charles Morison, of Cashiobury, and it is said he gave each of them £100,000 for a marriage portion. He left £200 to the poor of Kensington, founded almshouses at Campden, and left large sums to the Mercers' Company. That celebrated preacher, Baptist Noel, son of the Earl of Gainsborough, Viscount Campden, derived his singular Christian name from the rich mercer of Soper Lane. Sir Baptist's great house at Kensington (with sixty rooms), burnt in 1816, was, it is said, won by him from Sir Walter Cope, in a game of chance. The Viscountess Campden, the widow of Sir Baptist, left vast sums in charity, some of which bequests, being illegal, were seized by the Parliament.

The sessions hall built by Sir Baptist was a mean square brick house, with a stone portico, and annexed to the hall was a round-house, and close by was a pillory. At Hicks's Hall criminals were dissected. This court has been the scene of some great historical trials. The twenty-nine regicides were tried there, and so were many of the conspirators in the so-called Popish Plot; and here also Count Königsmarck was tried for murdering

his rival, Mr. Thynne, and was acquitted. Hicks's Hall is referred to in "Hudibras:"—

"An old dull sot, who told the clock
For many years at Bridewell dock,
At Westminster and Hicks's Hall,
And *hiccius doccius* played in all."

When Sir John Hawkins, a builder, the father of Dr. Johnson's spiteful biographer, used to go to Hicks's Hall, as chairman of the Middlesex Quarter Sessions, he used to drive pompously from his house at Highgate, in a coach and four horses.

In 1777 Hicks's Hall became so ruinous that it was proposed to rebuild it, at an expense of £12,000. This was opposed in Parliament, the traffic of Smithfield rendering the place too noisy and inconvenient. A new sessions house was therefore built on the west side of Clerkenwell Green, in 1782, and the old hall was pulled down, but for a long time afterwards the new hall went by the old name. Large additions were made on the south side in 1876, when the new Clerkenwell Road was formed.

St. John Street, Clerkenwell, is one of the most ancient of the northern London streets, and is mentioned in a charter of confirmation as early as the year 1170. It seems originally to have been only a way for pack-horses. It was first paved in the reign of Richard II. In the reign of Henry VIII. it had become "very foul, full of pits and sloughs, very perilous and noyous," and very necessary to be kept clean for the avoiding of pestilence. In Stow's time this road was used by persons coming from Highgate, Muswell Hill, &c., but grand persons often took to the fields, in preference, as we find Elizabeth, James I., and Charles I. doing; and no doubt St. John Street was a deep-rutted, dirty country road, something like a neglected plank road in Kentucky, or a suburban street in a Russian country town.

There was, in early times, a raised and paved causeway leading from St. John Street to Islington Church, which was called the "Long Causeway." About 1742 numerous footpads prowled about here. On the fortification of London during the civil wars, in 1642-3, a battery and breastworks were erected at the south end of St. John Street; Captain John Eyre, of Cromwell's Regiment, superintended them. There were also fortifications at Mountmill (the plague-pit spot before mentioned), in Goswell Street Road, a large fort, with four half bulwarks, at the New River upper pond, and a small redoubt near Islington Pound.

What is now Red Lion Street, Clerkenwell, was formerly an open piece of ground belonging to St. John's Priory, subsequently called Bocher or Butt

Close, and afterwards Garden Alleys. The houses were chiefly built about 1719, by Mr. Michell, a magistrate, who lived on the east side of Clerkenwell Green. His house was afterwards occupied by Mr. Wildman, the owner of that unparalleled racehorse, Eclipse, who sold him to lucky Colonel O'Kelly for 1,700 guineas. This horse, which was never beaten, and said to be a "roarer," could run four miles in six minutes and four seconds.

In the house at the north-west corner of Red Lion Street, the "Jerusalem" Tavern, recently demolished on the formation of the new Clerkenwell Road, that industrious compiler, Mr. John Britton, was bound apprentice to Mr. Mendham, a wine-merchant, an occupation which nearly killed the young student. In snatches of time stolen from the fuming cellar, Britton used to visit Mr. Essex, a literary dial-painter, who kindly lent him useful books, and introduced him to his future partner in letters, Mr. Edward Brayley, and to Dr. Trusler and Dr. Towers, the literary celebrities of Clerkenwell.

This Dr. Trusler was a literary preacher, who, in 1787, resided at No. 14, Red Lion Street, and supported himself by selling MS. sermons to the idle clergy. His father had been proprietor of the fashionable "Marybone Gardens," and his sister made the seed and plum-cake for that establishment. Trusler, a clever, pushing man, was at first an apothecary and then a curate. Cowper, in "The Task," laughed at Trusler as "a grand caterer and dry nurse of the church." He seems to have been an impudent projector, for when told by Dr. Terrick, Bishop of London, that he offered his clergy inducements to idleness, Trusler replied that he made £150 a year by his manuscript sermons, and that, for a benefice of the same value he would willingly discontinue their sale. He afterwards started as printer, at 62, Wardour Street, and published endless ephemeral books on carving, law, declamation, farming, &c.—twenty-five separate works in all. He died in 1820. In 1725 a Jew rag-merchant of this street died, worth £40,000. Early in the century an Arminian Jew named Simons lived here. He made some £200,000, but, ruined by his own and his son's extravagance, died at last in the parish workhouse. In 1857 an old lady named Austin died in this street (No. 22), aged 105.

It was to a printer named Sleep, in St. John Street, that Guy Fawkes, *alias* Johnson, used to come stealthily, in 1605, to meet fellow-Romanists, Jesuits, and other disaffected persons. St. John Street was a great place for carriers, especially those of Warwickshire and Nottingham, and the "Cross Keys,"

one of their houses of call, was one of Savage's favourite resorts, and there probably his sworn friend, Johnson, also repaired. The "Pewter Platter," the "Windmill," and the "Golden Lion" were well enough, but some of these St. John Street hostelries, in 1775, seem to have been much frequented by thieves and other bad characters.

St. John's Square occupied, says Mr. Pinks, the exact area of the court of the ancient priory. In the reign of James II., a Father Corker built a convent here, which was pulled down by Protestant rioters, in 1688, and several 'prentice boys were shot here by the Horse Guards in the riots. The Little Square, as the north-western side is called, was formerly known as North's Court, from its builder, a relation of Lord Keeper North, in Charles II.'s time. Sir John North resided here in 1677 and 1680. Dr. William Goddard, one of the Society of Chemical Physicians, who lived in St. John's Close, as it was then called, was one of those who had Government permission to sell remedies for the Great Plague. At the south-west corner of Jerusalem Passage stood the printing-office of Mr. Dove, whose neat "English Classics" are still so often seen at old bookstalls. On the south side of the square was the Free-Thinking Christians' Meeting House. This body seceded from the Baptists, and built a chapel here, about the year 1830. They were at first in Old Change, then in Cateaton Street (now Gresham Street), but were persecuted by Bishop Porteus. They held discussions on passages of the Bible, but no public prayers or ceremonies whatever.

In 1661 Charles Howard, first Earl of Carlisle, resided in the precincts of St. John's Square. This useful partisan of Charles II., ennobled at the Restoration, was our ambassador in Russia, Sweden, and Denmark, and was subsequently Governor of Jamaica. At the same period Arthur Capel, Earl of Essex, resided here, until 1670. He was afterwards Viceroy of Ireland, and First Lord of the Treasury. Persecuted for his doubtful share in the Rye House Plot, he killed himself in the Tower. Here also lived the first Lord Townshend, one of the five Commoners deputed by Parliament to go over to Holland and beg Charles II. to return. Another eminent resident was a staunch Commonwealth man, Sir William Fenwicke, who died in 1676. To these noble names we have to add that of Sir William Cordell, Master of the Rolls in the times of Mary and Elizabeth. He was Solicitor-General at the trial of Sir Thomas Wyatt. Queen Elizabeth visited him at his estate in Suffolk, when the Duke of Alençon sent to sue for her hand.

The following epitaph on Sir William Cordell is thus translated by Fuller from the tomb in Long Melford Church, Suffolk :—

> " Here William Cordal doth in rest remain,
> Great by his birth, but greater by his brain ;
> Plying his studies hard his youth throughout,
> Of causes he became a pleader stout.

manufactory. His father, Israel Wilkes, a rich distiller, lived in a handsome old brick house, approached by a paved court with wide iron gates, north of the church. There had been a distillery here as early as 1747. The old distiller who lived here, like a generous and intelligent country squire, drove a coach and six horses, and cultivated the

EDWARD CAVE. *From the Portrait by Hogarth.*   (*See page* 321.)

> His learning deep such eloquence did vent,
> He was chose Speaker of the Parliament ;
> Afterwards Queen Mary did him make (knight),
> And counsellor, State work to undertake ;
> And Master of the Rolls, well worn with age,
> Dying in Christ, heaven was his upmost stage ;
> Diet and clothes to poor he gave at large,
> And a fair almshouse founded on his charge. "

The site of the birthplace of that clever but unprincipled demagogue, John Wilkes, is now a clock

society of philosophers, men of letters, noblemen, and merchants. The house, which was pulled down about 1812, was at one time occupied by Colonel Magniac, who rendered himself famous by the automaton clocks he made for the Emperor of China.

Clerkenwell is noted for its clock-makers, and here armies of busy and intelligent men spend their lives in brass-casting, silvering dials, wheel-cutting, pinion-cutting, and glass-bending; and at No. 35, Northampton Square, Clerkenwell, is the British Horological Institute, for the cultivation of the science of horology, and its kindred arts and manufactures. In Northampton Road is the office of the Goldsmiths' and Jewellers' Annuity

latterly a poor bricked passage leading to Ledbury Place, which stood on the site of the bishop's old garden, was approached by several steps, and boasted a portico consisting of two Tuscan columns supporting a moulded entablature. In course of time the house lost caste, till, in 1817, it was

THE CRYPT OF ST. JOHN'S CLERKENWELL. (*See page* 310.)

Association, for relieving the decayed members of the two trades.

A special feature of this part of Clerkenwell was, till recently, Burnet House, which formerly stood on the west side of St. John's Square. It was originally a noble mansion of two storeys in height, and was lighted in front by fourteen square-headed windows. The forecourt, upon which shops were built, in 1859, was a garden. The grand entrance,

shared between an undertaker and a hearth-rug maker. The old staircases had long vanished, but in the basement were the original kitchens and cellars. "In several of the rooms," wrote Mr. Pinks, shortly before its demolition, "are very handsome mantelpieces, different in design, the ornaments in relief upon them consisting of flowers and leaves in festoonings, medallions, interlacing lines, and groups of female figures. The chimney jambs are of white marble, as are also the hearths. The old stoves have been all removed, and replaced by smaller ones of more recent date. There was formerly a very curious back to one of the grates in this mansion; it was a bas-relief in iron of Charles I., with the date of 1644 upon it, and represented that monarch triumphantly riding over a prostrate female figure, the Spirit of Faction. On each side were pillars, encircled with bay-leaves and a scroll of palm-branches. On the top were the royal crown, and the initials, 'C. R.,' and below the effigies of two women, seated on low stools, having baskets of fruit before them. Nothing is known of this device by the subsequent inmates, and it was probably either burnt out or removed. In the north-east corner of the yard of the right wing of the house, raised about eighteen inches from the ground on two piers of brickwork, was an old leaden cistern, the dimensions of which are four feet two inches in length, twenty and a half inches in width, and two feet six and a half inches in depth, with a mean thickness of half an inch. The cistern, which was a massive piece of cast work, was ornamented with several devices in low relief. On the front, and at either end, was a figure of the Goddess of Plenty, recumbent, by the side of a cornucopia overflowing with flowers and fruits, and behind her was a sheaf of full-eared wheat. Within a panel there was also a shield, quite plain, and over this, as a crest, was a lion passant, the dexter paw resting on a blazing star. Near the upper edge of the cistern was the date of its casting, 1682, with the initials, 'A. B. M.,' doubtless those of an occupier antecedent to Burnet's tenancy of the premises.

"There was until recently another cistern on the premises, similar to the above, bearing the date of 1721, and the initial 'G.,' for Gilbert, surmounted by a mitre. This may have been re-cast by one of Burnet's successors, as a memorial of him. Recently, having fallen from its position, it was removed altogether off the premises, and sold for old metal, and it is said to have weighed four hundredweight."

Bishop Burnet, the son of an Edinburgh lawyer, was born in 1643. He was educated in Aberdeen; in 1669 he became professor of divinity at Glasgow, and when only twenty-six years old was offered a Scottish bishopric, which he modestly declined. In 1674, when he had already married a daughter of the Earl of Cassilis, he came to London, and was appointed preacher at the Rolls' Chapel by Sir Harbottle Grimstone, and soon after was chosen lecturer at St. Clement Danes. In 1679 appeared the first folio volume of the chief work of his life,

the "History of the Reformation." Charles II. offered him the bishopric of Chichester, if he would only turn Tory, but Burnet, though vain, and fond of money, conscientiously refused, and even wrote a strong letter to the king, animadverting on his flagrant vices. At the execution of the good Lord William Russell, in Lincoln's Inn Fields, Burnet bravely attended him on the scaffold, and in consequence instantly lost the preachership at the Rolls and the lectureship of St. Clement's.

On the accession of James II. Burnet retired to the Continent, and travelled; but on the accession of the Prince of Orange was rewarded by the bishopric of Salisbury. According to some writers, Burnet was the very paragon of bishops. Two months every year he spent in traversing his diocese. He entertained his clergy, instead of taxing them with dinners, and helped the holders of poor benefices. He selected promising young men to study in Salisbury Close under his own eye; and was active in obtaining Queen Anne's Bounty for the increasing small livings.

Burnet died at his Clerkenwell house in 1715, and was buried near the communion-table of St. James's, Clerkenwell, the base Tory rabble flinging stones and dirt at the bishop's hearse.

In conversation Burnet is described as disagreeable, through a thick-skinned want of consideration. One day, during Marlborough's disgrace and voluntary exile, Burnet, dining with the duchess, who was a reputed termagant, compared the duke to Belisarius. "How do you account for so great a man having been so miserable and deserted?" asked the duchess. "Oh, madam," replied the bishop, "he had, as you know, such a brimstone of a wife." Burnet was opposed to the clergy enjoying a plurality of livings. A clergyman of his diocese once asked him if, on the authority of St. Bernard, he might hold two livings. "How will you be able to serve them both?" inquired Burnet. "I intend to officiate by deputy in one," was the reply. "Will your deputy," said Burnet, "be damned for you too? Believe me, sir, you may serve your cure by proxy, but you must be damned in person."

Burnet was extravagantly fond of tobacco and writing, and to enjoy both at the same time, he perforated the brim of his large hat, and putting his long pipe through it, puffed and wrote, and wrote and puffed again.

How far Burnet's historical writings can be relied on is still uncertain. He was a wholesale Whig, and seems to have been a vain, credulous man, who, according to Lord Bathurst, listened too much to flying gossip. Swift, in his violent and ribald way, denounced Burnet as a common liar, but, on the whole, we are inclined to think that he was only a violent party man, who, however, had a conscience, and tried his best to be honest. There is no doubt, however, from a letter discovered in the Napier charter chest, that on the discovery of the Rye House Plot, Burnet made many timid advances to the cruel and corrupt court.

In Burnet's house afterwards lived that remarkable man, Dr. Joseph Towers, the son of a poor bookseller in Southwark, who was born in the year 1737. Failing as a bookseller himself, Towers turned dissenting minister. He compiled the first seven volumes of "British Biography," and wrote fifty articles for Kippis's "Biographia Britannica." In 1794 Towers was arrested for his connection with the Society for Constitutional Information, of which Sheridan, Erskine, and the Duke of Norfolk were members. He died at this house, in St. John's Square, in 1799. Dr. Adam Clarke, the learned and pious author of the well-known Bible commentary, frequently lodged at No. 45, St. John's Square, where his sons carried on a printing business. He spent fifteen years in passing his eight quarto volumes through the press. He died in 1832, and was buried in the rear of the City Road Chapel, near Wesley. The Wesleyan chapel in St. John's Square was erected in 1849, at a cost of £3,800, by the transplanted congregation of Wilderness Row Chapel. The old-established printing offices of Messrs. Gilbert and Rivington were started in St. John's Square about 1757, and the firm still bears the name of Rivington.

St. John's Lane was, in the Middle Ages, the chief approach to the Hospital of St. John from the City. About 1619 this quarter was fashionable, numbering Lord Berkeley, Lady Cheteley, Sir Michael Stanhope, Sir Anthony Barker, and Lord Chief Justice Keeling among its noble and influential inhabitants. This last disgrace to the Bench was the base judge who sent John Bunyan to prison for three months, for being an upholder of conventicles. Some persons were once indicted before him for attending a conventicle; and, "although it was proved that they had assembled on the Lord's Day, with Bibles in their hands, without prayer-books, they were acquitted. He therefore fined the jury 100 marks a-piece, and imprisoned them till the fines were paid. Again, on the trial of a man for murder, who was suspected of being a Dissenter, and whom he had a great desire to hang, he fined and imprisoned all the jury, because, contrary to his directions, they brought in a verdict of manslaughter." Retribution came at last to this unjust judge. He was cited to the bar of the House of Commons in 1667, for constantly vi'ifying Magna

Charta, and only obtained mercy by the most abject submission. He retired to his house in Clerkenwell, disgraced, drew up a volume of divers cases in pleas of the Crown, and died in 1671.

In this same memorable lane resided, in 1677, that hard theological student, Matthew Poole, the compiler of the great Biblical synopsis, in five volumes folio. During the sham disclosures of Titus Oates, Poole's name was said to be down for immediate assassination. He fled to Holland in dismay, and died there the same year.

The "Old Baptist's Head," in St. John's Lane, a very historical house, was part of an old Elizabethan mansion, and the residence of Sir Thomas Forster, one of the judges in the Court of Common Pleas, who died here in 1612 (James I.) The quaint sign of the house was "John the Baptist's Head on a Charger." The inn formerly boasted bay windows of stained glass, and in the tap-room a carved stone mantelpiece, with what was supposed to be the Forster arms in the centre. In 1813 the rooms still had panelled wainscoats, and in the tap-room hung a picture of a Dutch revel, by Heemskerke, an imitator of Brauwer. In later years the "Old Baptist's Head" became a halting-place for prisoners, on their way from Newgate to the New Prison, Clerkenwell. In 1716 one of the celebrated Whig mug-houses was in St. John's Lane; and at the south-west corner of St. John's Lane, just beyond the boundary-mark of the parish, stood the "Queen's Head." It bore the date 1595, and in a niche of the gable-ended front was a bust of Queen Elizabeth, carved in stone.

In 1627-28 (Charles I.) a secret Jesuits' College was discovered near Clerkenwell Church, in a house where the Earl of Marlborough had formerly lived. Sir John Coke, then Secretary of State, drew up a report of the discovery, which was edited by Mr. J. G. Nichols, and re-published in the "Camden Miscellany." Sir John's narrative commences thus: "About Christmas last Humphrey Cross, one of the messengers in ordinarie, gave mee notice that the neighbours in St. John's saw provisions carried into the corner house uppon the broadway above Clerkenwel, but knewe none that dwelt there. In March following, about the beginning of the Parliament, Crosse brought word that divers lights were observed in the howse, and that some companie were gathered thither. The time considered, I thought fitt to make noe further delay, and therefore gave warrant to the sayd Crosse and Mr. Longe, and the constables next adjoyning to enter the house, and to search what persons resorted thither, and to what end they concealed their being there. At their entrie they found one that called himselfe Thomas Latham, who pretended to be keeper of the howse for the Earle of Shrewsburie. They found another, named George Kemp, said to be the gardener; and a woman, called Margaret Isham. But when they desired to go further, into the upper roomes, which (whilst they had made way into the hall) were all shutt upp and made fast, Latham tould them plainly that if they offred to goe further they would find resistance, and should doe it at their perils. They there-uppon repared to my house and desired more help, and a more ample warrant for their proceedings. And then both a warrant was granted from the councell boorde, and the Sheriffes of London were sent for theire assistance. But by this protraction they within the upper roomes gott advantage to retire themselves by secret passages into theire vaults or lurkinge-places, which themselves called their securities; so as when the officers came up they found no man above staires save only a sick man in his bed, with one servant attending him. The sick man called himselfe by the name of Weeden, who is since discovered to be truely called Plowden; and the servant named himselfe John Penington. More they found not, til, going downe againe into the cellars, Crosse espied a brick wall, newly made, which he caused to be perced and there within the vault they found Daniel Stanhop, whom I take to be Father Bankes, the Rector of their college, George Holland, alias Guy Holt, Joseph Underhill, aiias Thomas Poulton, Robert Beaumond, and Edward Moore, the priest; and the next day, in the like lurkinge-place, they found Edward Parre."

CHAPTER XLI.

CLERKENWELL—(continued).

Bowls and Bowling-greens—Clerkenwell Close—Thomas Weaver—Sir Thomas Challoner—The Fourth Earl of Clanricarde—A Right Mad Doctor—Newcastle Place and its Inhabitants—Clerkenwell Green—Izaak Walton—Jack Adams, the Clerkenwell Simpleton—The Lamb and Flag Ragged School—The Northampton Family—Miss Ray—The Bewicks—Aylesbury House and its Associations—The Musical Small-coal Man—Berkeley Street—"Sally in our Alley"—Red Bull Theatre—Ward's Public-house—The Old and New Church of St. James.

BOWLING-GREENS were once numerous in Bowling Green Lane, Clerkenwell. In 1675, says Mr. Pinks, there were two at the north-east corner. The bowling-alleys were both open and covered, and were laid with turf or gravel. The bowls were flat or round, and the simple object was to lay your bowl so many times nearest the jack, or mark. The pleasant game is repeatedly mentioned by Shake-speare, and furnished his quick fancy with innu-merable metaphors. There was also a game of ground balls, which were driven through an arch. This game expanded became Charles II.'s favourite diversion, "Pall Mall," and, contracted and com-plicated, it changed into our modern "Croquet." In 1617 (James I.) the Groom Porters' Office issued licences for thirty-one bowling-alleys, fourteen tennis-courts, and forty gambling-houses in London, Westminster, and their suburbs, all to be closed on Sundays. In 1675 there were only six houses in this lane, and at the south-west corner was the churchyard of St. James's. The "Cherry Tree" public-house was well known in 1775, and there were cherry-trees still there in 1825. At the south-west corner of Bowling Green Lane, in 1675, stood one of those mountain heaps of cinders and rubbish which disgraced old London. At one end of the lane there once stood a whipping-post for petty offenders. An old name for this lane was Feather Bed Lane, but why we do not know, unless boys like Defoe's Colonel Jack lolled, burrowed, and gambolled on the huge dust-heap.

Clerkenwell Close teems with old legends and traditions; and well it may, for was it not part of the old convent cloisters, and afterwards a portion of the glebe of the church of St. James? The house now No. 22, says Mr. Pinks, the Stow of Clerkenwell, was originally the parsonage house. The "Crown Tavern," at the south-west corner of the Close, was rebuilt in the early part of this century. The mummy of a poor cat, which some mason of John or Richard's reign had cruelly buried alive in one of the walls of St. James's Church, used to be solemnly shown there. Formerly the southern en-trance to the Close was small, and squeezed in between a butcher's shop and the "Crown Tavern."

That good plodding "old mortality," John Weever, lived in Clerkenwell Close in 1631 (Charles I.), and to that place brought home many a pocket-load of old epitaphs, to adorn his good old book, "Ancient Funeral Monuments." His house was the next one northward of No. 8. It is large, and double-fronted, and has fine old staircases, and foliated ceilings. Weever was a friend of Cotton and Selden, and therefore not lightly to be despised, but Anthony à Wood pronounces him credulous, and he is said to be careless in his dates. The following is Weever's epitaph, in St. James's, Clerkenwell :—

> " Lancashire gave me breath,
>   And Cambridge education ;
> Middlesex gave me death,
>   And this church my humation ;
> And Christ to me hath given
>   A place with Him in heaven."

In the Close, opposite the convent, according to Weever, resided Sir Thomas Challoner, in a house which either Thurlow or Cromwell himself afterwards occupied. On the front of the mansion, which stood in a large garden, were written four Latin lines, which have been thus Englished :—

> " Chaste faith still stays behind, though thence be flown
>   Those veiled nuns who here before did nest;
> For reverend marriage wedlock vows doth own,
>   And sacred flames keep here in loyal breasts."

This Sir Thomas Challoner, of Clerkenwell Close, was a gallant gentleman, who fought beside the Emperor Charles V., in Algiers ; on his return he was made by Henry VIII. first clerk of the Council, and in the reign of Edward VI. he won the favour of the proud Protector Somerset. By Elizabeth he was sent as a trusty ambassador to Ferdinand, Emperor of Germany, and afterwards to the court of Philip of Spain, where he was vexed by every possible indignity. He returned home in 1564, and spent the rest of his life quietly in the Close, completing his great work, " The Right Ordering of the English Republic," which he dedicated to his friend Burleigh. Sir Thomas, son of this wise courtier, married a daughter of Sir William Fleetwood, the well-known Recorder of London. His study of science in Italy enabled him to enrich himself by the discovery of alum on his own estate, near Gisborough, in Yorkshire. He became a friend of James I., who placed Prince Henry under his tuition, for which he received £4,000, " as a free gift." Two of this learned man's sons sat as judges at the trial of Charles I., and one was bold enough to sign the king's death-warrant. This latter Challoner Cromwell openly denounced as a drunkard when he dissolved the obstructive Parliament.

Near the Challoners, in the Close, in the year 1619, resided the fourth Earl of Clanricarde. This nobleman married the widow of Sir Philip Sidney. At the Restoration there were thirty-one good houses in Clerkenwell Close, Sir John Cropley and Dr. Theophilus Garenciers being the most distinguished residents. The latter gentleman was a Protestant refugee from Normandy, and kindly taught the " musical small-coal man " chemistry. He wrote some books on tapeworms and tincture of coral, and translated the nonsensical prophecies of Nostradamus. In 1668 Dr. Everard Maynwaring resided in the Close. He was a kinsman of the wife of Ashmole, the antiquary, and wrote a book to show that tobacco produced scurvy.

" An old writer, Aubrey," says Mr. Pinks, " who compiled an amusing volume on the superstitions of his countrymen, when treating of a fatality believed to attach to certain houses, says :—' A handsome brick house, on the south side of Clerkenwell Churchyard, has been so unlucky for at least forty years, that it was seldom tenanted, and at last nobody would adventure to take it.' This was written in 1696. Here also was once a private madhouse, of which the public was apprised by advertisement, as follows :— ' In Clerkenwell Close, where the figures of mad people are over the gate, liveth one who, by the blessing of God, cures all lunatick, distracted, or mad people. He seldom exceeds three months in the cure of the maddest person that comes in his house ; several have been cured in a fortnight, and some in less time. He has cured several from Bedlam, and other madhouses in and about this city, and has conveniency for people of what quality soever. No cure, no money.' Such equitable dealing as this, there can be little doubt, secured for the proprietor of this asylum a fair share of patronage from the friends of the insane."

Newcastle Place was the site of old Newcastle House, built upon the ruins of the convent, which had, at the dissolution, become the property of the Cavendish family. One likes to believe that a curse fell on those greedy nobles who stole what good and charitable men had left in trust for the poor, but that the trust had been sometimes abused, who is hardy enough to deny ? But the abuses of the priests could surely have been corrected better than by confiscation. The duke's garden extended as far as the present St. James's Walk, and contained six arches of the southern cloister of the old building. One cloister is described in the *Gentleman's Magazine* of 1785 as having at its west end an arched door communicating with the church. The roof resembled that of Exeter Cathedral, and the keystones were carved into the form of flowers. Over the cloister was a wareroom, and on the east side of the garden was the site of the ancient cemetery of the nuns. In 1773, according to Noorthouck, the nuns' hall, which still stood at the north-east end of the cloisters, had been turned into a double range of workshops. Two bricked-up arched windows, and the hood moulding of a Gothic doorway are visible in the sketch of the hall in Crowle's " Pennant."

The Duke of Newcastle, William Cavendish, and

his blue-stocking and eccentric wife, Margaret, the youngest daughter of Sir Charles Lucas, who was shot by the Parliamentarians at the surrender of Colchester, were the most memorable residents in this great Clerkenwell mansion. The duke was a gallant and chivalrous cavalier, whose white regiment of cavalry, generally known to the Cromwellians as the "Newcastle Lambs," did good service for wilful King Charles during the Civil War. In disgust at the loss of the battle of Marston Moor by the mad rashness of Prince

justice in Eyre, and Duke of Newcastle. He died at his house at Clerkenwell in 1676, aged eighty-four. The duchess, a *femme savante* of the deepest dye, wrote ten folio volumes of learned trifles and fantastic verses. A footman always slept on a truckle bed in a closet of her bedroom, and whenever a thought struck her in the night, she used to call out, " John !" and poor John had to scramble out in the cold, light a candle, and bind the fugitive fancy fast on paper. "The whole story," writes Pepys, " of this lady is a romance, and all she does

BURNET HOUSE, 1866. (*See page* 325.)

Rupert, the duke retired to the Continent, and there, with his faithful wife, during eighteen years' exile, endured many hardships while lodging at Antwerp, in a house which belonged to the widow of Rubens.

In the duchess's memoir of her brave husband, on whom she doated, and whom she seems to have considerably bored, she states that at one time of their exile they were both forced to pawn their clothes for a dinner. While abroad the duke produced a luxurious folio on horsemanship. During his absence the Parliament levied, it is computed, £733,579 on his estate. At the Restoration this faithful loyalist was made a chief

is romantic." "April 26, 1667.—Met my Lady Newcastle, with her coaches and footmen, all in velvet, herself, whom I never saw before, as I have heard her often described, for all the town-talk is nowadays of her extravagance, with her velvet cap, her hair about her ears, many black patches, because of pimples about her mouth, naked-necked, without anything about it, and a black *just au corps*.

"May 1, 1667.—She was in a black coach, adorned with silver, instead of gold, and snow-white curtains, and everything black and white. Staid at home, reading the ridiculous history of my Lord Newcastle, wrote by his wife, which shows her to be a mad, conceited, ridiculous woman, and him an asse to suffer her to write what she writes to him and of him."

"On the 10th April, 1667," says Mr. Pinks, Charles and his queen came to Clerkenwell, on a visit to the duchess. On the 18th, John Evelyn went to make court to the noble pair, who received him with great kindness; and another time he dined at Newcastle House, and was privileged to sit discoursing with her grace in her bedchamber, after dinner. Referring to her literary employments, when writing to a friend, she says, 'You will find

which set the whole family by the ears. The Earl of Thanet, another son-in-law, fought a duel with the Earl of Clare, in consequence, in Lincoln's Inn Fields, in which both combatants were wounded. The Earl of Clare, for his loyal service to William III., was, in 1694, created Duke of Newcastle, and enjoyed the favour of Queen Anne.

Newcastle House, at one period, was the residence of the eldest daughter of the old duke, the Duchess of Albemarle, a woman crazed with pride, who married General Monk's son, and drove him

NEWCASTLE HOUSE, 1770.   (*See page* 329.)

my works, like infinite Nature, that hath neither beginning nor end; and as confused as the chaos, wherein is neither method nor order, but all mixed together, without separation, like light and darkness.'" It will be remembered that Sir Walter Scott, in his "Peveril of the Peak," has cleverly sketched the old-fashioned high-flown duchess, and contrasted her with the gay and wanton beauties of England's corruptest court. The wise and foolish woman died in 1676, and was buried by her husband in Westminster Abbey.

Henry Cavendish, Master of the Robes to Charles II., left the bulk of his estates, realising about £9,000, to his son-in-law, the Earl of Clare,

by her folly to a liquid remedy, which killed him in his youth. At his death the duchess was so immensely wealthy, that pride crazed her, and she vowed never to marry any one but a sovereign prince. In 1692 the Earl of Montagu, disguising himself as the Emperor of China, won the mad woman, whom he then kept in constant confinement at Montagu House (the site of the British Museum). She survived her second husband thirty years, and at last died at Newcastle House, in 1734, aged ninety-six years. Her body lay in state in the Jerusalem Chamber, Westminster Abbey, and at midnight was privately interred near her father-in-law, General Monk, in Henry VII.'s

Chapel. It is said that up to the time of this mad woman's decease she was always served on the knee, as if she had really been the empress she believed herself.

Newcastle House, in Pennant's time, was a cabinet-maker's, and the garden was strewn with the defaced monuments of Prior Weston, and other worthies. About 1793 Mr. Carr, who built the present church of St. James, erected on the site of the duke's mansion the row of houses called Newcastle Place. Every trace of the convent then disappeared, except a small portion of a wall, the jamb of a Gothic window of the nuns' hall (now the side wall of a house at the north end of Newcastle Street). The old house was a sombre, monotonous brick structure, having its upper storey adorned with stone pilasters. The east and west wings stood forward, and there was a large courtyard in front.

Clerkenwell Green, long gay enough, even as lately as the latter part of the seventeenth century, was environed by mansions of the noble and rich. In Roques's huge Map of London in 1747 there were lofty trees on either side of the Green, and two at the north-east corner of Aylesbury Street. The last tree on the north side of the Green was blown down by a storm in July, 1796. The old pillory, where Mr. John Britton had seen a man fastened and pelted, used to stand on the western slope of the Green, near the bottom; and in 1787 a woman who had committed perjury was nearly killed at this place of punishment. A turnstile stood at the entrance of the close, prior to the houses being taken down to form a better approach to the church. A raised circle of stone with lamp-posts, near the middle of the green, and close to the drinking-fountain, marks, says the best of the local historians, the spot where the old watch-house once stood.

On the north side of the Green, a low brick house, now divided into three shops, was formerly the Welsh Charity School, founded in 1718. The house was built in 1737, and the charity removed to the Gray's Inn Road in 1772, and after that to Ashford, near Staines. There used to be a painted figure of a Welsh boy in a niche in the front of the school. Pennant, a warm-hearted Welshman, intended to have devoted the profits of his great work on "British Zoology" to this school, but its expenses were so great that he was unable to do so, and he gave instead the sum of £100.

Of the chief residents of Clerkenwell Green we can only select the most eminent. Amongst these we may mention Sir Richard Cheverton, the Lord Mayor in 1657, who proclaimed Richard Cromwell Protector. He lived long, and was styled the Father of the City. Sir William Bolton, an alderman, knighted by Charles II., also resided on the Green; and in 1670 we find, in the list of rich residents, Sir William Bowles, Bart., Sir Edward Smith, and Lady Windham.

Above all these aldermen and city magnates, however, rejoice, Clerkenwell, because that good and gentle spirit, Izaak Walton, once lived in thy midst, and often paced his guileless path, pondering on mighty barbel in the muddy depths of the pleasant river Lea. On his retirement from the snug little linendrapers' shops, first at the Exchange and then in Fleet Street, Walton, before the year 1650, says Sir Harris Nicolas, took a house at Clerkenwell. That delightful book, "The Compleat Angler; or, the Contemplative Man's Recreation," sold by Richard Marriot, in St. Dunstan's Churchyard, Fleet Street, appeared in 1653. The good, pious old fisherman lived at Clerkenwell, it is supposed, till 1661. He went to Worcester after that, and died at Winchester, at the house of a son-in-law of his, a prebendary, in 1683. In his will the worthy old man left forty-two mourning-rings to his friends, and (could human forgiveness go further?) £10 to his publisher, Richard Marriot.

George Sawbridge, an eminent bookseller of 1670, who published a book by Culpeper, the herbalist, also dwelt on Clerkenwell Green. He left £40,000 to be divided among his four daughters. Elias Ashmole records that he was a friend of Lilly, the sham astrologer.

Jack Adams, a Clerkenwell simpleton, who lived on the Green, became a notorious street character in the reign of Charles II. This half fool, half knave (like many of Shakespeare's jesters) is constantly mentioned in pamphlets of Charles II.'s reign. In an old work, called "The Wits; or, Sport upon Sport" (published in 1682), the writer describes the excellent comedians at the Red Bull Theatre, in Red Bull Yard, now Woodbridge Street. On one occasion, when Robert Cox, a celebrated low comedian, played "Simpleton the Smith," he used to come in munching a huge slice of bread-and-butter; Jack Adams, seeing it, cried out, "Cuz, cuz, give me some! give me some!" to the great amusement of all the spectators. This Adams seems to have turned astrologer and fortune-teller. You got a better fortune from him for five guineas than for five shillings, and he appears to have been as willing to cheat as his dupes were to be cheated. The conjuror of Clerkenwell seems, after this, to have generally adopted this popular name. There is an old print of Jack Adams, in which he is represented with a tobacco-pipe in his girdle, and standing by a table, on which lie a horn-book and " Poor Robin's Almanack."

In 1644, during the Civil Wars, Lady Bullock's house, on Clerkenwell Green, was attacked by soldiers, who stole fifty pieces of gold, and tore five rich rings from her ladyship's fingers. Dr. Sibbald, the incumbent of Clerkenwell, who resided near, remonstrated with the Parliamentary soldiers from his window, but the only reply was three musket-bullets at his head, which they narrowly missed. A servant of Lady Bullock was wounded by the soldiers.

In 1844 the Lamb and Flag Ragged School was established on Clerkenwell Green. Since that time day-schools, night-schools, and Sunday-schools have been added to it.

At the corner of Ashby Street, which leads from St. John's Street Road to Northampton Square, stands the old manor house of Clerkenwell, the residence of the Northampton family till nearly the end of the seventeenth century. The first baron was Sir Henry Compton, of Warwickshire, summoned to Parliament among the nobles in 1572 (Elizabeth). The second Lord Compton was created Earl of Northampton in 1618 (James I.), and also K.G. and Lord President of the Marches of Wales.

How that nobleman carried off the daughter of rich Lord Mayor Spencer, in a baker's basket, from Canonbury, we have before related. The wife of the second earl had the courage to attend her lord to the battle of Edgehill, where she witnessed the daring and danger of her three Cavalier sons. Spencer Compton fell at the battle of Hopton Heath, in 1643. The third earl resided at Clerkenwell in 1677; his estates, which had been confiscated, were returned to him at the Restoration. He is said to have had a troop of 200 retainers, who wore his livery of blue and grey, and he was one of the king's Privy Council and Constable of the Tower. This earl's youngest brother, after being a cornet of horse, was made Bishop of London, and was entrusted with the education of the Princesses Mary and Ann. After being suspended by James II., he performed the coronation service for William of Orange, and was appointed one of the commissioners for revising the Liturgy. His toleration of Dissenters rendered him unpopular with the Tories. He died in 1713. Joshua Alwyne Spencer, the tenth earl and second marquis, was the President of the Royal Society.

At the end of the seventeenth century the old manor-house of the Spencers was converted into a private lunatic asylum, by Dr. Newton. Thoresby,

the Leeds historian, speaks doubtfully of this doctor's honesty. He published a herbal, which Cave printed, and seems to have had a botanic garden behind the madhouse. It was here that strange fanatic and false prophet, Richard Brothers, was confined. This man had been a lieutenant in the Royal Navy, but left the service in 1789, and refusing, from conscientious scruples, to take the necessary oath, he lost his half-pay. He then became poor, and had to take refuge in a workhouse. In 1790 he became insane, believed himself a prophet sent from God, and warned all who called him mad, an impostor, or a devil, that they were guilty of blasphemy. In 1792 he sent letters to the king, the ministers, and the speaker, saying he was ordered by God to go to the House of Commons, and inform the members, for their safety, that the time was come for the fulfilment of the seventh chapter of Daniel. He went accordingly, and met with the rough reception that might have been expected. Soon after Brothers prophesied the death of King George, the overthrow of the monarchy, and the delivery of the crown into his own hands; this being treasonable, he was sent to Newgate. On his release, he persuaded many weak people to sell their goods and prepare to accompany him, in 1795, to the New Jerusalem, which was to be built on both sides of the river Jordan, and to become the capital of the world. In 1798 the Jews were to be restored, and he was to be revealed as their prince and ruler, and the governor of all nations, a post for which Brothers had even refused the divine offer of the Chancellorship of the Exchequer. Brothers at last got too troublesome, even for English toleration, and was confined as a lunatic in Clerkenwell; he was released in 1806, by the zealous intercession of his great disciple, John Finlayson, with whom he afterwards resided for nine years. Brothers died suddenly, of cholera, in 1824. His last words were addressed to Finlayson, asking if his sword and hammer were ready, referring to the building of the New Jerusalem. In 1817 the old manor-house was turned into a ladies' boarding-school.

Albemarle Street was so called from General Monk, Duke of Albemarle, during whose popularity the street was built. Albion Place was erected in 1822. In this street, in 1721, lived Christopher Pinchbeck, an inventor of "astronomico-musical clocks," and the peculiar compound metal to which he gave the name. We have already briefly mentioned this ingenious man in our chapter on Fleet Street. Pinchbeck made musical automata that played tunes and imitated birds, like the curious Black Forest clocks now so familiar to us. He also sold self-playing organs, to save the expense of organists in country churches, and he also condescended to mend clocks and watches.

Miss Ray, that unfortunate mistress of Lord Sandwich, who was shot by her lover, Hackman, the clergyman, served her time with a mantua-maker in St. George's Court, Albion Place. A pleasant memory of those delightful old engravers, the Bewicks, is also associated with St. George's Court; for here, about 1780, lived a bookseller named Hodgson, for whom they worked. In the same obscure yet honoured locality also lived that sturdy old antiquary, Dr. Thomas Birch, the son of a Quaker coffee-mill maker, of Clerkenwell. Birch eventually, after being usher to Mr. Besse, a Quaker in St. George's Court, took orders in the Church of England, and married the daughter of a clergyman. Lord Hardwicke patronised him, and in 1734 he became domestic chaplain to the unfortunate Jacobite Earl of Kilmarnock, who, joining in the luckless rebellion of '45, was beheaded on Tower Hill. In 1743 he was presented to the united rectories of St. Michael, Wood Street, and St. Mary Staining. He worked much for Cave, and was killed by a fall from his horse, near Hampstead, in 1760. He bequeathed his valuable library and manuscripts to the British Museum, and the residue of his small property to increase the salaries of the three assistant librarians.

Aylesbury Street, close by, is so called because in bygone times the garden-wall of the house of the Earls of Aylesbury skirted the south side of the thoroughfare. Aylesbury House was probably a name given to part of the old Priory of St. John, where the Earls of Elgin and Aylesbury resided about 1641. Robert Bruce, second Earl of Elgin, who lived here in 1671, was a devoted Cavalier, and an ardent struggler for the Restoration, and was made Earl of Aylesbury in 1663 by that not usually very grateful king, Charles II., to whom he was privy councillor and gentleman of the bedchamber. At the coronation of that untoward monarch, James II., the Earl of Aylesbury bore in procession St. Edward's staff, eight pounds nine ounces in weight, and supposed by credulous persons to contain a piece of the true cross. The earl died in 1685, the year he had been appointed Lord Chamberlain of the Royal Household. Anthony à Wood sums up the earl as a good historian and antiquary, a friend to the clergy, and a "curious collector of manuscripts."

But a far more interesting resident in Aylesbury Street was Thomas Britton, the "musical small-coal man," who, though a mere itinerant vendor of small coal, cultivated the highest branches of music, and drew round him for years all the great musicians of the day, including even the giant Handel. This singular and most meritorious person, born in Northamptonshire, brought up to the coal trade, and coming to London, took a small stable at the south-east corner of Jerusalem Passage, on the site now occupied by the "Bull's Head" public-house, and commenced his humble business. His coal he kept below, and he lived in a single room above, which was ascended by an external ladder. From Dr. Garenciers, his neighbour, this active-minded man obtained a thorough knowledge of practical chemistry, and in his spare time he acquired an extensive practical and theoretical knowledge of music. This simple-minded man founded a musical club, which met at his house for nearly forty years, and at first gave gratuitous concerts, afterwards paid for by an annual subscription of ten shillings, coffee being sold to his distinguished visitors at a penny a cup. The idea of the club is said to have been first suggested by Sir Roger l'Estrange. Dr. Pepusch, or the great Handel, played the harpsichord; Bannister, or Medler, the first violin. Hughes, a poet, and Woolaston, a painter, were also members, while Britton himself played excellently on the viol di gamba. The musical invitation to these concerts ran thus:—

> "Upon Thursdays repair to my palace, and there
>   Hobble up stair by stair, but I pray you take care
> That you break not your shins by a stumble;
> And without e'er a souse, paid to me or my spouse,
>   Sit still as a mouse at the top of the house,
> And there you shall hear how we fumble."

Britton's friend, Ned Ward, describes these pleasant Thursday evening concerts, which, he says, were as popular as the evenings of the Kit-Cat Club. Thomas Britton, in his blue frock, with a measure twisted into the mouth of his sack, was as much respected as if he had been a nobleman in disguise.

"Britton," says our Clerkenwell historian, "besides being a musician, was a bibliomaniac, and collector of rare old books and manuscripts, from which fact we may infer that he had cultivated some acquaintance with literature. It often happened that, on Saturdays, when some of these *literati* were accustomed to meet at the shop of one Christopher Bateman, a bookseller, at the corner of Ave Maria Lane, Paternoster Row, Britton, who had usually completed his morning round by twelve o'clock at noon, would, despite his smutty appearance and blue smock, after pitching his sack of small coal on the bulk of Bateman's shop, join the literary conclave, and take part in the conversation, which generally lasted an hour. Often as he walked the streets some one who knew him would point him out, and exclaim, 'There goes the small-coal man, who is a lover of learning, a performer of music, and a companion for gentlemen.' The circumstances of Britton's death are as remarkable as those of his life; he was literally frightened out of his life by a practical joke which was played on him by one Robe, a justice of the peace, and a frequenter of his concerts, who one day introduced as his friend a man who had the sobriquet of the 'Talking Smith,' but whose real name was Honeyman. This man possessed the power of ventriloquism, and when he saw Britton he, by a preconcerted arrangement, announced in a solemn voice, which seemed to come from a long distance, the death of Britton in a few hours, unless he immediately fell upon his knees and repeated the Lord's Prayer. Britton, in the terror of his soul, instinctively obeyed; but the chord of his life was unstrung by this sudden shock. A brief illness supervened, and in a few days he died. His death occurred in September, 1714, when he was upwards of sixty years of age. On the 1st of October his remains were followed to the grave by a great concourse of people, and interred in St. James's churchyard." Though Britton was honest and upright, ill-natured people, says Walpole, called him a Jesuit and an atheist, and said that the people attended his meetings to talk sedition and practise magic. At his death the worthy small-coal man left 1,400 books, twenty-seven fine musical instruments, and some valuable music.

Berkeley Street, formerly called Bartlett Street, was so named from its chief pride, Berkeley House, which stood at the corner facing St. John's Lane. The advanced wings of the mansion enclosed a spacious forecourt, and at the rear was a large garden. Sir Maurice Berkeley, who lived here, was standard-bearer to Henry VIII., Edward VI., and Queen Elizabeth. He it was who, when Sir Thomas Wyatt was beaten back from Ludgate to Temple Bar, yet would not surrender, induced Wyatt to mount behind him on his horse, and ride to Whitehall. In this house lived and died that pious Lord Berkeley, who, in Charles II.'s time was called "George the Traveller," and "George the Linguist." The first Earl of Berkeley obtained the titles of Viscount Dursley and Earl of Berkeley as a reward for his loyalty to Charles II. When the English prisoners were to be released from Algiers he offered to advance the money for their redemption. He bestowed on Sion College a valuable library, and he wrote some religious meditations, which obtained for him a eulogy

from Waller. He died in 1698. His second daughter, Lady Theophila, married the pious and learned Robert Nelson, author of "Fasts and Festivals." At what period Berkeley House was pulled down is unknown, but in the year 1856 a moulded brick, stamped with a lyre, supposed to be a relic of the old mansion, was found in Berkeley Street.

At the south-east end of Ray Street, a broken iron pump, let into the front wall of a dilapidated tenement, marks, as nearly as possible, the site of the ancient Clerks' Well, used by the brothers of St. John and the Benedictine nuns, and the place where, as the old chronicler says, the London parish clerks performed their miracle plays. In Stow's time this fine spring was cared for and sheltered with stone. In Aggas's map (about 1560) there is a conduit-house at the south-west corner of the boundary wall of St. Mary's nunnery, and the water falls into an oblong trough, which is enclosed by a low wall. In 1673 the Earl of Northampton gave this spring for the use of the poor of the parish of St. James, but it was at once let to a brewer. Strype, writing about 1720, describes the well as at the right-hand side of a lane which led from Clerkenwell to Hockley-in-the-Hole, and it was then enclosed by a high wall, which had been built to bound Clerkenwell Close. Hone, in 1823, writing of the mystery plays of the Middle Ages, points out that as the priory stood about half way down the slope from Clerkenwell Green to the Fleet, people stationed on the rising ground near could have easily seen the quaint performances at the well. Near the pump, erected in 1800, to mark the old well, stood one of the parish watch-houses, erected in 1794.

Vineyard Walk, Clerkenwell, is supposed to mark the site of one of the old priory vineyards. The ground was called the Mount, and against the western slopes grew vines, row above row, there being a small cottage at the top. It existed in this form as late as 1752. There was also a vineyard in East Smithfield as late as the reign of Stephen. It is said that the soil of this Mount Pleasant was sold, in 1765, for £10,000.

That remarkable man, Henry Carey, the author of "Sally in our Alley," one of the very prettiest of old London love songs, lived and died at his house in Great Warner Street. Carey, by profession a music-master and song-writer for Sadler's Wells, was an illegitimate son of the Marquis of Halifax, who presented the crown to William III. He was for long supposed to have written "God Save the King," but the composition has now been traced much further back. The origin of Carey's great

CLERKENWELL GREEN IN 1789. (*See page 332.*)

hit, "Sally in our Alley," was a 'prentice day's holiday, witnessed by Carey himself. A shoe-maker's apprentice making holiday with his sweetheart, treated her with a sight of Bedlam, the puppet-shows, the flying chairs (ups and downs), and all the elegancies of Moorfields, and from thence proceeding to the Farthing Pye House, he gave her a collation of buns, cheesecakes, stuffed beef, and bottled ale; through all of which scenes the author dodged them. Charmed with the sim-

Edward Alleyn, founder of Dulwich College, played here in 1617. In 1627 we find the king's company obtaining an injunction from the Master of the Revels, forbidding the use of Shakespeare's plays by the Red Bull company. Some of the earliest female performers upon record in this country appeared at the Red Bull. The theatre was rebuilt and enlarged in 1633, when it was, probably for the first time, roofed in, and decorated somewhat elaborately, the management particularly

THE OLD CHURCH OF ST. JAMES, CLERKENWELL.   (*See page* 338.)

plicity of their courtship, he wrote his charming song of "Sally in our Alley," which has been well described as one of the most perfect little pictures of humble life in the language. Reduced to poverty or despair by some unknown cause, Carey hung himself in 1743. Only a halfpenny was found in his pocket.

The Red Bull Theatre, a house as well known in Elizabeth's time as the Globe or the Fortune, stood at the south-west corner of what was afterwards a distillery, in Woodbridge Street. At the commencement of the reign of James I. the queen's servants, who had been the Earl of Worcester's players, performed at this house. In 1613, George Wither, the poet, speaks disparagingly of the place.

priding itself on a stage curtain of "pure Naples silk." We find Carew, in some commendatory lines on a play of Davenant, denouncing the Red Bull performances as bombast and non-sense.

During the Commonwealth, when the victorious zealots prohibited stage plays, the Red Bull company were permitted to produce drolls and farces. From a print dated 1622 we see that the stage was at that time lighted by chandeliers, and that there were boxes for spectators behind the actors. At the Restoration the king's players acted for a few days at the Red Bull, and then went to a new playhouse built for them in Vere Street, Clare Market. Pepys speaks of the Red Bull as a low theatre, and of the performances as bad. The house was closed in 1663, and was then turned into a fencing-school.

In the same street as the Red Bull Theatre, in Queen Anne's reign, Ned Ward, a coarse, but clever writer, whom we have often quoted, kept a public-house. In his poetical address to the public he says, with indistinct reference to the Red Bull Theatre—

> " There, on that ancient, venerable ground,
>   Where Shakespeare in heroic buskins trod,
> Within a good old fabrick may be found
>   Celestial liquors, fit to charm a god ;
> Rich nectar, royal punch, and home-brewed ale,
>   Such as our fathers drank in time of yore.
>
> *   *   *   *   *   *
>
> Commodious room, with Hampstead air supplied.
>
> *   *   *   *   *   *
>
>   No bacchanalian ensigns at the door,
> To give the public notice, are displayed,
>   Yet friends are welcome. We shall say no more,
> But hope their friendship will promote a trade."

Ward, who retorted an attack of Pope in the " Dunciad," was, as we have mentioned, a friend of the musical coal-man, and at his public-house Britton's books and musical instruments were sold after his death.

The old church of St. James, Clerkenwell, was only a fragment in Stow's time. No. 22 in the Close was the original rectory house. The church was sold in 1656 to trustees for the parish. The steeple fell down in 1623, after having stood for five centuries, and, being badly rebuilt, fell again, when nearly repaired, the bells breaking in the roof and gallery, and all the pews. There was no organ in the church till within sixty years of its demolition. The old building was pulled down in 1788, and a fine monument of Sir William Weston, the last prior of St. John's, was sold to Sir George Booth, and removed to Burleigh. The prior's effigy represented a skeleton. There was also a fine brass over the monument of Dr. John Bell, Bishop of Worcester in the time of Henry VIII., to whom it is said he acted as secretary. He was engaged by the king in the matter of his divorces from Catherine of Arragon and Anne of Cleves. " He was buried," says Green, the historian of Worcestershire, " like a bishop, with mitre and odours, things that belong to a bishop, with two white branches, two dozen staves, torches, and four great tapers, near the altar," in the old church of St. James, Clerkenwell. On the north side of the church stood a costly stone altar-tomb, with Corinthian pillars, to the memory of Lady Elizabeth Berkeley, whose effigy lay in state, with the head of a negro at her feet. This lady was a gentlewoman to the Princess Elizabeth, in the Tower, and refusing to go to mass, was so threatened that she was compelled to fly to Geneva, where she remained in exile till the death of Queen Mary. There was also the monument of Thomas Bedingfield, one of Queen Elizabeth's gentlemen pensioners, the son of that worthy Governor of the Tower who treated Elizabeth with such kindness and forbearance when, in her earlier years, she was a prisoner in his care.

The old church also contained a marble tablet, affixed to a chancel pillar, to the memory of that patient old antiquary, John Weever, who collected a great volume of epitaphs and inscriptions. A tomb to the memory of Elizabeth, Countess of Exeter, who married the grandson of the famous Burleigh, and died in 1653, is now in the vaults of the new church. On a painted board near this tomb it was stated that the venerable countess was grandmother to thirty-two children, and great-grandmother to thirty-three. In the old chapter-house, which had been turned into a vestry, was buried Sir Thomas Holt, father of the famous Lord Chief Justice Holt. Near the south-east corner of the church was a black and white marble monument, which had been erected in memory of George Strode, an old Cavalier officer, and a great benefactor to the poor of Clerkenwell.

The new church of St. James, which cost nearly £12,000, was consecrated by Bishop Porteus, in 1792. The church contains several interesting monuments, including one erected to the memory of Bishop Burnet, in 1715, who, as we have already stated, was buried beneath the altar in the old church. The plain blue slab, carved with his arms, surrounded by the garter, is now preserved in the vault. Against the wall, on the gallery staircase, is a memorial stone to the famous Clerkenwell archer, Sir William Wood, captain of the Finsbury archers, who died in 1691. He was the wearer of many a prize-badge, and the author of "The Bowman's Glory," a curious little book in praise of archery. He lived to the age of eighty-two, and three flights of whistling arrows were discharged over his grave.

CHAPTER XLII.

SMITHFIELD.

Bartholomew Fair—A Seven Days' Tournament—Duels and Trial by Ordeal in Smithfield—Terrible Instances of the *Odium Theologicum*—The Maid of Kent—Foxe's Account of the Smithfield Martyrs—The Smithfield Gallows—William Wallace in Smithfield—Bartholomew Priory—The Origin of Bartholomew Fair—St. Bartholomew becomes popular with Sailors—Miscellaneous Occupiers of Smithfield—Generosity of English Kings to St. Bartholomew's—A Religious Brawl—The London Parish Clerks in Smithfield—The Court of Pie-poudre.

SMITHFIELD, or "Smoothfield," to follow the true derivation, was from the earliest times a memorable spot in old London. Bartholomew Fair, established in the reign of Henry II., in the neighbourhood of the priory and hospital founded by Rayer, the king's worthy jester, brought annually great crowds of revellers to the same place where, in Mary's brief reign, so many of her 277 victims perished. Smithfield, in the reign of the early Edwards, was a chosen place for tournaments, and here many a spear was splintered on breastplate and shield, and many a stout blow given, till armour yielded or sword shattered.

In 1374 Edward III., then sixty-two, enamoured of Alice Perrers, held a seven days' tournament in Smithfield, for her amusement. She sat beside the old man, in a magnificent car, as the Lady of the Sun, and was followed by a long train of plumed knights, careless of the disgrace, each leading by the bridle a beautiful palfrey, on which was mounted a gay damsel.

In 1390 that young prodigal, Richard II., wishing to rival the splendid feasts and jousts given by Charles of France, on the entry of his consort, Isabella of Bavaria, into Paris, invited sixty knights to a tilt in Smithfield, commencing on the Sunday after Michaelmas Day. This tournament was proclaimed by heralds in England, Scotland, Hainault, Germany, Flanders, and France. The Sunday was the feast of the challengers. About three p.m. came the procession from the Tower —sixty barbed coursers, in full trappings, each attended by a squire of honour, and after them sixty ladies of rank, mounted on palfreys, "most elegantly and richly dressed," and each leading by a silver chain a knight, completely armed for tilting, minstrels and trumpeters attending the procession to Smithfield. Every night there was a magnificent supper for the tilters at the bishop's palace, where the king and queen were lodged, and the dancing lasted till daybreak. On Tuesday King Edward entertained the foreign knights and squires, and the queen the ladies. On Friday they were entertained by the Duke of Lancaster, and on Saturday the king invited all the foreign knights to Windsor.

That great historical event, the death of Wat Tyler, we have elsewhere described, but it is necessary here to touch upon it again. Wrongs, no doubt, his followers had, but they were savage and cruel, and intoxicated with murder and plunder. They had beheaded the Archbishop of Canterbury, and held London in terror for seven days. Wat Tyler's insolent behaviour at the meeting in Smithfield (June 15, 1381) greatly alarmed the king's friends. He came towards Richard, throwing his dagger in the air, and he even ventured to hold the king's bridle. Walworth, in the alarm of the moment, ran his sword into the rough rebel's throat, and at the same instant a squire stabbed Wat in the side. It was then that Richard II. courageously, and with great presence of mind, led off the rebels to Islington Fields, where the mayor and a thousand men soon scattered them to the winds.

Smithfield was frequently chosen as the scene of mediæval duels, and of the ordeal by battle. The combat, in the reign of Henry VI., between the master and the 'prentice who had accused him of treason, will be remembered by all readers of Shakespeare. The ordeal was, perhaps, hardly fairly tried in this case, as the poor armourer had been plied with liquor by his over-zealous friends; but there is one comfort, according to the poet, he confessed his treason in his dying moments.

Smithfield was, at one time, a place of torture peculiarly in favour with theologians. Here that stern tyrant, Henry VIII., burnt poor wretches who denied his ecclesiastical supremacy; here Mary burnt Protestants, and here Elizabeth burnt Anabaptists. In 1539 (Henry VIII.) Forest, an Observant friar, was cruelly burnt in Smithfield, for denying the king's supremacy, the flames being lit with "David Darvel Gatheren," a once sacred image from Wales. Latimer preached patience to the friar, while he hung by the waist and struggled for life. And here, too, was burnt Joan Boucher, the Maid of Kent, for some theological refinement as to the incarnation of Christ, Cranmer almost forcing Edward VI. to sign the poor creature's death-warrant. "What, my lord!" said Edward, will ye have me send her quick to the devil, in her error? I shall lay the charge therefore upon you, my Lord Cranmer, before God."

Of the last moments of the Smithfield martyrs, Foxe, their historian, has left a narrative, so plainly told, so simple in tone, and so natural in every detail, as to guarantee its truth to all but partisans. A few passages from Foxe will convey a perfect impression of these touching scenes, and of the faith wherewith these firm, resolute men embraced death. Speaking of Roger Holland, a Protestant martyr, Foxe says, with a certain exultation:— "The day they suffered a proclamation was made that none should be so bold to speak or talk any word unto them, or receive anything of them, or to touch them upon pain of imprisonment, without either bail or mainprize; with divers other cruel threatening words, contained in the same proclamation. Notwithstanding the people cried out, desiring God to strengthen them; and they, likewise, still prayed for the people, and the restoring of His word. At length Roger, embracing the stake and the reeds, said these words:—'Lord, I most humbly thank Thy Majesty that Thou hast called me from the state of death unto the light of Thy heavenly word, and now unto the fellowship of Thy saints, that I may sing and say, Holy, holy, holy, Lord God of hosts! And Lord, into Thy hands I commit my spirit. Lord, bless these Thy people, and save them from idolatry.' And so he ended his life, looking up into heaven, praying and praising God, with the rest of his fellow-saints: for whose joyful constancy the Lord be praised."

The end of three more of the same army Foxe thus gives:—"And so these three godly men, John Hallingdale, William Sparrow, and Master Gibson, being thus appointed to the slaughter, were, the twelfth day after their condemnation (which was the 18th day of the said month of November, 1557), burnt in Smithfield in London. And being brought thither to the stake, after their prayer made, they were bound thereunto with chains, and wood set unto them; and after wood, fire, in the which being compassed about, and the fiery flames consuming their flesh, at the last they yielded gloriously and joyfully their souls and lives into the holy hands of the Lord, to whose tuition and government I commend thee, good reader. Amen."

Of the heroic death of John Rogers, the proto-martyr in the Marian persecution, Foxe gives the following account:—

"After that John Rogers," he says, "had been long and straitly imprisoned, lodged in Newgate amongst thieves, often examined and very uncharitably treated, and at length unjustly and most cruelly, by wicked Winchester, condemned. The 4th of February, A.D. 1555, being Monday in the morning, he was warned suddenly by the keeper's wife of Newgate, to prepare himself to the fire; who, being then sound asleep, scarce with much shogging could be awaked. At length, being raised and waked, and bid to make haste, 'Then,' said he, 'if it be so I need not tie my points;' and so was had down first to Bonner to be degraded. That done, he craved of Bonner but one petition. And Bonner asking what that should be: 'Nothing,' said he, 'but that I might talk a few words with my wife before my burning.' But that could not be obtained of him. 'Then,' said he, 'you declare your charity, what it is.' And so he was brought into Smithfield by Master Chester and Master Woodroofe, then sheriffs of London, there to be burnt; where he showed most constant patience, not using many words, for he could not be permitted; but only exhorting the people constantly to remain in that faith and true doctrine which he before had taught and they had learned, and for the confirmation whereof he was not only content patiently to suffer and bear all such bitterness and cruelty as had been showed him, but also most gladly to resign up his life, and to give his flesh to the consuming fire, for the testimony of the same. . . . The Sunday before he suffered he drank to Master Hooper, being then underneath him, and bade them commend him unto him, and tell him, 'There was never little fellow better would stick to a man than he would stick to him,' presupposing they should both be burned together, although it happened otherwise, for Master Rogers was burnt alone. . . Now, when the time came that he, being delivered to the sheriffs, should be brought out of Newgate to Smithfield, the place of his execution, first came to him Master Woodroofe, one of the aforesaid sheriffs, and calling Master Rogers unto him, asked him if he would revoke his abominable doctrine and his evil opinion of the sacrament of the altar. Master Rogers answered and said, 'That which I have preached I will seal with my blood.' 'Then,' quoth Master Woodroofe, 'thou art a heretic.' 'That shall be known,' quoth Rogers, 'at the day of judgment.' 'Well' quoth Master Woodroofe, 'I will never pray for thee.' 'But I will pray for you,' quoth Master Rogers; and so was brought the same day, which was Monday, the 4th of February, by the sheriffs towards Smithfield, saying the psalm 'Miserere' by the way, all the people wonderfully rejoicing at his constancy, with great praises and thanks to God for the same. And there, in the presence of Master Rochester, Comptroller of the Queen's Household, Sir Richard Southwell, both the sheriffs, and a wonderful number of people, the fire was put unto him; and when it had taken hold both upon his legs and shoulders, he, as one feeling no smart, washed his hands in the flame as though it had been in cold water. And, after lifting up his hands unto heaven, not removing the same until such time as the devouring fire had consumed them, most mildly this happy martyr yielded up his spirit into the hands of his heavenly Father. A little before his burning at the stake his pardon was brought if he would have recanted, but he utterly refused. He was the first martyr of all the blessed company that suffered in Queen Mary's time, that gave the first adventure upon the fire. His wife and children, being eleven in number, and ten able to go, and one sucking on her breast, met him by the way as he went towards Smithfield. This sorrowful sight of his own flesh and blood could nothing move him; but that he constantly and cheerfully took his death, with wonderful patience, in the defence and quarrel of Christ's Gospel."

The chosen place for executions before Tyburn was the Elms, Smithfield, between "the horsepond and Turnmill brook," which, according to Stow, began to be built on in the reign of Henry V. The gallows seems to have been removed to Tyburn about the reign of Henry IV. In Stow's time none of the ancient elms remained. Here that brave Scotch patriot and guerilla chief, Sir William Wallace, was executed, on St. Bartholomew's Eve, 1305. After many cruel reprisals on the soldiers of Edward I., and many victories, this true patriot was betrayed by a friend, and surrendered to the conquerors. He was dragged from the Tower by horses, and then hung, and, while still conscious, quartered. Here also perished ignominiously Mortimer, the cruel favourite of the queen, the murderess of her husband, Edward II. Edward III., then aged eighteen, seized the regicide, Mortimer, at Nottingham Castle, and he was hung at the Elms, the body remaining on the gibbet, says Stow, "two days and nights, to be seen of the people."

The account of Bartholomew Priory and of Bartholomew Fair, so admirably narrated by Mr. Henry Morley, is an interesting chapter in the history of Smithfield. The priory was founded by Rayer, a monk, who had been jester and revel-master to Henry I., a specially superstitious monarch. Rayer was converted by a vision he saw during a pilgrimage to Rome, where he had fallen grievously sick. In his vision Rayer was borne by a beast with four feet and two wings, up to a high place,

whence he saw the mouth of the bottomless pit. As he stood there, crying out and trembling, a man of majestic beauty, who proclaimed himself St. Bartholomew the Apostle, came to his succour. The saint said that, by common favour and command of the celestial council, he had chosen a place in the suburbs of London where Rayer should found a church in his name. Of the cost he was to doubt nothing; it would be his (St. Bartholomew's) part to provide necessaries.

On Rayer's return to London he told his friends and the barons of London, and by their advice made his request to the king, who at once granted it, and the church was founded early in the twelfth century. It was an unpromising place, though called the King's Market, almost all marsh and dirty fens, and on the only dry part stood the Elms gibbet. Rayer, wise in his generation, now feigned to be halfwitted, drawing children and idlers together, to fill the marsh with stones and rubbish. In spite of his numerous enemies, many miracles attended the building of the new priory. At evensong a light appeared on the new roof; a cripple recovered the use of his limbs at the altar; by a vision Rayer discovered a choral book which a Jew had stolen; a blind boy recovered his sight. In the twelfth year of his prelacy Rayer obtained from King Henry a most ample charter, and leave to institute a three days' fair on the Feast of St. Bartholomew, forbidding any but the prior to levy dues on the frequenters of the fair during those three days. Fairs, as Mr. Morley has most learnedly shown, generally originated in the assembling of pilgrims at church festivals, and St. Bartholomew's Fair was no exception to the rule.

Rayer, after witnessing endless miracles, and showing a most creditable invention, and a true knowledge of his supernatural art, died in 1143, leaving a little flock of thirteen monks, living very well on the oblations of the rich Londoners. The miracles continued very well. The saint became a favourite with seamen, and the sailors of a Flemish ship, saved by prayers to the saint of Smithfield, presented a silver ship at his altar. The saint appeared to a sailor on a wreck, and led a wrecked Flemish merchant to land in safety. He cured madmen, and was famous in cases of fires and possession by devils.

Fragments of the old Norman priory existed till recently in Bartholomew Close and the dim thoroughfare called Middlesex Passage. This latter place, a fragment of the old priory, was overhung by the wreck of the great priory hall, the site of which is now occupied by the pay-office of the City of London Union. On each side of this passage there was access to separated portions of the crypt. The crypt was divided into aisles by two rows of Norman arches, supporting a high vaulted ceiling, all traces of which are now gone. The entrance to the crypt was by a descent of twenty-five feet. There is a tradition that at the end of this long subterranean hall there used to be a door opening into the church; now the visitor to the shrine will only find, through an alley a door and bit of church wall hemmed in between factories. The present arches, the zig-zag ornaments of the early Normans, are still as when Rayer eyed them with crafty triumph.

The site of the priory was chosen with a true monkish wisdom. The saint had included in his wishes a piece of the king's Friday Market, and horses, oxen, sheep, and pigs would all bring grist in one way or another to the great monastic mill. Already Smithfield was the great horse-market of London, as it continued to be for many

PLACE OF EXECUTION IN OLD SMITHFIELD. (*See page* 340.)

church is the choir of the old priory, and the nave is entirely gone; the last line of the square of cloisters had been turned into a stable, and fell down some forty years ago. The apse is shorn off, and a base brick wall closes that forlorn space. "Half-way," says Mr. Morley, "between capital and base of the pillars of that oratory of the Virgin which a miracle commended once to reverence, now stands the floor of the vestry of the parish church." The walls and aisles on either side of the church are still nearly in the same state as when Rayer's miracles were all over, and he took a last glance at the great work of his singular life, and the house raised to God and the builder's own vanity. The high aspiring columns and solid

long centuries. On Shrove Tuesday every school-boy came here to play football; and it was also the "Rotten Row" of the horsemen of the Middle Ages. It was the great Campus Martius for sham-fights and tilts. It was a ground for bowls and archery; the favourite haunt of jugglers, acrobats, and posture-makers. There were probably, in early times, says Mr. Morley, two Bartholomew Fairs, one held in Smithfield, and one within the priory bounds. The real fair was held within the priory gates, and in the priory churchyard; where, too, on certain festivals, schoolmasters used to bring their boys, to hold in public logical controversies. The churchyard fair seems from the first to have been chiefly a draper's and clothiers'

THE "HAND AND SHEARS."

A CASE BEFORE THE COURT OF PIE-POUDRE. *From a Drawing dated* 1811.   (*See page* 344.)

fair; and the gates were locked every night, and guarded, to protect the booths and stands.

The English kings did not forget the hospital. In 1223 we find that King Henry III. gave an old oak from Windsor Forest as fuel for the infirm in the Hospital of St. Bartholomew, the generous grant to be renewed every year. In 1244 (Henry III.) a disgraceful religious brawl occurred at the very gate of the West Smithfield Priory. Boniface, the Provençal Archbishop of Canterbury, came to visit Rayer's friars, and was received with solemn procession. The bishop was rather angry at the state, and told the canons that he passed not for honour, but to visit them as part of the duties of his office. The canons, irritated at his pride, replied that having a learned bishop of their own, they desired no other visitation. The archbishop, furious at this, smote the sub-prior on the face, crying, "Indeed! indeed! doth it become you English traitors so to answer me?" Then, bursting with oaths, this worthy ecclesiastic fell on the unfortunate sub-prior, tore his rich cope to shreds, trampled them under foot, and then thrust the wearer back with such force against a chancel pillar as nearly to kill him. The canons, alarmed at this furious onslaught, pulled the archbishop on his back, and in so doing discovered that he was armed. The archbishop's Provençal attendants, seeing their master down, fell in their turn on the Smithfield canons, beat them, rent their frocks, and trod them under foot.

The canons then ran, covered with blood and mire, to the king, at Westminster, but he refused to interfere. The citizens, by this time roused, would have rung the common bell, and torn the foreign archbishop to pieces, had he not fled over the water to Lambeth. They called him a ruffian and a cruel brute, and said he was greedy for money, unlearned and strange, and, moreover, had a wife.

The early miracle-plays seem to have been often performed at Smithfield. In 1390 the London parish clerks played interludes in the fields at Skinner's Well, for three consecutive days to Richard II., his queen, and court. In 1409 (Henry IV.) the parish clerks played *Matter from the Creation of the World* for eight consecutive days; after which followed jousts. In those early times delegates of the merchant tailors, with their silver measure, attended Bartholomew Fair, to try the measures of the drapers and clothiers.

"From the earliest times of which there is record," says Mr. Morley, whose wide nets few odd facts escape, "the Court of Pie-poudre, which had jurisdiction over offences committed in the fair, was held within the priory gates, the prior being lord of the fair." It was held, indeed, to the last, close by, in Cloth Fair. After 1445 the City claimed to be joint lord of the fair with the prior, and four aldermen were always appointed as keepers of the fair and of the Court of Pie-poudre.

CHAPTER XLIII.

SMITHFIELD AND BARTHOLOMEW FAIR.

The Mulberry-garden at St. Bartholomew's—Prior Bolton—The Growth of Bartholomew Fair—Smithfield reduced to order—"Ruffians' Hall"— Ben Jonson at Bartholomew Fair—A Frenchman's Adventures there—Ned Ward's Account—The *Beggars' Opera*—"John Audley"— Garrick meets a brother Actor—A Dangerous Neighbourhood—Old Smithfield Market—Remains of the Smithfield Burnings—Discovery of Human Remains.

A GREAT part of the priory was rebuilt in the reign of Henry IV., and it became famous for its mulberry-garden, one of the first planted in England. That garden stood to the east of the present Middlesex Passage, and it was under its great leafy trees that scholars at fair-time held their logical disputations. Within the gates the northern part of the priory ground was occupied by a large cemetery with a spacious court, now Bartholomew Close. After the time of Henry IV. the City established a firm right to all fair-tolls outside the priory enclosure. The last prior of St. Bartholomew who was acknowledged by the English kings died in office, and was the last prior but one of the Black Canons of West Smithfield. This was

that same Prior Bolton who built the oriel in the church for the sacristan to watch the altar-lights; and he built largely, as we have already shown, at Canonbury. He had two parishes, Great St. Bartholomew and Little St. Bartholomew, within his jurisdiction. At the dissolution the priory and the hospital were torn apart by greedy hands for ever.

In 1537 Sir Thomas Gresham, then Lord Mayor, prayed that the City might govern St. Mary, St. Thomas, and St. Bartholomew Hospitals, "for the relief, comfort, and aid of the helpless poor and indigent." In 1544 the king established a new Hospital of St. Bartholomew, under a priest as master, and four chaplains; but the place was mismanaged, and King Henry VIII. founded it anew, "for the continual relief and help of a hundred sore and diseased."

At the dissolution the privileges of the fair were shared by the corporation and Lord Rich (who died 1568), ancestor of the Earls of Warwick and Holland. The Cloth Fair dwindled away in the reign of Elizabeth, when the London drapers found wider markets for their woollens, and the clothiers, as roads grew better, started to wider fields. The three days' fair soon grew into a fourteen days' carnival, to which all ranks resorted. We find the amiable and contemplative Evelyn writing of his having seen "the celebrating follies" of Bartholomew; and that accumulative man, Sir Hans Sloane, sending a draughtsman to record every *lusus naturæ* or special oddity. In 1708 (Queen Anne), the nuisance of such licence becoming intolerable to the neighbourhood, the fair was again restricted to three days. The saturnalia were always formally opened by the Lord Mayor, and the proclamation for the purpose was read at the entrance to Cloth Fair. On his way to Smithfield it was the custom for the mayor to call on the keeper of Newgate, and on horseback partake of "a cool tankard of wine, nutmeg, and sugar;" the flap of the tankard lid, it will be remembered, caused the death of the mayor, Sir John Shorter, in 1688, his horse starting, and throwing him violently. The custom ceased in the second mayoralty of Sir Matthew Wood.

"In 1615,"* says Howes, "the City of London reduced the rude, vast place of Smithfield into a faire and comely order, which formerly was never held possible to be done, and paved it all over, and made divers sewers to convey the water from the new channels which were made by reason of the new pavement; they also made strong rayles round about Smithfield, and sequestered the middle part of the said Smithfield into a very faire and civill walk, and rayled it round about with strong rayles, to defend the place from annoyance and danger, as well from carts as all manner of cattell, because it was intended hereafter that in time it might prove a faire and peaceable market-place, by reason that Newgate Market, Moorgate, Cheapside, Leadenhall, and Gracechurche Street were unmeasurably pestred with the unimaginable increase and multiplicity of market folks. And this field, commonly called West Smithfield, was for many years called 'Ruffians' Hall,' by reason it was the usual place of frayes and common fighting during the time that sword and bucklers were in use. But the ensuing deadly fight of rapier and dagger suddenly suppressed the fighting with sword and buckler."

Shakespeare has more than one allusion to the horse-fair in Smithfield, and of these the following is the most marked :—

Falstaff. Where's Bardolph?

Page. He's gone into Smithfield, to buy your worship a horse.

Falstaff. I bought him in Paul's, and he'll buy me a horse in Smithfield; an I could get me but a wife in the stews, I were manned, horsed, and wived.—*Second Part of Henry IV.*, Act i., Sc. 2.*

That fine, vigorous old satirist, Ben Jonson, the dear friend and protégé of Shakespeare, named one of his best comedies after this great London fair, and has employed his Hogarthian genius to depict the pickpockets, eating-house-keepers, protesting Puritans, silly citizens, and puppet-show proprietors of the reign of James I. Some extracts from his amusing play, *Bartholomew Fair*, 1613 (written in the very climax of the author's power), are indispensable in any history, however brief, of this outburst of national merriment. The following extract from Mr. Morley's "History of Bartholomew Fair" contains some of the most characteristic passages :—

"Nay," says Littlewit, "we'll be humble enough, we'll seek out the homeliest booth in the fair, that's certain; rather than fail, we'll eat it on the ground." "Aye," adds Dame Purecroft, "and I'll go with you myself. Win-the-Fight and my brother, Zeal-of-the-Land, shall go with us, too, for our better consolation." Then says the Rabbi, "In the way of comfort to the weak, I will go and eat. I will eat exceedingly, and prophecy. There may be a good use made of it, too, now I think on't, by the public eating of swine's flesh, to profess our hate and loathing of Judaism, whereof the brethren stand taxed. I will therefore eat, yea, I will eat exceedingly." So these also set off for the fair.

In the fair, as I have said, is Justice Overdue, solemnly establishing himself as a fool, for the benefit of public morals. There are the booths and stalls. There is prosperous Lanthorn Leatherhead, the hobby-horse man, who cries, "What do you lack? What is't you buy? What do you lack? Rattles, drums, halberts, horses, babies o' the best, fiddles of the finest!" He is a too proud pedler, owner also of a famous puppet-show, the manager, indeed, for whom Proctor Littlewit has sacrificed to the Bartholomew muses. Joan Trash, the gingerbread-woman, keeps her stall near him, and the rival traders have their differences. "Do you hear, Sister Trash, lady of the basket! sit farther with your gingerbread progeny, there, and hinder not the prospect of my shop, or I'll have it proclaimed in the fair what stuff they

---

* The work began, Anthony Munday informs us, on the 4th of February, 1614-15. "The citizens' charge thereof (as I have been credibly told by Master Arthur Strangewaies) amounting well near to sixteen hundred pounds."

* This, it may be added, is in allusion to a proverb often quoted by old writers—"Who goes to Westminster for a wife, to St. Paul's for a man, and to Smithfield for a horse, may meet with a queane, a knave, and a jade."

are made on." "Why, what stuff are they made on, Brother Leatherhead? Nothing but what's wholesome, I assure you." "Yes, stale bread, rotten eggs, musty ginger, and dead honey, you know." "I defy thee, and thy stable of hobby-horses. I pay for my ground, as well as thou dost. Buy any gingerbread, gilt gingerbread! Will your worship buy any gingerbread? Very good bread, comfortable bread!"

The cries of the fair multiply. "Buy any ballads? new ballads! Hey!"

> "Now the fair's a filling!
> Oh, for a tune to startle
> The birds o' the booths here billing
> Yearly with old Saint Bartle!"

"Buy any pears, pears, fine, very fine pears!" "What do you lack, gentlemen? Maid, see a fine hoppy-horse for your young master. Cost you but a token* a week his provender."

"Have you any corns on your feet and toes?"

"Buy a mousetrap, a mousetrap, or a tormentor for a flea?"

"Buy some gingerbread?"

"What do you lack, gentlemen? fine purses, pouches, pin-cases, pipes? What is't you lack? a pair o' smiths, to wake you in the morning, or a fine whistling bird?"

"Ballads! ballads! fine new ballads!"

> "Hear for your love, and buy for your money,
> A delicate ballad o' the ferret and the coney;
> A dozen of divine points, and the godly garters,
> The fairing of good counsel, of an ell and three quarters."

"What do you lack, what do you buy, mistress? A fine hobby-horse, to make your son a tilter? A drum, to make him a soldier? A fiddle, to make him a reveller? What is't you lack? little dogs for your daughters, or babies, male or female?"

"Gentlewomen, the weather's hot; whither walk you? Have a care of your fine velvet caps; the fair is dusty. Take a sweet, delicate booth with boughs, here in the way, and cool yourselves in the shade, you and your friends. The best pig and bottle-ale in the fair, sir. Old Ursula is cook. There you may read—'Here be the best pigs, and she does roast them as well as ever she did'"—(there is a picture of a pig's head over the inscription, and)—"the pig's head speaks it."

"A delicate show-pig, little mistress, with shweet sauce and crackling, like de bay-leaf i' de fire, la! Tou shalt ha' the clean side o' the table-clot, and di glass vash'd with phatersh of Dame Annèsh Cleare."†

In "Wit and Drollery: Jovial Poems," 1682, the writer has hit off several of the chief rarities of the fair:—

> "Here's that will challenge all the fair.
> Come, buy my nuts and damsons, and Burgamy pears!
> Here's the *Woman of Babylon, the Devil, and the Pope*,
> And here's the little girl, just going on the rope!
> Here's *Dives and Lazarus*, and the *World's Creation*;
> Here's the Tall Dutchwoman, the like's not in the nation.
> Here is the booths, where the high Dutch maid is;
> Here are the bears that dance like any ladies;
> Tat, tat, tat, tat, says little penny trumpet;
> Here's Jacob Hall, that does so jump it, jump it;

> Sound, trumpet, sound, for silver spoon and fork,
> Come, here's your dainty pig and pork."

In the year 1698, a Frenchman, Monsieur Sorbière, visiting London, says, "I was at Bartholomew Fair. It consists mostly of toy-shops, also finery and pictures, ribbon-shops—no books; many shops of confectioners, where any woman may commodiously be treated. Knavery is here in perfection, dextrous cutpurses and pickpockets. I went to see the dancing on the ropes, which was admirable. Coming out, I met a man that would have took off my hat, but I secured it, and was going to draw my sword, crying, 'Begar! You rogue! Morbleu!' &c., when on a sudden I had a hundred people about me crying, 'Here, monsieur, see *Jephthah's Rash Vow*.' 'Here, monsieur, see the Tall Dutchwoman.' 'See The Tiger,' says another. 'See the Horse and no Horse,' whose tail stands where his head should do.' 'See the German Artist, monsieur.' 'See *The Siege of Namur*.' So that betwixt rudeness and civility I was forced to get into a *fiacre*, and with an air of haste and a full trot, got home to my lodgings."

In 1702, the following advertisement appeared relative to the fair:—

"At the Great Booth over against the Hospital Gate, in Bartholomew Fair, will be seen the famous company of rope-dancers, they being the greatest performers of men, women, and children that can be found beyond the seas, so that the world cannot parallel them for dancing on the low rope, vaulting on the high rope, and for walking on the slack and sloaping ropes, outdoing all others to that degree, that it has highly recommended them, both in Bartholomew Fair and May Fair last, to all the best persons of quality in England. And by all are owned to be the only amazing wonders of the world in everything they do. It is there you will see the Italian Scaramouch dancing on the rope, with a wheelbarrow before him with two children and a dog in it, and with a duck on his head, who sings to the company, and causes much laughter. The whole entertainment will be so extremely fine and diverting, as never was done by any but this company alone."

Ned Ward, as the "London Spy," went, of course, to the fair, but in a coach, to escape the dirt and the crowd; and at the entrance, he says, he was "saluted with Belphegor's concert, the rumbling of drums, mixed with the intolerable squeaking of catcalls and penny trumpets, made still more terrible with the shrill belches of lottery pickpockets through instruments of the same metal with their faces." The spy, having been set down with his friend at the hospital gate, went into a convenient house, to smoke a pipe and drink small beer bittered with colocynth. From one of its windows he looked down on a crowd rushing, ankle-deep in filth, through an air tainted by fumes of tobacco and of singeing, over-roasted pork, to

---

* Tokens were farthings coined by tradesmen for the convenience of change, before farthings were issued as king's money by Charles II. in 1672.

† A favourite well near Hoxton, that of Agnes le Clare.

see the Merry Andrew. On their galleries strutted, in their buffoonery of stateliness, the quality of the fair, dressed in tinsel robes and golden leather buskins. "When they had taken a turn the length of their gallery, to show the gaping crowd how majestically they could tread, each ascended to a seat agreeable to the dignity of their dress, to show the multitude how imperiously they could sit."

A few years before this the fair is sketched by Sir Robert Southwell, in a letter to his son (26th August, 1685). "Here," he says, "you see the rope-dancers gett their living meerly by hazarding of their lives; and why men will pay money and take pleasure to see such dangers, is of separate and philosophical consideration. You have others who are acting fools, drunkards, and madmen, but for the same wages which they might get by honest labour, and live with credit besides. Others, if born in any monstrous shape, or have children that are such, here they celebrate their misery, and, by getting of money, forget how odious they are made. When you see the toy-shops, and the strange variety of things much more impertinent than hobby-horses of ginger-bread, you must know there are customers for all these matters; and it would be a pleasing sight could you see painted a true figure of all these impertinent minds and their fantastic passions, who come trudging hither only for such things. 'Tis out of this credulous crowd that the ballad-singers attrackt an assembly, who listen and admire, while their confederate pickpockets are diving and fishing for their prey.

"'Tis from those of this number who are more refined that the mountebank obtains audience and credit; and it were a good bargain if such customers had nothing for their money but words, but they are best content to pay for druggs and medicines, which commonly doe them hurt. There is one corner of this Elizium field devoted to the eating of pig and the surfeits that attend it. The fruits of the season are everywhere scattered about, and those who eat imprudently do but hasten to the physitian or the churchyard."

"In the year 1727-28," says Mr. Morley, "Gay's *Beggar's Opera* was produced, and took the foremost place among the pleasures of the town. It took a foremost place also among the pleasures of the next Bartholomew Fair, being acted during the time of the fair by the company of comedians from the new theatre in the Haymarket, at the 'George' Inn in Smithfield. William Penkethman, one of the actors who had become famous as a booth-manager, was then recently dead, and the Haymarket comedians carried the *Beggar's Opera* out of Bartholomew into Southwark Fair, where 'the late

Mr. Penkethman's great theatrical booth' afforded them a stage. One of the managers of this speculation was Henry Fielding, then only just of age, a young man who, with good birth, fine wit, and a liberal education, both at Eton and at Leyden University, was left to find his own way in the world. His father agreed to allow him two hundred a year in the clouds, and, as he afterwards said, his choice lay between being a hackney writer and a hackney coachman. He lived to place himself, in respect to literature, at the head of the prose writers of England, I dare even venture to think, of the world."

"A writer in the *St. James's Chronicle* (March 24, 1791) wished to place upon record the fact that it was Shuter, a comedian, who, in the year 1759, when master of a droll in Smithfield, invented a way, since become general at fairs, of informing players in the booth when they may drop the curtain and dismiss the company, because there are enough people waiting outside to form another audience. The man at the door pops in his head, and makes a loud inquiry for 'John Audley.'" The ingenious contriver of this device is the Shuter who finds a place in "The Rosciad" of Churchill :

"Shuter, who never cared a single pin
Whether he left out nonsense, or put in."

"There lived," says Mr. Morley, "about this time a popular Merry Andrew, who sold ginger-bread nuts in the neighbourhood of Covent Garden, and because he received a guinea a day for his fun during the fair, he was at pains never to cheapen himself by laughing, or by noticing a joke, during the other 362 days of the year."

"Garrick's name," says the same writer, "is connected with the fair only by stories that regard him as a visitor out of another world. He offers his money at the entrance of a theatrical booth, and it is thought a jest worth transmitting to posterity that he is told by the checktaker, 'We never takes money of one another.' He sees one of his own sturdy Drury Lane porters installed at a booth-door, where he is pressed sorely in the crowd, and calls for help. 'It's no use,' he is told, 'I can't help you. There's very few people in Smithfield as knows Mr. Garrick off the stage.'"

In "Oliver Twist" Dickens sketches with his peculiar power the dangerous neighbourhood of Smithfield, which lay between Islington and Saffron Hill, the lurking-place of the Sykeses and Fagins of forty years ago :—

"As John Dawkins," writes Dickens, "objected to their entering London before nightfall, it was nearly eleven o'clock before they reached the turnpike at Islington. They crossed from the 'Angel' into St. John's Road, struck down the small street which terminates at Sadler's Wells Theatre, through Exmouth Street and Coppice Row, down the little court by the side of the workhouse, across the classic ground which once bore the name of very narrow and muddy, and the air was impregnated with filthy odours. There were a good many small shops, but the only stock-in-trade appeared to be heaps of children, who, even at that time of night, were crawling in and out at the doors, or screaming from the inside. The sole places that

THE CHURCH OF ST. BARTHOLOMEW-THE-GREAT, 1737. (*See page* 351.)

Hockley-in-the-Hole, thence into Little Saffron Hill, and so into Saffron Hill the Great, along which the Dodger scudded at a rapid pace, directing Oliver to follow close at his heels.

"Although Oliver had enough to occupy his attention in keeping sight of his leader, he could not help bestowing a few hasty glances on either side of the way, as he passed along. A dirtier or more wretched place he had never seen. The street was seemed to prosper amid the general blight of the place were the public-houses, and in them the lowest orders of Irish were wrangling with might and main. Covered ways and yards, which here and there diverged from the main street, disclosed little knots of houses where drunken men and women were positively wallowing in the filth, and from several of the doorways great, ill-looking fellows were cautiously emerging, bound, to all appearance, upon no very well-disposed or harmless errands."

The enormous sale of roast pork at Bartholomew Fair ceased, says Mr. Morley, with all the gravity of a historian, about the middle of the last century, and beef sausages then became the fashion. Thomas Rowlandson's droll but gross pictures of the shows, in 1799, show those sickening boat-swings and crowds of rough and boisterous sight-seers. He writes on one of the show-boards the

came to their windows with lights, alarmed at the disturbance. In 1807 the place grew even more lawless, and a virago of an actress, who was performing Belvidera in *Venice Preserved*, knocked down the august king's deputy-trumpeter, who applied for his fees. Richardson's shows were triumphant still, as in 1817 was Toby, "the real learned pig," who, with twenty handkerchiefs over his eyes, could tell the hour to a minute, and pick out a card from a pack. In one morning of

OLD SMITHFIELD MARKET, 1837.

name of Miss Biffin, that clever woman who, through the Earl of Morton's patronage, succeeded in earning a name as a miniature painter, though born without either hands or arms. In 1808 George III. paid for her more complete artistic education, and William IV. gave her a small pension, after which she married, and, at the Earl of Morton's request, left the fair caravans for good.

This great carnival, a dangerous sink for all the vices of London, gradually grew unbearable. In 1801 a mob of thieves surrounded any respectable woman, and tore her clothes from her back. In 1802 "Lady Holland's Mob," as it used to be called, robbed visitors, beat inoffensive passers-by with bludgeons, and pelted harmless persons who

September, 1815, there were heard at Guildhall forty-five cases of felony, misdemeanour, and assault, committed at Bartholomew Fair. Its doom was fixed. Hone, in 1825, went to sketch the dying festival, and describes Clarke from Astley's, Wombwell's Menagerie, and the Living Skeleton. The special boast of Wombwell, who had been a cobbler in Monmouth Street, was his Elephant of Siam, who used to uncork bottles, and decide for the rightful heir, in a very brief Oriental melodrama. The shows, which were now forced to close at ten, had removed to the New North Road, Islington. Lord Kensington, in 1827, had offered to remove the fair, and in 1830 the Corporation bought of him the old priory rights. In 1839 Mr. Charles

Pearson recommended more restrictions, and the exclusion of theatrical shows followed. The rents were raised, and in 1840 only wild beast shows were allowed. The great fair at last sank down to a few gilt gingerbread booths. In 1849 the fair had so withered away that there were only a dozen gingerbread stalls. The ceremony of opening since 1840 had been very simple, and in 1850 Lord Mayor Musgrove, going to read the parchment proclamation at the appointed gateway, found that the fair had vanished. Five years later the ceremony entirely ceased, but the old fee of 3s. 6d. was still paid by the City to the rector of St. Bartholomew-the-Great, for a proclamation in his parish. The fair had outlived its original purpose.

Smithfield Market was condemned in 1852 by law to be moved to Islington, the noise, filth, and dangers of the place having at last become intolerable, and half a century having been spent in discussing the annoyance.

"The original extent of Smithfield," says Mr. Timbs, "was about three acres; the market-place was paved, drained, and railed in, 1685; subsequently enlarged to four and a half acres, and since 1834 to six and a quarter acres. Yet this enlargement proved disproportionate to the requirements. In 1731 there were only 8,304 head of cattle sold in Smithfield; in 1846, 210,757 head of cattle, and 1,518,510 sheep. The old City laws for its regulation were called the "Statutes of Smithfield." Here might be shown 4,000 beasts and about 30,000 sheep, the latter in 1,509 pens; and there were fifty pens for pigs. Altogether, Smithfield was the largest live market in the world."

The old market-days were, Monday for fat cattle and sheep; Tuesday, Thursday, and Saturday, for hay and straw; Friday, cattle and sheep, and milch cows; and at two o'clock for scrub-horses and asses. All sales took place by commission. The customary commission for the sale of an ox of any value was 4s., and of a sheep, 8d. The City received a toll upon every beast exposed for sale of 1d. per head, and of sheep at the rate of 1s. per score. Smithfield salesmen estimated the weight of cattle by the eye, and from constant practice they approached so near exactness that they were seldom out more than a few pounds. The sales were always for cash. No paper was passed, but when the bargain was struck the buyer and seller shook hands, and closed the sale. £7,000,000, it was said, were annually paid away in this manner in the narrow area of Smithfield Market. "The average weekly sale of beasts," said Cunningham in 1849, "is said to be about 3,000, and of sheep about 30,000, increased in the Christmas week to about 5,000 beasts, and 47,000 sheep. The following return shows the number of cattle and sheep annually sold in Smithfield during the following periods:—

	Cattle.	Sheep.
1841	194,298	1,435,000
1842	210,723	1,655,370
1843	207,195	1,817,360
1844	216,848	1,804,850
1845	222,822	1,539,660
1846	210,757	1,518,510

In addition to this, a quarter of a million pigs were annually sold."

The miseries of old Smithfield are described by Mr. Dickens, in "Oliver Twist," in his most powerful manner. "It was market morning," he says; "the ground was covered nearly ankle-deep with filth and mire, and a thick steam perpetually rising from the reeking bodies of the cattle, and mingling with the fog which seemed to rest upon the chimney-tops, hung heavily above. All the pens in the centre of the large area, and as many temporary ones as could be crowded into the vacant space, were filled with sheep; and tied up to posts by the gutter-side were long lines of oxen, three or four deep. Countrymen, butchers, drovers, hawkers, boys, thieves, idlers, and vagabonds of every low grade, were mingled together in a dense mass. The whistling of drovers, the barking of dogs, the bellowing and plunging of beasts, the bleating of sheep, and grunting and squeaking of pigs; the cries of hawkers, the shouts, oaths, and quarrelling on all sides, the ringing of bells, and the roar of voices that issued from every public-house, the crowding, pushing, driving, beating, whooping, and yelling, the hideous and discordant din that resounded from every corner of the market, and the unwashed, unshaven, squalid, and dirty figures constantly running to and fro, and bursting in and out of the throng, rendered it a stunning and bewildering scene, which quite confused the senses."

"Smithfield Market, on a rainy morning in November, twenty-five years ago," writes Aleph, in the *City Press*, "was a sight to be remembered by any who had ventured through it. It might be called a feat of clever agility to get across Smithfield, on such a greasy muddy day, without slipping down, or without being knocked over by one of the poor frightened and half-mad cattle toiling through it. The noise was deafening. The bellowing and lowing of cattle, bleating of sheep, squeaking of pigs, the shouts of the drovers and often, the shrieks of some unfortunate female who had got amongst the unruly, frightened cattle, could not be forgotten. The long, narrow lanes of pavement that crossed the wider part of the market, opposite the hospital, were always lined with cattle, as close together as they could stand, their heads tied to the rails on either side of the scanty pathway, when the long horns of the Spanish breeds, sticking across towards the other side, made it far from a pleasant experience for a nervous man to venture along one of these narrow lanes, albeit it was the nearest and most direct way across the open market. If the day was foggy (and there were more foggy days then than now), then the glaring lights of the drover-boys' torches added to the wild confusion, whilst it did not dispel much of the gloom. It was indeed a very great change for the better when at last the City authorities removed the market into the suburbs."

In March, 1849, during excavations necessary for a new sewer, and at a depth of three feet below the surface, immediately opposite the entrance to the church of St. Bartholomew-the-Great, the workmen laid open a mass of unhewn stones, blackened as if by fire, and covered with ashes and human bones, charred and partially consumed. This was believed to have been the spot generally used for the Smithfield burnings, the face of the victim being turned to the east and to the great gate of St. Bartholomew, the prior of which was generally present on such occasions. Many bones were carried away as relics. Some strong oak posts were also dug up; they had evidently been charred by fire, and in one of them was a staple with a ring attached to it. The place and its former history were too significant for any doubt to exist as to how they had been once used. Gazing upon them thoughtfully, one was forcibly reminded of the last words of Bishop Latimer to his friend Ridley, as they stood bound to the stake at Oxford: " Be of good comfort, Master Ridley, and play the man; we shall this day light such a candle, by God's grace, in England, as I trust shall never be put out." And the good Latimer's words have come true.

Some years ago, on removing the foundations of some old houses, on the south side of Long Lane, a considerable quantity of human remains were discovered—skulls and other portions of the skeletons. This spot was understood to be the north-west corner of the burying-ground of the ancient priory of St. Bartholomew. The skulls were thick and grim-looking, with heavy, massive jaws, just as one would expect to find in those sturdy old monks, who were the schoolmen, artists, and sages of their time.

CHAPTER XLIV.

THE CHURCHES OF BARTHOLOMEW-THE-GREAT AND BARTHOLOMEW-THE-LESS.

The Old Bartholomew Priory—Its Old Privileges—Its Revenues and Early Seals—The Present Church—The Refectory of the Priory—The Crypt and Chapel—Various Interesting Remains of the Old Priory—The Monuments of Rayer, the Founder, Robert Chamberlain, and Sir Walter Mildmay—The Smallpage Family—The Old and New Vestry-rooms—The Monument to Abigail Coult—The Story of Roger Walden, Bishop of London—Dr. Francis Anthony, the Physician—His *Aurum Potabile*—The Priory of St. Bartholomew-the-Great as an Historical Centre—Visions of the Past—Cloth Fair—The Dimensions of St. Bartholomew-the-Great—Old Monuments in St. Bartholomew-the-Less—Injudicious Alterations—The Tower of St. Bartholomew-the-Less—The Tomb of Freke, the Eminent Surgeon.

IN 1410, when the priory was rebuilt, it was entirely enclosed with walls, the boundaries of which have been carefully traced out by many diligent antiquaries. The north wall ran from Smithfield along the south side of Long Lane, to its junction with the east wall, about thirty yards west from Aldersgate Street. This wall is mentioned by Stow, and delineated by Aggas, who has marked a small postern gate in it, which stood opposite Charterhouse Square, where there is now (says a writer in 1846) the entrance to King Street, Cloth Fair. The west wall commenced at the south-west corner of Long Lane, and continued along Smithfield and the middle of Duc Lane (now Duke Street) to the south gate, or Great Gate House, now the principal entrance to Bartholomew Close.

The south wall, starting from this spot, ran eastward in a direct line to Aldersgate Street, where it formed an angle, and passed southwards about forty yards, then resumed again its eastern course, and joined the corner of the east wall, which ran parallel with Aldersgate Street, at the distance of about twenty-six yards. The priory wall was fronted by the houses of Aldersgate Street, London House among others, between which and the wall ran a ditch. At the demolition of this wall various encroachments took place, which led to great disputes (especially in 1671) about the boundaries between the privileged parish of St. Bartholomew and the City. The old privileges of Rayer's Priory and precinct were that the parishioners were not to serve on juries, and could appoint their own constables; paid few City rates, taxed themselves, and were not required to become free of the City on starting in business.

When, in 1539, Sir Richard Rich purchased the church and priory for £1,064 11s. 3d., the thirteen frozen-out canons received annuities of £6 13s. 4d. each.   Queen Mary granted the church to the Black Friars, but they had but a short reign, and the Riches, Earls of Warwick and Holland, came again into unrighteous possession.   The priory, at the dissolution, was valued at £653 15s. a year. The revenues were principally derived from small houses in the parishes of St. Nicholas and St. Sepulchre, and also from country property, such as land at Stanmore, and in Canonbury, as before mentioned.   The chantries were very rich, and the alms and oblations were abundant.   The old seals of the priory, necessary to render legal any alienation of rents or possessions, were kept by the prior under three keys, which were in charge of the prior and two brethren specially chosen.   The earliest seals of the priory which are preserved are attached to a life-grant of the church of St. Sepulchre, from Rayer to Haymon, priest, and dated in 1137. The seal of the reign of Edward III. represents St. Bartholomew standing on a lion, holding a knife (symbol of martyrdom) in his left hand, and a book in his right.   On either side of him is a shield, on which are three lions, guardant, passant.   This was the common seal of the hospital.   On the seal, which bears date 1341, St. Bartholomew is seated on a throne, as before, holding a knife in his left hand; around him are the heavens, with moon in crescent, and twelve stars; on the reverse is a boat, with a church in it.   In what was probably the last seal, the saint stands under a canopy, which is supported by two pillars.

The ruins of the old priory were less hidden and obliterated when the writer on the Priory and Church of St. Bartholomew in Knight's "London" searched for them than they are now.   The present church is merely the choir of the old priory church. Its front was probably originally in a line with the small gateway yet remaining, and which formerly led to the southern aisle of the nave, now entirely destroyed.   The gateway was a finely-fronted arch of four ribs, each with receding mouldings, alternating with Norman zigzag ornaments, springing from a cluster of sculptured heads.   In Knight's time the south wall, once the wall of the south aisle, belonged to a public-house which had rooms with arched ceilings, a cornice with a shield extending through three of them, and a chalk cellar.   These had belonged to the priory.   Among costermongers' houses and sheds, and near a smith's workshop,

were the arches of the east cloister.   The roof and part of the wall fell in many years ago, but five arches of the east and one of the west side still remained.   A fine Norman arch leading into the aisle was walled up.   In several parts of the ruins of the cloister the groins and key-stones and elaborately carved devices were still visible.   It was calculated by the writer in Knight's "London" that the cloisters of St. Bartholomew's were nearly fifteen feet broad, and once extended round the four sides of a square of nearly 100 feet.

The same writer describes the refectory of the priory, then a tobacco-manufactory, divided into two or three stories, as originally a room some forty feet high, thirty feet broad, and 120 feet long, finely roofed with oak.   The ceilings and floors of the three stories were evidently temporary, and formed of huge timbers plucked from the original roof. The crypt, which ran below the refectory, still exists.   It is of immense length, with a double row of beautiful aisles, and in perfect preservation.   A door in this vault is traditionally supposed to lead to Canonbury.   Perhaps, says one writer, it was really used as a mode of escape by the Nonconformist ministers who occupied the adjoining chapel during part of the sixteenth and seventeenth centuries.   "It opened till lately," says Mr. Delamotte, in 1846, "into a cellar that extended beneath the chapel, and where the fire broke out, in 1830, that destroyed the latter, and some other interesting parts of the old priory."   The chapel formed part of the monastic buildings, but what part, is unknown.   It had an ancient timber roof, and a beam projecting across near the centre, and in a corner there is said to have been an antique piece of sculpture, representing a priest with a child in his arms, probably some saint and the infant Jesus.   In several parts of the walls were marks of private doors.   This chapel had been occupied by Presbyterian ministers till 1753, when Wesley obtained possession of it, and opened it for his followers.   It is supposed that Lord Rich's house occupied the site of the prior's stables and wood-yard, and that an old house with a vaulted ceiling and a fine carved mantelpiece marks the spot, near Middlesex Passage, where the mulberry-garden stood, the last tree in which was cut down about 1846.

At the back of the present church, and between it and Red Lion Passage, stood the prior's house. It may still be traced by its massive walls, square flat pillars, and fluted capitals, and the old dormitory, which some years ago was occupied by gimp-spinners.   There are also remains of the south transept, and the ruins still heaped there comprise also the chapter-house, which stood between the old vestry and the transept. There were traces formerly of the once beautiful arch that led into the chapter-house, and there is also a fragment of the wall of the transept. The picturesque-looking low porch, with its deep pent-house, says one writer on the subject, now the entrance into the church from the transept, was formerly an entrance into St. Bartholomew's Chapel. In Cloth Fair a narrow passage points to the position of the north transept. Extending from the sides of the choir north and south, and partly over the aisles, were buildings used as schools; that on the south was burnt in the fire of 1830; the other still exists, and it contains two of the fine circular arches that form the second tier of the choir.

Within the porch of St. Bartholomew's are the remains of a very elegant pointed arch, that probably led into the cloisters. The aisles are separated from the choir by solid pillars and square piers indifferently, from which spring five semicircular arches on either side. The arches next the choir are adorned with billet moulding, which does not cease with the arch, but, in some places, is continued horizontally over the cap of the column, until it meets the next arch. The triforium has similar arches, each opening being divided into four compartments by small Norman columns and arches, formerly bricked up, but now re-opened. The prior's state pew is a bay, or oriel, probably added by Prior Bolton, on the south side. His rebus is upon it. This oriel communicated with the priory, and was where the prior assisted at the service, in all the pride of state and pomp, and from this point of vantage he could watch his thirteen canons. There are similar oriels, says Mr. Godwin, in Malmesbury Abbey, and in Exeter Cathedral.

There is a clerestory above the triforium, with pointed windows, and a passage the whole length of the building. The roof is of timber, divided into compartments by a tie-beam and king-post, the corbels resting on angels' heads. There also remains a portion of the transepts.

"One of the most interesting features of the choir," says Mr. Delamotte, " is the long-continued aisle, or series of aisles, which entirely encircle it, opening into the former by the spaces between the flat and circular arch-piers of the body of the structure. It is about twelve feet wide, with a pure arched and vaulted ceiling, in the simplest and truest Norman style, and with windows of different sizes, slightly pointed. The pillars against the wall, opposite the entrance into the choir, are flat, apparently made so for the convenience of the sitters. One of the

most beautiful little architectural effects, of a simple kind that we can conceive is to be found at the north-eastern corner of the aisle. Between two of the grand Norman pillars, projecting from the wall, is a low postern doorway, and above, rising on each side from the capitals, a peculiarly elegant arch, something like an elongated horse-shoe. The connection between two styles so strikingly different in most respects, as the Moorish, with its fantastic delicacy (?), variety, and richness, and the Norman, with its simple (occasionally uncouth) grandeur, was never more apparent. That little picture is alone worth a visit to St. Bartholomew's." The postern leads into a curious place, enclosed by the end of the choir (or altar end) on one side, and the circular wall of the eastern aisle on the other. It is supposed by Mr. Godwin to have been the chancel of the original building, and no doubt it was, if we are to suppose that the altar wall has undergone great changes. At present the space is so narrow, and so dark, that it need not surprise us to hear that it is called the Purgatory. We have no doubt that this part has been visible, in some way, from the choir, and not, as it is now, entirely excluded from it; for a pair of exactly similar pillars, with a beautiful arch above, standing at the south-east corner of the aisle, are, in a great measure, shut in here.

The monument of Rayer (or Rahere), the founder of the priory, the pious jester of Henry I., is in the north-east corner of the church, next the altar, and almost exactly opposite Prior Bolton's beautiful oriel window. Bolton restored this tomb with pious care, and may have placed his window so as to command a perpetual view of that *memento mori*. This monument is of a much later date than the period of Rayer's death. It consists of a highly-wrought stone screen, of pointed Gothic, enclosing a tomb, on which, under a canopy, rests the prior's effigy. The roof of the tomb is exquisitely groined. Except a few of the pinnacles, the monument is still uninjured, and Time has watched kindly over the good man's grave. A crowned angel kneels at Rayer's feet, and monks of his order pray by his side. Each of the monks has a Bible before him, open at Isa. li., which contains the following verse, so applicable to the church built on the marsh :—"The Lord shall comfort Zion : he will comfort all her waste places ; and he will make her wilderness like Eden, and her desert like the garden of the Lord ; joy and gladness shall be found therein, thanksgiving, and the voice of melody."

"Besides the choir of the old church," says Mr. Godwin, "there remains a portion of the transepts, and of the nave, at their junction with it, over which rose a tower. At the commencement of each transept, a large arch, spanning its whole width, springs from the capitals of slender clustered columns, and, at the end of the nave and commencement of the choir, other arches (the width of the church) spring from corbels, sculptured to represent the capitals of similar columns. The four arches are surrounded by zigzag ornaments. Of these arches, those at the intersection of the tran-

of Robert Chamberlain. It is of very dark brown marble, and consists of a figure of a man in complete armour, kneeling in state under an alcove, while two angels are drawing aside the curtains. The monument of James Rivers bears the date 1641 (eve of the Civil War), and bears this inscription—

"Within this hollow vault there rests the frame
Of the high soul which once informed the same ;
Torn from the service of the State in 's prime
By a disease malignant as the time ;

RAYER'S TOMB.   (*See page* 353.)

septs are pointed, and have been referred to as among the various instances of the *incidental* use made of the pointed arch in early buildings, before it became a component part of a system, at least in England." "The cause for this," says Mr. Britton, the famous antiquary, "was evident; for those sides of the tower being much narrower than the east and west divisions, which are formed of semicircular arches, it became necessary to carry the arches of the former to a point, in order to suit the oblong plan of the intersection, and, at the same time, make the upper mouldings and lines range with the corresponding members of the circular arches."

One of the finest monuments in the choir is that

Whose life and death designed no other end
Than to serve God, his country, and his friend ;
Who, when ambition, tyranny, and pride
Conquered the age, conquered himself, and died."

Beyond is a sumptuous and curious transitional monument, half-classic, half-Gothic, in memory of Sir Walter Mildmay, 1689. This gentleman, the generous founder of Emanuel College, Cambridge, held offices under Henry VIII. and Edward VI.; and, though not compliant enough, was made by Elizabeth Chancellor of the Exchequer.

In the corner next to Sir Walter's monument is that to the memory of the Smallpage family (1558), which is of very dark marble. It contains two busts, one of a male, the other of a female. The

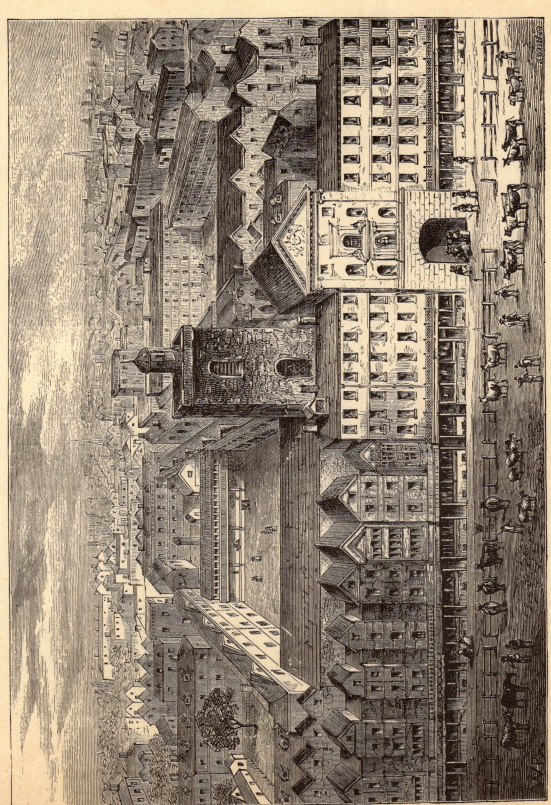

ST. BARTHOLOMEW'S HOSPITAL IN 1750. (*See page* 359.)

former has a fine face and a double-peaked beard; the latter, in a full ruff, looks rather a Tartar.

In the spandrils of some of the arches of this church there are ornaments which resemble the Grecian honeysuckle, and which are unusual in Gothic work. A small bit of the old nave is now used as the organ-loft; and over what was once part of the aisle of the nave rises the poor brick tower, built in 1628. The vestry-room is part of the south transept, and a magnificent chapel once stood on the east side of this transept. When the ill-judged classic altar-piece was taken down, some years ago, the stone wall was found painted bright red, and spotted with black stars. The chamber between the choir and the east aisle, early in this century, contained several thousand bones.

Near the junction of the south and east aisles is the old vestry-room, a solemn, ancient place, probably once an oratory. The present vestry, a mere place for registers and surplices, is built over the southern aisle. Here is a beautiful Norman semicircular arch, forming one of a range of arches by which the second storey of the choir was probably continued at a right angle along the sides of the transept. "Among the monuments of the aisles is one in the form of a rose, with an inscription to Abigail Coult, 1629, who died "in the sixteenth year of her virginity." Her father, Maximilian Coult, or Colte, was a famous sculptor of the time, and was employed by James I. in various public buildings. In the office-book of the Board of Works appears the line, "Max. Colte, Master Sculptor, at £8 a year, 1633." Filling up the beautiful horse-shoe arch, which it thus conceals, at the south-eastern corner, is the monument of Edward Cooke. There appears to have been attached to the northern aisle—probably corresponding in position with the old vestry—another chapel.

In Walden Chapel, on the north side of the altar, Roger Walden, Bishop of London, was buried, instead of in St. Paul's—but why, no one can guess. "Never had any man," says Weever, "better experience of the uncertainty of worldly felicity." "Raised," says Mr. Delamotte, "from the condition of a poor man by his industry and ability, he became successively Dean of York, Treasurer of Calais, Secretary to the King, and Treasurer of England. When Archbishop Arundel fell under the displeasure of Richard II., and was banished, Walden was made Primate of England. On the return of Arundel, in company with Bolingbroke, and the ascent of the latter to the throne, Arundel of course resumed his archiepiscopal rank and functions, and Roger Walden became again a private individual. Arundel, however, behaved very nobly to the man whom he must have looked on as a usurper of his place, for he conferred on him the bishopric of London. Walden did not live long to be grateful for this very honourable and kindly act, for he died within the ensuing year. 'He may be compared to one so jaw-fallen,' says Fuller, in his usual quaint, homely style, 'with over-long fasting, that he cannot eat meat when brought unto him; and his spirits were so depressed with his former ill-fortunes, that he could not enjoy himself in his new unexpected happiness.'"

In St. Bartholomew-the-Great was buried, in 1623, Dr. Francis Anthony, a learned physician and chemist of the reign of James I., who was frequently fined and imprisoned by the London College of Physicians for practising physic without a licence. Dr. Anthony, who seems to have been a generous and honest man, prided himself on the discovery of a universal medicine, which he called *aurum potabile*, or potable gold, which he mixed with mercury.

"Dr. Anthony," says Mr. Delamotte, "published a very learned and modest defence of himself and his *aurum potabile*, in Latin, written with great decency, much skill in chemistry, and with an apparent knowledge in the theory and practice of physic. In the preface he says 'that after inexpressible labour, watching, and expense, he had, through the blessing of God, attained all he had sought for in his inquiries.' In the second chapter of his work he affirms that his medicine is a kind of extract or honey of gold, capable of being dissolved in any liquor whatsoever, and referring to the common objection of the affinity between the *aurum potabile* and the philosopher's stone, does not deny the transmutation of metals, but still shows that there is a great difference between the two, and that the finding or not finding of the one does not at all render it inevitable that the other shall also be discovered, or remain hidden. The price of the medicine was five shillings an ounce. Wonderful cures, of course, are displayed in the doctor's pages. His publication produced quite a controversy on the merits of *aurum potabile*. We need not wonder to find that Dr. Anthony had implicit believers in the value of his nostrum, when we see the great chemist and philosopher, Boyle, thus commenting on such preparations: 'Though I have long been prejudiced against the pretended *aurum potabile*, and other boasted preparations of gold, for most of which I have still no great esteem, yet I saw such extraordinary and surprising effects from the tincture of gold I spake of (prepared by two foreign physicians) upon persons of great note with whom I was particularly acquainted, both before they fell desperately sick and after their strange recovery, that I could not but change my opinion for a very favourable one as to some preparations of gold.'"

A local antiquary, who is as learned as he is imaginative, has furnished us with some notes on the priory and its neighbourhood, of which we gladly avail ourselves :—

"Excepting the tower and its immediate neighbourhood," says the writer, "there is no part of London, old or new, around which are clustered so many events interesting in history, as that of the Priory of St. Bartholomew-the-Great, and its vicinity. There are narrow, tortuous streets, and still narrower courts, about Cloth Fair, where are hidden away scores of old houses, whose projecting eaves and overhanging floors, heavy cumbrous beams, and wattle and plaster walls, must have seen the days of the Plantagenets and the earlier Tudors. There are remains of groined arches, and windows with ancient tracery, strong buttresses, and beautiful portals, with toothed and ornate archways, belonging to times long anterior to Wycliffe and John of Gaunt, yet to be found lurking behind dark, uncanny-looking tenements. To the real lover of the past history of our great City ; to the earnest inquirer into the rise and progress of our present civilisation ; to the pious student of the earlier times of our English Church, and her struggles after freedom, there is no part of modern London that will better reward a careful survey than that now under our consideration.

"Note that dark archway yonder. Fully seven centuries have passed since the hand of some good lay brother traced its bold outline, and worked with cunning mallet and chisel the beautiful beading and its toothed ornaments. And in the old times, when Chaucer was young, and his Canterbury Pilgrims were men and women of the period, processions of cowled monks and chanting boys, with censers and crucifix, wended their way from the old priory to that of the Black Friars, by the Thames ; and not unfrequently, when Edward III. and his favourite Alice Perrers had spent the morning in witnessing the tournay of mailed knights in Smithfield, have they and their attendants, with all the pomp and pageantry of chivalry, passed beneath this old gateway to the grand entertainments provided by the good prior for their delectation, in the great refectory beyond the south cloisters. Rhenish and Cyprus wines, with sack and strong waters, were there in plenty, and geese, swans, bustards, and lordly peacocks, graced the well-filled board, with venison pasties and the boar's head ready at hand ; whilst all such fruits as were then naturalised amongst us were reared by the careful fathers in their garden at Canonbury, for the use of the good prior's table.

"In later years the solemn, weather-worn stones of this old archway have had sad scenes to frown upon, and yet, nearer our own day, merry parties have gambolled and frisked beneath the ancient portal, as they wended their way to the pandemonium of mirth and folly in Bartholomew Fair.

"In the Great Close, where is now a row of dilapidated houses, was once the west cloister of the priory; and here, as we turn, was the south cloister, just beyond which was, until quite lately, the remains of the great refectory. Beneath it was much of the ancient crypt, with its deep groined arches, more than half buried under the débris of ages. Some portion of this is still left us, beneath the modern buildings erected on the spot.

"As we go round the Great Close, towards the other end of the church, we pass by some very old houses, that occupy the place where was once the east cloister. Behind these houses used to be a great mulberry-tree, only removed in our own time. This was formerly the centre of the cloister court. You fancy you see a tall, bareheaded man, in monkish garb of grey, his rosary dangling by his side, as he stands near a pillar of the cloister, deeply immersed in the breviary he holds in his hand. See his sandalled feet, and his long grey beard ; he is the personal friend of the good Prior Rayer. Now he moves, and silently steps across the grass towards the big mulberry-tree, where he sits down upon a stone seat beneath its umbrageous branches, and laying down his book, he takes from the folds of his habit a scroll. Slowly he unrolls it, and carefully studies the curious lines, curves, and ornaments drawn thereon. That old monk is the good Alfune, the builder of St. Giles's, Cripplegate.

"See here, is the prior's house, its big stones hidden under a casing of bricks and stucco, whilst here and there, like big rocks, a buttress crops out, an enormity quite unsuited to the gingerbread buildings of modern times. But these good monkish architects built more for the future than for themselves. Look above : there, where is now a row of windows to a fringe factory was once the dormitory, or 'dormite,' of the monks. They needed looking-after sometimes, so the prior wisely kept them near himself at night.

"Let us go along this dark and narrow passage. Now we are in Cloth Fair. This is where the ancient cloth fair was held, to which came merchants from Flanders and Italy, with their precious wares for the sons and daughters of old London. How aged some of these houses are ! floor leaning over floor, until you may fancy they are toppling upon you. Now come with me under this low gateway, and take my hand, for it is quite dark here, and we must walk in Indian file, the space is so narrow. Between the houses and the low wall, as your eyes become used to the deep gloom, you will notice that the first floor entirely covers the narrow court behind, and is supported on posts, and the next leaning over the one beneath it. These houses have seen many generations of tenants, and in some of them the old cloth business is still carried on. Now peep over the wall on your left. You will find the level much lower there, for they have lately been clearing away some of the accumulated rubbish, and 'dust and ashes' of past ages, and have exposed to view some beautiful windows, that formed part of the prior's house, perhaps the infirmary, or 'firmary,' as that was under the same roof, or a portion of the crypt, used for such a purpose mayhap. Past these very windows the old priors of the monastery must have gone to the service in the church. Let us follow, and note, as we step into the ancient Norman aisle, the finely-curved semicircular arches, and the curious nooks and crannies, only to be found in such places. See, we have to go through that small door near the purgatory into the choir.

"What a blaze of light! There are scores of tapers on the altar, the crucifix, emblazoned banners, and the rich vestments of the officiating priests; and as they cross and recross the tessellated floor of the chancel, note that they make each time low genuflexions towards the altar. Mark the incense-bearers, swinging the spicy odour to and fro, which is wafted towards us, and mingles, as it were, with the loud pealing of the organ and the sweet chanting of the boy choristers, and the low responses of the cowled brethren of the priory.

"Now they pass in procession round the church, along the choir, and down the lofty nave, towards the beautiful entrance-gate. Anon they return, and on reaching the altar-tomb of their founder, Rayer, they stop, a priest swings a censer to and fro before it, whilst all kneel and cross themselves; then again they move towards the altar, and as the choir ceases chanting, the last notes of the organ are heard reverberating along the lofty roof. The brethren follow each other slowly towards the door, the tapers are extinguished one by one, and thus the pageant fades from our imagination; and once more we find ourselves in Smithfield, outside the Cloth Fair gate of the ancient Priory of St. Bartholomew."

The dimensions of this most interesting church, half Norman, half early English, are generally given

thus: The height about 40 feet, the breadth 60 feet, the length 138 feet; add to this 87 feet for the length of the destroyed nave, and we have 225 feet as the entire length of the church of Rayer's priory. The church was much injured in the fire of 1830, when a portion of the middle roof of the south aisle fell.

When Rayer, on his return from doing penance at Rome, built a hospital in Smithfield, in performance of a vow made in sickness, he added to it that chapel which is now called St. Bartholomew-the-Less, which, after the dissolution, became a parish church for those living within the hospital precinct. In Stow's time the church seems to have been full of old monuments and brasses of the fifteenth and later centuries, a few of which only have been preserved.

Among those which no longer remain were two brass effigies, "in the habit of pilgrims," with an inscription, commencing—

" Behold how ended is
The poor pilgrimage
Of John Shirley, Esquire,
With Margaret, his wife,"

and ending with the date 1456. "This Shirley," says Mr. Godwin, "appears to have been a traveller in various countries. He collected the works of Chaucer, John Lydgate, and other learned writers, 'which works he wrote in sundry volumes, to remain for posterity.' 'I have seen them,' says Stow, 'and partly do possess them.' Such of the epitaphs as Stow omitted to mention were recorded by Weever, in his 'Funeral Monuments.' The earliest of them was as follows:—

' The xiiii.c. yere of our Lord and eight,
Passyd Sir Robart Greuil to God Almight,
The xii. day of April; Broder of this place,
Jesu for his mercy rejoice him with his grace.'

"The length of the church, at the beginning of the eighteenth century, was 99 feet, and the breadth was 42 feet, except in the chancel, the narrowness of which latter, however, was more than counterbalanced by a chapel on the north side."

In 1789, Mr. George Dance, the architect and surveyor to the hospital, repaired the church, by first destroying the whole interior, leaving only the old walls, the vestibule, and the square tower. Dry rot very soon setting in, in an aggravated form, Mr. Hardwick, in 1823, commenced the rebuilding, turning out Mr. Dance's timber octagon, and replacing it with stone and iron. It was then found that Mr. Dance, in his contempt for Gothic architecture, had ruthlessly cut away altar-tombs and such mediæval trifles. The result of all this incompetent tinkering is a compo tower and an iron roof. In the east window are several saints, the arms of Henry VIII. and the hospital, and those of various hospital treasurers. North of the communion-table is a tablet in memory of the wife of Thomas Bodley, Elizabeth's ambassador in France and Germany, and the generous founder of the great library at Oxford. In this church there is also a monument to Henry Earle, surgeon, of St. Bartholomew's, which was erected to this amiable man in 1838. In the lobby that leads to the western porch, where a sexton hung himself in 1838, there is a canopied altar-tomb and several relics of old Gothic sculpture. Among others, a niche containing the figure of an angel bearing a shield, and beneath it the arms of Edward the Confessor, impaled with those of England.

Near Mr. Earle's tablet is a large monument, presenting a kneeling figure beneath an entablature, supported on two columns, and inscribed to Robert Balthrope :—

"Who Sergeant of the Surgeons sworn
Near thirty years had been.
He dyed at sixty-nine of years,
December's ninth the day ;
The year of grace eight hundred twice,
Deducting nine away."

The tower of St. Bartholomew-the-Less contains some fine Norman and early English arches and pillars. The piscina from the ancient church is used as a font. A beautiful chancel has been built, in the style of the Lady chapels in Normandy. The pulpit and reredos are marble and alabaster, with bas-relief of the Sermon on the Mount, and the stained glass windows are by Powell. The parish register records the baptism of the celebrated Inigo Jones, son of a Welsh clothworker, residing at or near Cloth Fair ; and the burial, in 1664, of James Heath, a Cavalier chronicler of the Civil Wars, who slandered Cromwell, and has been branded by Carlisle, in consequence, as "Carrion Heath." He was buried near the screen door, says Aubrey.

Upon entering the chapel there is, immediately upon your left hand, a remarkably curious tomb of the fireplace kind, most elaborately wrought. It is the tomb of Freke, the senior surgeon of St. Bartholomew's Hospital, who wrote many works upon surgery, still to be found in its library. His bust is to be seen in the museum of the hospital, and he is represented by Hogarth, in the last plate of "The Stages of Cruelty," presiding aloft over the dissecting-table, and pointing with a long wand to the dead "subject," upon whom he is lecturing to the assembled students. There is likewise in the office of St. Bartholomew's a curious large wooden chandelier, which Freke carved with his own hand.

CHAPTER XLV.

ST. BARTHOLOMEW'S HOSPITAL.

Its Early History—The Presidency of the Royal Hospitals—Thomas Vicary—Harvey, the Famous Physician—The Great Quadrangle of the Hospital Rebuilt—The Museums, Theatres, and Library of St. Bartholomew's—The Great Abernethy—Dr. Percival Pott—A Lucky Fracture—Great Surgeons at St. Bartholomew's—Hogarth's Pictures—Samaritan Fund—View Day—Cloth Fair—Duck Lane.

ST. BARTHOLOMEW'S HOSPITAL was founded by Rayer, the jester or minstrel of Henry I. At the dissolution the fat, greedy hands of Henry VIII., that spared no gold that would melt, whether it was God's or man's, soon had a grip of it; but, for very shame, at the petition of Sir Richard Gresham, Lord Mayor and father of the builder of the Royal Exchange, he turned it over to the City. The king then, in 1546, says Mr. Timbs, "vested the Hospital of St. Bartholomew in the mayor, commonalty, and citizens of London, and their successors, for ever, in consideration of a payment by them of 500 marks a year towards its maintenance, and with it the nomination and appointment of all the officers. In September, 1557, at a general court of the governors of all the hospitals, it was ordered that St. Bartholomew's should henceforth be united to the rest of the hospitals, and be made one body with them, and on the following day ordinances were made by the corporation for the general government of all the hospitals. The 500 marks a year have been paid by the corporation since 1546, besides the profit of many valuable leases."

From a search made in the official records of the City, it appears that for more than 300 years—namely, since 1549—an alderman of London had always been elected president of St. Bartholomew's Hospital. Until 1854, whenever a vacancy occurred in the presidency of the royal hospitals (St. Bartholomew's, Bethlehem, Bridewell, St. Thomas's, or Christ's Hospitals), it was customary to elect the Lord Mayor for the time being, or an alderman who had passed the chair. This rule was first broken when the Duke of Cambridge was chosen president of Christ's Hospital, over the head of Alderman Sidney, the then Lord Mayor; and again, when Mr. Cubitt, then no longer an alderman, was elected president of St. Bartholomew's in preference to the then Lord Mayor. The question

physician to the hospital for thirty-four years, and here, in 1619 (James I.), he first lectured upon his great discovery.

The executors of Whittington had repaired the hospital, in 1423 (Henry VI.), but it had to be taken down in 1730, when the great quadrangle

INTERIOR OF ST. BARTHOLOMEW-THE-GREAT, 1868. (*See page* 353.)

is, however, contested by the foundation-governors, or the corporation, and the donation-governors."

The first superintendent of the hospital was Thomas Vicary, serjeant-surgeon to Henry VIII., Edward VI., Mary, and Elizabeth, and one of the earliest English writers on anatomy. The great Harvey, the physician of Charles I., and the first discoverer of the circulation of the blood, was

was rebuilt by Gibbs, the ambitious architect of St. Martin's-in-the-Fields, and the first stone laid June 9th, 1730. The gate towards Smithfield, a mean structure (with the statue of Henry VIII. and the inscription, "St. Bartholomew's Hospital, founded by Rahere, A.D. 1102; re-founded by Henry VIII., 1546."), was built in 1702. On the pediment of the hospital are two figures—Lameness and

Sickness.   The cost of the work in 1730 was defrayed by public subscription, Dr. Radcliffe being generously prominent among the donors, and leaving £500 a year for the improvement of the general diet, and £100 a year to buy linen.

The museums, theatres, and library of this noble charity are very large.   A new surgery was added in 1842.   The lectures of the present day were established by the great Abernethy, who was elected assistant-surgeon in 1787.

with the patient's wishes, but complimented him on the resolute manner he adopted.

Abernethy made but little distinction between a poor and a rich patient, but was rather more attentive to the former; and, on one occasion, gave great offence to a certain peer, by refusing to see him out of his turn.   On entering his apartment, the nobleman, having indignantly asked Abernethy if he knew who he was, stated his rank, name, &c., when Abernethy, it is said, replied, with

PIE CORNER IN 1789.   *From a Drawing in Mr. Gardner's Collection.*   (See page 363.)

Sir Astley Cooper used to say, "Abernethy's *manner* was worth a thousand a year to him." Some of his patients he would cut short with, "Sir, I have heard enough!   You have heard of my book?"   "Yes."   "Then go home and read it." To a lady, complaining of low spirits, he would say, "Don't come to me; go and buy a skipping-rope;" and to another, who said she felt a pain in holding her arm over her head, he replied, "Then what a fool you must be to hold it up!" He sometimes, however, met with his match, and cutting a gentleman short one day, the patient suddenly locked the door, slipped the key into his pocket, and protested he would be heard, which so pleased Abernethy that he not only complied

the most provoking *sang froid*, "And I, sir, am John Abernethy, surgeon, lecturer of St. Bartholomew's Hospital, &c.; and if you wish to consult me, I am now ready to hear what you have to say in your turn."   The Duke of Wellington having insisted on seeing him out of his usual hours, and abruptly entering his parlour one day, was asked by the doctor how he got into the room.   "By the door," was the reply.   "Then," said Abernethy, "I recommend you to make your exit by the same way."   He is said to have given another proof of his independence, by refusing to attend George IV. until he had delivered his lecture at the hospital; in consequence of which he lost a Royal appointment.

That eminent surgeon, Percival Pott, was also one of the shining lights of St. Bartholomew's. The following is the story told of the celebrated fracture, which he afterwards learned to alleviate, and to which he gave his name:—In 1756, while on a visit to a patient in Kent Street, Southwark, he was thrown from his horse, and received a compound fracture of the leg. This event produced, perhaps, one of the most extraordinary instances of coolness and prudence on record. Aware of the danger of rough and injudicious treatment, he would not suffer himself to be raised from the pavement, but sent a messenger for two chairmen. When they arrived, he directed them to nail their poles to a door, which he had purchased in the interim, on which he was then carefully placed, and borne to his residence in Watling Street, near St. Paul's. A consultation was immediately called, and amputation of the limb was resolved on; but, upon the suggestion of a humane friend, who soon after entered the room, a successful attempt to save the limb was made. This accident confined Mr. Pott to his house for several weeks, during which he conceived, and partly executed, his "Treatise on Ruptures."

In 1843 the authorities founded a collegiate establishment for the resident pupils within the college walls: a spacious casualty room has also been added. In 1878 a new lecture theatre, a lofty and imposing structure, with the usual offices attached, was built at the corner abutting upon Giltspur Street. In 1736 the grand staircase was painted gratuitously by Hogarth, whose heart always warmed to works of charity. The subjects are "The Good Samaritan" and "The Pool of Bethesda." These two pictures, for which he was made a life governor, were, as he tells us himself in his autobiographical sketch, his first efforts in the grand style.

"Before I had done anything of much consequence in this walk (*i.e.*, the painting and engraving of modern moral subjects)," says the sturdy painter, "I entertained some hopes of succeeding in what the puffers in books call 'the great style of history painting;' so without having had a stroke of this grand business before, I quitted small portraits and familiar conversations, and, with a smile at my own temerity, commenced history painter, and on a great staircase at St. Bartholomew's Hospital painted two Scripture stories, 'the Pool of Bethesda' and 'the Good Samaritan,' with figures seven feet high."

"This hospital receives," says Mr. Timbs, in 1868, "upon petition, cases of all kinds, free of fees; and accidents, or cases of urgent disease, without letter,

at the surgery, at any hour of the day or night. There is also a 'Samaritan Fund,' for relieving distressed patients. The present buildings contain twenty-five wards, consisting of 650 beds, 400 being for surgical cases, and 250 for medical cases and the diseases of women. Each ward is presided over by a 'sister' and nurse, to the number of nearly 180 persons. In addition to a very extensive medical staff, there are four resident surgeons and two resident apothecaries, who are always on duty, day and night, throughout the year, to attend to whatever may be brought in at any hour of the twenty-four. It further possesses a college within itself, a priceless museum, and a first-class medical school, conducted by thirty-six professors and assistants. The 'View-day,' for this and the other royal hospitals of the City, is a day specially set apart by the authorities to examine, in their official collective capacity, every portion of the establishment, when the public are admitted."

"In January, 1846," says the same writer, "the election of Prince Albert to a governorship of the hospital was commemorated by the president and treasurer presenting to the foundation three costly silver-gilt dishes, each nearly twenty-four inches in diameter, and richly chased with a bold relief of— 1. The election of the Prince; 2, the Good Samaritan; 3, the Plague of London. The charity is ably managed by the corporation. The qualification of a governor is a donation of one hundred guineas."

In the court-room is one of the many supposed original portraits of Henry VIII. by the copiers of Holbein, who is venerated here—and in Mr. Froude's study—if nowhere else.

St. Bartholomew's contained in 1880 676 beds. About 6,000 in-patients are admitted every year, besides 100,000 out-patients. The average income of the hospital is £45,000, derived chiefly from rents and funded property. The number of governors exceeds 300.

Dr. Anthony Askew, one of the past celebrities of St. Bartholomew's, a contemporary of Freke, was scarcely more famous in medicine than in letters. The friend of Dr. Mead, Hogarth, and other great people, he was a notable personage in Georgian London, and, like Pitcairne and Freke, was a Fellow of the Royal Society. He employed Roubillac to produce the bust of Mead, which he presented to the College of Physicians, the price arranged being £50. In his delight at the goodness of the work, Askew sent the artist £100 instead of £50, whereupon Roubillac grumbled that he was not paid enough, and sent in a bill to his employer for £108 2s. Askew contemptuously paid the bill, even to the odd shillings, and sent the receipt to Hogarth. Dr. Pate, a physician of St. Bartholomew's of the same period, lived in Hatton Garden, which, like Ely Place, was long a great place for doctors. Dr. Pitcairne, his colleague, lived in Warwick Court, till he moved into the treasurer's house in St. Bartholomew's. He was buried in the hospital church. The posthumous sale of Dr. Askew's printed library, in 1775, by Baker and Leigh, and which lasted twenty days, was *the* great literary auction of the time. There was a subsequent sale of his MSS. in 1789, which also produced a great sum.

Among the modern physicians of St. Bartholomew's we must notice Dr. Baly (Queen's physician, killed in a fearful railway accident) and Dr. Jeaffreson, notable chiefly for his pleasant manners, his skill in whist, billiards, and shooting, and his extraordinary popularity. Wonderfully successful in practice, he was everybody's favourite; but, though a most enlightened man, he did nothing for science, either through literature or investigation.

Among the modern surgeons to be noticed are Sir William Lawrence, Bart.; Mr. Skey, C.B., who was famous for recommending stimulants and denouncing boat-racing, and other too violent sports; and Thomas Wormald, who died lately. Skey and Wormald were favourite pupils of Abernethy, and imitators of their great master's jocular manner and pungent speech. Tommy Wormald, or "Old Tommy," as the students called him, was Abernethy over again in voice, style, appearance, humour. "Done for," was one of his pithy written reports on a "bad life" to an insurance company, whose directors insisted that he should write his reports instead of giving them verbally. He once astounded an apothecary, who was about to put him and certain physicians off with a single guinea fee, at a consultation on a rich man's case, by saying, "A guinea is a lean fee, and the patient is a fat patient. I always have fat fees from fat patients. Pay me two guineas, sir, instantly. Pay Dr. Jeaffreson two guineas, instantly, sir. Sir, pay both the physicians and me two guineas each, instantly. Our patient is a fat patient." Some years since, rich people of a mean sort would drive down to St. Bartholomew's, and get gratuitous advice, as out-patients. Tommy was determined to stop this abuse, and he did it by a series of outrageous assaults on the self-love of the offenders. Noticing a lady, dressed in silk, who had driven up to the hospital in a brougham, Tommy raised his rich, thunderous, sarcastic voice, and, to the inexpressible glee of a roomful of young students, addressed the lady thus:—"Madam, this charity is for the poor, destitute, miserable invalids of London. So you are a miserable invalid in a silk dress —a destitute invalid, in a rich silk dress—a poor invalid, in a dress that a duchess might wear. Madam, I refuse to pay attention to miserable, destitute invalids, who wear rich silk dresses. You had better order your carriage, madam." The lady did not come again.

A few remaining spots round Smithfield still remain for us to notice, and foremost among these is Cloth Fair, the great resort in the Middle Ages of country clothiers and London drapers. Strype describes the street as even in his day chiefly inhabited by drapers and mercers; and Hatton mentions it as in the form of a T, the right arm running to Bartholomew Close, the left to Long Lane.

This latter lane, originally on the north side of the old priory, reaches from Smithfield to Aldersgate Street, and in Strype's time was known for its brokers, its second-hand linen, its upholstery, and its pawnbrokers. Congreve, always witty, makes Lady Wishfort, in his *Way of the World*, hope that one of her admirers will one day "hang in tatters, like a Long Lane pent-house or a gibbeted thief;" and good-natured Tom Brown declares that when the impudent rag-sellers in Barbican and Long Lane suddenly caught him by the arm and cried, "What do you lack?" he who feared the sight of a bailiff worse than the devil and all his works, was mortally scared.

In Duck Lane we part good friends with Smithfield. R. B., in Strype, describes it as coming out of Little Britain and falling into Smithfield, and much inhabited by second-hand booksellers. Howell, in his "Letters," mentions finding the Poet-Laureate Skelton, "pitifully tattered and torn," skulking in Duck Lane; and Garth, in his pleasant and graphic poem, says—

> "Here dregs and sediment of auctions reign,
> Refuse of fairs, and gleanings of Duck Lane."

And Swift, in one of the best of his short poems (that on his own death), writes—

> "Some country squire to Lintot goes,
> Inquires for Swift, in verse and prose.
> Says Lintot, 'I have heard the name;
> He died a year ago.' 'The same!'
> He searches all the shop in vain;
> 'Sir, you may find him in Duck Lane:
> I sent them with a load of books,
> Last Monday, to the pastrycook's.'"

At the Giltspur Street end of Smithfield stands Pie Corner, worthy of note as the spot where the Great Fire, which began in Pudding Lane, reached its limits: the figure of a fat boy still marks the spot.

CHAPTER XLVI.

CHRIST'S HOSPITAL.

The Grey Friars in Newgate Street—The Origin of Christ's Hospital—A Fashionable Burying-Place—The Mean Conduct of Sir Martin Bowes—Early Private Benefactors of Christ's Hospital—Foundation of the Mathematical School—Rebuilding of the South Front of Christ's Hospital—The Plan of Christ's Hospital—Famous Pictures in the Hall—Celebrated Blues—Leigh Hunt's Account of Christ's Hospital—The "Fazzer"—Charles Lamb—Boyer, the Celebrated Master of Christ's Hospital—Coleridge's Experiences—Erasmus—Singular Legacies—Numbers in the School—The Education at Christ's Hospital—Eminent Blues—The Public Suppers—Spital Sermons—Ceremony on St. Matthew's Day—University Exhibitions—The Diet—"Gag-eaters"—The Rebuilding in 1803.

LIVES there a Londoner who has not, at some stray hour or other, leant against the tall iron gates in Newgate Street, and felt his golden youth return, as he watched the gambols of the little bareheaded men in blue petticoats and yellow stockings? Can any man of thought, however hurried Citywards, but stop a moment to watch and see the "scrouge," the mad rush after the football, the dashing race to rescue prisoners at the bases? Summer or winter, the yellow-legged boys form a pleasant picture of perpetual youth; nor can one ever pass a strapping young Grecian in the streets without feeling some veneration for the successor of Coleridge and Charles Lamb, Hazlitt and Leigh Hunt.

Where the fine old school now stands was the site of a convent of Grey (or Mendicant) Friars, who, coming to London in the thirteenth century, after a short stay in Holborn and Cornhill, were, in 1225, housed on the north side of Newgate Street, on a good plot of ground next St. Nicholas Shambles, by John Ewin, a pious and generous mercer, who eventually became a lay brother. The friars of St. Francis, aided by men like Ewin, throve well on the scraps of Holborn and Cheapside, and their chapel soon grew into a small church, which was rebuilt in 1327 with great splendour. The Grey Friars' church, says Pennant, was reckoned "one of the most superb of the conventual establishments of London," and alms poured fast into its treasury. It received royal offerings and sheltered royal dead. In 1429 the immortal Whittington built the studious friars of Newgate Street a library, 129 feet long and 31 broad, with twenty-eight desks, and eight double settles. In three years it was filled with books, costing £556 10s., whereof Richard Whittington gave £400, and Dr. Thomas Winchilsey, one of the friars, the rest, adding an especial 100 marks for the writing out the works of D. Nicholas de Lyra, in two volumes, to be chained there. Among the royal contributors to the Grey Friars we may mention Queen Margaret, second wife of Edward I., who gave in her lifetime 2,000 marks, and by will 100 marks, towards building a choir; John Britaine, Earl of Richmond, gave £300 towards the church building, besides jewels and ornaments; Mary, Countess of Pembroke, sent £70, and Gilbert de

Clare, Earl of Gloucester, twenty great oak beams from his forest at Tunbridge and £20; the good Queen Philippa, wife of Edward III., £62; and Isabel, queen-mother of Edward III., £70.

The founder of the school is by most people supposed to have been Edward VI., but it was really his father, Henry VIII., and it was one of the few works of mercy which originated in that cruel tyrant. At the dissolution, when sacramental cups and crucifixes were being melted down by the thousand, to maintain a bad king in his sumptuous splendour, the English Sultan, in one of his few good moments, near the end of his reign, gave the Grey Friars' church to the City, to be devoted to the relief of the poor. The building had previously been used as a storehouse for plunder taken from the French. The gift, confirmed by the pious young king, Edward VI., was announced by Dr. Ridley, Bishop of Rochester, at a public sermon at Paul's Cross. The parishes of St. Ewin, St. Nicholas, and part of St. Sepulchre's were at this time compressed into one large parish, and called Christ Church.

The good work remained in abeyance, till, in 1552, the worthy Ridley, preaching before the young king, his subject being "mercy and charity," made, says Stow, "a fruitful and godly exhortation" to the rich to be merciful to the poor, and also to move those who were in authority to strive, by charitable ways and means, to comfort and relieve them. The young king, always eager to do good, hearing that London swarmed with impoverished and neglected people, at once sent for the bishop to come to him after sermon. The memorable interview between Ridley and Edward took place in a great gallery at Westminster, where the king and bishop were alone. A chair had been already provided for the bishop, and the king insisted on the worthy prelate remaining covered. Edward first gave the bishop hearty thanks for his good sermon and exhortation, and mentioned the special points which he had noted. "'Truely, truely,' remarks Ridley (for that commonly was his oath), 'I could never have thought that excellency to have been in his Grace, but that I beheld and heard it in him.' At the last the king's majestie much commended him for his exhortation for the reliefe of the poore. 'For, my lord,' quoth he, 'you willed such as are in authority to bee careful thereof, and to devise some good order for theire reliefe, wherein I think you mean mee; for I am in highest place, and therefore am the first that must make answer unto God for my negligence, if I should not be careful therein, knowing it to bee the expresse commandment of Almighty God to have compassion of his poore and needy members, for whom we must make an account unto him. And truely, my lord, I am (before all things else) most willing to travaile that way, and doubting nothing of your long and approved wisdome and learning, who have such good zeale as wisheth health unto them; but also that you have had some conference with others what waies are best to be taken therein, the which I am desirous to understand; I pray you therefore to say your minde.'"

The bishop, amazed to hear the wisdom and earnest zeal of the child-king, confessed that he was so astonished that he hardly knew what to reply; but after a pause, he urged the special claims of the poor of London, where the citizens were wise, and, he doubted not, pitiful and merciful, and would carry out the work. The king, not releasing Ridley till his letter to the mayor was written, signed, and sealed, sent his express commandment to the mayor that he should inform him how far he had proceeded. Ridley, overjoyed at such youthful zeal, went that night to Sir Richard Dobbes, the Lord Mayor, and delivered the king's letter and message. The mayor, honoured and pleased, invited the bishop to dine the next day with two aldermen and six commoners, to discuss the charitable enterprise. On the mayor's report to the king, Edward expressed his willingness to grant a charter to the new governors, and to be proclaimed as founder and patron of the new hospital. He also confirmed his father's grant of the old Grey Friars' monastery, and endowed it (to bring the charity at once into working order) with lands and tenements that had belonged to the Savoy, of the yearly value of about £450. He also consented to the City's petition that they might take, in mortmain or otherwise, without licence, lands to the yearly value of ———. Edward filled up the blank with the words "4,000 marks," and then, before his whole council, exclaimed, with his usual pious fervour, "Lord, I yield Thee most hearty thanks that Thou hast given me life thus long, to finish this work to the glory of Thy name."

Edward, says the Rev. W. Trollope, the historian of Christ's Hospital, lived about a month after

signing the Charter of Incorporation of the Royal Hospitals. The citizens, roused by the king's fervour, and touched by his untimely death, set to work with gold and steel, and in six months the old Grey Friars' monastery was patched up sufficiently to accommodate 340 boys, a number increased to 380 by the end of the year.

As the Grey Friars' churchyard was thought, in the Middle Ages, to be peculiarly free from ghosts and flying demons of all sorts, it soon became a fashionable burying-place, and almost as popular as the great abbey even with royalty. Four queens lie there, among countless lords and ladies, brave knights, and godly monks—Margaret, second wife of Edward I., and Isabella, the infamous wife and part-murderess of Edward II., both, as we have before mentioned, benefactors to the hospital; Joan, daughter of Edward II. and wife of David Bruce, King of Scotland; and, lastly, Isabella, wife of William, Baron Fitzwarren, titular Queen of Man. The English Queen Isabella, as if to propagate an eternal lie, was buried with the heart of her murdered husband on her breast. Her ghost, according to all true "Blues," still haunts the cloisters.

Here also rest other knights and ladies, almost equally illustrious by birth; among others, Isabella, daughter of Edward III. and wife of Ingelram de Courcy, Earl of Bedford; John Hastings, the young Earl of Pembroke, slain by accident at a Christmas tournament in Woodstock Park, 1389; John, Duke of Bourbon, one of the noble French prisoners taken at Agincourt, who had been a prisoner in the Tower eighteen years; Walter Blount, Lord Mountjoy, Lord Treasurer to Edward IV.; and the "gentle Mortimer," the wretched paramour of Queen Isabella, who was hung at Tyburn, and left two days withering on the gallows. Lastly, those two rapacious favourites of Richard II., Sir Robert Tresilian, Chief Justice of England, and Sir Nicholas Brembre, Lord Mayor of London, both hung at Tyburn. Tradition goes that they could not hang Tresilian till they had removed from his person certain magic images and the head of a devil.

The friars' churchyard seems also to have been fashionable with state criminals of the Middle Ages, for here also lies Sir John Mortimer, an unhappy Yorkist, hung, drawn, and quartered at Tyburn by the Lancastrian party in 1423, the second year of the reign of the child-king, Henry VI. To the same bourne also came a victim of Yorkist cruelty, Thomas Burdet, for speaking a few angry words about a favourite white buck which Edward IV. had carelessly killed. A murderess, too, lies here, a lady named Alice Hungerford, who, for murdering her husband in 1523, was carted to Tyburn, and there hung. All these ancient monuments and tombs were basely and stupidly sold, in 1545, by Sir Martin Bowes, Lord Mayor, for a poor fifty pounds. The Great Fire of 1666 destroyed the Grey Friars' church, which Wren shortly afterwards rebuilt, a little further to the east; and in the old church perished the tomb of the beautiful Lady Venetia Digby, whom Ben Jonson celebrated, and who, it was absurdly sup-

of boyish happiness, was rebuilt by Sir C. Wren. In 1673, Charles II., at the suggestion of our old friend Pepys, Sir Robert Clayton, and Lord Treasurer Clifford, founded a mathematical school for the instruction of forty boys in navigation, and appointed Pepys one of the governors. King Charles endowed the school with £1,000 for seven years, and added an annuity of £370 out of the Exchequer, for the educating and sending to sea ten boys annually, five of whom pass an examina-

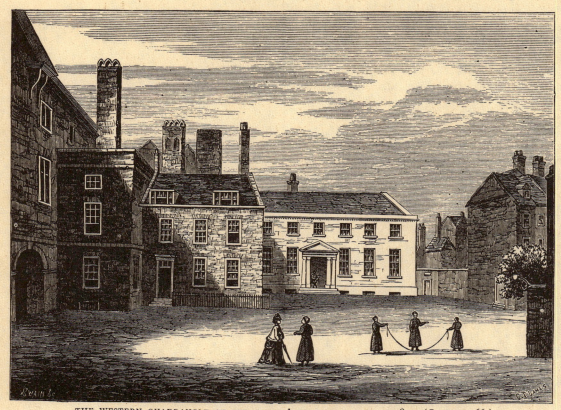

THE WESTERN QUADRANGLE OF OLD CHRIST'S HOSPITAL, ABOUT 1780. (See page 366.)

posed, perished from viper-broth, administered by her husband to heighten her beauty.

One of the earliest private benefactors of this hospital was Sir William Chester, Lord Mayor in 1554, who built the walls adjoining to St. Bartholomew's Hospital; and the next was John Calthrop, draper, who, at his own expense, arched and vaulted the noisome town ditch, from Aldersgate to Newgate. Nor must we forget that worthy though humble benefactor, Castell, the shoemaker, from his early habits generally known as "the Cock of Westminster," who left to the hospital £44 a year from his hard-earned store. The greater part of the school (except the venerable cloisters) so often echoing with the merry shouts

tion before the Elder Trinity Brothers every six months. These boys used to be annually presented by the president to the king, upon New Year's Day, when that festival was observed at court, and afterwards, upon the queen's birthday. They wear, says Mr. Trollope, a badge upon the left shoulder, the figures upon which represent Arithmetic, with a scroll in one hand, and the other placed upon a boy's head; Geometry, with a triangle in her hand; and Astronomy, with a quadrant in one hand and a sphere in the other. Round the plate is inscribed, "Auspicio Caroli secundi Regis, 1673." The dye is kept in the Tower.

Mr. Stone, a governor, to supplement the king's grant, left a legacy for the maintenance of a preliminary class of twelve boys, who were to be taught navigation. The "Twelves" wear a badge on the right shoulder, the king's boys wearing theirs on the left. Sir Robert Clayton, after a severe illness, in 1675, built the south front of the hospital, which had been in ruins since the Great Fire, and, on

Hertford (where all the younger children are educated), to which a large hall was added in 1800. In 1694 Sir John Moore, alderman, built a writing-school. The good work went on, for, in 1724, Samuel Travers gave the hospital an estate for the maintenance of forty or fifty sons of lieutenants,

THE MATHEMATICAL SCHOOL, CHRIST'S HOSPITAL. *From a View published by N. Smith*, 1793. (See page 368.)

the death of his partner, Mr. Morrice, who had offered to halve the expense, Sir Robert secretly paid the whole £5,000, which was not known till the Tories had deprived him of the mayoralty and of the governorship of the hospital.

In 1680 Sir John Frederick, the president, rebuilt the great hall, which the Fire had injured, at a cost of more than £5,000; and, three years after, the governors erected a branch building at

to be educated for the navy. Later, John Stock, Esq., left £3,000 to the school, for the maintenance of four boys, children of naval lieutenants, to be educated, two as sailors and two as tradesmen. In 1783 John Smith, Esq., left money to build a new grammar-school, and several masters' houses were afterwards pulled down, and a good entrance made from Little Britain.

This re-disposition of the ground made room

for three playgrounds—the ditch, the garden, and the new playground. The site of the grammar-school was taken from the south side of the ditch. The following used to be a sufficiently accurate account of the school premises:—On the south side of the entrance from Little Britain is the treasurer's house, and the other houses in this play-ground are occupied by the matron, masters, and beadles. Proceeding in an easterly direction leads to the south-east entrance from King Edward Street, Newgate Street, and in this space (which is called the counting-house yard) stands the counting-house, and several other houses, which are inhabited by the clerks and some of the masters. The treasurer has also a back entrance to his house, at the end of the counting-house, and his garden runs at the back of all the houses on the east side of this yard. The opposite building is occupied by the boys, and in a niche in the centre, fronting the door of the counting-house, is a statue of King Edward (con-sidered the most perfect one), which represents his majesty, who stands on a black marble slab, in the act of delivering the charter.

The mathematical school is over the old west entrance, now closed up, and was built by Wren, with a ward for the foundation boys over it. A robed statue of Charles II., dated 1672, stands over the gateway. The entrance leads to the north-west corner of the cloisters, which form the four shady sides of the garden playground, and have porticoes, with Gothic arches all round. The walls are supported by abutments of the old priory. Wren repaired the cloisters, which are useful to the young blue monks for play and promenade in wet weather.

The great dining-hall is every way worthy of the grand old City school. It was erected from designs of John Shaw, architect, and stands partly on the foundations of the ancient refectory, and partly on the site of the old City wall. The style is pure Gothic, and the southern or principal front is built of Portland stone with cloisters of Heytor granite, running beneath a portion of the dining-hall. Nine large and handsome windows occupy the entire front. On the ground storey are the governors' room, the wardrobe, the buttery, and other offices; and the basement storey contains, besides cellars, &c., a spacious kitchen, 69 feet long by 33 feet wide, supported by massive granite pillars. The hall itself, with its lobby and organ-gallery, occupies the entire upper storey, which is 187 feet long, $51\frac{1}{2}$ feet wide, and $46\frac{1}{2}$ feet high. It was at one time (and perhaps still is) famous for its rats, who, attracted by the crumbs and frag-ments of food, foraged about after dark in hundreds.

It used to be the peculiar pride of an old "Blue" to catch these rats with his hands only, traps being considered cowardly aids to humanity and unworthy of the hospital. The old dusty picture-frames are favourite terraces for these vermin.

The two famous pictures in the hall—neither of them of much real merit, but valuable for their portraits—are those of Edward VI. renewing his father's gift of the hospital, and of St. Thomas and Bridewell, to the City, falsely ascribed to Holbein, who died seven or eight years before the event took place; and "sprawling" Verrio's picture of James II. receiving an audience of Christ's Hospital boys and girls. The pseudo-Holbein and the painting by Verrio are both well described by Malcolm. The so-called Holbein " adorns the west wall, and is placed near the entrance, at the north end of the hall. The king is seated on a throne, elevated on two steps, with two very clumsy brackets for arms, on which are fanciful pilasters, adorned with carving, and an arch; on the left pilaster, a crowned lion holding a shield, with the letter 'E'; a dragon on the other has another inscribed 'R.' Two angels, reclining on the arch, support the arms of England. The hall of audience is represented as paved with black and white marble; the windows are angular, with niches between each. As there are statues in only two of those, it seems to confirm the idea that it is an exact resemblance of the royal apartment.

" The artist has bestowed his whole attention on the young monarch, whose attitude is easy, natural, and dignified. He presents the deed of gift with his right hand, and holds the sceptre in his left. The scarlet robe is embroidered, and lined with ermine, and the folds are correct'y and minutely finished. An unavoidable circumstance injures the effect of this picture, which is the diminutive stature of the infant-king, who shrinks into a dwarf, compared with his full-grown courtiers; unfortu-nately, reversing the necessary rule of giving most dignity and consequence to the principal person in the piece.

" The chancellor holds the seals over his crossed arms at the king's right hand. This officer and three others are the only standing figures. Ridley kneels at the foot of the throne, and shows his face in profile with uplifted hands. On the right are the mayor and aldermen, in scarlet robes, kneeling. Much cannot be said in praise of those worthies. The members of the Common Council, &c., on the other side, are grouped with more skill, and the action is more varied. The heads of the spectators are generally full of anxious attention.

" But five of twenty-eight children who are intro-duced in the foreground turn towards the king; the remainder look out of the picture. The matron on the girls' side (if a portrait) was chosen for her mental and not her personal qualifications. Such are the merits and defects of this celebrated painting, which, though infinitely inferior to many of Holbein's Dutch and Italian contemporaries, is a valuable, and in many respects an excellent, historic composition.

"Verrio's enormous picture" of James II. and the Bluecoat children "must originally have been in three parts : the centre on the end wall, and the two others on the adjoining sides. Placed thus, the perspective of the depths of the arches would have been right ; as it is at present, extended on one plane, they are exactly the reverse. The audience-chamber is of the Ionic order, with twenty pilasters, and their entablatures and arches. The passage, seen through those, has an intersected arched ceiling. The king sits in the centre of the painting, on a throne of crimson damask, with the royal arms embroidered on the drapery of the canopy, the front of which is of fringed white cloth of gold. The footstool is of purple cloth of gold, and the steps of the throne are covered by a rich Turkey carpet, not remarkably well painted. The king holds a scroll in his left hand, extends the right, and seems to address a person immediately before him. The position of his body and the fore-shortened arm are excellent, and the lace and drapery are finely drawn and coloured. On the sides of the throne are two circular portraits.

"The painter has committed a strange error in turning the king's face from the Lord Mayor, who points in vain to an extended map, a globe, and all the kneeling figures, exulting in the progress of their forty boys in the mathematics, who are busily employed in producing their cases and definitions. Neither in such an attitude could the king observe fourteen kneeling girls, though their faces and persons are handsome and graceful, and the matron and her assistant seem eager to place them in the monarch's view. Verrio has stationed himself at the extreme end of the picture, and his expression appears to inquire the spectators' opinion of his performance. On the opposite side a yeoman of the guard clears the way for some person, and a female seems alarmed at his violence, but a full-dressed youth before him looks out of the picture with the utmost indifference. There is one excellent head which speaks earnestly to a boy. Another figure, probably the master or steward, pulls a youth's hair with marks of anger. Several lords-in-waiting are correct and good figures.

"At the upper end of the room, and on the same west wall, is a large whole-length of Charles II.

descending from his throne, a curtain from which is turned round a pillar. The king holds his robe with his right hand, and points with the left to a globe and mathematical instruments.

"Some years past"—the date of Malcolm's writing is 1803—"an addition was made to the hall, by taking part of the ward over the south cloister into it. In this are several portraits. Queen Anne, sitting, habited in a gown of cloth of gold with a blue mantle laced with gold and lined with ermine. Her black hair is curled, and without ornament ; the arms are too small, but the neck and drapery are good. She holds the orb in her left hand, rested on the knee ; the right crosses her waist."

"Although Christ's Hospital is, and has been from its foundation, in the main a commercial seminary," says Mr. Howard Staunton, "the list of ' Blues' who have acquired celebrity in what are called the ' liberal professions' would confer honour upon a school of much loftier pretensions. Notably among the earliest scholars are the memorable Jesuit, Edmund Campian, a man whose unquestionable piety and marvellous ability might well have saved him from a horrible and shameful death ; the great antiquary, William Camden, though the fact of his admission is not satisfactorily authenticated ; Bishop Stillingfleet (according to the testimony of Pepys) ; David Baker, the ecclesiastical historian ; John Vicars, a religious controversialist of considerable learning and indefatigable energy, but whose fanaticism and intolerance have obtained him an unenviable notoriety from the pen of the author of ' Hudibras ;' Joshua Barnes, the Greek scholar ; John Jurin, another scholar of great eminence, and who was elected President of the College of Physicians ; Jeremiah Markland, a man of distinction, both as scholar and critic ; Richardson, the celebrated novelist ; Bishop Middleton, of Calcutta ; Samuel Taylor Coleridge, and Robert Allen."

In the present century Christ's Hospital can boast of Thomas Mitchell, the well-known translator of Aristophanes ; William Henry Neale, Master of Beverley School ; Leigh Hunt, Charles Lamb, George Dyer, James White, James Scholefield, Regius Professor of Greek in Cambridge ; the Rev. George Townsend ; Field Marshal Lord Seaton ; and Thomas Barnes, editor of the *Times*, than whom no man, if he had cared for it, could have been more certain of distinction.

"In the cloisters," says Leigh Hunt, "a number of persons lie buried, besides the officers of the house. Among them is Isabella, wife of Edward II., the ' she-wolf of France.' I was not aware of this circumstance then; but many a time, with a recollection of some lines in Blair's 'Grave' upon me, have I run as hard as I could, at night-time, from my ward to another, in order to borrow the next volume of some ghostly romance. In one of the cloisters was an impression resembling a gigantic foot, which was attributed by some to the angry stamping of the ghost of a beadle's wife!"

"Our dress," says the same pleasant author, "was of the coarsest and quaintest kind, but was respected out of doors, and is so. It consisted of a blue drugget gown, or body, with ample skirts to it; a yellow vest underneath, in winter-time; small-clothes of Russia duck; worsted yellow stockings; a leathern girdle; and a little black worsted cap, usually carried in the hand. I believe it was the ordinary dress of children in humble life, during the reign of the Tudors. We used to flatter ourselves that it was taken from the monks; and there went a monstrous tradition that at one period it consisted of blue velvet with silver buttons. It was said, also, that during the blissful era of the blue velvet we had roast mutton for supper, but that the smallclothes not being then in existence, and the mutton suppers too luxurious, the eatables were given up for the ineffables. . . .

"Our routine of life was this: We rose to the call of a bell at six in summer and seven in winter; and after combing ourselves and washing our hands and faces, went at the call of another bell to breakfast. All this took up about an hour. From breakfast we proceeded to school, where we remained till eleven, winter and summer, and then had an hour's play. Dinner took place at twelve. Afterwards was a little play till one, when we again went to school, and remained till five in summer and four in winter. At six was the supper. We used to play after it in summer till eight: in winter we proceeded from supper to bed. On Sundays, the school-time of the other days was occupied in church, both morning and evening; and as the Bible was read to us every day before every meal and on going to bed, besides prayers and graces, we rivalled the monks in the religious part of our duties. . . .

"When I entered the school," says Leigh Hunt, speaking of the Grecians, "I was shown three gigantic boys—young men, rather (for the eldest was between seventeen and eighteen)—who, I was told, were going to the university. These were the Grecians. They were the three head boys of the grammar-school, and were understood to have their destiny fixed for the Church. The next class to these—like a college of cardinals to those three popes (for every Grecian was in our eyes infallible)—were the deputy-Grecians. The former were supposed to have completed their Greek studies, and were deep in Sophocles and Euripides. The latter were thought equally competent to tell you anything respecting Homer and Demosthenes."

The "fazzer," in Leigh Hunt's time, was the mumbo-jumbo of the hospital. The "fazzer," says this author, "was known to be nothing more than one of the boys themselves. In fact, he consisted of one of the most impudent of the bigger ones; but as it was his custom to disguise his face, and as this aggravated the terror which made the little boys hide their own faces, his participation of our common human nature only increased the supernatural fearfulness of his pretensions. His office as fazzer consisted in being audacious, unknown and frightening the boys at night, sometimes by pulling them out of their beds, sometimes by simply *fazzing* their hair ('fazzing' meant pulling or vexing, like a goblin); sometimes (which was horriblest of all) by quietly giving us to understand, in some way or other, that the 'fazzer was out,' that is to say, out of his own bed, and then being seen (by those who dared to look) sitting, or otherwise making his appearance, in his white shirt, motionless and dumb."

Charles Lamb talks of the earlier school in a different vein, and with more poetry and depth of feeling. "I must," he says, "crave leave to remember our transcending superiority in those invigorating sports, leapfrog and basting the bear; our delightful excursions in the summer holidays to the New River, near Newington, where, like otters, we would live the long day in the water, never caring for dressing ourselves when we had once stripped; our savoury meals afterwards, when we came home almost famished with staying out all day without our dinners; our visits, at other times, to the Tower, where, by ancient privilege, we had free access to all the curiosities; our solemn processions through the City at Easter, with the Lord Mayor's largess of buns, wine, and a shilling, with the festive questions and civic pleasantries of the dispensing aldermen, which were more to us than all the rest of the banquet; our stately suppings in public, when the well-lighted hall, and the confluence of well-dressed company who came to see us, made the whole look more like a concert or assembly than a scene of a plain bread and cheese collation; the annual orations upon St. Matthew's Day, in which the senior scholar, before he had done, seldom failed to reckon up among those who had done honour to our school, by being educated in it, the names of those accomplished critics and

Greek scholars, Joshua Barnes and Jeremiah Markland (I marvel they left out Camden, while they were about it). Let me have leave to remember our hymns and anthems, and well-toned organ; the doleful tune of the burial anthem, chanted in the solemn cloisters upon the seldom-occurring funeral of some schoolfellow; the festivities at Christmas, when the richest of us would club our stock to have a gaudy-day, sitting round the fire, replenished to the height with logs, and the penniless and he that could contribute nothing partook in all the mirth and some of the substantialities of the feasting; the carol sung by night at that time of the year, which, when a young boy, I have so often lain awake to hear, from seven (the hour of going to bed) till ten, when it was sung by the older boys and monitors, and have listened to it in their rude chanting, till I have been transported in fancy to the fields of Bethlehem, and the song which was sung at that season by angels' voices to the shepherds.

"Nor would I willingly forget any of those things which administered to our vanity. The hem-stitched bands and town-made shirts, which some of the most fashionable among us wore; the town girdles, with buckles of silver or shining stone; the badges of the sea-boys; the cots, or superior shoe-strings, of the monitors; the medals of the markers (those who were appointed to hear the Bible read in the wards on Sunday morning and evening), which bore on their obverse, in silver, as certain parts of our garments carried, in meaner metal, the countenance of our founder, that godly and royal child, King Edward the Sixth, the flower of the Tudor name—the young flower that was untimely cropt, as it began to fill our land with its early odours—the boy-patron of boys—the serious and holy child, who walked with Cranmer and Ridley, fit associate, in those tender years, for the bishops and future martyrs of our Church, to receive or (as occasion sometimes proved) to give instruction :—

    ' But, ah ! what means the silent tear?
        Why, e'en mid joy, my bosom heave?
    Ye long-lost scenes, enchantments dear !
        Lo ! now I linger o'er your grave.

    ' Fly, then, ye hours of rosy hue,
        And bear away the bloom of years !
    And quick succeed, ye sickly crew
        Of doubts and sorrows, pains and fears !
    Still will I ponder Fate's unalter'd plan,
    Nor, tracing back the child, forget that I am man.' "

Of the hospital Charles Lamb says:—"I remember L—— at school, and can well recollect that he had some peculiar advantages which I and others of his schoolfellows had not. His friends lived in town, and were near at hand; and he had the privilege of going to see them, almost as often as he wished, through some invidious distinction, which was denied to us. The present worthy sub-treasurer to the Inner Temple can explain how that happened. He had his tea and hot rolls in a morning, while we were battening upon our quarter of a penny loaf—our 'crug'—moistened with attenuated small beer, in wooden piggins, smacking of the pitched leathern jack it was poured from. Our Monday's milk porridge, blue and tasteless, and the pease-soup of Saturday, coarse and choking, were enriched for him with a slice of ' extraordinary bread and butter ' from the hot loaf of the Temple. The Wednesday's mess of millet, somewhat less repugnant—(we had three banyan to four meat days in the week)—was endeared to his palate by a lump of double-refined, and a smack of ginger (to make it go down the more glibly), or the fragrant cinnamon. In lieu of our *half-pickled* Sundays, or *quite fresh* boiled beef on Thursdays (strong as *caro equina*), with detestable marigolds floating in the pail, to poison the broth—our scanty mutton scrags on Fridays, and rather more savoury but grudging portions of the same flesh, rotten roasted or rare, on the Tuesdays (the only dish which excited our appetites and disappointed our stomachs in almost equal proportion)—he had his hot plate of roast veal, or the more tempting griskin (exotics unknown to our palates), cooked in the paternal kitchen (a great thing), and brought him daily by his maid or aunt ! I remember the good old relative (in whom love forbade pride), squatted down upon some odd stone in a by-nook of the cloisters, disclosing the viands (of higher regale than those cates which the ravens ministered to the Tishbite), and the contending passions of L—— at the unfolding. There was love for the bringer; shame for the thing brought and the manner of its bringing; sympathy for those who were too many to share in it, and, at top of all, hunger (eldest, strongest of the passions !) predominant, breaking down the strong fences of shame, and awkwardness, and a troubling over-consciousness. . . . .

"Under the stewardship of Perry, can L—— have forgotten the cool impunity with which the nurses used to carry away openly, in open platters, for their own tables, one out of two of every hot joint which the careful matron had been seeing scrupulously weighed out for our dinners ? . . . .

"I was a hypochondriac lad; and the sight of a boy in fetters, upon the day of my first putting on the blue clothes, was not exactly fitted to assuage the natural terrors of initiation. I was of tender years, barely turned of seven, and had only read of such things in books, or seen them but in dreams. I was told he had *run away*. This was the punishment for the first offence. As a novice, I was soon after taken to see the dungeons. These were little square Bedlam cells, where a boy could just lie at his length upon straw and a blanket—a mattress, I think, was afterwards substituted—with a peep of light, let in askance, from a prison orifice at top, barely enough to read by. Here the poor

pated. With his pale and frightened features, it was as if some of those disfigurements in Dante had seized upon him. In this disguisement he was brought into the hall (L——'s *favourite state-room*), where awaited him the whole number of his schoolfellows, whose joint lessons and sports he was henceforth to share no more; the awful presence of the steward, to be seen for the last time; of the executioner-beadle, clad in his state robe for the occasion; and of two faces more, of direr

THE CLOISTERS, CHRIST'S HOSPITAL. *From a View published in* 1804. (*See page* 368.)

boy was locked in by himself all day, without sight of any but the porter, who brought him his bread and water, *who might not speak to him*, or of the beadle, who came twice a week to call him out to receive his periodical chastisement."

"The culprit who had been a third time an offender, and whose expulsion was at this time deemed irreversible, was brought forth, as at some solemn *auto da fé*, arrayed in uncouth and most appalling attire, and all trace of his late 'watchet weeds' being carefully effaced, he was exposed in a jacket resembling those which London lamplighters formerly delighted in, with a cap of the same. The effect of this divestiture was such as the ingenious devisers of it must have antici-

import, because never but in these extremities visible. These were governors, two of whom, by choice or charter, were always accustomed to officiate at these *ultima supplicia*—not to mitigate (so, at least, we understood it), but to enforce the uttermost stripe. Old Bamber Gascoigne and Peter Aubert, I remember, were colleagues on one occasion, when the beadle turning rather pale, a glass of brandy was ordered to prepare him for the mysteries. The scourging was, after the old Roman fashion, long and stately. The lictor accompanied the criminal quite round the hall. We were generally too faint with attending to the previous disgusting circumstances to make accurate report with our eyes of the degree of corporal suffering inflicted. After scourging he was made over, in his *san benito*, to his friends, if he had any, or to his parish officer, who, to enhance the effect of the scene, had his station allotted to him on the outside of the hall gate."

Of Boyer, the celebrated master of Christ's hands hung out of the sleeves, with tight wristbands, as if ready for execution; and as he generally wore grey worsted stockings, very tight, with a little balustrade leg, his whole appearance presented something formidably succinct, hard, and mechanical. In fact, his weak side, and un-

SUPPER AT CHRIST'S HOSPITAL. (*See page* 376.)

Hospital, Leigh Hunt says :—"The other master, the upper one, Boyer—famous for the mention of him by Coleridge and Lamb—was a short, stout man, inclining to punchiness, with large face and hands, an aquiline nose, long upper lip, and a sharp mouth. His eye was close and cruel. The spectacles which he wore threw a balm over it. Being a clergyman, he dressed in black, with a powdered wig. His clothes were cut short; his

doubtedly his natural destination, lay in carpentry, and he accordingly carried, in a side-pocket made on purpose, a carpenter's rule.

"Jeremy Boyer had two wigs, both pedantic, but of different omen—the one, serene, smiling, fresh-powdered, betokening a mild day; the other, an old, discoloured, unkempt, angry caxon, denoting frequent and bloody execution. Woe to the school when he made his morning appearance in his *passy*, or *passionate* wig. No comet expounded surer. Jeremy Boyer had a heavy hand. I have known him double his knotty fist at a poor trembling child (the maternal milk hardly dry upon its lips), with a 'Sirrah, do you presume to set your wits at me?' Nothing was more common than to see him make a headlong entry into the school-room, from his inner recess or library, and, with turbulent eye, singling out a lad, roar out, 'Od's my life, sirrah !'—his favourite adjuration,—'I have a great mind to whip you;' then, with as sudden a retracting impulse, fling back into his lair, and, after a cooling lapse of some minutes (during which all but the culprit had totally forgotten the context), drive headlong out again, piecing out his imperfect sentence, as if it had been some devil's litany, with the expletory yell, '*and I* WILL, *too !*'"

Of Coleridge at school Charles Lamb says :— "Come back into memory, like as thou wert in the dayspring of thy fancies, with hope, like a fiery column, before thee — the dark pillar not yet turned—Samuel Taylor Coleridge, logician, metaphysician, bard ! How have I seen the casual passer through the cloisters stand still, entranced with admiration (while he weighed the disproportion between the *speech* and the *garb* of the young Mirandola), to hear thee unfold, in thy deep and sweet intonations, the mysteries of Jamblichus or Plotinus (for even in those years thou waxedest not pale at such philosophic draughts), or reciting Homer in his Greek, or Pindar, while the walls of the old Grey Friars re-echoed to the accents of the *inspired charity-boy !* Many were the 'wit-combats' (to dally awhile with the words of old Fuller) between him and C. V. Le Grice, 'which, too, I behold, like a Spanish great galleon and an English man-of-war. Master Coleridge, like the former, was built far higher in learning, solid, but slow in his performances. C. V. L., with the English man-of-war, lesser in bulk, but lighter in sailing, could turn with all tides, tack about, and take advantage of all winds, by the quickness of his wit and invention.'"

"The discipline at Christ's Hospital, in my time," says Coleridge, in his "Table-Talk," in 1832, "was ultra-Spartan; all domestic ties were to be put aside. 'Boy!' I remember Boyer saying to me once, when I was crying, the first day of my return after the holidays, 'boy! the school is your father; boy! the school is your mother; boy! the school is your brother; the school is your sister; the school is your first cousin, and your second cousin, and all the rest of your relations. Let's have no more crying!' No tongue can express good Mrs. Boyer. Val Le Grice and I were once

going to be flogged for some domestic misdeed, and Boyer was thundering away at us by way of prologue, when Mrs. B. looked in, and said, 'Flog them soundly, sir, I beg!' This saved us. Boyer was so nettled at the interruption, that he growled out, 'Away! woman, away!' and we were let off."

"The upper grammar-school was divided into four classes, or forms. The two under ones were called Little and Great Erasmus; the two upper were occupied by the Grecians and Deputy-Grecians. We used to think the title of Erasmus taken from the great scholar of that name ; but the sudden appearance of a portrait among us, claiming to be the likeness of a certain Erasmus Smith, Esq., shook us terribly in this opinion, and was a hard trial of our gratitude. We scarcely relished this perpetual company of our benefactor, watching us, as he seemed to do, with his omnipresent eyes. I believe he was a rich merchant, and that the forms of Little and Great Erasmus were really named after him. It was a poor consolation to think that he himself, or his great uncle, might have been named after Erasmus. Little Erasmus learned Ovid ; Great Erasmus, Virgil, Terence, and the Greek Testament. The Deputy-Grecians were in Homer, Cicero, and Demosthenes ; the Grecians in the Greek plays and the mathematics."

"I have spoken," says Leigh Hunt, speaking of Charles Lamb, "of the distinguished individuals bred at Christ's Hospital, including Coleridge and Lamb, who left the school not long before I entered it. Coleridge I never saw till he was old. Lamb I recollect coming to see the boys, with a pensive, brown, handsome, and kindly face, and a gait advancing with a motion from side to side, between involuntary consciousness and attempted ease. His brown complexion may have been owing to a visit in the country ; his air of uneasiness, to a great burden of sorrow. He dressed with a quaker-like plainness. I did not know him as Lamb ; I took him for a Mr. 'Guy,' having heard somebody address him by that appellative, I suppose in jest."

Soon after the foundation of the schools, says the latest writer on the subject, we find lands and legacies pouring in for the benefit of the charity ; many, however, of the gifts being for the blind and aged, for exhibitions, for apprenticing, and for many other objects not strictly attached to the hospital, considered merely as a school. In the same manner many persons left estates and moneys to the governors, on condition that a certain number of scholars should be taken from the ranks of certain City companies, or from certain particular parishes, or should be nominated by some public body, fixed by the donor. From these causes the present property of the trust is encumbered with many charges for purposes which, in the present day, are unnecessary, and often impracticable. Thus, one person left a legacy on condition that a certain number of boys should receive pairs of gloves, on which should be printed, "Christ is risen," and these were to be worn in the various processions in which the school took part in Easter week. The gloves are still given, but instead of being printed on the glove, a little badge is worn, with the words required by the founder. A certain Mary Hunt gave £100, that £3 yearly should be expended for a dinner of boiled legs of pork, while several other persons left moneys to be expended on roast beef and mutton, one of them expressly stating that his gift was to be in addition to the ordinary meat provided for the scholars. If Charles Lamb is to be believed—and he himself was a "Blue"—the gifts of extra meat were, at that date, very much needed; and we are also told that in addition to the quantity being small, the quality also was then far from good. No such complaints can be made in the present day. Many of the contributions given for the hospital were very large, that of Lady Mary Ramsey, wife of a Lord Mayor of London, being now worth over £4,000 a year; and within the last few years Mr. Richard Thornton bequeathed a large sum to the charity. One cannot, therefore, be astonished to find, particularly when we remember that the school is especially connected with the Corporation of London, that the present gross income of Christ's Hospital is now about £75,000 per annum, of which about £50,000 is expended on education.

The Schools' Inquiry Commissioners hesitate to disturb the old dress, which Charles Lamb has declared it would be a kind of sacrilege to change; it is, however, very distasteful to the "Grecians," or senior boys.

The number of boys in the school at present is, as a rule, about 1,200, of whom somewhat less than 700 are at the premises in Newgate Street; the remainder—the younger boys—being kept at Hertford for from one to three years before being sent to the London institution. As a general rule the boys are supposed to leave at fifteen years of age, the Grecians and Deputy-Grecians, with a few of the Mathematical boys, who require a further time for their studies, remaining longer in the school. The age of admission is eight, the boys, as is well known, being nominated by the various members of the governing body. In addition to the fixed body of governors there are a large number of presentation governors, who have each paid £500 to the funds of the charity. This payment, indeed,

is not supposed necessarily to cause the donor to be elected a governor, but as the privilege has rarely been withheld, it is practically the fact that such a gift will, in all reasonable probability, secure an appointment as governor with its corresponding benefits. It has been calculated that a governor so appointed has, in twelve years from his appointment, through his nominees, received a benefit of over £900 from the charity. Whether the charity was founded with this intention, we leave our readers to judge. No doubt, in many cases the *quasi*-purchased presentations relieve distressed parents; but there can be no doubt that many of the children in the school (we might almost say the larger number) belong to a class of persons perfectly able to support them, without any appeal to the funds of the charity.

The education given at the hospital is of a superior class, and many of the past students have taken high honours at both universities. Between twenty and thirty masters are employed as the London staff, of whom we remark that the head master receives what appears a very small sum for such a position.

The eminent "Blues" of former times, whom we have before epitomised, deserve a word or two to themselves. Edmund Campian, the celebrated Jesuit, after a quiet life as a professor of rhetoric in a Catholic college at Prague, came to England proselytising, but being seized by Walsingham, Elizabeth's zealous Secretary of State, was tried, found guilty, and hung at Tyburn, in 1581. William Camden, that patriarch of English antiquaries, whose indefatigable researches and study of Saxon rendered his work of special value, was finally appointed by Sir Fulke Greville, his friend, to a post in the Heralds' College. Camden, as a herald, was consulted by Bacon as to the ceremonies for creating him viscount. In his old age Camden founded a history lecture at Oxford, and died at his house at Chiselhurst, in Kent (afterwards occupied by the French ex-emperor), in 1623. Camden's papers relative to ecclesiastical affairs belonged to Archbishop Laud, and were, it is supposed, destroyed by Prynne and Hugh Peters. Camden seems to have been an easy, unruffled man. He was accused by his enemies of borrowing too freely, and without acknowledgment, from his predecessor, Leland. He wrote some by no means indifferent Latin poetry, and an epitaph on Mary Queen of Scots. Joshua Barnes, Greek professor at Cambridge, was another shining light of the Bluecoats. His editions of Homer and Anacreon were in their time celebrated. He died in 1712, and on the old scholar's monument it is recorded that he had read his small English Bible through 121 times. Dr. Bentley used to say of Joshua Barnes that "he understood as much of Greek as an Athenian cobbler." In Emmanuel Library great bundles of Barnes's Greek verses fade and gather dust, together with a part of a Latin-Greek lexicon never finished. Jeremiah Markland, a learned scholar and critic, was another memorable "Blue." He vindicated Addison's character against Pope's satire, was sneered at by Warburton, and edited many editions of classical works. Latterly, this worthy scholar lived in retirement, near Dorking, and twice refused the Greek professorship. Poor George Dyer, Lamb's friend, a true "Blue" indeed, was originally a reporter and private tutor. He wrote some weak poems, and edited Valpy's unsuccessful Delphin classics. Dr. Middleton, Lord Bishop of Calcutta, another "Blue," was early in life vicar of St. Pancras. Val Le Grice, mentioned so lovingly by Charles Lamb, afterwards became a perpetual curate at Penzance, where he helped to found a geological society, and was an opponent of the Methodist revival. James White, another "Blue" of this epoch, for some time filled a post in the hospital country house. His "Letters of Falstaff," were much applauded by the Lamb set. Meyer, nephew of Hoppner, an eminent engraver, was placed in the hospital by Boydell's interest. He was an eminent portrait painter, and a friend of George Dyer. Another great credit to the Blue-coat School was the Rev. Thomas Mitchell, the admirable translator and commentator upon the plays of Aristophanes. Previous to his dexterous rendering, only two out of the extant comedies of Aristophanes had been translated into English.

Among the pictures in the dining-hall we should not forget a simple-hearted representation of Sir Brook Watson (Lord Mayor,) escaping when a boy from the shark that bit his leg off while bathing. This is the work of Copley, the father of Lord Lyndhurst. A wit of the time had the cruelty, from personal knowledge of this worthy Lord Mayor, to observe that if the shark had got hold of Sir Brook Watson's skull instead of his leg, the shark would have got the worst of it.

There is a curious history attached to the portrait of a Mr. John St. Amand, the grandfather of a benefactor to the hospital, which hangs in the treasury. By the terms of James St. Amand's will all the money he left passes to the University of Oxford if this picture is ever lost or given away ; and the same deprivation occurs if this picture is not produced once a year at the general court, and also shown, on requisition, to the Vice-Chancellor

or his deputy. As the St. Amands had intermarried, in the reign of Henry III., with the luckless Stuarts, there is a tradition in the school that this picture is the portrait of the Pretender, but this is an unfounded notion.

A very old feature of Christ's Hospital is the public supper on the six Thursday evenings preceding Easter, for which pleasant sight the treasurer and governors have the right of issuing tickets. It is a pretty quaint ceremony of the old times, and was witnessed by Queen Victoria and Prince Albert, in 1845. The long tables are laid with plates of bread and butter, and vessels containing milk. Formerly the supper consisted of bread and cheese and beer. The interesting ceremony commences by the steward rapping a table three times with a hammer. The first stroke is for taking places, the second for silence, the third is the signal for a Grecian to read the evening lesson from the pulpit, which lesson is followed by appropriate prayers. The Lord Mayor, as President, is seated in a state chair made of oak from old St. Katherine's Church. A psalm is then sung, which is followed by a short grace. The "amen" at the end of the prayers, pronounced by nearly 800 voices, has an electrical effect. The visitors walk between the tables, and mark the happy, excited faces and the commensurate appetite of youth. After supper, about which there is no "coy, reluctant, amorous delay," an anthem is sung, and the boys then pass before the president's chair in procession, bow, and retire.

The wards are each headed by their special nurses, who formerly, when the public suppers began at Christmas and ended at Easter, were each preceded by a little Bluecoat holding two high candlesticks, the "trade boys" of each ward carrying the bowls, candlesticks, tablecloths, breadbaskets, and knife-baskets. The sight is at all times a pretty one, and the ceremony makes one young again to witness it.

The Spital sermons are annually preached in Christchurch, Newgate Street, on Easter Monday and Tuesday before the Lord Mayor and corporation, and the governors of the five royal hospitals ; the bishops in turn preaching on Monday, and usually his lordship's chaplain on Tuesday. On Tuesday the children go to the Mansion House, and pass through the Egyptian Hall before the Lord Mayor, each boy receiving a glass of wine, two buns, and a shilling, the monitors half-a-crown each, and the Grecians a guinea. The boys formerly visited the Royal Exchange on Easter Monday, but this has been discontinued since the burning of the last Exchange in 1838. They also formerly went to the Mansion House on Easter Monday, but this has likewise been discontinued.

"At the first drawing-room of the year," writes John Timbs, "forty 'mathematical boys' are presented to the sovereign, who gives them £8 8s. as a gratuity. To this other members of the Royal Family formerly added smaller sums, and the whole was divided among the ten boys who left the school in the year. During the illness of George III. these presentations were discontinued, but the governors of the hospital continued to pay £1 3s., the amount ordinarily received by each, to every boy on quitting. The practice of receiving the children was revived by William IV."

Each of the "mathematical boys," having passed his Trinity House examination, and received testimonials of his good conduct, is presented with a watch, in addition to an outfit of clothes, books, mathematical instruments, a quadrant, and sea-chest, and twenty-five pounds after three years' service.

On the annual prize-day, in July, the Grecians deliver orations before the Lord Mayor, corporation, governors, and their friends, this being a relic of the scholars' disputations in the cloisters. "Christ's Hospital," says an author we have already quoted, "by ancient custom possesses the privilege of addressing the sovereign, on the occasion of his or her coming into the City to partake of the hospitality of the corporation of London. On the visit of Queen Victoria in 1837 a booth was erected for the hospital boys in St. Paul's Churchyard, and on the royal carriage reaching the cathedral west gate the senior scholar, with the head master and treasurer, advanced to the coach-door and delivered a congratulatory address to Her Majesty, with a copy of the same on vellum."

The annual amount of salaries in London and Hertford is about £5,000. About 200 boys, says Mr. Timbs in 1868, are admitted annually. By the regulations passed at a court in 1809 it was decreed "that no children of livery servants (except they be freemen of the City of London), and no children who have *any adequate* means of being educated or maintained, and no children who are lamed, crooked, or deformed, or suffering from any infectious or incurable disease, should be admitted. Also, that a certificate from a minister, church-warden, and three principal inhabitants of the parish be required with every child, certifying its age, and that it has no adequate means of being educated or maintained." How far this rule of the old charity has been carried out, and in what way the rigour of such a binding form has been evaded, it

is not for us to say; but one thing is certain, that in spite of the fact that Christ's Hospital was originally intended to educate dependent children, very many of the boys brought up here are the sons of well-to-do gentlemen.

Mr. Howard Staunton, writing in 1869, says: "On an average four scholars are annually sent to Cambridge with an Exhibition of £80 a year, tenable for four years, and one to Oxford with £100 a year for the like period. Besides these there are the 'Pitt Club' Scholarship and the 'Times' Scholarship, each of £30 a year for four years, which are awarded by competition to the best scholar in classics and mathematics combined, and held by him in addition to his general Exhibition. Upon proceeding to the university each Grecian receives an allowance of £20 for books, £10 for apparel, and £30 for caution-money and settling-fees." Five boys are now sent annually to each university for four years, with an allowance of £90.

The dietary of the boys is still somewhat monastic. The breakfast, till 1824, was plain bread and beer, and the dinner three times a week consisted only of milk-porridge, rice-milk, and pea-soup. The old school-rhyme, imperishable as the Iliad, runs—

> " Sunday, all saints ;
> Monday, all souls ;
> Tuesday, all trenchers ;
> Wednesday, all bowls ;
> Thursday, tough Jack ;
> Friday, no better ;
> Saturday, pea-soup with bread and butter."

The boys, like the friars in the old refectory, till lately ate their meat off wooden trenchers, and ladled their soup with wooden spoons from wooden bowls. The beer was brought up in leather jacks, and retailed in small piggins. Charles Lamb, as we have seen before, does not speak highly of the food. The small beer was of the smallest, and tasted of its leather receptacle. The milk-porridge was blue and tasteless; the pea-soup coarse and choking. The mutton was roasted to shreds; the boiled beef was poisoned with marigolds.

There was a curious custom at Christ's Hospital in Lamb's time never to touch "gags" (the fat of the fresh boiled beef), and a "Blue" would have blushed, as at the exposure of some heinous immorality, to have been detected eating that forbidden portion of his allowance of animal food, the whole of which, while he was in health, was little more than sufficient to allay his hunger. The same, or even greater refinement, was shown in the rejection of certain kinds of sweet cake. What gave rise to these supererogatory penances, these self-denying ordinances? The "gag-eater" was held as equivalent to a ghoul, loathed, shunned, and insulted. Of a certain juvenile monster of this kind Lamb tells us one of his most charming anecdotes, droll and tender as his own exquisite humour. A "gag-eater" was observed to carefully gather the fat left on the table, and to secretly stow away the disreputable morsels in the settle at his

up four flights of stairs, and the wicket was opened by an old woman meanly clad. Suspicion being now certainty, the spies returned with cruel triumph to tell the steward. He investigated the matter with a kind and patient sagacity, and the result was, that the supposed mendicants turned out to be really the honest parents of the brave gag-eater. "This young stork, at the expense of his own good name, had all this while been only feeding the old

THE HALL OF CHRIST'S HOSPITAL.   (See page 368.)

bedside. A dreadful rumour ran that he secretly devoured them at midnight; but he was watched again and again, and it was not so. At last, on a leave-day, he was marked carrying out of bounds a large blue check handkerchief. That, then, was the accursed thing. It was suggested that he sold it to beggars. Henceforward he moped alone. No one spoke to him; no one played with him. Still he persevered. At last two boys traced him to a large worn-out house inhabited by the very poor, such as then stood in Chancery Lane, with open doors and common staircases. The "gag-eater" stole

birds." "The governors on this occasion," says Lamb, "much to their honour, voted a present relief to the family, and presented the boy with a silver medal. The lesson which the steward read upon rash judgment, on the occasion of publicly delivering the medal, I believe would not be lost upon his auditory. I had left school then, but I well remember the tall, shambling youth, with a cast in his eye, not at all calculated to conciliate hostile prejudices. I have since seen him carrying a baker's basket. I think I heard he did not do so well by himself as he had done by the old folks."

"There were some school-rhymes," says Leigh Hunt, "about 'pork upon a fork,' and the Jews going to prison. At Easter a strip of bordered paper was stuck on the breast of every boy, containing the words, 'He is risen.' It did not give us the slightest thought of what it recorded; it only reminded us of an old rhyme which some of the boys used to go about the school repeating—

'He is risen, he is risen,
　All the Jews must go to prison.'

Those who became Grecians always went to the university, though not always into the Church, which was reckoned a departure from the contract. When I first came to school, at seven years old, the names of the Grecians were Allen, Favell, Thomson, and Le Grice, brother of the Le Grice above mentioned, and now a clergyman in Cornwall. Charles Lamb had lately been Deputy-Grecian, and Coleridge had left for the university."

In 1803 it was resolved by degrees to rebuild

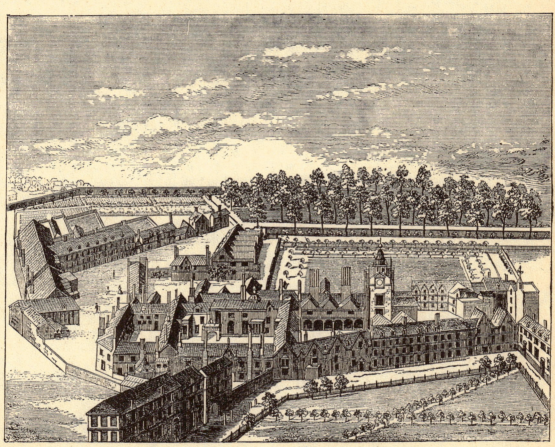

BIRD'S-EYE VIEW OF THE OLD CHARTERHOUSE. (See page 388.)

A beautiful Christian deduction! Thus has charity itself been converted into a spirit of antagonism; and thus it is that the antagonism, in the progress of knowledge, becomes first a pastime and then a jest.

"When a boy," says the same writer, "entered the upper school, he was understood to be in the road to the university, provided he had inclination and talents for it; but, as only one Grecian a year went to college, the drafts out of Great and Little Erasmus into the writing-school were numerous. A few also became Deputy-Grecians without going farther, and entered the world from that form.

Christ's Hospital. Part of the revenues were laid aside for a building-fund, and £1,000 was given by the corporation. The first stone of the great Tudor dining-hall was laid by the Duke of York, April 28, 1825, John Shaw being the architect. The back wall stands in the ditch that surrounded old London, and is built on piles driven twenty feet deep. In excavating, some Roman coins and a pair of Roman sandals were discovered. The southern front, facing Newgate Street, is supported by buttresses, and has an octagonal tower at each extremity, and is embattled and pinnacled in a trivial and unreal kind of way. The great metal gates of the playground are enriched with the arms of the hospital, argent, a cross gules in the dexter chief, a dagger of the first on a chief azure between two fleurs-de-lis, or, a rose argent. Behind the hall is the large infirmary, built in 1822, and on the east and west sides of the cloisters are the dormitories.

"In the year 1552," says Stow, "began the repairing of the Grey Friars' house, for the poor fatherless children; and in the month of (23) November, the children were taken into the same, to the number of almost four hundred. On Christmas Day, in the afternoon, while the Lord Mayor and aldermen rode to Paules, the children of Christ's Hospital stood from St. Lawrence Lane end, in Cheape, towards Paules, all in one livery of russet cotton, three hundred and forty in number; and in Easter next they were in blue at the Spittle, and so have continued ever since."

A few years ago a dinner given to Mr. Tice, late head beadle of the hospital, to present him with a purse of seventy guineas, strongly marks the brotherhood that prevails among old "Blues." The first toast drank was to the grand old words—"The religious, royal, and ancient foundation of Christ's Hospital. May those prosper who love it, and may God increase their number." One of the speakers said—"Mr. Tice had an immense amount of patronage in his hands, for he promoted him to be 'lavatory-boy' and 'jack-boy,' till at last he rose to the height of his ambition, and was made 'beer-boy.' He remembered there was a tradition amongst all the boys who went to Peerless Pool, that unless they touched a particular brick they would inevitably be drowned. The grandest days of all, though, were the public suppings, at which Mr. Tice had to precede the Lord Mayor in the procession, and people used to be always asking who he was. He was taken for the French Ambassador, for Garibaldi, and indeed for everybody but Mr. Tice."

Under the scheme for the administration of the foundation and endowments of Christ's Hospital, drawn up in conformity with the Endowed Schools Act of 1869, it is proposed that the residue of income of the general fund, if any, may be applied for the purposes of the Exhibitions Fund, or otherwise for the benefit of the schools of the foundation, or any of them, in improving the accommodation or convenience of the school buildings or premises, or generally in extending or otherwise promoting the objects and efficiency of the schools. Whatever shall not be so applied shall, on passing the yearly accounts, be treated as unapplied surplus, and be deposited in a bank on account of the governors, in order that, when it amounts to a suitable sum, it may be used in augmentation of the general endowment. It has been proposed to abolish the Hertford school.